Reforming Asian Socialism

Reforming Asian Socialism

The Growth of Market Institutions

edited by
John McMillan and
Barry Naughton

Ann Arbor

THE UNIVERSITY OF MICHIGAN PRESS

Copyright © by the University of Michigan 1996
All rights reserved
Published in the United States of America by
The University of Michigan Press
Manufactured in the United States of America
∞ Printed on acid-free paper

1999   1998   1997   1996   4   3   2   1

A CIP catalog record for this book is available from the British Library.

Library of Congress Cataloging-in-Publication Data

Reforming Asian socialism : the growth of market institutions / edited
  by John McMillan and Barry Naughton.
        p.   cm.
    "This book is a result of a conference held at the Graduate School
of International Relations and Pacific Studies, University of
California, San Diego in May 1993"—Pref.
    Includes bibliographical references and index (p.   ).
    ISBN 0-472-10661-9 (hardcover : acid-free paper)
    1. Asia—Economic policy—Congresses.   2. Socialism—Asia—
Congresses.   3. China—Economic policy—1976- —Congresses.
4. Socialism—China—Congresses.   I. McMillan, John, 1951–
II. Naughton, Barry.   III. University of California, San Diego.
Graduate School of International Relations and Pacific Studies.
HC412.R437   1996
338.95—dc20   96-4313
                                                                        CIP

Preface

This book is the result of a conference held at the Graduate School of International Relations and Pacific Studies, University of California, San Diego in May 1993. The editors are grateful for support from the University of California's Pacific Rim Research Program.

Contents

Part 1
Building a New
Economic System

CHAPTER 1

Elements of Economic Transition

John McMillan and Barry Naughton

President Vaclav Havel of the Czech Republic describes the endpoint of economic reform with his customary eloquence:

> [T]he only economic system that works is a market economy, in which everything belongs to someone—which means that someone is responsible for everything. It is a system in which complete independence and plurality of economic entities exist within a legal framework, and its workings are guided chiefly by the laws of the marketplace. This is the only natural economy, the only kind that makes sense, the only one that leads to prosperity, because it is the only one that reflects the nature of life itself. The essence of life is infinitely and mysteriously multiform, and therefore it cannot be contained or planned for, in its fullness and variability, by any central intelligence.[1]

What is the best way to move from an inefficient centrally planned economy to the prosperity promised by Havel's "only natural economy"?

Fierce debate has divided those who advocate shock therapy or big-bang reform, as implemented in Russia and Eastern Europe, and those who contend that a gradual, evolutionary approach, of the sort followed by China, will produce a more effective transformation. The Czech Republic's other leading politician, Prime Minister Vaclav Klaus, has put this debate in perspective. Responding to accusations that he had applied shock therapy to what was then Czechoslovakia, he said:

> I reject the term "shock therapy." It's a false dilemma, shock therapy versus gradualism. It's absolutely wrong. The economic transformation has many layers, many dimensions. Some have zero time horizon, and some have a time horizon of weeks, months, years.[2]

---

1. Havel 1992, 62.
2. *New York Times,* May 3 1992, 11.

Which aspects of the reforms can move quickly, which adjustments can only be made slowly, and why? What are the various "layers" and "dimensions" of the transition? How, in practice, does the transition away from a centrally planned economy proceed? What new institutions are created? To what extent can new institutions evolve spontaneously, and to what extent must they be guided by the government? Answering questions such as these requires detailed empirical examination of how transition economies are actually adjusting. The chapters that follow look closely at how markets are being created where they did not exist before.

This book examines aspects of the reform process in China and Vietnam, looking also, for comparison, at Poland and Ukraine, as well as at North Korea, a country that has not yet begun to reform. China is disproportionately represented. China and Vietnam started reforms in the late 1970s, a decade or more before any other communist country.[3] The reform processes in China and Vietnam share some important aspects, but China's experience has been much better studied. Because there has been so much more time to observe what is happening in China, much more is known about the reform process in China than elsewhere, and the chapters to follow reflect this. Some fascinating experiments in novel institutional forms have occurred in Chinese rural industry: firms that, by comparison with textbook models and Western market economy practice, have highly unusual ownership structures have proven to be remarkably successful. China serves as a useful laboratory for the study of transition processes: much can be learned by asking how, and why, a particular reform process is similar to, or different from, what has happened in China.

The present study goes beyond the big-bang versus gradualism policy debates to examine empirically the processes that must take place in any

---

3. If a broader definition of reform is used, reforms in communist economies of course began during the 1960s in Eastern Europe, or even as early as 1958 in Czechoslovakia. The most significant of the early reforms was the "New Economic Mechanism" adopted in Hungary in 1968. Early reforms faced critical limitations, not only politically, but economically as well. In no case did these early reforms allow a real transition away from planner sovereignty to genuine market allocation of resources. Restrictions on entry into key sectors were always maintained, prices were never market-determined, and the principle of enterprise subservience to the government bureaucracy was universally upheld. These early reforms were thus very different from the reforms of the 1980s and the 1990s in Eastern Europe, the former Soviet states, and Asia. It is unfortunate that there exists no obvious terminology distinguishing between the partial and tentative reforms of the 1960s that attempted to ameliorate the planned economies of the day and the dramatic adoption of market institutions and market allocation of resources that characterized all significant reforms after the beginnings of Chinese reform in 1978. The reasons for the failures and occasional successes of the European reforms of the 1960s certainly deserve study, but for the purpose of this volume, attention is concentrated on substantial reforms that introduced market allocation, market prices, and new institutions required to support market transactions. There is no question that the earliest reforms, in this sense, began in China at the end of 1978.

reforming economy: the development of market institutions. There are numerous common processes that characterize all transitions, including entry of new firms, creation of market institutions, and restructuring of state-owned industry. The authors of this volume seek to shed light on specific processes: on the elements of the transition toward a market economy. The first objective of the volume is thus to reveal the concrete processes of institutional change and creation that make up the more general process of transition. In this sense, the study of China and Vietnam is part of an effort to develop a more general understanding of the transition as a whole, and the individual chapters of this volume should be seen as building blocks for the construction of a general account of the transition to a market economy.

In addition, the study of the microeconomics of transition has implications for policy making. The overwhelming experience of the early 1990s was that big-bang reforms in Eastern Europe were surprisingly painful, leading to unexpectedly large and persistent reductions in output, while reforms in China and Vietnam were surprisingly successful, leading to significant accelerations in output growth. It is not appropriate to draw overly simple conclusions about policy from this contrast: there are far too many differences between the contrasting cases to permit simplistic generalizations. But the new information about reform outcomes challenges us to develop better interpretations of the reform process: What are the fundamental causes of the contrast in outcomes? Are there lessons for policy from this contrast? One approach, taken by Sachs and Woo (1994), has been to stress the macroeconomic and structural differences between China and Vietnam, on the one hand, and the European former socialist states on the other. From their perspective, there are no lessons from comparative experience because the differences are simply too great. The approach taken in this volume is quite different. We believe there are important lessons for economic reform, and for economic policy making in general, that can be derived from the Chinese and Vietnamese experiences. A microeconomic approach to the institutions and incentives required by the transition is the most efficient way to draw those lessons. The choice of reform strategy is constrained by the need for the development of market institutions, some of which take time to develop. These are taken for granted in a fully functioning market economy, but their absence in the early stages of transition can seriously hamper development. Institutional development takes a considerable length of time. Comparative, cross-country research into the detailed elements of the transitions is needed in order to cast light on what is feasible.

The chapters to follow address questions such as: What new market institutions are being created? To what extent are they developing spontaneously? To what extent is the government playing a role? What kinds of restructuring of state firms are actually occurring? What is the organizational structure of the new firms? How are they being financed? How are contracts made and enforced in the absence of a market-oriented legal system? What are the similarities and differences across the different countries in the micro-economics of transition? Is there an Asian, as opposed to European, model of reform, or are all the reforms—in practice if not in rhetoric—similar in some fundamental way?

This research has implications for economic theory. Modern principal-agent theory, being a theory of incentives, is tailor-made for examining many of the issues raised by the transition. Moreover, the reforms represent a gigantic economic experiment that provides an opportunity to enrich the theo-retical literature. Economic theory has sometimes been used as the basis of prescriptions for economic reform. But a careful look at reform can also shed new light on economic theory, by giving us opportunities to test the realism of our hypotheses and generating new insights that can be incorporated into further theorizing.

Building a New Economic System

Reforming an economy means replacing an old system with a new system. All the institutions of the planned economy were developed as component parts of that system: they are mutually consistent, but incompatible with a true market economy. The microeconomic institutions as well as the macroeconomic— fiscal and monetary systems in particular—must all be changed. The price, ownership, and incentive systems in the planned economy are internally con-sistent. This consistency is one of the messages of Gates, Milgrom, and Roberts (chap. 2). The focus there is on complementarities among reform measures, but this chapter can also be read to show the consistency between price and incentive parameters under the old system: given government con-trol of prices and the government's unwillingness to give agents a stake in future profitability, low-powered incentives are actually socially optimal.

We learned during the 1980s that it is not hard to destroy the old system. In Eastern Europe and the Soviet Union, the system collapsed under the impact of a few hard shocks. China's initially tentative reforms led steadily toward a market economy. Precisely because the planned economy system is an integral whole, the removal of certain crucial constituent elements can cause the whole edifice to tumble. One essential component of the planned system, for example, is the state's monopoly over industry. A reform that permits new firms to enter an industry and compete with the state-run firms is extremely subversive to the planned system. In the countryside in China and Vietnam, the dissolution of collectives and the return to household farming had a similar effect in undermining the planned economy.

Such reforms can touch off a powerful process of change. New economic agents are created, often having high-powered incentives. These new agents are not under the control of the planners, and often compete with existing state-controlled agents. The state is forced to seek new incentive systems within the state sector in order to allow its agents to respond more effectively to new competitors.

Reforms in both China and Vietnam were marked by early attention to the incentives facing economic agents at the grassroots level. Rural and urban producer organizations were restructured in ways that made them more responsive to economic opportunity. Only then—and partially in response to pressures created by these new grassroots elements—was the overall economic environment reformed to permit more general competition and more efficient markets.

With the further development of competition, state control over the price system erodes. This new environment creates conditions under which entrepreneurship is rewarded and learning about market economies proceeds rapidly. As many of the individual chapters of this volume stress, these processes occur within the former state sector as well as outside it. State agents seek to adapt existing institutions to the new environment.

These successes create new challenges. Markets must start to operate where they did not exist before. New organizational forms must be improvised. Property rights must be defined and a law of contract instituted. A market-oriented financial system must come into being. Income and sales taxes must be designed. Macroeconomic institutions must be changed. Not only must these and other institutions emerge, but they must also fit together. The new system must work as a system. Reforms are often complementary: one reform is more effective if another reform is already in place. In particular, as Gates, Milgrom, and Roberts show, strengthening managerial incentives has a complementary effect with reforming prices, which in turn has a complementary effect with any reform that increases product-market competition.

A given reform might be useless or even counterproductive if introduced in isolation, and have beneficial effects only if it is introduced as part of a package of reforms. The Gates-Milgrom-Roberts theory can be applied to the partial reforms attempted in Eastern Europe in the 1960s. It suggests that they failed because they were too partial. The early attempts at reform typically took the form of strengthening the incentives facing state-owned firms' managers, while in other respects the planners maintained their control, fixing prices and prohibiting the emergence of any product-market competition. The complementarities among incentives, prices, and competition mean that reforming one in isolation has few or no beneficial effects. China's 1980s reforms are also commonly described as partial, but they have been highly successful. While far from being comprehensive or big-bang reforms, they were, in fact, far broader than Eastern Europe's early reform attempts: beginning in the early 1980s, prices and incentives systems were reformed and competition was allowed to develop. The fact that China's reforms encompassed the package of complementary variables identified by Gates, Milgrom, and Roberts may account for their success.

It is significant that these complementarities are microeconomic: they operate at the level of the individual firm or household. Thus, they do not necessarily lead to prescriptions for reform "packages" or optimal sequences of reform measures. Instead, they lead us to conclude that incremental reforms, so long as they reach a certain critical mass, can lead into a broader transition to the market as progress in one area creates pressure for complementary measures in related areas. This contrasts with the more usual way that economists look at the reform process. One familiar analytic approach has been to analyze reform as a two-stage process: first, prices are freed and become much more informative, such that the overall incentive environment is rapidly transformed; second, a gradual process of institution building is begun. Prices and incentives (which can quickly be changed) are treated separately from institutions (which cannot). However, the interdependence of institutional change and incentive developments described by many of our authors suggests that this simplification sacrifices too much of reality. The underdevelopment of institutions means that incentives won't be "right" during much of the transition, in any case. By contrast, with gradual institution building and strengthening of incentives, the two processes can be mutually supportive.

Most advisers to reforming economies from the West stress the paramount need for the introduction of a new legal system—in particular a law of contract. China has not revamped its legal system, as Clarke shows (chap. 3). Well-defined laws of property and contract simply do not exist. Perhaps this means that China's growth is unsustainable. Or perhaps it means that the role of the law has been exaggerated. Contracts in China are less legal than relational. Businesspeople in China keep their promises (most of the time) not because they are required to by the law, but because they care for their reputation: reneging on a "contract" is likely to destroy the businessperson's ability to do business in the future. Just as the success of China's nonstate firms requires us to rethink some of our notions of why ownership matters, so China's economic growth in the face of what would seem to be inadequate legal institutions requires us to rethink our Western-oriented notions of the relationship between the law and economic success.

Building and Adapting Institutions

The reform environment creates a demand for institutional innovation. A recurrent theme in the following chapters is that the introduction of powerful incentives creates a demand for new institutions. Yet scarce resources of capital and expertise must be used up in creating new institutions. Indeed, markets themselves are institutions. A market is not an abstraction in which a demand curve spontaneously intersects a supply curve (contrary to what might be inferred from elementary economics textbooks). A market is a living institution, which needs rules and customs in order to work. Given the disparate goals of the market participants and the uneven distribution of information among them, the rules of exchange must be craftily structured for a market to operate smoothly (Wilson 1987). In functioning market economies, these rules and customs differ widely from market to market. In a transition economy, these rules and customs must either be consciously designed or they must evolve. Markets do not automatically come into being as soon as laws prohibiting market activity are abolished.

The transition economy must make do, at least temporarily, with the institutions left over from the planned economy. They cannot be discarded until new institutions have been created to take their place. How can the old institutions be reformed? How can new institutions be improvised from the remnants of the old? Many of the following chapters describe a process of institutional adaptation and improvisation. In many cases, these solutions fall short of optimal performance. Yet they work, in the sense that they permit economic agents to resolve short-run conflicts and go on making the long-run decisions about production, saving, and investment that are crucial to the successful functioning of a modern economy. An important part of the story of economic reform in China and Vietnam is the relative absence of catastrophic institutional failure. Many reforms have miscarried and been abandoned. On many occasions, the reform process has been delayed until important conflicts could be resolved. But ultimately, adequate institutions were developed to permit the evolutionary process of reform to proceed. (On this process, see especially Whiting [Chap. 4]; Rozelle [Chap. 9]; and Gitomer [Chap. 10].) by contrast, in the former Soviet states, many organizations have simply collapsed. Their failure to provide basic services has rippled through the rest of the economy, depressing output and incomes. The avoidance of institutional failure is an important aspect of evolutionary reform processes.

Institutional Innovation in Industry

The chapters on industrial reform focus primarily on industrial firms and their relation to governmental bodies. Creating new economic activities and reforming existing activities are complementary aspects of the transition process. Modern industrial production requires the existence of large industrial firms. Large industrial firms, adapted to perform efficiently in a market environment, are scarce in the transition process. Such firms can only come from a limited number of sources. New private firms are created rapidly in all transitions, but these firms are initially small in scale and are able to account for only a fraction of production for the first few years after the initiation of the reforms. Most production continues to come from firms that trace their origins back to the state-controlled sector. Privatizing these firms is necessarily a slow process. In the meantime, state-owned firms must be restructured.

A unique Chinese innovation is the "township and village enterprise" (or TVE). Outside the state sector, rural township and village enterprises have been the source of much of the dynamism in China's economic reforms. The entry of these new firms illustrates the vitality of market forces. Despite impressive impediments—little law of contract, weak property rights, under-developed capital markets—when the restrictions on the activities of nonstate firms were loosened in the early 1980s, a huge amount of entrepreneurial investment occurred, with striking success. The nonstate sector by 1990 accounted for half of China's industrial output.

China's nonstate firms have unusual ownership forms and organizational structure, as Whiting (chap. 4), Nee and Su (chap. 5), and Qian and Stiglitz (chap. 8), describe. Some are private, in roughly the Western sense. But most are run by communities of a few hundred or a few thousand people. China's township enterprises are an improvised organizational form. They are neither purely private nor purely publicly run: there is a certain fuzziness about property rights. This imprecision in property rights does impede the operation of these firms, as Whiting shows. Nevertheless, they have been remarkably successful, as their growth indicates. In part, this is because of the smallness of the communities that own the firms. The continuity of personnel and control relationships, Nee and Su argue, permits successful operation in the face of inadequately specified property rights. Continuity minimizes conflict over ownership and provides sharing of incremental returns.

Further impetus for efficient operation comes from the product-market and capital-market disciplines facing these firms. Product-market discipline comes in the standard form: most firms compete with other nonstate firms, and in some cases state firms, to sell their outputs, and the competition is often fierce. The financial-market discipline is unusual. Most of the investment capital in established firms comes from the firms' own retained earnings, and additional funds come from the local community, either in the form of government funds or as local savings channeled through the Rural Credit Cooperatives. The local community thus has a large stake in the success of its community firms, and the local township government intervenes in capital markets to protect its investments. As Whiting shows (chap. 4), this results in a certain "softening" of the firms' budget constraints, and capital markets fall short of operating with textbook efficiency. However, operating on a local scale, the community government seems to be better informed about a firm's potential than a provincial or national industrial bureau controlling a state firm would be, and so has more effective control. Since the community government's resources are limited and most of its revenue (needed, among other things, to pay the salaries of community government officials) comes from these enterprises, it is motivated to protect its investment by inducing the firm to maximize its profits.

Community-owned firms have served as a useful transitional device. They have succeeded in generating large amounts of investment in an environment in which, with financial markets almost nonexistent, private firms might have been unable to generate much capital. Indeed, the very imperfections in the capital markets that Whiting documents can be seen as a potential advantage to community-owned firms during the transition. Financial institutions inherited from the old economic system are ill-prepared to provide capital to risky private businesses starting up, and those firms are typically starved for capital. Community firms, by contrast, benefit from the intermediary role of (increasingly entrepreneurial) community governments, which facilitates more rapid diversion of society's savings toward new activities that are risky but have a high average rate of return.

It remains to be seen whether community-owned firms are a permanent feature of China's economy, or merely a step on the way to a fully privately owned economy. But the decade-long success of these firms suggests that the common belief that efficient production requires firms to be structured like Western firms, with clearly defined ownership, is overly simple.

In Vietnam, according to Ronnås (chap. 6), private firms are emerging quite rapidly. This seems to be a common feature of transitions generally: once private business is allowed, it grows quite rapidly regardless of the form of the transition as a whole. However, the growth of the private sector is hampered in Vietnam, according to reports from the entrepreneurs themselves, by the slow development of market institutions. The expansion of firms is slowed by capital constraints—the absence of a financial market—and market constraints—poor sales channels, transport problems, and so on. Again, these limitations seem to be a common feature of the transition process. Indeed, one of the reasons for the success of China's TVEs may be that they are well situated to overcome capital market limitations because the sponsorship and support of community governments facilitates their access to formal credit markets.

In the planned economy, almost all industrial production was done by state-owned firms, which were notoriously inefficient. What to do about these state-owned firms is perhaps the biggest headache for the reformers. Should the government sell them off to private owners as quickly as possible, leaving it to the new owners to restructure them? Or should the government commercialize them—that is, change the forms of their regulation imposed from above so that their internal incentives resemble those of a privately owned firm—and only later privatize them? Czechoslovakia and China exemplify the two policy extremes. Czechoslovakia's state firms were privatized before being restructured; China's state firms were restructured before being privatized. The new democratic government in Czechoslovakia initiated a massive privatization scheme. The Chinese government restructured its state-owned firms through the 1980s, and only began some timid attempts at privatization in the early 1990s. China's restructuring was successful, in that managers' and workers' incentives were greatly strengthened, and as a result the productivity of these firms significantly improved, as McMillan and Naughton show (chap. 7).

Each ordering of reform leaves many unresolved difficulties. In the Czech Republic and Slovakia, the dispersed stock ownership that the voucher privatization produced and the slow development of a functioning capital market may blunt the managers' incentives to restructure the firms. In China, the continued subsidization of some chronically loss-making state-owned firms raises questions of whether successful privatization is possible. Which should come first, privatization or restructuring? Only time will tell which ordering works best.

The contributions by Qian and Stiglitz (chap. 8) and by Nee and Su (chap. 5) both stress the fact that innovative hybrid property forms have developed both within and outside of the state sector. Clearly, a prerequisite for this process was the development of a certain level of ownership of productive facilities on the part of local governments. But once local governments obtained a certain level of secure, though informal, property rights, the process of institutional innovation took off. For example, Nee and Su argue that the introduction of profit sharing from the top down within the state sector led to the creation of informal property rights, which in turn led state officials to create new hybrid enterprise forms.

Rural Institutional Innovation

Perhaps the most interesting institutional development in the transition processes anywhere has occurred in the Chinese countryside. The first-ever clear success in reforming a communist-economy institution was in Chinese agriculture. Spectacular output gains occurred when collective farming was abolished, and replaced by what were, in all but name, private plots, as Rozelle (chap. 9) discusses. The noteworthy features of this transformation include the speed with which it achieved initial success—actually abolishing the communes took about three years—and the ease with which it happened—the peasants generally welcomed the change, in many cases even abolishing the communes before receiving government approval. This initial success, however, merely reflected the inefficiencies of the old commune system. The creation of a market economy in the Chinese countryside actually took several more years.

In China, agricultural reform was crucial to the rest of the reform program; the increase in agricultural productivity spurred the growth of nonstate industry by generating a pool of savings and surplus labor. In the former Soviet Union, in contrast, farm reform seems to have been slow or nonexistent, despite the collapse of central planning. Why has agricultural reform proven to be difficult to achieve in the former Soviet Union? In Ukraine, according to Johnson and Minton-Beddoes (chap. 11), in the early 1990s there has been little demand by farm workers for private family farms. This is because of the power of two groups left over from Stalinist agriculture: farm managers and large, monopsonistic food-processing firms have, at least so far, effectively sabotaged the reforms. The incentives facing the farm managers have not been reformed despite nominal attempts at reform. Juxtaposing Rozelle's chapter with that of Johnson and Minton-Beddoes reveals the critical importance of reform and adaptation of marketing networks in agriculture. In neither case was the simple abolition of the collectives and vesting of property rights in households sufficient to make the rural reforms succeed. The differences between China and Ukraine might be sought not so much in the technological conditions of farming (though this might also be important) as in the supply and marketing environment within which farmers operate.

Gitomer (chap. 10) points out that the revival of household farming created new demands for effective irrigation services that could only be met by newly structured irrigation firms. New institutions are improvised in response to these new demands. Some services that have partial public good or natural monopoly character—such as irrigation in rural areas, and transportation everywhere—are so crucial that supply must be maintained without interruption throughout the transition process. When the state withdraws its support for such services, a solution must be improvised. The failure of Russia's transportation sector has been a major source of Russia's economic difficulties in the early 1990s: food rots in the countryside because it is impossible to get it into the cities. Gitomer provides an example of an apparently successful improvisation: irrigation in rural China. The market provision of irrigation is often problematic, even in well-functioning market economies, because of large economies of scale and the difficulty of monitoring users. The problems of irrigation supply seem to have been effectively resolved in China. Because irrigation supply has relatively high fixed and low marginal costs, efficiency requires that a low price be charged to customers and fixed costs be covered elsewhere. The private firms that have emerged to supply irrigation are regulated by the local government to prevent them from overcharging farmers for the water. They cover their fixed costs by being permitted to engage in related profit-generating activities, such as raising fish. By contrast, attempts to provide substitutes for the former system of providing rural health care have met with a more mixed response, and cannot really be termed successful at this time.

The Politics and Economics of Reform Strategies

Machiavelli said "the reformer has enemies in all those who profit by the old order, and only lukewarm defenders in all those who would profit by the new order. . . . Thus it arises that on every opportunity for attacking the reformer, his opponents do so with the zeal of partisans, the others only defend him half-heartedly, so that between them he runs great danger."[4] The political weakness of a reforming government, and its inability to credibly commit itself to continuing with the policies it announces, constrain the choice of reform policies, according to Fang (chap. 15). If the reformers are in a relatively weak political position, then support for the reform program can be purchased by adopting step-by-step reforms. A gradual reform policy has the advantage that the initial reforms can be directed at areas where there will be a quick and sure payoff (such as agriculture in China). This initial success then strengthens the political support for reform, and more difficult and painful reforms can be attempted. A firmly pro-reform government, according to this argument, can succeed with a big-bang strategy; a government whose commitment to reform is weaker should adopt gradual reforms.

A reforming government may not have the luxury of choice. The timing and the components of the reform package might be, in large part, dictated by economic feasibility—certain policies, such as devaluation of the currency, are fast-acting, while others, such as development of market institutions, are slow to take effect.

China, having started its reforms in the late 1970s, has more experience with reform than any other communist or ex-communist economy, and therefore more data to offer those who study reform. What exactly is the Chinese model? By the early 1990s, China was still far short of being an efficient market economy; but its 1980s reforms were strikingly successful, as measured by high rates of economic growth. The components of China's provisional reform success were, as Naughton (chap. 13) discusses, first, the rapid dissolution of collective agriculture and the consequent spurt in agricultural output; second, the massive entry of nonstate industrial firms following the elimination of restraints on such firms; and third, improvements in the productivity of state-owned firms by the introduction of several mutually reinforcing incentive mechanisms.

---

4. Machiavelli 1950, 21–22.

Vietnam started its reforms shortly after China, and in some respects (such as full price reform) outstripped China, as Dawkins and Whalley (chap. 13) show. As in China, there were successes with agricultural reform and the entry of new firms. Vietnam's relative poverty, however, makes the task of reform even more daunting than usual. The sequence of reforms in Vietnam differs from that in China, but many of the elements are similar. Whether this similarity is caused by imitation or by a more fundamental complementarity of reform measures remains to be determined.

North Korea is at the opposite extreme, having, by the early 1990s, implemented only timid reforms, as Lee (chap. 14) shows. In North Korea, reforms in managerial incentives were attempted in the 1980s. As in Eastern Europe in the 1960s and 1970s, state control over prices was not loosened and competition was not permitted to emerge. North Korea's lack of success is explicable in terms of the Gates-Milgrom-Roberts theory: the complementary reforms, necessary to the success of managerial reforms, were not enacted.

Conclusion

When the transition processes of the various formerly planned economies are looked at close-up, as is done in the chapters to follow, the similarities are more noticeable than the differences. In any formerly planned economy, new institutions must be developed and old institutions reformed. Markets must be created where they did not exist before. The various reforms interact with each other; any given reform may fail if another, complementary, reform is not already in place. The building of market institutions is a fundamentally similar process everywhere. The transition process may be punctuated by "big bangs" and other apparently discontinuous events. But in spite of these up-heavals, the transition process is best thought of as a process that takes a decade or two, and is composed of many strands that are common to all transition processes.

REFERENCES

Havel, Vaclav. *Summer Meditations*. New York: Knopf, 1992.
Machiavelli, Niccolo. *The Prince and The Discourses*. New York: Modern Library, 1950.
Sachs, Jeffrey, and Wing T. Woo. "Structural Factors in the Economic Reforms of China, Eastern Europe, and the Former Soviet Union." *Economic Policy* 18 (April 1994): 101–45.
Wilson, Robert. "Game-Theoretic Analyses of Trading Processes." In T. Bewley, ed., *Advances in Economic Theory*. Cambridge: Cambridge University Press, 1987.

CHAPTER 2

Complementarities in the Transition from Socialism: A Firm-Level Analysis

Susan Gates, Paul Milgrom,
and John Roberts

Most descriptions of economic reform in the former communist economies describe the benefits of the various reform elements in a piecemeal way. Thus, private ownership of a firm increases the incentive to produce highly valued outputs, to economize on inputs, and to protect the value of assets; price liberalization/rationalization and the elimination of subsidies encourage managers to choose the right mix of inputs and outputs; free trade forces managers to face international competition, drives them to activities where they have a comparative advantage, and permits them to achieve greater economies of scale; and competition policy prevents large state firms from using their scale to distort market outcomes. From these descriptions, one might observe that the various proposed reforms are all designed to enhance managerial performance incentives and, from this, be tempted to conclude that they are substitutes for one another, with diminishing returns to additional reforms. Not only is this position wrong, but the reverse conclusion is actually more accurate. There are significant complementarities among these various reforms. Correspondingly, each individual reform makes undertaking the others more attractive.

The idea that there may be complementarities among the individual reform elements within an economic reform package is not new. Indeed, the idea has sometimes been offered as a logical underpinning for the "big bang" strategy for economic reform, in contrast to any policy of partial or gradual reform. As Lipton and Sachs put it:

> The transition process is a seamless web. Structural reforms cannot work without a working price system; a working price system cannot be put in

We thank Simon Johnson, John McMillan, Barry Naughton, and especially Barry Weingast for helpful comments and the Institute for Policy Reform for financial support. Gates is from the Rand Corp. and Milgrom and Roberts are from Stanford University.

17

place without ending excess demand and creating a convertible currency; and a credit squeeze and tight macroeconomic policy cannot be sustained unless prices are realistic, so that there is a rational basis for deciding which firms should be allowed to close. At the same time, for real structural adjustment to take place under the pressures of this demand, the macroeconomic shock must be accompanied by other measures, including selling off state assets, freeing up the private sector, establishing procedures for bankruptcy, preparing a social safety net, and undertaking tax reform. Clearly, the reform process must be comprehensive. (1990b)

This idea has been repeated and made the basis of policy prescriptions. For example, the *Economist* (1991) notes that "[b]ecause all the required reforms are so interlinked, trying to identify the best sequence was always a phony goal. No single measure can bring much benefit without at least some progress towards the other reforms." These arguments, however, are all informal ones. The relationships among the various reform elements are not well defined, and the implications of those relationships are not rigorously explored. To what extent are all these economic reforms complementary? Does such complementarity really imply that the "big-bang" reform strategy is optimal, or does that argument entail some additional implicit assumptions?

The word *complementarity* has various uses and meanings within economics, but we shall use it only in a particular, formal sense. A pair of reforms or policies or activities is complementary if (1) adopting one does not preclude adopting the other and (2) whenever it is possible to implement each reform separately, the sum of the benefits to doing just one or the other is no greater than the benefit of doing both together. An equivalent phrasing of the second condition is that the incremental return to implementing any one of the reforms is greater if the other has already been implemented. It is a theorem (Topkis 1978) that if each pair of reforms in a package is complementary, then implementing any subset of the reforms raises the incremental return to implementing the remaining ones.

While the case for complementarity among the incentive-oriented reforms is not an unqualified one, some plausible sources of pairwise complementarities are easy to identify. First, a policy that strengthens management's incentive to generate profits may cause managers to devote more effort to low value-added or even negative value-added activities when profits are measured using artificial, administered prices, but the very same policy may inspire increased efforts for highly valued activities after prices have been rationalized. Or, what is really just the flip side of the same effect, price rationalization has a greater salutary effect on managers' decisions if the managers are first given incentives to maximize profits.

The rise and fall of private Polish greenhouses demonstrates this phenomenon. In the late 1980s, the Polish government relaxed restrictions on cooperative and private enterprises. Enterpreneurs soon realized that they could make large profits by building greenhouses, heating them with energy that was heavily subsidized by the state, and growing tropical flowers to be sold domestically at uncontrolled prices, or exported. With the price liberalization of 1990 and the subsequent increase in energy prices, the entrepreneurs quickly fled the tropical flower business, presumably directing their resources and efforts toward more socially valuable activities.

A second plausible complementarity is that between privatizing firms and promoting competition, whether by breaking up oligopolies, encouraging entry, or opening up markets to international competition. The reason is much the same as that which makes price rationalization and privatization complementary: managerial incentives to increase output are based on marginal revenues, rather than the competitive price of output, and policies to promote competition in an industry reduce the gap between price and marginal revenue. If the other prices in the economy are set competitively, this is an unambiguous improvement.

A third complementarity may be found between privatization policies implemented in different sectors or at different times. Setting different incentives for different sectors encourages managers to shift effort and even capital toward the high-incentive sector. Similarly, delayed implementation of a privatization policy encourages activities that shift profits forward in time, when the managers' shares are larger. In both cases, managers are encouraged to reallocate resources without regard to the efficiency of the resulting allocation.

In Poland, these perverse incentives associated with piecemeal, delayed privatization are evident in the wave of *nomenklatura* privatization that occurred between 1987 and 1989. In 1987 and 1988, the communist government of Poland legalized stock issue by state-owned firms to transform themselves into joint stock companies. Slay (1992, 53) notes that "managers who had links with the PUWP [Polish United Workers' Party] *nomenklatura* could legally transform state enterprises into private joint-stock companies. This meant that party-state officials controlled the composition and price of issues of stock during these transformations and used their positions as insiders to become owners of the previously state-owned enterprises." These firms came to be known as *nomenklatura* companies. Staniszkis (1991) reports that in 1987, there were already 80 such companies in Poland, and by the beginning of 1990, there were over 40,000. These *nomenklatura* companies generally enjoyed success at the expense of the state enterprise. In many cases, the managers would expropriate only the profitable elements of the state firm, leaving the rest in state hands.

This wave of *nomenklatura* privatization triggered outrage among the population and debate among academics over both the ethics and efficiency of such privatization. For our thesis, the important point of this episode is that it illustrates the reason why increasing incentives for some activities makes it important to increase the incentives for all. For while the plundering of state assets inherent in *nomenklatura* privatization may actually have led to improved efficiency at some of the newly created firms, it also resulted in both resource misallocation among sectors and overtime and an unnecessary loss of revenue for the government.

To analyze timing, it is helpful to take an abstract point of view, regarding policy stances this year and next year as separate policy instruments. For example, there may be private appropriability of returns this year and next, or just next year; there may be price rationalization this year and next, or just next year (or perhaps just this year); and so on. The arguments we have already made then suggest that there is complementarity between privatization and price rationalization within a given year, between privatization this year and next, and between privatization in one sector and in another. The threat of hoarding induces a complementarity between price rationalization this year and next. To the extent that input price rationalization for a firm requires effective antitrust policies to be applied to suppliers, those policies are complementary as well. The whole reform package is rife with complementarities at the level of the firm.

This chapter attempts a detailed theoretical study of the joint effect of various policies on the behavior of a firm's managers in order to formalize the kinds of arguments made above. The general problem is, of course, quite complex, and we need to abstract from some of its complexities to obtain a tractable representation. Our formal approach to studying issues of complementarity follows Milgrom and Roberts 1990 while our modeling of incentives draws mostly from Holmstrom and Milgrom 1987.[1] The formal analysis tends to confirm that complementarities among reform policies of the sorts just discussed are possible, but that the conclusions we derive depend on certain assumptions about the conditions prevailing at the time of transition of the former socialist economy. The analysis also identifies some likely cases of substitute policies.

We emphasize that the mere finding of complementarities across reforms (or other kinds of activities) does *not* by itself imply that the reforms (or activities) should all be installed simultaneously. This is most clearly illus-

---

1. Holmstrom and Milgrom 1994 introduced the idea that different incentive instruments used to regulate employees and agents are complements. The main differences between the two analyses are ones of context, which determine the incentive instruments and the way they are used.

trated by taking the argument to a ridiculous extreme. Observe that work experience and productive work are complementary, because working certainly does not preclude gaining experience and experience increases the productivity of work. Yet, it would be absurd to argue from this alone that inexperienced workers should not be permitted to work, for work must precede the accumulation of experience. It is similarly absurd to argue on the basis of complementarities alone that it is unwise to rationalize prices without privatization, or that one should prohibit the creation of new private enterprises until the government can create a suitable means of taxing them.

The logic that supports big-bang policies involves two elements besides complementarity among reform instruments. The first is *complementarity over time*. For example, the mere fact that price rationalization is expected for tomorrow makes it valuable to implement it today, in order to prevent distortions such as hoarding and dumping. Such complementarity of reforms over time is a reason for speedy implementation. The second element is *nonconvexities,* which are endemic in incentive problems. These nonconvexities make it quite possible that each reform individually has an adverse effect on managerial performance, even though the whole package of reforms has a decidedly salutary effect. We illustrate this possibility in an otherwise well-behaved example in our later discussion of complementarity among incentive instruments, using a concave production function and a convex cost function. This possibility implies that piecemeal implementation of reforms can add to the costs of transition and increase pressures to reverse reforms that are already in place.

A second important caveat is that the analysis offered here is built on the particular structure of the reforms. Generalization to other reform packages is unwarranted and, indeed, we see no reason to suppose that all packages of reforms must be characterized by extensive complementarities. China's dramatic successes since the late 1970s with its partial reforms (McMillan and Naughton 1992) indicate the extreme degree to which details determine the conclusion of the analysis. Agricultural reforms in China, implemented in an environment where capital and effort were not fungible across agricultural and industrial activities, did not suffer the disadvantages we have described. Provided that the government is strong enough to enforce fulfillment of the plan, we find no reason to suppose that price reforms allowing only output beyond the plan to be traded at uncontrolled prices will be complementary to price reform for the remaining planned units as well, even though the two parts together constitute what might be called full price liberalization.

The following section gives an account of the incentives for managers in Poland just before and during the recent transition. In addition, we discuss the problem of monopoly power and look at the various ways in which the Polish government tried to improve competitiveness. The Polish experience provides the motivation for several of our modeling decisions. The simplest version of our formal model, which excludes trade and competition policies, is developed in the third section. Readers who wish to skip the technicalities can omit this section and proceed directly to the next. Complementarities within the formal model are developed and described in nontechnical language in the fourth section. This section also includes an example showing the possibility of a "policy-by-policy optimum" that is not a global optimum.[2] That is, we illustrate a collection of policies that are coherent in the sense that any change in one policy alone would be undesirable even though a package of changes is desirable. The next section extends our analysis to include the effect of trade and competitiveness policies, along with price reform, privatization, and timing. We conclude with a discussion of the lessons of the model.

Managerial Incentives in Poland

A series of reforms were introduced in Poland during the communist era, in an attempt to improve profit-making incentives for managers (Frydman and Wellisz 1991). That attempt was generally regarded as a failure. The continuation of price controls, enterprise subsidies, and reverse taxation rendered any sort of profit-based "managerial incentive plan" ineffective as a means of motivating managers. According to Fan and Schaffer (1991), the "profit" upon which the profit tax and wage bonus were based was profit after the subtraction of turnover taxes and the addition of subsidies. Such manipulations of the final profit of firms were widespread and were normally used to make sure that most (if not all) state firms were profitable on paper, no matter how poor their actual performance.

These subsidies were quite extensive, suggesting that the government spent a lot of money in order to maintain the "profitability" of various state firms. Holzmann reports that in the 1980s Eastern European governments spent about 15 percent of GDP on budgetary subsidies. Western countries, on average, spend less than 5 percent on direct subsidies. Moreover, the subsidies to Eastern European enterprises (through artificially low prices on inputs, negative turnover tax, etc.) were generally much larger than were direct subsidies to consumers. The main reason for this disparity is that as the Eastern European governments abandoned strict quantity-planning mechanisms, tax preferences and other subsidies became a substitute method of control. "Since most prices were initially administered, differences between

---

2. Similar messages can be found in Murphy, Shleifer, and Vishny 1992 and Shleifer and Vishny 1992, who argue that partial price reform in the context of a planned economy can distort the allocation between the public and private sectors, leading to worse overall economic performance.

prices and costs resulting from the distorted price structure had to be compensated for. Consequently, producer subsidies (and taxes) were generally used to bring enterprise accounts into balance." (Holzmann 1991, 158).

In a detailed study of subsidization in the 500 largest Polish firms for 1988, Schaffer (1990) notes that not a single firm was a loss maker after its subsidies were included. There were two major types of subsidy given to Polish enterprises. The first was a product-specific subsidy, which was supposed to compensate enterprises for any unfavorable implications of price controls. The second was an enterprise-specific subsidy, "which might be paid, for example, to enterprises with old equipment and therefore high operating costs. . . . There is, however, anecdotal evidence that nearly all these subsidies were allocated according to a number of informal, enterprise-specific criteria, in particular profitability" (Schaffer 1990, 190). The discretion the government exercised in determining subsidies to individual firms weakened the link between managerial compensation and the real value of the firm's activities.

The reform package of January 1990 included reforms releasing enterprises from central control and significantly reducing subsidies. The discretionary tax subsidies were abolished. Although profits might now be a better signal of managerial performance, the compensation system was not designed to reward managers for such performance. In addition to these reforms, the Polish government introduced a tax on excessive wages in state enterprises. This tax applied to both worker and managerial wages and bonuses. The policy for 1990 called for the partial indexation of a firm's total wage bill to inflation. Each month, the government established a maximum allowable wage bill increase, or wage norm. The norms provided for wage increases that were smaller than the rate of inflation. Any firm whose wage bill exceeded that norm was subject to a tax of between 100 percent and 500 percent on those excesses (Coricelli and Revenga 1992). Although this policy was designed to force a decline in real wages and prevent the return of the wage-price spiral that plagued Poland throughout 1989, it had the additional effect of limiting incentive pay in state enterprises. Also, because the excessive wage tax did not apply to private enterprises, many workers and managers viewed the ability to increase wages as a great incentive to privatize.

In summary, the Polish government has been trying to improve managerial performance incentives since the early 1980s. Although the reforms of the 1980s linked managerial compensation to firm profits, the reforms did not achieve the goal of increased production, for a variety of reasons. Importantly, firm profits were directly manipulated by the government through turnover taxes and subsidies, and profits were measured by controlled, centrally determined prices, so that measured profits bore little relation to real value added. Although these distortions were largely removed in 1990, it appears that direct profit-based incentives for state managers were weakened by policies that restricted wage payments (including bonuses for both workers and managers) at state firms. Since wages at private firms are not regulated, these managers do have higher-powered profit incentives. Many of those large firms currently under state ownership are targeted for participation in the mass privatization program.

Even if profit-based incentives are successfully instituted, however, the resulting managerial behavior may not be in the social interest. Many economists, e.g., Slay 1990, suggest that because of the high degree of industrial concentration in Eastern European countries, as well as trade restrictions that shield firms from international competition, incentive-based economic reforms may induce monopolists and oligopolists to continue restricting output while increasing prices to increase profits. Studies by Slay (1990) and Schaffer (1990) indicate that the industrial structure of Poland immediately prior to the "big-bang" reforms of January 1990 was oligopolistic, suffering from a lack of small competitors. Slay suggests that the lack of competition in many sectors (e.g., glass, printing, machine tools, and wood products) before 1990 was due in large part to government policies restricting the creation of private enterprise, state administrative restrictions, and underdeveloped supply networks. One would assume that market reforms alone would significantly improve competition in these sectors. However, Slay argues that other sectors, such as coal, paper, and metallurgy, are so highly concentrated and integrated that additional measures may be needed to introduce competitive forces into those industries.

Lipton and Sachs (1990a), in an early blueprint for privatization in Poland, argue that monopoly power is not an urgent problem in a country like Poland if trade restrictions are removed and domestic producers are subject to stiff foreign competition. In their view, trade liberalization is a perfect substitute for an active competitiveness policy. With the benefit of hindsight, Blanchard et al. (1991) argue that trade liberalization was not strong enough to prevent the exercise of market power by large state enterprises in Poland in 1990. Price liberalization gave state managers the ability to set prices at the monopoly level, and most state-owned enterprises took advantage of this opportunity.

> Anecdotal evidence has it that some firms, having always operated under excess demand conditions, thought it safe to choose a high price, only to discover over time that the price far exceeded even the monopoly price and that some price increases had to be rolled back. More quantitative evidence is provided by the behavior of profits of firms since the stabilization: profits have been unexpectedly high, especially so in the face of a sharp decrease in domestic demand, to which we return below. The

constraints on prices from convertibility and a fixed exchange rate do not appear to have been powerful enough to have prevented monopoly pricing in large segments of the economy, at least for the time being. (Blanchard et al. 1991, 18)

Blanchard et al. go on to recommend an extensive restructuring program for state industries that would, among other things, reduce monopoly power.

Studies of the behavior of Polish state enterprises after the "big bang" reach conflicting conclusions as to the extent to which these firms have exercised monopoly power. In a study of state-owned enterprises in Poland after the reforms, Schaffer (1992) examines aggregate trends in markup over cost for Polish state-owned enterprises and concludes that there is no evidence to support the notion that state enterprises restricted output in order to exercise monopoly power. It is not clear, however, that such general conclusions about the exercise of monopoly power in Poland follow from an analysis of aggregate data. Slay's 1992 study of industrial concentration in Poland suggests that firms in different industries respond to price liberalization and market reforms in different ways. Frydman and Wellisz (1991) argue that this is exactly what happened. State enterprises in the consumer goods sector, which faced strong competition from both domestic private firms and foreign firms, reacted to the decline in consumer demand by reducing production as well as markups. On the other hand, they note that, "the strongly monopolized producer goods industries, insulated to a large extent from market shocks, switched, under the impact of the stabilization measures, from a policy of below-market clearing to monopolistic pricing" (Frydman and Wellisz 1991, 144). Kharas (1991) argues to the contrary that "at a broad sectoral level, output changes correspond to what neoclassical theory would predict, rising in response to higher prices, and falling in sectors faced with higher costs and taxes" (1991,19). While noting that state-owned enterprises in Poland did not appear to be exercising monopoly power in 1990, Kharas stresses that there is a real danger of such power developing unless strong actions, in addition to trade liberalization, are taken to promote competition. "[A]lthough openness to international trade provides a considerable spur to competition, it is a blunt instrument whose effects are uneven across sectors. . . . Consumer goods industries, especially food-based products and other light industry goods, may be made competitive through trade, but in consumer durables, pharmaceuticals, producer goods and of course nontradables, international trade is less significant" (Kharas 1991, 30–31). Kharas goes on to suggest that trade liberalization policies should be supplemented with an active antimonopoly policy that looks at each firm on an individual basis, considering the potential economies of scale in the industry and the influence of foreign competition in the sector, and the potential for abuse of monopoly power. In his view, trade liberalization and competitiveness policies are substitutes, but the relative impact of each policy varies across sectors of the economy.

Whatever the actions of large state Polish firms in the immediate post-reform period, the exercise of some degree of monopoly power was of significant concern to the government, which responded with both trade liberalization and competitiveness policies. Trade liberalization was a central feature of the Polish "big bang." In addition to lifting the quantity restrictions and the restrictions on economic entities allowed to engage in foreign trade that existed in the communist era, the government also lowered tariff rates on most products.[3] Trade liberalization was accompanied by the establishment of full internal currency convertibility at a fixed rate. Given the hyperinflation that was plaguing Poland in 1989, the monetary stabilization program was naturally fraught with uncertainty. In hindsight, it appears that the fixed exchange rate, set in January 1990 and maintained until May of 1991, undervalued the Polish currency. This undervaluation served to dampen the competitive pressures of trade liberalization in 1990.

The Polish government has also focused attention on industrial concentration and monopoly in domestic production.[4] Apparently, there is good reason for such concern, as 80 percent of goods markets at a detailed product level are dominated by producers whose market share exceeds 30 percent (OECD 1992b, 60), The Antimonopoly Law of February 1990 renders various monopolistic and anticompetitive acts illegal, and provides for the creation of the Antimonopoly Office. This office is empowered to break up monopolistic enterprises and intervene actively in the pricing decisions of firms that have a dominant position in the market.[5]

Of course, the other aspect of competition policy, requiring little government intervention, is the development of the private sector through privatization of existing state enterprises and the entry of new businesses. The Polish mass privatization program continues to suffer delays due to political crisis.

---

3. Whereas the average tariff rate in January of 1989 was 18.3 percent, the average tariff rate in 1990 fell to 5.5 percent. In August of 1991, the Polish government raised tariffs once again, especially on agricultural goods and animal products, so that the average tariff rate on all goods rose to 18.4 percent, and the average tariff rate on nonagricultural goods is 16.3 percent (OECD 1992b, 134).

4. For detailed information on industrial concentration, see OECD 1992a.

5. The Antimonopoly Office appears to be taking its mandate quite seriously. In 1990 alone, 188 enterprises were broken up into 771 individual units. Most of these divisions occurred among enterprises under the control of the ministries of industry, transportation, and agriculture. (Kharas 1991, 8). In the first half of 1991, 84 firms were broken up into 190 units. In addition, the Antimonopoly Office blocked about 10 percent of the 1,100 proposals submitted by state enterprise attempting transformation (incorporation or liquidation). "In particular, 60 out of 200 requests for change of status to joint stock company were delayed in 1991 pending divestiture or reorganization of the company concerned" (OECD 1992b, 60).

Comprehensive mass privatization legislation finally passed the Sejm (parliament) in April of 1993 and was approved by President Walesa.[6] The legislation calls for the rapid commercialization and subsequent privatization of 400 large firms, including 170 manufacturing firms that account for 13.8 percent of manufacturing production. Meanwhile, the privatization of small shops and businesses and the entry of new small businesses proceeded rather rapidly. By the end of 1991, there were almost 1.5 million registered private businesses in Poland and by September of that year, 75 percent of trading firms, 45 percent of construction firms, and 80 percent of trucking firms were under private ownership. (OECD 1992a, 38). Even in the area of industrial production, where privatization has not proceeded as rapidly as expected, the private sector accounted for 24.1 percent of total industrial production in 1991, up from 16.2 percent in 1989.

In contrast to the piecemeal economic reform strategies of the communist era, reforms in postcommunist Poland have been more comprehensive, focusing not only on improved managerial incentives in state-owned enterprises, but also on privatization, price liberalization, and policies to promote competition. In order to investigate timing, as well as direct complementarities among policies, the formal model that is the basis of most of our analysis incorporates three policy instruments: current privatization, future privatization, and price rationalization. We will later expand the model in order to study how these policies relate to trade liberalization and competitiveness policies.

The Model

We consider a model in which the firm transforms a single marketed input and employee efforts into a single output, using a variety of production processes. For concreteness and simplicity, we represent all employees involved in running the firm by a single agent, whom we call "the manager."[7] The manager makes four choices in running the firm. He selects the levels, x_1 and x_2, of the input to use in the firm's two production processes and supplies two kinds of efforts, e_1 and e_2. The first kind of effort is used with the marketed input x_1 to produce current output according to the "effort intensive" production function $\min(e_1, x_1)$. The second kind of effort may represent an investment in intangibles or other assets that are not currently easily measured but that add output of value e_2 in a future period. Alternatively, e_2 can be used to represent effort

---

6. The implementation of this program has been delayed due to the collapse of the parliamentary government in May 1993. Further delays are expected under the new left-leaning governing parliamentary coalition, which took over in October 1993.

7. This reduced form approach is fully justified if the inside agents can monitor one another and contract perfectly among themselves (Holmstrom and Milgrom 1990).

expended in another sector of the economy, though we shall suppress that interpretation during the analysis of the model. In addition, there is a second production process using the marketed input that produces $g(x_2)$ units of output and that requires no managerial effort. Output of the two processes are indistinguishable. For compactness of notation, we sometimes represent output as a function of the effort, e_1, and the total input purchases, $x = x_1 + x_2$ as $f(e_1,x) = e_1 + g(x - e_1)$, with the convention that $g(z) = z$ for $z \leq 0$.

The motivation of this formulation is as follows. As we shall see, including output that is a joint function of effort and marketed inputs, where the two kinds of inputs are complementary, allows the state to use a low input price to promote managerial effort.[8] The min operator creates an especially tractable complementarity (between x_1 and e_1) when managerial effort is used in production. It is also reasonable to suppose that manipulating the input price, p_x, will affect the firm's input mix; including the $g(x_2)$ term accomplishes that. The two kinds of effort allow the possibility of a similar distortion in effort provision. For example, an increase in the incentive for current output may cause effort to be shifted away from its other valuable use, namely, investing in intangibles that create future output.

The central planner is assumed to provide incentives to managers for current output by sharing a fraction, α_1, of current net earnings with the manager.[9] This may be done through an explicit performance contract, or the planner might blink when some fraction of the firm's net resources is diverted by managers to their personal use. Sharing profits is an alternative to privatization, but not a perfect substitute. One possible difference is political or ideological constraints that limit state managers' incomes more than those of private managers, making it easier to set α_1 higher in privately owned firms than in state-owned ones. A second difference lies in the possibilities for opportunistic behavior. Even a planner that can commit to sharing current income in excess of some target may still be unable to commit to future targets, and that makes sharing the future returns arising from current effort investments problematical. We suppose that there is a separate constant, α_2, reflecting the share of returns on such investments that accrue to the firm's manager. We allow that α_2 may be zero.

The manager has quasi-linear preferences and constant absolute risk aversion, that is, utility is given by $U(w,e) = -\exp[-r(w - C(e))]$. In this expression, $C(e)$ is the "cost of effort," w is the manager's "wage," and r is the

---

8. Litwack and Qian (1993) have similarly observed that subsidizing complementary inputs—in their case public inputs—can supply an incentive for increased effort by a firm's managers.

9. In this reduced form model, we simply assume that the compensation contract is linear in form. This linearity can be justified as the form of the optimal contract in a certain fully specified dynamic model. See Holmstrom and Milgrom 1987.

coefficient of absolute risk aversion. This utility specification has two main advantages. First, it implies that transfers made to or from the manager affect neither his willingness to bear a given risk nor his willingness to expend a given level of effort for a given level of pay. These properties add tractability to the analysis of incentives. Equally importantly, when combined with a similar assumption about other agents in the economy, the specification means that cash transfers among agents do not affect the total certainty equivalent of the parties. This achieves a complete separation of distributional issues from efficiency issues within the model. The total certainty equivalent in this context is an unambiguous neoclassical index of efficiency: Given any two productive arrangements with different values of this index, there is a potential Pareto improvement to be achieved by moving from the low index arrangement to the higher index arrangement and making appropriate transfers, but no potential Pareto improvement by moving in the other direction. The index for the overall economy is the sum of the firm-level efficiency indexes. This separation of distributional from efficiency issues is very useful analytically: it allows us to isolate and study the issues of how various reform policies combine to affect the efficiency of firms' operations. At the same time, one must remember that what is being analyzed is just one important aspect of the actual reform problem.

We also assume that the cost of effort function is convex quadratic, as follows: $C(e_1,e_2) = \frac{1}{2}c_1e_1^2 + \frac{1}{2}c_2e_2^2 + c_{12}e_1e_2$. The significance of the quadratic form has been discussed at length by Holmstrom and Milgrom (1994). Essentially, the linearity of production in effort combined with the quadratic effort-cost function results in a separable effort-supply function, so that the level of incentives for one activity does not affect the slope of effort supply for the other activity. This simplifies the analysis by eliminating an effect of ambiguous sign, and thus also limits the generality of the conclusions we obtain. We further assume that c_1, c_2, c_{12}, $\Delta > 0$, where $\Delta = c_1c_2 - c_{12}^2$. That c_{12} is positive means that the two kinds of efforts are substitutes in cost for the agent: a higher level of effort in one activity raises the marginal cost of effort in the other. That the determinant Δ is positive means that the cost function is convex.

The firm's profits are $\pi = p_yf(e_1,x) - p_xx + \epsilon$, where p_y is the output price, $p_x < p_y$ is the input price, and ϵ is a normally distributed error term with variance σ^2. The requirement that $p_x < p_y$ means that the production process requiring managerial inputs is potentially viable. The manager thus chooses x, e_1, and e_2 to maximize his certainty equivalent, which is:

$$\alpha_1[p_yf(e_1,x) - p_xx] + \alpha_2e_2 - C(e_1,e_2) - \frac{1}{2}r\alpha_1^2\sigma^2 .$$

If we further specify that the function g is smooth and concave on $\mathbf{R}_+$ and satisfies $\lim_{z \downarrow 0} g'(z) \geq 1$ and $\lim_{z \uparrow \infty} g'(z) \to 0$, then clearly x will be chosen to be strictly larger than e_1. The firm's demand for the input is then $e_1 + x_2$, where x_2 is determined by:

$$g'(x_2) = p_x/p_y .$$ (1)

It is not difficult to show that the effort supply functions are then:

$$e_1 = e_1(\alpha_1(p_y - p_x),\alpha_2) = c_2\Delta^{-1}(p_y - p_x)\alpha_1 - c_{12}\Delta^{-1}\alpha_2$$ (2)

$$e_2 = e_2(\alpha_1(p_y - p_x),\alpha_2) = -c_{12}\Delta^{-1}(p_y - p_x)\alpha_1 + c_1\Delta^{-1}\alpha_2 .$$ (3)

Notice from equation 2 that incentives for current effort can be provided either by increasing α_1 or by increasing the spread between input and output prices, $p_y - p_x$. Since we are not modeling the uses of output, the distortions from manipulating p_y are omitted from our model. For that reason, we shall regard p_x, but not p_y, as an incentive instrument for the planner and assume that $p_y = p_y^*$.

Although reducing p_x is a substitute for increasing α_1 in providing incentives, it can be an inferior substitute. For suppose the actual shadow price of the input in the economy is p_x^*. Then providing incentives by setting $p_x < p_x^*$ does tend to encourage more use of effort e_1 and a correspondingly higher level of input x_1 in the first production process, but it also leads the firm to use too much of the input x_2 in the second production process. In mathematical terms, for any fixed level of e_1, the firm chooses x to maximize $p_y^*g(x - e_1) - p_xx$, but the social optimum involves choosing x to maximize $p_y^*g(x - e_1) - p_x^*x$. With $p_x < p_x^*$, the optimal level of x is no smaller in the second problem, and is strictly larger whenever equation 3 applies. Thus, manipulating incentives using input prices induces an extra distortion in the economy. (Notice, though, that we have not yet described the cost of using α_1.)

The low price of certain basic inputs, such as energy, in the socialist economies is consistent with a policy of encouraging effort devoted to the production of final goods when those who control a firm are not residual claimants. Later, for our formal comparisons of policies, we will assume that pretransition input prices were set optimally given the institutionally imposed restrictions on α_1 and α_2. In particular, this implies that the actual input price is set below the corresponding economy-wide shadow price or the price at which the input might be sold in the world market, if that is the relevant opportunity cost: $p_x < p_x^*$.

The social objective in our model is to maximize the total certainty equivalent of the manager and the rest of society. This total consists of the social value of the present and future outputs produced, minus the value of inputs used, and minus the cost of managerial effort and any risk premium that the manager bears. Thus, the social objective is:

$$p_y^* f(e_1, x) - p_x^* x + e_2 - C(e_1, e_2) - \tfrac{1}{2} r \alpha_1^2 \sigma^2 . \tag{4}$$

This is to be controlled choosing the input price p_x and the incentive coefficients α_1 and α_2, subject to the constraints of effort and inputs and chosen consistently with equations 1–3. Later, we shall also introduce competition policy, consisting of antitrust policy and trade policy, into the model.

Complementarity Among Incentive Instruments

The analysis of the model is conducted by substituting the constraints (1)–(3) into the objective function (4). We first consider complementarities among incentives for the two activities. Let $a_1 = \alpha_1(p_y - p_x)$, $a_2 = \alpha_2$, and $a = (a_1, a_2)$. Obviously, the manager's optimum entails $x_1 = e_1$. So, we may rewrite the social objective as:

$$\begin{aligned} \Omega = (p_y^* - p_x^*) e_1(a) &+ p_y^* g(x_2(p_x/p_y)) - p_x^* x_2(p_x/p_y) + e_2(a) \\ &- C(e_1(a), e_2(a)) - \tfrac{1}{2} r a_1^2 \sigma^2 / (p_y^* - p_x^*)^2 . \end{aligned} \tag{5}$$

Here, we regard Ω as $\Omega(a_1, a_2, p_x)$: performance depends on the control instruments.

PROPOSITION 1. *Incentives for current and future output are complementary, that is,* $\partial^2 \Omega / \partial a_1 \partial a_2 > 0$.

PROOF. The linearity of the effort supply functions, $e_i(a) = (c_j a_i - c_{12} a_j)/\Delta$ implies that $\partial^2 \Omega / \partial a_1 \partial a_2 = \partial^2 C(e_1(a), e_2(a)) / \partial a_1 \partial a_2$. Substituting the effort supplies into the quadratic cost function and evaluating the cross partial yields $\partial^2 \Omega / \partial a_1 \partial a_2 = -\partial e_2 / \partial a_1 = c_{12} \Delta^{-1} > 0$. □

If we imagine that privatization amounts to increasing α_1 and α_2 toward unity (with unity representing the firm's manager and employees being full residual claimants), then the implication of this is that from the point of view of managerial incentives, announcing a privatization reform for the future makes it more worthwhile to take steps that increase current incentives. Such steps may include making privatization immediate. In the alternate interpretation, the proposition also implies that if there are no restrictions on the flow of resources (such as capital and effort) out of state firms, it is imperative to match increased incentives in the private sector with increased incentives in the state sector.

The intuitive explanation for this result is as follows. If the two different kinds of agent efforts are substitutes in the agent's cost function, as we have assumed, then increases in the incentive a_2 for investment tend to divert effort away from current production. The marginal opportunity cost of this diversion is zero if the effort devoted to current output is efficient (that is, if the marginal value of additional effort in producing current output equals the marginal cost), but is positive if the efforts devoted to current output are inefficiently low. The stronger the incentives for current output, the lower the opportunity cost of the diverted effort. Notice that the magnitude of this effect hinges on the strength of the substitution effect, for $\partial^2 \Omega / \partial a_1 \partial a_2 = -\partial e_2 / \partial a_1$.

PROPOSITION 2. *Starting from a "socialist equilibrium" defined by the condition that the current input price, p_x, is already optimized for the pre-transition values of $\alpha_1 < 1$ and $\alpha_2 \leq 1$, privatization (setting $\alpha_1 = 1$) and price rationalization (setting $p_x = p_x^*$) are complementary reforms.*

PROOF. By definition, at the socialist equilibrium, increasing p_x to p_x^* has a negative payoff. However, if privatization has occurred in the current period, so that $\alpha_1 = 1$ while $\alpha_2 \leq 1$, then the three effects of increasing p_x to p_x^* in equation 5 are all positive. The increase eliminates excess use of the marketed input (reduces x_2); reduces a_1 to its optimal value, $p_y^* - p_x^*$, leading to value increasing changes in both e_1 (which is reduced) and e_2 (which is increased); and reduces the risk premium (which is proportional to a_1^2). □

PROPOSITION 3. *It is possible in this formulation for there to be a policy-by-policy optimum at the socialist equilibrium. In that case, changes in any one of the policy instruments α_1, α_2, or p_x can only reduce value, yet simultaneous increases in all three instruments would increase value.*

PROOF. Possibility is proved by giving an example. Let $c_1 = 1/5$, $c_2 = 1/6$, and $c_{12} = 1/8$. Let the social values of the input and output be $p_y^* = 10$ and $p_x^* = 8.5$, the coefficient of absolute risk aversion $r = 1/2$ and the variance $\sigma^2 = 1/16$. Finally, let $g(\cdot)$ be a piecewise linear concave production function with slope 1 on [0,3], 3/4 on [3,5], 1/4 on [5,7], and 0 for $x_2 \geq 7$. In that case, one can show that $(\alpha_1, \alpha_2, p_x) = (.106, 0, 2.5)$ is a policy-by-policy optimum, leading to choices $(e_1, e_2, x_1, x_2) = (7.5, 0, 7.5, 5)$ and social payoff $\Omega = 8.125$. In contrast, setting $p_x = p_x^* = 8.5$ and $\alpha_1 = \alpha_2 = 1$, leading to $(e_1, e_2, x_1, x_2) = (7.06, .71, 7.06, 3)$ and $\Omega = 10.13$. □

Notice, first, that the existence of an interior policy-by-policy optimum requires that the social welfare maximization problem be nonconvex. For otherwise, the first-order conditions of policy-by-policy optimization would also entail global maximization. This means that although C is quadratic and g is concave, the principal-agent incentive problem is not concave. Indeed, in our example, the agent's choice of x_2 is actually a discontinuous function of the price p_x, so the objective function is not even continuous in the policy variables. There is nothing unusual or strange about this. Nonconvexities of this sort are quite normal in principal-agent problems in general and in this sort of model in particular (Holmstrom and Milgrom 1991). There is no plausible reason to rule out, a priori, the possibility of such policy-by-policy optima.

Competition Policy

Thus far, we have assumed that firms operate in perfectly competitive markets, so that the marginal return to output from the point of view of the firm coincides with both the output price and marginal social value of that output ($MR_y = p_y = p_y^*$) both before and after price liberalization. However, our discussion of trade and competitiveness policy in Poland suggests that price liberalization can create opportunities for the exercise of monopoly power by domestic enterprises. Before price liberalization occurs, the government controls the price of output as well as the price of input, and sets the price of output so that it is equal to the marginal social value of that output. After price liberalization, the government no longer sets the price of output; instead, price is determined by what are usually imperfectly competitive market forces. To the extent that firms in a given industry are able to exercise such monopoly power, our assumption that $MR = p_y^*$ no longer holds. The purpose of this section is to examine the implications of monopoly power for our model, and to study the role of competitiveness policies in the overall reform package.

As the discussion in the second section indicates, there may be some sectors of the economy that are made effectively competitive by import competition, others that already consist of many small firms, others where the breakup of large firms to reduce market power is desirable, and still others where the emergence of new domestic competitors makes any government policy intervention unnecessary. There is little to be gained for our purposes by modeling all these possibilities in detail. Instead, we make a simple extension of our model, allowing that there may be a difference between the marginal return, MR_y, received by a firm for units of output and the social value of output, which is p_y^*. A firm with market power has a tendency to restrict output, which we may represent by the condition $MR_y < p_y^*$. A small firm in an industry where other firms are restricting output may find its marginal revenue is $MR_y > p_y^*$. In terms of the mathematical model, these possibilities are captured by replacing p_y^* by MR_y in the manager's first-order condition.

Within the formal model, competition policies are just policies to reduce or eliminate the difference between MR_y and p_y^*. In this formal sense, competition policy is an element of price rationalization. Price rationalization requires that the marginal return to intermediate and final goods (x and y) reflect the social value of that product. In the model of the previous section, the market for good y was perfectly competitive, so *price liberalization* was just the same as *price rationalization*. Then proposition 2, which states that price rationalization and privatization are complementary policies, also implies that price liberalization and privatization are complementary. When firms are able to exercise market power, the direct effect of price liberalization is more complicated. On one hand, it allows p_x to move to its optimal level, p_x^*; at the same time, it results in a divergence between p_y^* and MR_y. Thus, while price liberalization induces the manager to use inputs more efficiently, it can also distort the manager's output choice away from the socially optimal level. Therefore, while Proposition 2 assures that price rationalization is complementary to privatization, the relation between price liberalization and privatization is less clear. When firms have considerable market power, an effective competition policy may be necessary in order to obtain beneficial effects from price liberalization.

Conclusion

The main thrust of this chapter has been to examine how certain reforms that have been proposed and implemented in the transition from socialism interact, whether complementarities among policy instruments can be found at the level of the firm, and what the implications of those complementarities may be. Our analysis does indeed find likely complementarities at work between price rationalization and ownership reforms (privatization), a temporal complementarity that makes speedup of reforms desirable, and a complementarity between the package of ownership and price reforms and competitiveness policies of various kinds.

As its very definition indicates, complementarity is an attribute of the *interaction* among different policy instruments. Our conclusions about complementarities would remain unchanged if one were to enrich the analysis by introducing extra effects that alter the *separate* benefits or costs of using price controls, privatization, or competitiveness policy. This stability lends some robustness to our analysis, since quite large alterations of the model could be made without affecting the complementarity conclusion. This observation, however, is a two-sided coin. The fact that complementarity continues to hold even when one makes large changes in the costs and benefits of a certain policy implies that arguments about complementarity cannot alone determine the form of the optimal policy.

As we emphasized in the introduction, when reform is desirable, complementarity over time tends to reinforce the argument in favor of fast, comprehensive reform. But this is only a tendency. Contrary to the arguments sometimes made, complementarity among instruments does not by itself imply that fast, comprehensive reform—the "big bang"—is necessary or desirable, because there are also costs to implementing such a strategy.[10] Contrary to arguments that are sometimes made in favor of a more gradual approach to implementing reforms, we have shown that a policy-by-policy socialist equilibrium is possible. That is, regardless of scale economies, there may not exist any gradual reform path from the socialist equilibrium to the first-best policy that involves improved performance at each step of the way. Indeed, there may not even exist a first step involving a single policy that does not involve some temporary loss of output. The presence of complementarities alone does not determine the optimal path of reform.

REFERENCES

Blanchard, O., R. Dornbusch, P. Krugman, R. Layard, and L. Summers. 1991. *Reform in Eastern Europe*. Cambridge, MA: MIT Press.
Coricelli, F., and A. Revenga. 1992. "Wages and Unemployment in Poland: Recent Developments and Policy Issues." In *Wage Policy during the Transition to a Market Economy: Poland 1990–91*, World Bank Discussion Paper no. 158. Washington, DC: The World Bank.
Dewatripont, M., and G. Roland. 1992. "Economic Reform and Dynamic Political Constraints." *Review of Economic Studies* 59.
Economist. 1991. "Business in Eastern Europe Survey: Catch 22." *Economist*, September 21, 5.
Fan, Q., and M. Schaffer. 1991. "Enterprise Reforms in Chinese and Polish State-Owned Industries." *Economic Systems* 15, no. 2 (October).
Frydman, R., and S. Wellisz. 1991. "The Ownership-Control Structure and the Behavior of Polish Enterprises during the 1990 Reforms: Macroeconomic Measures and Microeconomic Responses." In V. Corbo, F. Coricelli, and J. Bossak, eds., *Reforming Central and Eastern European Economies: Initial Results and Challenges*. Washington, DC: The World Bank.
Hinds, Manuel. 1991. "Issues in the Introduction of Market Forces in Eastern European Socialist Economies." In Simon Commander, ed., *Managing Inflation in Socialist Economies in Transition*. Washington, DC: The World Bank.

---

10. For example, Dewatripont and Roland (1992) emphasize that political constraints can cause a too rapid reform to fail. McKinnon (1991) cites financial constraints on firms needing to upgrade their technologies as a reason to go slowly. Blanchard et al. (1991) cite both financial and labor market imperfections as raising the costs of rapid transition.

Holmstrom, Bengt, and Paul Milgrom. 1987. "Aggregation and Linearity in the Provision of Intertemporal Incentives." *Econometrica* 55, no. 2 (March): 303–28.

Holmstrom, Bengt, and Paul Milgrom. 1990. "Regulating Trade among Agents." *Journal of Institutional and Theoretical Economics* 146, no.1 (March): 85–105.

Holmstrom, Bengt, and Paul Milgrom. 1991. "Multitask Principal-Agent Analyses: Incentive Contracts, Asset Ownership and Job Design." *Journal of Law, Economics and Organization* 7 (Spring): 24–52.

Holmstrom, Bengt, and Paul Milgrom. 1994. "The Firm as an Incentive System." *American Economic Review* 84, no. 4 (September): 972–91.

Holzmann, Robert. 1991. "Budgetary Subsidies in Central and Eastern European Economies in Transition." *Economic Systems* 15, no. 2 (October).

Jorgensen, E., A. Gelb, and I. Singh. 1991. "Life after the Polish 'Big Bang': Representative Episodes of Enterprise Behavior." In V. Corbo, F. Coricelli, and J. Bossak, eds., *Reforming Central and Eastern European Economies: Initial Results and Challenges.* Washington, DC: The World Bank.

Kharas, Homi. 1991. "Restructuring Socialist Industry: Poland's Experience in 1990." World Bank Discussion Paper no. 142. Washington, DC: The World Bank.

Law No. 88 (Anti-Monopoly Law): 24 February 1990. Published in Dzennik Ustaw no.14, 88 13 Mar 1990, 170–74. Translated in JPRS-EER-90-115-S, 68.

Lipton, David, and Jeffrey Sachs. 1990a. "Privatization in Eastern Europe: The Case of Poland." *Brookings Papers on Economic Activity* 2.

Lipton, David, and Jeffrey Sachs. 1990b. "Creating a Market Economy in Eastern Europe: The Case of Poland." *Brookings Papers on Economic Activity* 1.

Litwack, John, and Yingyi Qian. 1993. "Economic Transition Strategies: Fiscal Instability Can Favor Unbalanced Investment." Working paper, February.

McKinnon, R. 1991. *The Order of Economic Liberalization.* Baltimore, MD: Johns Hopkins University Press.

McMillan, John, and Barry Naughton. 1992. "How to Reform a Planned Economy: Lessons from China." *Oxford Review of Economic Policy* 8, no. 1 (Spring).

Milgrom, Paul, and John Roberts. 1990. "The Economics of Modern Manufacturing: Technology, Strategy and Organization." *American Economic Review* 80, no. 3 (June): 511–28.

Murphy, K., A. Shleifer, and R. Vishny. 1992. "The Transition to a Market Economy: Pitfalls of Partial Reform." *Quarterly Journal of Economics* 107.

OECD. 1992a. *Industry in Poland: Structural Adjustment Issues and Policy Options.* Paris: OECD Publishers.

OECD. 1992b. *OECD Economic Surveys: Poland.* Paris: OECD Publishers.

Schaffer, M. 1990. "State-Owned Enterprises in Poland: Taxation, Subsidisation, and Competition Policies," *European Economy* no. 43 (March).

Schaffer, M. 1992. "The Polish State-Owned Enterprise Sector and the Recession in 1990." *Comparative Economic Studies* 34, no. 1 (Spring).

Shleifer, A., and R. Vishny. 1992. "Pervasive Shortages under Socialism." *RAND Journal of Economics* 9 (Summer).

Slay, Ben. 1990. "Monopoly and Marketization in Polish Industry." *Jahrbuch der Wirtschaft Osteuropas* 14, no. 1.

Slay, Ben. 1992. "Poland: The Role of Managers in Privatization." RFE/RL Research Report vol. 2, no. 12, April.

Staniszkis, Jadwiga. 1991. "'Political Capitalism' in Poland." *East European Politics and Societies* 5, no. 1.

Topkis, Donald M. 1978. "Minimizing a Submodular Function on a Lattice." *Operations Research* 26 (March–April): 305–21.

CHAPTER 3

The Creation of a Legal Structure for Market Institutions in China

Donald C. Clarke

Introduction

It is often supposed, by both advocates and critics, that the hallmark of a true free-market economy is the absence of governmental regulation: the less regulation, the freer the market. If this were so, then the task of reforming socialist economies would be fairly straightforward: once the political decision to move to a market economy had been made, one would simply dismantle the stultifying apparatus of state planning. Whatever was left afterward would be a market economy. To be sure, there would still be political decisions to be made about economic reform, but these would be largely tactical in nature: do gradualist measures, for example, ease the pain of transition or simply prolong it?

Unfortunately, "the market" is not a self-defining institution. At most, it connotes some kind of decentralized system of voluntary exchange subject to constraints. Yet even such a simple definition begs the most important questions: what counts as voluntary, for example, and what can be exchanged? The market cannot function without some institution capable of making and enforcing rules that answer such questions. If this institution is the state, then the delineation of the rules of the market is, in its own way, just as much "state intervention" as the delineation of the rules of planning. The rules of the market are much more than mere ground rules for fair exchanges: in defining what shall count as a protected entitlement and what can be traded, they can have an enormous influence upon the distribution of wealth and power in society. The decision to expand the role of the market in a society's economy, therefore, is only the first of many strategic political decisions that must be made along the way to any particular institutionalization of the market.

The picture is further complicated by the fact that a desire by policymakers to have a market system in general, or even some particular institutionalization of the market, does not automatically call forth the legal institutions necessary for the market to operate. It would be very surprising if the legal system created within a planned or largely planned economy happened to be suited to the needs of a market economy. The system that protected "state property," for example, cannot be counted on to protect private property just because the scope of permissible individual ownership has been broadened. A legal system is not only a set of definitions of rights, but also a set of procedures for doing things with those rights. Indeed, the treatment of what I have provisionally labelled rights may lead us to the conclusion that they should not have been called rights at all in the first place.

In short, the transition from traditional socialism by no means entails a retreat of the state from the economic sphere. The creation and maintenance of any particular set of market institutions requires that those institutions be defined and protected.

Market institutions can be thought of as having two legal facets. First, the law defines the institutions and rules of the market. The law defines what kind of natural persons can form contracts, and what type of organization can be considered equivalent to a natural person for contracting purposes; it defines what counts as property subject to purchase and sale and what kind of act will establish a binding contract. Obviously, different systems could have very different answers to these questions and still justifiably be called "market" systems. We can call these institutions and rules the substantive legal facet of market institutions.

Second, the law supplies—indeed, one could, following Holmes,[1] say the law *is*—the set of procedures for making these institutions a reality. This may be called the procedural legal facet of market institutions. These two facets are separable only conceptually. In practice, the contours of a substantive right depend crucially on the extent to which it can be realized. There is no difference between saying that you have no right to do X and saying that you have a right to do X but that no real-world consequences will follow from the existence of that right. If the substantive content of rights, and in particular rights appropriate to the functioning of market institutions, matters, then it is crucial to understand the procedural context within which those rights exist.

This chapter will examine the extent to which China has the kind of legal system (or any set of institutions, whether or not they are called legal) suited to the task of defining and enforcing rights appropriate to a market economy. It will show that in many respects, the reform of China's legal institutions lags far behind the reform of its economic system. The final section addresses the question of whether this lag really matters.

---

1. "The prophecies of what the courts will do in fact, and nothing more pretentious, are what I mean by the law." Oliver Wendell Holmes, *The Path of the Law,* 10 HARV. L. REV. 457, 461 (1897).

The "Traditional" (Post-1949) Legal System

Scholars and others have often questioned whether modern China has ever had anything that can justifiably be called a "legal system."[2] Obviously it all depends on what one means by "legal system." It is certainly true that in many important respects, the legal system of post-1949 China[3] was vastly different from the set of institutions known as "legal" in the industrialized West. That system was, not surprisingly, part and parcel of the economic system with which it coexisted, and the point of that system was state control over economic activity.

The legal system reflected this both in its substantive rules and in its procedures. Let us take as a case study a contract for the delivery of raw materials from coal mine to steel mill. The traditional (i.e., post-1949) Chinese legal system dealt with this phenomenon very differently from the way that a legal system designed for a market economy would.

The traditional model of the planned economy views the state as essentially one giant vertically integrated productive firm: "China, Inc."[4] The various ministries are divisions within the firm and enterprises are factories. The role of contracts prior to economic reform was essentially one of fleshing out the details of the plan.[5] Whether at the central or the regional level, state plans simply could not cover all the details of the production and allocation of all industrial products. Moreover, contracts were the form in which the planned transfer of products from one enterprise to another became specific, concrete

---

2. See, e.g., THOMAS B. STEVENS, ORDER AND DISCIPLINE IN CHINA: THE SHANGHAI MIXED COURT 1911–27 (University of Washington Press, 1992). When I reveal my academic specialty (Chinese law) to taxi drivers and other casual acquaintances in China, the response is almost always a snort of derision and disbelief—"There *is* no law in China"—followed by an anecdote in support of the proposition.

3. As well as pre–1949 China, but the point will not be argued here.

4. A brief description of the Chinese planning system can be found in Donald C. Clarke, *What's Law Got to Do with It? Legal Institutions and Economic Reform in China,* 10 U.C.L.A. PAC. BASIN L.J. 1, 5–6 (1991); for a fuller account, see Barry Naughton, *China's Experience with Guidance Planning,* 14 J. COMP. ECON. 743 (1990); and Barry Naughton, *Industrial Planning and Prospects in China,* in Eugene Lawson, ed. U.S.-CHINA TRADE: PROBLEMS AND PROSPECTS 179 (Praeger, 1988) [hereinafter B. Naughton, *Industrial Planning*].

5. "Various enterprises and business units give concreteness to the state plan and ensure its completion through signing economic contracts. Whether or not the state plan is actually feasible can be reflected through the implementation of contracts. Therefore, without contracts the plan will come to nothing; the fulfillment of contracts is precisely the implementation of the plan." *Jingji guanxi zhong de zhongyao zhunze* (An Important Standard in Economic Relationships), Renmin ribao (People's Daily), Dec. 17, 1981, at 1, quoted in PITMAN B. POTTER, POLICY, LAW AND PRIVATE ECONOMIC RIGHTS IN CHINA: THE DOCTRINE AND PRACTICE OF LAW ON ECONOMIC CONTRACTS 146 (Ph.D. diss., Univ. of Washington, 1986).

obligations.[6] Clearly, the contracts that fleshed out the details of the plan could not be entirely, or even mostly, free in the sense that the parties could simply decline to contract if the terms did not suit them. The means must be as mandatory as the ends. On the other hand, it is important to remember that plan targets themselves were formulated in a back-and-forth process that tried to take enterprise capabilities into account.[7] Consequently, it would be a mistake to draw too sharp a distinction between plans and contracts in the prereform system. Contracts were the continuation of the plan by other means.[8]

Because contracts were so closely tied to the plan, the state had no interest in enforcing them unless they worked to fulfill the goals of the plan. As long as contracts specified the details that the plan could not, the state would support their enforcement. As soon as the plan changed, however, and the transaction called for in the contract was no longer necessary or desirable from the standpoint of the plan, the state would not only permit, but would even require the contract to be changed to meet the new circumstances.[9] In addition, enterprises had little reason to be very worried about "damage"[10] caused by breached contracts. The state would make up for such damage by increasing subsidies or reducing relevant targets.[11]

A contract between a coal mine and a steel mill is thus entered into at the behest of their administrative superiors. It becomes legally valid not because

6. See RICHARD PFEFFER, UNDERSTANDING BUSINESS CONTRACTS IN CHINA, 1949–1963 20 (Harvard Univ. Press, 1973).

7. See generally Thomas P. Lyons, *Planning and Interprovincial Co-ordination in Maoist China,* 1990 CHINA Q. 37; B. Naughton, *Industrial Planning, supra* n. 4.

8. For a study of Chinese contract law and practice that emphasizes the voluntary aspects of contracting in China and disagrees with some of the characterizations made here, see Roderick Macneil, *Contract in China: Law, Practice, and Dispute Resolution,* 38 STAN. L. REV. 303 (1986).

9. See R. PFEFFER, *supra* n. 6, at 53.

10. I put the word "damage" in quotation marks for two reasons. First, the term must be understood in a new way because of the great significance of operational targets assigned to Chinese state-owned enterprises. To a Chinese enterprise manager, damage could mean reduced revenues and lost profits, but it could also mean increased difficulty in meeting any target set by superiors. Suppose a contract breach means the enterprise is unable to fulfill its output target. If the enterprise is a monopolist, reduced output might actually increase profits. Thus, no loss would be cognizable under Western contract law. In a Chinese state-owned enterprise, however, employees could suffer real losses in the form of reduced bonuses for failure to meet the output target.

Second, damages are not really damages at all as far as the enterprise is concerned if adjustments are somehow made to eliminate their effect on the enterprise.

11. See P. POTTER, *supra* n. 5, at 52. A case where the breach was handled as described is noted in R. PFEFFER, *supra* n. 6, at 54–55. The disinclination to enforce contractual rights is one consequence of the soft budget constraint analyzed in JANOS KORNAI, ECONOMICS OF SHORTAGE 75 (North-Holland Pub. Co., 1980).

it is the expression of the will of the parties, but because it has been authorized (and subsequently approved) by higher levels.

Second, the contract, like statutory law in general in such a system, does not grant "rights" as such. If a law says that X "shall" be done, you do not necessarily have a right to some kind of redress if X is not done and you are thereby damaged. If one is looking for rights, Chinese laws appear very poorly drafted indeed. "Should" is liberally used alongside of "must"; laws frequently state that X "should normally" or "should in principle" be done, but give no hint of when exceptions can be made.

The intention of the drafters becomes clear, however, if one considers the law as a crystallization of state policy directed to administrators. Most economic contracts must be approved by these administrators; they are the ones who must "obey" the law. Where the law says that contracts "should in general" contain a certain provision, is a contract without that provision invalid? Have its signers violated the law? The question is impossible to answer. The relevant question, for the state, is whether, when one looks at *all* of the contracts approved by the relevant authority, the rule of "in general" or "in principle" has been satisfied. What the law aims to establish is a kind of statistical regularity, not any particular individual's right to something.

Thus, if a steel mill believes that a delivery from a coal mine is not up to standard, the matter will not be resolved by reference to issues of rights or fault. The steel mill will first complain to government administrators, and the dispute, if not resolved earlier, will eventually rise to the first administrator with authority over both enterprises.[12] That official's primary concern is to take the action that will best fulfill the goals of the plan. If the coal is indeed of poor quality, which party is in the best position to do something about it? Can the steel mill's targets still be met with inferior coal? Fault comes into the picture only, if at all, when it is time to assess the performance of enterprise managers for the purpose of bonuses or promotions. (Indeed, because we are assuming that both enterprises are in the same industrial "system" (*xitong*), a promotion may take a manager from one enterprise to the other.)

Legal Institutions in a Market Economy

Let us now consider what has to be different in an economy attempting to move away from planning and toward a market. To understand that, however, we need to specify some reasons why a society might want to make the move.

---

12. This example is taken from, and more fully detailed in, John A. Spanogle and Tibor M. Baranski, Jr., *Chinese Commercial Dispute Resolution Methods: The State Commercial and Industrial Arbitration Bureau*, 35 AM. J. COMP. L. 761, 764–65 (1987), who label it "administered resolution."

As an economic reform strategy, the move to market allocation usually represents a recognition that planners simply cannot process the infinite number of facts about an economy that must be assimilated before a working plan can be formulated.[13] Decentralized decision making made by myriad actors, each responding to price signals, is viewed as superior. As a political reform strategy, market allocation may be favored over bureaucratic allocation because it reduces the dependence of citizens upon state officials for their daily needs. The following discussion will consider only the implications of the economic justification.

If the state seeks to establish market institutions as an economic reform measure, the key question is whether prevailing legal institutions make it possible for market institutions to function the way they must if there is to be any difference from the old system.

Perhaps the single most important feature of law and rights in a market economy is *general applicability*. The point of economic reform is to get rid of state micromanagement of enterprises according to a plan. Given this goal, regulation by enterprise-specific directives must yield to regulation by rules of general applicability. This is because the difference between laws of general application and enterprise-specific directives is that the latter need to be guided and coordinated; they need to have some rationale behind them to make sure that they have the desired effect; in short, they have to be part of a plan. But the plan is what we were trying to get rid of. Allocative decisions are to be made instead by decentralized actors responding to price signals. High-priced inputs, for example, are supposed to go to those enterprises that, because they produce a valuable product, can afford them, not to those that can persuade their supervisory government organ to supply them. The task for law in market-directed economic reform is to play a similar role: to function as an aspect of the environment in which enterprises operate. If all economic law is enterprise-specific and the product of bargaining between the enterprise and superior levels of administration, there can be no hope of making its content rational and internally consistent without something like a plan. If law is to be used in support of market institutions, it must apply indifferently to large numbers of economic actors. Otherwise the system will revert to the kind of ad hoc bargaining whose inadequacies led to the drive for reform in the first place.[14]

The key question, then, is whether there is any institution in China ready and able to undertake the task of uniform application of a set of rules defining

---

13. Vaclav Havel's philosophical expression of this view is quoted in the introduction to this volume: "The essence of life is infinitely and mysteriously multiform, and therefore it cannot be contained or planned for, in its fullness and variability, by any central intelligence." VACLAV HAVEL, SUMMER MEDITATIONS 62 (Knopf, 1992).

14. I make this argument more fully in Donald C. Clarke, *The Law, the State and Economic Reform*, in Gordon White, ed., THE CHINESE STATE IN THE ERA OF ECONOMIC REFORM 190 (M.E. Sharpe, 1991).

and protecting market institutions. For a number of reasons, the courts in China are the most likely candidate for this task—more likely, that is, than any other institution. They are, however, hampered in several ways that cast doubt on their ability to accomplish it.

Courts are the most likely candidate to undertake the uniform and general enforcement of rules because individual courts, not just the system as a whole, have the putative authority to issue orders cutting across bureaucratic and territorial boundaries. That is, a judge sitting in a Hunan county and appointed by the county People's Congress could, under proper circumstances, legitimately order a state-owned, city-run handicrafts factory in Harbin to pay a sum of money to a collectively owned, township-run sandalwood supplier in Guangxi.

No other institution in China, including the Communist Party, has this kind of formal authority. As noted earlier, the traditional way to solve disputes in China has been to find the common superior with jurisdiction over both parties. This principle applies not only to dispute resolution, but also sometimes to the most basic kinds of communications or cooperative relationships. If two units in different systems (*xitong*) would gain from some mutually beneficial arrangement, they can't just do it. They must go through proper channels. Enforcement of rules by any institution other than courts is inevitably going to run into the problems of particularism and bargaining that economic reform was intended to move away from.

There is another reason that courts have the potential to be more effective than the traditional bureaucracies in helping the government implement uniform and consistent policies. A pervasive problem in any authority system is ensuring that commands from the top are carried out at the lower levels of the system that interact directly with the object of regulation. There is a progressive loss of control as the organization becomes larger and the distance increases between policy makers at the top and policy implementers and enforcers at the bottom. The difficulties encountered by Chinese policy makers at the center in seeing their directives implemented are well known.

The key advantage of court-enforced policy (i.e., "law") over bureaucratically implemented policy is that, if the system works properly, it minimizes the number of layers between policy making and policy implementation. Parties come before the court with a specific dispute that the court has the power and the authority to resolve. The court resolves this dispute by direct reference to the original text of the policy issued by the relevant policy maker.[15] There is, in principle, no reason why this text cannot have been directly formulated and

---

15. I am speaking, of course, of the type of legal question that is so clear-cut that it never makes it into court in real life. I should not be understood as saying that where the issue is debatable, the court resolves it through a process of formal deduction from premises set forth in the texts.

approved by the central authorities. When a court resolves a dispute, there-fore, there is only one intermediate layer between the central policy makers and the regulated parties. Thus, court enforcement of rules has the potential to provide a much greater degree of uniformity and consistency than enforce-ment by other bureaucracies—provided the courts can actually command obedience and have a system for ensuring consistent enforcement.

Limitations of Courts as Guarantors of Market Institutions

The remarkable breadth of the formal authority of courts merely underscores its purely formal character. China's courts suffer from severe limitations as guar-antors of the generally applicable system of rights necessary to a complex market order because they are often unable or unwilling to enforce legal standards. First, judges may simply lack the education necessary to do the job competently. China now has some fifty "political-legal institutes" and univer-sity law departments that annually produce about 5,000 bachelor of law graduates.[16] Because very little legal education took place between the mid-1960s and the late 1970s, there is a great shortage of persons qualified to serve as judges. Recent graduates, in their early twenties, are simply too young. Many judges are demobilized army officers with little education; there is as yet no career judicial bureaucracy with clear, or even vague, standards of compe-tency. Until the 1995 promulgation of the Law on Judicial Officers, there were *no* objective qualifications that all judges had to have. As of 1993, one third (33.3 percent) of judicial personnel lacked postsecondary education.[17]

Judicial ignorance of the law is particularly devastating in a system such as China's because it is so difficult to remedy. Chinese judicial procedure is basically inquisitorial, leaving a great deal of initiative to the judge instead of to the parties and their lawyers. Just finding the applicable law can be an impossible task. Laws and regulations are promulgated by a bewildering variety of governmental and quasi-governmental bodies, and no comprehen-sive and up-to-date indexes are available. There is no regular system of case reporting that allows judges to see how other courts have handled similar problems.[18] Quite often there will simply be no statutory rule directly on

---

16. See *Legal Eagles,* China Daily, Mar. 4, 1993, at 3.

17. See Ren Jianxin, Supreme People's Court Work Report, March 22, 1993, in BRITISH BROADCASTING CORPORATION, SUMMARY OF WORLD BROADCASTS, PART 3: THE FAR EAST [SWB/FE], April 12, 1993, at C1 (report delivered by president of Supreme People's Court to first session of Eighth National People's Congress).

18. The Supreme People's Court does publish the *Supreme People's Court Gazette,* a periodical containing directives, interpretations, and cases (generally lower court decisions thought to be particularly instructive). In addition, judges no doubt have access to case reports that are not publicly available.

point, or there may exist contradictory rules. In these cases, there is simply no way of guessing how an untrained and ill-educated judge will choose to decide the issue and no sense of what sorts of arguments should or should not count.

Furthermore, even if judges have enough education to do the job, they may be corrupt or partial and unwilling to render a correct judgment. Official corruption is a serious problem in China—indeed, it was one of the griev- ances that sent the people of Beijing and other cities into the streets in the spring of 1989—and Chinese press reports make it clear that it extends to the judiciary. It is difficult, however, to quantify it in a rigorous enough way to provide meaningful comparative perspective. The number of news stories on the topic is a function of the government's wish to publicize the problem, not necessarily of its size. Without reliable data, it is possible only to note the existence of this obstacle to law implementation, not to specify its degree.

In addition, even if judges are able and willing to render a correct judgment, their decision may be overridden by higher authorities within the court. Courts at all levels have as part of their structure an Adjudication Committee headed by the president of the court. It is the highest decision- making body within the court as an institution. It is official policy that "judi- cial independence" means not that the particular judge or judges hearing the case should be independent from outside pressures (i.e., senior judges in the same court), but at most that the court *as an institution* should be free from outside pressures. The Adjudication Committee has the power, among other things, to override the decision of the judges who actually heard the case and conducted the trial and to order them to enter a different decision. Reports in the legal press show that in many courts it is routine for the Adjudication Committee to decide cases (often before the hearing), with the result that "those who try the case do not decide it, and those who decide the case do not try it" (*shenzhe bu pan, panzhe bu shen*).

Also, the court as a whole is subject to many outside pressures and is particularly vulnerable to local government direction. Judges can be threat- ened with various unpleasant consequences if they do not decide as the threat- ener wishes. I shall look here at only one kind of vulnerability with a specific institutional basis, that is, the power of the local party and government to dictate to courts how they shall decide cases.

The local party tends to judicial matters through its Political-Legal Com- mittee (*zheng-fa weiyuanhui*).[19] This committee has traditionally been in

---

19. According to the Notice of the Central Committee of the Chinese Communist Party on the Establishment of Political-Legal Committees (*Zhonggong zhongyang guanyu chengli zheng- fa weiyuanhui de tongzhi*) (Central Committee Doc. No. 5, 1980), the Political-Legal Committee, inter alia, "guides (*zhidao*) the work of the various political-legal departments" (this would include courts) and "properly disposes of important and difficult cases." This document, not to my knowledge publicly available, is cited in *Zhonggong zhongyang guanyu jiaqiang zheng-fa*

charge of the police, the procuracy, the courts, other aspects of judicial administration, and civil affairs. The Political-Legal Committee is often headed by the leader of the local police or of the local party and government.

It has long been the practice in China for local party secretaries or party committees to review and approve the disposition of cases by courts. This was the concrete manifestation of the principle of party leadership. The official theory now is that Party leadership is to be exercised at the level of legislation or general policy making, not in the adjudication of specific cases. But it has proved difficult to break old habits.

Judges may find themselves out of a job if they do not do as they are told by the Political-Legal Committee or other local power holder. The formal power of appointment and dismissal of court personnel is lodged in the local People's Congresses. In practice, however, they act as rubber stamps for the local party organizational department. The real power is in the hands of the local party leadership. "This personnel power exercised by a small group of leaders hangs like the sword of Damocles over those who would do things according to law."[20] "If the court insists on handling things according to law and disposes of certain cases in ways not satisfactory to these leaders, some of them will use their power to arbitrarily reassign the court's leadership."[21]

Finally, any judgment needs to be enforced, yet the courts are short on autonomous enforcement powers. It is frequently difficult to get court judgments enforced against any determined defendant, to say nothing of a well-connected and politically powerful defendant. Indeed, the president of the Supreme People's Court in 1988 described the failure to enforce court decisions as "the most outstanding problem in the administration of justice in the economic sphere."[22]

Why is it so difficult to execute judgments? First, there are few penalties for refusing to obey a court order. Chinese courts have no contempt power,

---

gongzuo de tongzhi (Chinese Communist Party Central Committee Notice on Strengthening Political-Legal Work), Jan. 13, 1982, reprinted in ZHONGGONG NIANBAO 1983–84 (Yearbook of Chinese Communism 1983–84) 8-3, 8-6 (Taipei 1984) [hereinafter 1982 Political-Legal Notice].

20. Zhao Zhenjiang, Zhou Wangsheng, Zhang Qi, Qi Haibin, and Wang Chenguang, *Lun falü shixiao* (On the Effectiveness of Laws), 2 ZHONG-WAI FAXUE (Chinese and Foreign Legal Studies), 1, 5 (1989).

21. Shi Youyong, *Shenpan zhong difang baohu zhuyi de chengyin ji duice* (Local Protectionism in Adjudication: Causes and Countermeasures), 6 FAXUE (Jurisprudence) 15 (1989).

22. See Zheng Tianxiang, *Zuigao renmin fayuan gongzuo baogao* (Supreme People's Court Work Report), 4 ZHONGHUA RENMIN GONGHEGUO QUANGUO RENMIN DAIBIAO DAHUI CHANGWU WEIYUANHUI GONGBAO (Gazette of the Standing Committee of the National People's Congress of the People's Republic of China) [NPCSC GAZETTE] 24, 29 (1988) (report delivered to 1st Session of 7th National People's Congress, April 1, 1988). Complaints about problems in implementing judgments are a regular feature of the annual Supreme People's Court work reports.

and it is not a crime to refuse to obey a court order. Article 157 of the Criminal Law makes it a crime to refuse to carry out a judgment if the refusal is by means of threats or violence. This covers the person who interferes with the actions of others carrying out a judgment, but does not cover the person who is ordered to do something and simply does not do it.

Article 77 of the 1982 Civil Procedure Law empowered the court to fine or detain those who "have a duty to assist in execution" of civil judgments and refuse to do so, but this probably did not refer to the actual object of the judgment, who is usually called "the executee" (*bei zhixing ren*). Evidently this lacuna was noted, for the 1991 revision provides in Article 102 that parties themselves (as well as others) may be fined or detained if they refuse to carry out a legally effective court judgment or ruling.[23] It remains to be seen, however, how well this provision will be enforced.

Second, courts often lack sufficient bureaucratic clout to enforce their judgments against administrative units. Any clout they have comes from the bureaucratic rank of individual judges. Although courts and governments at any given level are supposed to be equal, court presidents generally have a lower bureaucratic rank than the chief executive of the government at the same level.[24] This means, for example, that the latter has access to some documents from the center that the former cannot see. It is simply alien to the way China functions that a lower-level official from one bureaucracy should be able to give orders to a higher-level official from another.[25] A low-status judge does not have the prerogative to disobey, much less to command, a higher-status official. As one county party secretary is reported to have said, "Tell me what matters more: official rank or the law? I can definitely tell you, rank matters more. Law is made by man; without man, how could there be law? Without man, how could law matter at all? That's why I say that rank matters more."[26]

Third, the cooperation of local authorities is needed. Judicial independence is not of much use if it results in nothing more than the issuance of a

23. Refusal to carry out judgments is one of a list of acts in Article 102 that are said to subject the actor to criminal liability *if* they violate the Criminal Law. Aside from the fact that it is hardly necessarily to put into the Civil Procedure Law the truism that acts in violation of the Criminal Law will subject the actor to criminal liability, we have already seen that the mere refusal to carry out a court order does not appear to violate the Criminal Law.

24. See Fang Chengzhi, *Renmin fayuan zai guojia jigou zhong de diwei* (The Position of the People's Courts in the Structure of the State), 4 FAXUE ZAZHI (Jurisprudence Magazine) 15(1985); Tao-tai Hsia, The Concept of Judicial Independence 9 and n.23 (unpublished paper 1986).

25. See generally K. LIEBERTHAL AND M. OKSENBERG, POLICY MAKING IN CHINA: LEADERS, STRUCTURES, AND PROCESSES ch. 4 (Princeton Univ. Press, 1988) (discussing characteristics of the structure of state power).

26. See Fang Chengzhi, *supra* n. 24, at 16.

piece of paper. The enforcement of local court judgments may be supported by local authorities, if only because a judgment they opposed would likely not be issued in the first place. Nevertheless, courts are reluctant to move with force and authority against the truly recalcitrant defendant. In one case, an old man and his wife transferred their house to another and then wanted it back so they could give it to their son. To accomplish their purpose, they simply reoccupied the original house. The new owner took them to court and won both on first trial and on appeal. The defendants, however, refused to move out on the grounds that they were old. Fearing they would commit suicide, the court eventually ruled that they could stay until they died, at which time the court's judgment would take effect. The writer reporting this case criticizes the court, but displays the identical attitude when he says that where execution would "genuinely cause difficulty," one should consider an "appropriate post-ponement."[27]

The greater enforcement problem occurs with the execution of judgments from courts outside the jurisdiction of the local government. The enforcement of such judgments is essentially a voluntary matter for the local authorities.

Local courts in China are considered in fact, although not in law, to be simply arms of local government. Courts are dependent on local government for their financing, and their personnel serve de jure at the pleasure of the local People's Congress and de facto at the pleasure of the local party organization. This sets the stage for the conflict of two principles. A court, wherever located, is by law empowered to issue a judgment binding on anyone, provided it has proper jurisdiction. In the Chinese political system, however—and by no means only the Chinese—the government of County A in Province X cannot tell the government of County B in Province Y what to do. Because of the identification of courts with local governments, their judgments are subject to the latter principle, not the former.

Local authorities often oppose the enforcement of outside judgments. Under economic reform, localities are more dependent than before on their own resources. Local enterprises form the revenue base for local governments. Thus, it is important to protect their financial health. The president of the Supreme People's Court complained about this phenomenon:

> Some localities—mainly party and government leaders at the basic level—demand that when the court passes judgment, it be favorable to the party from the locality. If it is not, they accuse the court of "embracing outsiders" (*gebozhou wang wai guai*). If a court from outside the locality rules against a local party in a suit, requiring that party to bear

---

27. Su Nan, *Fayuan de panjue zai mouxie difang nan yi zhixing* (Court Judgments Are Difficult to Implement in Certain Places), Fazhi ribao (Legal System Daily), Jan. 3, 1989, at 4.

economic liability, to pay a debt, or to compensate for economic loss, certain leaders of the locality will obstruct the implementation of the court's judgment.[28]

The financial contract system, under which localities are obliged to turn over a fixed amount of revenues to the center each year,[29] has made it even less likely that local authorities will permit resources to flow out of the jurisdiction. Since local governments are usually the primary claimants on the enterprise's income, they bear the loss when their enterprise pays out to an outside party.

If it is common for local courts to rule against outsiders, it is easy to see why even the most upright local authorities would have good reason to be suspicious of the impartiality of an outside judgment against a local enterprise. They would naturally be reluctant to help enforce it. Sometimes outside court personnel will actually make a trip (at the winner's expense) to the loser's district to execute the judgment. But without the cooperation of local authorities, outside court personnel are simply strangers in a strange land. They have no connections, no authoritative letters of introduction, no influence, and no power.

It can be very difficult to obtain local court cooperation if the local authorities are dead set against it. Contracts across jurisdictions can be unenforceable. In one case, a local court refused to help enforce an outside judgment despite two specific orders from the Supreme People's Court to do so.[30]

In the face of this protectionism, local governments have begun to make treaties pledging to protect each other's enterprises as their own. Shanghai, for example, is reported to have signed agreements "on the protection of the legitimate rights and interests of enterprises" with nine provinces.[31] These treaties can play a useful role as long as the parties have an interest in

---

28. Shi Youyong, *supra* n. 21, at 15 (citing a speech made by Supreme People's Court president Ren Jianxin in October 1988). Ren's predecessor made the same complaint in almost identical terms (and using the same colloquial expression) in April of 1986. See Zheng Tianxiang, *Zuigao renmin fayuan gongzuo baogao* (Supreme People's Court Work Report) (report delivered to 4th Session of 6th National People's Congress, April 8, 1986), reprinted in Zhongguo fazhi bao (Chinese Legal System News), April 23, 1986, at 2, 3.

29. See K. LIEBERTHAL AND M. OKSENBERG, *supra* n. 25, at 139.

30. See Chen Shibin, *Dawu xian fayuan jianchi difang baohu zhuyi, tuoyan san nian ju bu xiezhu zhixing waidi panjue* (Dawu County Court Persists in Local Protectionism; After Delaying Three Years, Still Refuses to Assist in the Execution of an Outside Judgment), Fazhi ribao (Legal System Daily), June 4, 1988, at 1.

31. See Yang Jisheng, *"East-West Dialogue" in China—the Strategy of Unbalanced Economic Development on the Mainland in Perspective*, 9 LIAOWANG (Outlook) (overseas edition) 5 (1989), in FOREIGN BROADCAST INFORMATION SERVICE, DAILY REPORT: CHINA [FBIS], Apr. 10, 1989, at 37, 39.

continued cooperation, and are more practical than the usual pious exhorta-
tions to local authorities.[32] They are, however, essentially unenforceable.

Rules, Rights, and Economic Development

The establishment and maintenance of market institutions in the reforming
Chinese economy requires—or at least is substantially aided by—a particular
kind of rule making and rule application. This rule making and application is
characterized by generality and should be understood in opposition to the
traditional system of ad hoc bargaining between individual enterprises and
their superiors.

The problem with a system of general rules is that there is currently no
system of institutions in China willing and able to enforce them. First, there is
a chicken-and-egg problem. In the absence of complete economic reform,
economic activity does not take place on a level playing field. Thus, applying
general rules without taking individual differences into account is not only
seen as unfair, but actually *is* so. Moreover, it may be counterproductive as
well, if efficient enterprises that nevertheless lose money find themselves in
trouble, for example, under the Enterprise Bankruptcy Law. However, the
development of a market economy is obstructed to the extent that the principle
of particularism reigns.

Second, making general rules stick implicates important questions of
political power. It means drastically weakening the power of some institutions
to grant exemptions and building institutions that can enforce the rules. Courts
have seemed the natural candidate for the task because of their sweeping
formal authority and their ability to keep to a minimum the amount of noise in
policy transmission. They are not, however, capable of carrying it out as
currently structured.

Power in China flows within bureaucratic systems, not across them.
Rules that purport to operate horizontally, across bureaucracies, are essentially alien to the system and are difficult to enforce. Without the creation of
an enforcement institution that transcends the traditional system of state
power, any law promoting fundamental economic reform that purports to be
generally applicable is unlikely to be effective.

While the legal system has undergone significant reforms in the last
decade, in many crucial areas it remains as before and thus unable to perform
the task of enforcing the rules of economic reform. First, there is no evidence
to suggest that courts have more real power now than they did a decade ago.

---

32. See, for example, the "solution" proposed by one writer: "The best way of solving the
problem [of court judgments not being implemented] is for the relevant units and personnel to
truly do things according to law" (Su Nan, *supra* n. 27, at 4).

The observance of court judgments for many institutions remains essentially voluntary. Yet establishing a system where courts have real power involves grasping some very thorny political nettles. Second, courts remain essentially the creatures of the level of government that appointed their personnel. They cannot be used to overcome the obstacles to reform posed by local protectionism and particularism when they are part of the very structure causing the problem.

The prominence of local and regional centers of political power on the list of obstacles to economic reform in China may shed light on the question of the proper role of the state in the establishment of economically efficient social institutions. Recent writing in law and economics has attacked the "legal-centralist" view, attributed to scholars from Hobbes to Calabresi, that the state is the exclusive creator of property rights.[33] Instead, these writers say, property rights may arise "anarchically out of social custom" and "from the workings of non-hierarchical social forces."[34]

It may be, of course, that the debate will turn out to be about what the participants mean by "rights." Just how compulsory must the corresponding duty be before we will find that a "right" exists? Ellickson's study of norms established spontaneously in the whaling industry hardly disproves the legal-centralist thesis when the writer concedes that the system broke down as economic pressures led some whalers simply to defect.[35] The assurance of enforcement, the confidence that others *cannot* defect at will, is the whole point of having a right, and the key to the arguments of Douglass C. North and others that well-defined rights are necessary for sustained economic development to occur.[36]

If we adopt a strong definition of "rights," however, the Chinese case suggests that the spontaneous-rights thesis, while not necessarily wrong, has limits in a complex economy. Efficient economic organization doesn't just happen: there are powerful political forces opposed to it that can be overcome only by more powerful political forces. State intervention is just as necessary

---

33. See Robert C. Ellickson, *A Hypothesis of Wealth-Maximizing Norms: Evidence from the Whaling Industry,* 5 J. L. ECON. & ORG'N 83 (1989); R. Zerbe, The Development of Institutions and the Joint Production of Fairness and Efficiency in the California Gold Fields (Right Makes Might) (May 8, 1990) (unpublished manuscript).

34. See R. Ellickson, *supra* n. 33, at 83.

35. See R. Ellickson, *supra* n. 33, at 95 n.39.

36. "[W]ithout institutional constraints, self-interested behavior will foreclose complex exchange [and the economic growth that it makes possible], because of the uncertainty that the other party will find it in his or her interest to live up to the agreement." DOUGLASS C. NORTH, INSTITUTIONS, INSTITUTIONAL CHANGE, AND ECONOMIC PERFORMANCE 33 (Cambridge Univ. Press, 1990). On the relationship between economic growth and property and contract rights generally, see *id.* and DOUGLASS C. NORTH AND ROBERT PAUL THOMAS, THE RISE OF THE WESTERN WORLD (Cambridge Univ. Press, 1973).

to a complex market economy as it is to a planned economy. Local governmental power made the Commerce Clause necessary in the U.S. Constitution; federal governmental power is needed to enforce it.

A second issue raised by the weakness of rights-enforcing institutions in China is the extent to which that observed weakness challenges the connection made by North and others between economic development and well-defined and enforceable rights of property and contract. The intuitive appeal of the hypothesis is undeniable: it seems beyond dispute that the unavailability or unenforceability of property rights is going to deter useful investment that would otherwise occur. Consider the predicament of the Chinese peasant interviewed below:

> When asked, Mr. Yang says that agricultural production and income could increase even further if the family made some irrigation improvements, terraced more of their land, and planted fruit trees. Mr. Yang, though, is unwilling to make such capital improvements to the land. The profits from such investments would only be realized after several years, and Mr. Yang considers his family's use rights to the land too uncertain. Although the local leaders told him they could use the land for at least fifteen years, the [Yang family's] land use contract has no such term. And Mr. Yang notes that his neighbors were required to give up a portion of their land, on which they had recently planted fruit trees, for a road. The neighbors received no compensation.[37]

One might interpret the much-vaunted consumption boom in the Chinese countryside as evidence of agricultural investments forgone for the reasons cited by Mr. Yang.

On the other hand, nobody who was in China fifteen years ago can doubt the reality of the tremendous economic growth and rise in prosperity that has occurred since that time. How can that undeniable fact be reconciled with the finding of this chapter that legal institutions remain essentially unreformed and ill-suited to the institutions of a market economy, that property and contract rights are not well defined and reliably enforced?

---

37. Tim Hanstad, *The Effects of Rural Reforms on a Chinese Family,* RURAL DEVELOPMENT INSTITUTE REVIEW, Spring 1993, at 1, 2. In another work based on the same set of interviews, the researchers write:

> If land is taken, little legal assurance is afforded the farmer in obtaining compensation—either for the disturbance of his usership or for improvements he may have made in the land. It appears that only nominal compensation, if any, is given. . . . [T]he farmer will not keep the continuing benefit of long-term improvements. . . .

ROY L. PROSTERMAN AND TIM HANSTAD, LAND REFORM IN CHINA: A FIELDWORK-BASED APPRAISAL 37 (Rural Development Institute, 1993).

It is possible, of course, that this chapter is simply wrong: perhaps, despite surface appearances, legal institutions in China provide far more predictability and stability than they appear to.

Second, perhaps both the North hypothesis and the findings of this chapter are right. China's current growth could then be explained as taking place *in spite of* the absence of appropriate legal institutions. The tremendous advance over the prereform period is explained not as a function of how hospitable the current institutional structure is to economic development, but instead as a function of how unimaginably inhospitable and restrictive the prereform system was. The thunderclap of growth we have witnessed over the past several years is, in this view, nothing more than the air of entrepreneurship rushing in to fill a vacuum. It is, essentially, a one-time-only advance that will stall out when further gains from exchange can be obtained only from a division of labor and institutional complexity not supported by China's legal institutional structure.

Finally, the North hypothesis may simply be wrong: perhaps stable and predictable rights of property and contract are only a small part of the explanation of why economic growth occurs. It may be that while these rights matter at the margin, reasonably effective institutional substitutes are available and other factors are much more important contributors to economic development. Macauley, for example, demonstrated the discontinuity between contract law and the contracting practices of businesses in the United States; what mattered more to the parties than the law was that they were in a relationship that was beneficial to both.[38] According to this theory, I keep my promise to you not because of the threat of legal sanctions, but because I want to do business again, either with you or with those who would hear about any promises I broke.

This theory, of course, has its limits. If the promise of further business is the only glue that holds contractual relations together, then an entire class of necessary and useful contracts—those between parties who have no need or desire for anything more than a one-shot deal—will be unenforceable and thus discouraged. There are, however, reasons for thinking that in China this class of contract is relatively rare, and that therefore this problem is relatively unimportant, at least for the moment.

First of all, China's population is not very mobile. Although mobility has increased tremendously in the economic reform era, changing one's residence is still difficult. Therefore, a party who prepays on a contract has less reason

---

38. See Stewart Macauley, *Non-Contractual Relations in Business: A Preliminary Study,* 28 AM. SOC. REV. 55 (1963). On the theory of relational contracting, see Ian Macneil, *Contracts: Adjustment of Long-Term Economic Relations under Classical, Neo-Classical, and Relational Contract Law,* 72 NW. U.L. REV. 854 (1978).

(although not of course *no* reason) to fear that the other party will simply disappear with the money.

Second, only a small percentage of economic activity measured by value is conducted by individual entrepreneurs, with most of the rest conducted by units of government at various levels.[39] These are much more likely to be known quantities to a prospective business partner. Altogether, then, it may be that relational contracting can carry economic development in China a long way even in the absence of a well-functioning formal system.

A further question raised by the North hypothesis is whether we might expect to see not economic development as a response to institutional innovation, but rather institutional innovation as a response to economic development. Can demand create supply? Under this conjecture, the growth and increasing complexity of economic activity in China will eventually tend to generate the institutions needed to keep it going. The difficulty here is supplying a mechanism whereby demand elicits supply. Many societies in history would have been much better off with a well-developed legal system, but they didn't all get one.

The most plausible scenario may be one founded on the increasing power of regional governments coupled with an increased mobility of capital. While the central government has not so far shown much capacity for creating a set of institutions that can effectively enforce property rights, it may be more possible for the provinces (and perhaps governments at even lower levels) to do so. Why should they want to? The answer here lies in competition for resources. The region that provides the most hospitable environment for economic activity will reap the rewards of increased employment and tax revenues.[40] This may be one of the reasons behind the judicial cooperation agreements signed by Shanghai with several other cities in the late 1980s[41] and more recently by courts of several cities along the Yangtse.[42] The key to this

---

39. See figure 1 in Barry Naughton, *Distinctive Features of Economic Reform in China and Vietnam,* chapter 12 in this volume. A small percentage of output is attributable to joint ventures and wholly foreign-owned enterprises.

40. One should also note that in the absence of strong, *enforceable* central policies on environmental protection, such competition is likely to lead to severe pollution that "will make Eastern Europe look like a nature park." Ann McIlroy, *An Economic Boom Is Fuelled by Environment-Destroying Material,* Vancouver Sun, May 1, 1993, at B2 (quoting Western diplomat in Beijing).

41. See n. 31 *supra.*

42. *Xiang-E liushisi-jia fayuan lianshou gongpo yidi zhixing nan guan jian xiao* (Sixty-Four Courts in Hunan and Hubei Join Hands, Achieve Results in Overcoming the Problem of Executing Judgments in Other Regions), Fazhi ribao (Legal System Daily), July 24, 1991, at 1 (reporting mutual execution agreement among courts of several cities along the Yangtse); Peng Changlin, *Jianli jingji shenpan sifa xiezhu zhidu, xieshou gongke anjian yidi zhixing nanti* (Establish a System for Judicial Cooperation in Economic Adjudication; Join Hands to Conquer the Problem of Executing Judgments in a Different Locality), *Jingji fazhi* (Economic Legal System), No. 7, 1992, at 30–32 (enthusiastically praising same agreement).

scenario is that provinces must be independent enough to be able to offer meaningful differences in economic environment, but not independent enough to obstruct the free movement of capital.

REFERENCES

Chen Shibin. "Dawu xian fayuan jianchi difang baohu zhuyi, tuoyan san nian ju bu xiezhu zhixing waidi panjue" ("Dawu county court persists in local protectionism; after delaying three years, still refuses to assist in the execution of an outside judgment"). *Fazhi ribao (Legal System Daily)*, 4 June 1988, 1.
Clarke, Donald C. "What's Law Got to Do with It? Legal Institutions and Economic Reform in China." *U.C.L.A. Pacific Basin Law Journal* 10, no. 1 (1991): 1–76.
Clarke, Donald C. "The Law, the State and Economic Reform." In Gordon White, ed., *The Chinese State in the Era of Economic Reform*, 190–211. (Armonk, N.J.: M. E. Sharpe, 1991).
Ellickson, Robert C. "A Hypothesis of Wealth-Maximizing Norms: Evidence from the Whaling Industry." *Journal of Law, Economics & Organization* 5, no. 1 (1989): 83–97.
Fang Chengzhi. "Renmin fayuan zai guojia jigou zhong de diwei" ("The position of the people's courts in the structure of the state"). *Faxue zazhi (Jurisprudence Magazine)*, no. 4 (1985), 15–16.
Hanstad, Tim. "The Effects of Rural Reforms on a Chinese Family." *Rural Development Institute Review*, no. 2 (Spring 1993): 1–2.
Havel, Vaclav. *Summer Meditations* (New York: A. A. Knopf, 1992).
Holmes, Oliver Wendell. "The Path of the Law." *Harvard Law Review* 10, no. 8 (1897): 457–78.
Kornai, Janos. *Economics of Shortage* (Amsterdam, New York: North-Holland Pub. Co., 1980).
"Legal Eagles." *China Daily*, 4 March 1993, 3.
Lieberthal, Kenneth, and Michael Oksenberg. *Policy Making in China: Leaders, Structures, and Processes* (Princeton, N.J.: Princeton University Press, 1988).
Lyons, Thomas P. "Planning and Interprovincial Co-ordination in Maoist China." *China Quarterly*, no. 121 (March 1990): 37–60.
Macauley, Stewart. "Non-Contractual Relations in Business: A Preliminary Study." *American Sociological Review* 28, no. 1 (1963): 55–67.
Macneil, Ian. "Contracts: Adjustment of Long-Term Economic Relations under Classical, Neo-Classical, and Relational Contract Law." *Northwestern University Law Review* 72, no. 6 (1978): 854–905.
Macneil, Roderick. "Contract in China: Law, Practice, and Dispute Resolution." *Stanford Law Review* 38, no. 2 (1986): 303–97.
McIlroy, Ann. "An Economic Boom Is Fuelled by Environment-Destroying Material." *Vancouver Sun*, 1 May 1993, B2.
Naughton, Barry. "Distinctive Features of Economic Reform in China and Vietnam." Chapter 12 in this volume.

Naughton, Barry. "China's Experience with Guidance Planning." *Journal of Comparative Economics* 14, no. 4 (1990): 743–67.

Naughton, Barry. "Industrial Planning and Prospects in China." In Eugene Lawson, ed., *U.S.-China Trade: Problems and Prospects*, 179–193 (New York: Praeger, 1988).

North, Douglass C. *Institutions, Institutional Change, and Economic Performance* (Cambridge: Cambridge University Press, 1990).

North, Douglass C., and Robert Paul Thomas. *The Rise of the Western World: A New Economic History* (Cambridge: Cambridge University Press, 1973).

Peng Changlin. "Jianli jingji shenpan sifa xiezhu zhidu, xieshou gongke anjian yidi zhixing nanti" ("Establish a system for judicial cooperation in economic adjudication; join hands to conquer the problem of executing judgments in a different locality"). *Jingji fazhi (Economic Legal System)*, no. 7 (1992): 30–32.

Pfeffer, Richard. *Understanding Business Contracts in China 1949–1963*. (Cambridge, Mass.: Harvard University Press, 1973).

Potter, Pitman B. *Policy, Law and Private Economic Rights in China: The Doctrine and Practice of Law on Economic Contracts* (Ph.D. diss., University of Washington, 1986).

Prosterman, Roy L., and Tim Hanstad. *Land Reform in China: A Fieldwork-Based Appraisal* (Seattle: Rural Development Institute, 1993).

Ren Jianxin. "Supreme People's Court Work Report," 22 March 1993. British Broadcasting Corporation, *Summary of World Broadcasts, Part 3: The Far East*, 12 April 1993, C1/9–17.

Shi Youyong. "Shenpan zhong difang baohu zhuyi de chengyin ji duice" ("Local protectionism in adjudication: Causes and countermeasures"). *Faxue (Jurisprudence)*, no. 6 (1989) 15–18.

Spanogle, John A., and Tibor M. Baranski, Jr. "Chinese Commercial Dispute Resolution Methods: The State Commercial and Industrial Arbitration Bureau." *American Journal of Comparative Law* 35, no. 4 (1987): 761–99.

Stevens, Thomas B. *Order and Discipline in China: The Shanghai Mixed Court 1911– 27* (Seattle and London: University of Washington Press, 1992).

Su Nan. "Fayuan de panjue zai mouxie difang nan yi zhixing" ("Court judgments are difficult to implement in certain places"). *Fazhi ribao (Legal System Daily)*, 3 January 1989, 4.

Tao-tai Hsia. "The Concept of Judicial Independence" (1986).

"Xiang-E liushisi-jia fayuan lianshou gongpo yidi zhixing nan guan jian xiao" ("Sixty-four courts in Hunan and Hubei join hands, achieve results in overcoming the problem of executing judgments in other regions"). *Fazhi ribao (Legal System Daily)*, 24 July 1991, 1.

Yang Jisheng. "'East-West Dialogue' in China—the Strategy of Unbalanced Economic Development on the Mainland in Perspective." *Liaowang (Outlook)* (overseas edition), no. 9 (1989), 5–7. Foreign Broadcast Information Service, *Daily Report: China*, 10 April 1989, 37–43.

Zerbe, Richard. *The Development of Institutions and the Joint Production of Fairness and Efficiency in the California Gold Fields (Right Makes Might)* (8 May 1990).

Zhao Zhenjiang, Zhou Wangsheng, Zhang Qi, Qi Haibin, and Wang Chenguang. "Lun falü shixiao" ("On the Effectiveness of Laws"). *Zhong-wai faxue (Chinese and Foreign Legal Studies),* no. 2 (1989): 1–7, 29.

Zheng Tianxiang, "Zuigao renmin fayuan gongzuo baogao" ("Supreme People's Court work report"). *Zhonghua renmin gongheguo quanguo renmin daibiao dahui changwu weiyuanhui gongbao (Gazette of the Standing Committee of the National People's Congress of the People's Republic of China)* no. 4 (1988): 24–37.

Zheng Tianxiang. "Zuigao renmin fayuan gongzuo baogao" ("Supreme People's Court work report"). *Zhongguo fazhi bao (Chinese Legal System News),* 23 April 1986, 2, 3.

"Zhonggong zhongyang guanyu jiaqiang zheng-fa gongzuo de tongzhi" ("Chinese Communist Party Central Committee notice on strengthening political-legal work"), 13 January 1982. In *Zhonggong nianbao 1983–84 (Yearbook of Chinese Communism 1983–84)* (Taipei 1984), §8, 3–6.

Part 2
Reforming Industry

CHAPTER 4

Contract Incentives and Market Discipline in China's Rural Industrial Sector

Susan H. Whiting

Introduction

Rural enterprise, comprising both private and collective ownership forms, is one of the driving forces behind the dynamism of the Chinese economy under reform. Rural industrial output has grown at an average annual rate of 25 percent per year since the initiation of reform in 1978 and already accounts for nearly one-third of the national total. This chapter focuses on one component of rural industry—collectively owned, township- and village-run enterprises. Specifically, it examines the sources of discipline on enterprise behavior contained in managerial contracts and labor, capital, and product markets, which represent forces for increased efficiency. At the same time, the chapter demonstrates the ways in which the political interests of local governments reduce the effectiveness of these forces.

The findings can be summarized as follows: Contract incentives are effective, as demonstrated by the fact that pay and performance vary together, but performance indicators create incentives for managers to maximize output rather than profits, while contracts for township officials contain explicit targets for performance on social as well as economic indicators, thus diverting attention away from purely economic considerations. Similarly, the labor market for township officials rewards them for promoting community welfare as well as economic growth, while the labor market for managers is highly segmented and rewards managers for their ability to achieve the goals of

I would like to thank Robert Dernberger, Barry Naughton, Craig O'Neill, Yingyi Qian, and Christine Wong for their comments on earlier drafts. Research was supported by grants from the Committee for Scholarly Communications with the People's Republic of China and from the Joint Committee on Chinese Studies of the American Council of Learned Societies and the Social Science Research Council, with funds provided by the Chiang Ching-kuo Foundation. The Shanghai Academy of Social Sciences, Fudan University, and the Universities Service Centre of the Chinese University of Hong Kong provided institutional support.

township leaders. With respect to the capital market, the phenomenal growth of rural collectives can be understood only in light of the ready supply of cheap credit, fueled by an increasing rural savings rate. At the same time, credit allocation is often subordinated to the goals of township leaders, who channel funds to rural collectives based on a mix of economic and social priorities, thereby undermining capital market discipline to some degree. Finally, extreme competition in product markets imposes significant constraints on the behavior of both township leaders and enterprise managers.

The chapter begins by introducing the performance record of rural enterprises in the second section. The next section outlines the relevant elements of principal-agent theory and introduces the analogy between a township and a large diversified corporation. Then I examine in detail the incentives and constraints imposed by managerial contracts and labor, capital, and product markets. The main empirical focus of the chapter is on capital market discipline, which is covered in the greatest detail. This study differs from other analyses by using interview data to examine the process of credit allocation.[1] The chapter concludes with an assessment of the overall incentives and constraints facing township- and village-run enterprise at the current stage of reform in China.

Background: The Record of Rural Enterprise

The rural enterprise sector as a whole encompasses a wide array of ownership forms. This chapter focuses exclusively on collectively owned township- and village-run enterprises (TVEs). TVEs are operated by the appointed leaders of township governments or villagers' committees, and these leaders depend on TVEs as their primary source of revenue. Put in perspective, TVEs account for the lion's share of rural industrial output, although they represent only a small portion of the total number of rural industrial enterprises. The share of rural enterprises accounted for by TVEs declined from 100 percent in 1978 to about 17 percent in 1985 and only 12 percent in 1991. By contrast, TVEs still accounted for 75 percent of rural industrial output in 1991, down from about

---

1. In addition to published statistics, documents, and research reports, the discussion employs interview data collected by the author between September 1991 and August 1992 at research sites under the Wuxi (Jiangsu Province), Wenzhou (Zhejiang Province), and Shanghai municipalities. At each site interviews were conducted with enterprise managers and accountants, as well as with an array of officials representing various government bureaus and bank/credit cooperative offices at the county, township, and (where applicable) village levels. Over 200 interviews were conducted in total. Ideally, both research sites and enterprises would have been selected by means of a random sample. However, because of official restrictions, it was not possible to implement this sampling procedure; therefore, the data cannot be considered truly representative, and the conclusions are not strictly generalizable. The township names used in the chapter are pseudonyms.

80 percent in 1985.[2] The following paragraphs document the remarkable growth record of TVEs and their contribution to community welfare.[3]

Measured in terms of gross value of output, TVEs grew over 20 percent per year between 1985 and 1991; industrial output alone grew at nearly 24 percent per year over the same period. (See tables 1 through 4.) Exports by TVEs, which were valued at only 4 billion yuan in 1985, grew even faster, with average annual growth of about 50 percent per year, reaching nearly 67 billion yuan by 1991. However, profitability, measured here by profits and taxes as a percentage of fixed-assets, declined from 37.3 percent in 1985 to 25.3 percent in 1991.[4] The same pattern occurs for TVEs in the industrial sector, with profitability declining from 28.4 percent in 1987 to 23.7 percent in 1991.

Assessments of TVE efficiency are a matter of debate among economists. Recent research suggests that rural industry made improvements in enterprise efficiency during the 1980s. According to Gary Jefferson and Thomas Rawski,

> Although efforts to measure productivity growth in the collective sector are impeded by inadequate output deflators and inconsistencies between statistical measures of output and employment, the growth of output per worker, output per unit of capital, and total factor productivity in the collective sector, and especially among township and village enterprises, appears to have outstripped comparable measures for the state sector.[5]

For the period 1984–88, the authors estimate the annual growth of total factor productivity at 6.6 percent for township and village industry, compared to 3 percent for state industry. Chenggang Xu estimates that the growth of total factor productivity accounted for between one-third and one-half of TVE output growth between 1984 and 1987.[6] That estimate may be high, however. Research by Jefferson, Rawski, and Yuxin Zheng covering both urban and township collectives during the period 1980–88 shows that increases in total factor productivity accounted for only 27 percent of output growth, with

---

2. These data are drawn from Nongyebu xiangzhen qiyesi, ed., *Zhongguo xiangzhen qiye tongji zhaiyao 1992* (China's township and village enterprise statistical abstract 1992) (Beijing: State Statistical Bureau).

3. The following discussion refers to TVEs in primary, secondary, and tertiary sectors unless explicitly identified as referring to industry. Tables 1 and 2 are comprised of data from all three sectors, while tables 3 and 4 are comprised of data from industry alone. As is clear from the tables, comparably complete information was not available for industrial TVEs alone.

4. Including working capital funds in the base would further reduce profitability as measured here.

5. Gary H. Jefferson and Thomas G. Rawski, "Enterprise Reform in Chinese Industry," *Journal of Economic Perspectives* 8 (Spring 1994): 47–70.

6. Chenggang Xu, "Growth, Productivity and Bureaucratic Control of Chinese Rural Industry," manuscript, London School of Economics. January 1990.

TABLE 1. Performance of Township- and Village-Run Enterprises

Item	1985	1986	1987	1988	1989	1990	1991
	(billion current yuan, unless noted)						
Number of firms (mil)	1.8	1.7	1.6	1.6	1.5	1.5	1.4
Employment (mil)	43.3	45.4	47.2	48.9	47.2	45.9	47.7
Total wages	30.1	35.6	43.0	54.1	58.1	60.7	70.7
Average wages (yuan)	697	783	911	1106	1230	1321	1482
Gross value of output	204.9	251.6	323.7	436.3	485.6	625.4	771.3
Gross value, industrial output	147.8	189.2	261.0	343.8	461.5	524.1	651.8
Exports	3.9	9.9	16.2	26.9	37.1	48.6	67.0
Statutory tax bill	10.9	13.7	16.9	23.7	27.2	27.5	33.4
Community welfare payments	11.3			16.4	16.2	18.3	21.4
Gross profits	28.0	31.0	37.6	52.7	53.3	54.1	66.5
Net profits	17.1	16.1	18.8	25.9	24.0	23.3	28.5
Remitted profits	6.8		7.3	9.4	9.1	8.8	10.2
Enterprise welfare payments	1.2			2.5	2.4	2.4	3.1
Original value of fixed assets	75.0	94.7	123.2	158.4	192.1	220.2	262.6
Profits + taxes / fixed assets (%)	37.3	32.7	30.5	33.3	27.8	24.5	25.3

Sources: *Zhongguo xiangzhen qiye nianjian 1978–87, 1989, 1990, 1991* (China's township and village enterprise yearbook 1978–87, 1989, 1990, 1991) (Beijing: State Statistical Bureau); *Zhongguo xiangzhen qiye tongji zhaiyao 1992* (China's township and village enterprise statistical abstract 1992) (Beijing; State Statistical Bureau).

TABLE 2. Growth of Township- and Village-Run Enterprises

Item	1986	1987	1988	1989	1990	1991
	(percentage increase)					
Number of firms	−6.6	−8.4	0.5	−3.4	−5.3	−0.8
Employment	5.0	3.9	3.7	−3.6	−2.7	3.8
Total wages	17.9	20.9	25.9	7.3	4.5	16.4
Average wages	12.4	16.3	21.4	11.2	7.4	12.2
GVO (nominal)	22.8	28.7	34.8	11.3	28.8	23.3
GVIO (nominal)	28.0	38.0	31.7	34.2	13.6	24.4
Exports	155.1	62.8	65.9	38.2	30.7	37.9
Statutory tax bill	26.5	23.3	39.6	15.2	1.1	21.2
Community welfare payments				−1.0	13.1	16.8
Gross profits	10.7	21.4	40.2	1.1	1.4	23.0
Net profits	−6.0	17.0	37.5	−7.3	−3.1	22.3
Remitted profits			29.2	−3.1	−3.4	16.5
Enterprise welfare payments				−3.5	2.0	25.9
Original value of fixed assets	26.2	30.2	28.6	21.2	14.6	19.3
Profits + taxes / fixed assets (%)	−12.3	−6.7	9.2	−16.5	−11.9	3.3

Sources: Same as Table 1.

TABLE 3. Performance of Township- and Village-Run Industry

Item	1987	1988	1989	1990	1991
	(billion current yuan, unless noted)				
Number of firms (mil)	1.0	1.0	1.0	0.9	0.9
Employment (mil)	33.4	35.1	34.5	34.0	35.5
Total wages	30.2		42.7	46.5	54.5
Average wages (yuan)	904		1236	1368	1534
GVIO	261.0	343.8	461.5	524.0	651.8
Gross profits	28.9		42.8	43.0	54.3
Net profits	13.3		17.8	16.9	21.3
Remitted profits	5.3		6.7	6.6	7.6
Enterprise welfare payments			1.8	1.8	2.3
Original value of fixed assets	102.0		164.1	190.7	228.9
Profits + taxes / fixed assets (%)	28.4		26.1	22.5	23.7

Sources: Same as Table 1.

expansions in material inputs accounting for the largest share of output growth (57 percent).[7] In her study of Jiangsu Province, Penelope Prime uses both gross and net output to estimate total factor productivity for the period 1981– 88. Using gross output, she finds that productivity growth was higher in collective than in state industry, with increases of 6.2 and 4.1 percent, respectively. However, using net output, she finds higher productivity growth in state industry, with an increase of 2.3 percent compared to only 1.7 for collective industry. She suggests that one explanation for this difference may be that inputs of both capital and labor "increased substantially faster in collective industry than in state industry." Thus, she concludes,

> the results comparing productivity change between state and collective industry in Jiangsu are inconclusive. However, they do suggest caution in interpreting the fast growth in collective industrial output as evidence that reforms have made China's economy more efficient.[8]

It is beyond the scope of this chapter to assay an independent estimate regarding the efficiency of TVEs; rather, it examines the extent to which contractual incentives and labor, capital, and product markets create pressure to improve efficiency.

One of the most important characteristics of TVEs is the great extent to

---

7. Gary H. Jefferson, Thomas G. Rawski, and Yuxin Zheng, "Growth, Efficiency, and Convergence in China's State and Collective Industry," *Economic Development and Cultural Change* 40, no. 2 (January 1992): 239–66.

8. Penelope B. Prime, "Industry's Response to Market Liberalization in China: Evidence from Jiangsu Province," *Economic Development and Cultural Change* 41, no. 1 (October 1992): 38.

TABLE 4. Growth of Township- and Village-Run Industry

Item	1988	1989	1990	1991
	(percentage increase)			
Number of firms	2.9	−1.5	−4.8	−0.7
Employment	5.0	−1.6	−1.5	4.4
Total wages			9.1	17.1
Average wages			10.7	12.1
GVIO	31.7	34.2	13.6	24.4
Gross profits			0.5	26.3
Net profits			−4.7	26.0
Remitted profits			−2.0	16.2
Enterprise welfare payments			1.7	26.5
Original value of fixed assets			16.2	20.0
Profits + taxes / fixed assets (%)			−13.7	5.3

Sources: Same as Table 1.

which they contribute to community development and welfare. These enterprises, through locally retained tax payments, fees, and profit remittances, are the main source of revenue for township governments. TVE taxes totaled 33.4 billion yuan in 1991, although in 1990 (the most recent year for which this information is available) actual payments of sales and income taxes represented only 75 percent of taxes owed.[9] TVEs also paid fees in support of community welfare totalling 21.4 billion yuan in 1991 and remitted profits totalling 10.2 billion yuan to townships and villages.[10] These figures do not include fees paid to township government industrial corporations, which William Byrd and Lin Qingsong estimate to have equalled approximately 2 billion yuan in 1985.[11] In addition, TVEs employed nearly 48 million people (equivalent to about 11 percent of the rural labor force) and committed 3.1 billion yuan to educational and welfare benefits within the firm during 1991. The impact of these burdens on enterprise operations is discussed in detail below.

There is no doubt that the development of TVEs has markedly improved the standard of living in China's rural areas, whether via increasing individual incomes or expanding community welfare expenditures funded by TVE revenues. Moreover, the evident success of rural collectives documented previ-

---

9. Zhongguo xiangzhen qiye nianjian bianji weiyuanhui, *Zhongguo xiangzhen qiye nianjian 1991* (China's township and village enterprise yearbook 1991) (Beijing: Nongye chubanshe, 1992): 194–96.

10. In the Shanghai suburban counties, for example, there are four officially sanctioned community fees, including fees to support agriculture, agricultural sidelines, rural education, and general social welfare expenditures (such as pension funds, cultural centers, etc.). Informant 56.

11. William A. Byrd and Lin Qingsong, "China's Rural Industry: An Introduction," in William A. Byrd and Lin Qingsong, eds., *China's Rural Industry: Structure, Development, and Reform* (Oxford: Oxford University Press, published for the World Bank, 1990), 15.

ously, particularly in terms of the rapid expansion of output and the explosive growth of exports, suggests that there are some effective incentives at work and that market forces shape the behavior of township leaders and enterprise managers to a significant degree. The task of this chapter is to identify what those incentives and market forces are and show how the political interests of local government officials interact with them. The following section lays out the framework for analysis.

Analytical Framework

Principal-agent theory is a theory of incentives and constraints; it is about "how one person, the *principal,* can make it in the interest of another person, the *agent,* to behave as the principal wants."[12] Applied to the modern corporation, the theory focuses on the ways in which owners constrain managers to serve the owners' interests, which are usually assumed to center on efficient profit maximization. According to the theory, four main forces constrain the behavior of managers: managerial contracts, and labor, capital, and product market discipline. By linking performance (as defined by the principal) and rewards, contracts create incentives for managers to behave as profit maximizers. Competition in labor, capital, and product markets forces managers to pursue profits as efficiently as possible.[13] This chapter applies this theory to the Chinese case. It examines the nature of the incentives contained in managerial contracts and the extent to which the markets in which rural firms participate constrain managerial behavior. The remainder of this section shows that the Chinese township functions essentially as a corporation— although with certain distinctive characteristics.[14] The analogy between a township and a corporation provides the basis for the application of principal-agent theory in the context of China's rural industrial sector.

The township (formerly the commune) resembles a corporation in that township officials, as de facto owners of TVE assets, exercise significant control over the firms under their jurisdiction. Such control is a legacy of the commune era, when party, government, and economic management functions were combined under a single commune administration. Township officials

---

12. John McMillan, "Creating Incentives: Principal-Agent Contracts in Practice," *Taiwan Economic Review* 20, no. 1 (March 1992): 81.

13. For a review of some of the extensive literature on this topic, see Bengt R. Holmstrom and Jean Tirole, "The Theory of the Firm," in R. Schmalensee and R. D. Willig, eds., *Handbook of Industrial Organization,* vol. 1 (Elsevier Science Publishers, 1989).

14. This analogy has also been employed by others. See, for example, Byrd and Lin, "China's Rural Industry: An Introduction," 5–6; Victor Nee, "Organizational Dynamics of Market Transition: Hybrid Forms, Property Rights, and Mixed Economy in China," *Administrative Science Quarterly* 37 (March 1992): 1–27; and Jean C. Oi, "Fiscal Reform and the Economic Foundations of Local State Corporatism in China," *World Politics* 45, no. 1 (October 1992): 99–126.

are de facto owners because the township government has (1) authority to decide how enterprise assets will be used, including control over the appointment and remuneration of managers, the nature and scale of investment, the size of the work force, and so on; (2) effective claim on all collective enterprise profits (although official regulations technically limit this claim to 40 percent of net profits);[15] and (3) authority to dispose of enterprise assets by transfer, sale, or dissolution of the firm.[16] According to William Byrd and N. Zhu,

> At the community [township] level the industrial corporations responsible for supervising community enterprises [TVEs] function in many ways like financial conglomerates, holding companies, or the headquarters of loosely managed multidivisional corporations. The key financial roles of the industrial corporations include pooling enterprises' after-tax profits for investment and directing other resources (from local banks and credit cooperatives) to particular investment projects; cushioning subordinate enterprises from short-term fluctuations; serving as a short-term financial intermediary by transferring funds from enterprises with surpluses to those with deficits; and facilitating the issuance of short-term bonds to local residents.[17]

However, the township also differs from the corporation in four important respects. First, township officials owe their positions not to de jure ownership of capital but to the county-level officials who appoint them.[18] The power that township officials exercise as de facto owners of TVEs lasts only as long as they hold political office. Unlike real owners, therefore, the maximand of township officials is determined in part by the performance criteria

---

15. "Zhonghua renmin gongheguo xiangcun jiti suoyouzhi qiye tiaoli (People's Republic of China regulations on township and village collectively owned enterprises, June 3, 1990)," in Nongyebu, *"Zhonghua renmin gongheguo xiangcun jiti suoyouzhi qiye tiaoli" xuexi zhidao* ("People's Republic of China regulations on township and village collectively owned enterprises" study guide) (Beijing: Renmin Chubanshe, 1991), 345–54. The relevant section is chapter 5, article 32.

16. This paragraph draws on Susan H. Whiting, "The Comfort of the Collective: The Political Economy of Rural Enterprise in Shanghai," presented at the Annual Meeting of the Association for Asian Studies, Los Angeles, March 25–28, 1993; and idem, "Zizhuquan: xiangzhen qiye zouxiang shichang de qianti (Autonomy: A prerequisite for township and village enterprises to move towards the market)," *Shanghai jiaoxian gongye (Shanghai Suburban Industry)*, no. 3 (1992). These essays detail the division of control between township officials and enterprise managers in terms of enterprise autonomy.

17. William A. Byrd and N. Zhu, "Market Interactions and Industrial Structure," in William A. Byrd and Lin Qingsong, eds., *China's Rural Industry: Structure, Development, and Reform* (Oxford: Oxford University Press, published for the World Bank, 1990), 89.

18. Technically, TVEs are owned by all residents of the township or village, respectively. In theory, township officials represent the interests of all residents in managing township assets.

(kaohe zhibiao) associated with their political office, which encourage township officials to maximize output rather than profits. Moreover, as community leaders, township officials themselves pursue goals other than profit maximization. One survey of township and village leaders identified increasing the incomes of local residents, increasing local employment opportunities, and producing revenues to finance government activities as their top three goals with respect to rural enterprises.[19]

Second, the township derives revenues from its enterprises via many channels besides profit remittances. Specifically, the township retains a share of the direct and indirect taxes paid by the TVEs under its jurisdiction;[20] it also receives an array of legally mandated fees and illegal exactions paid by these TVEs. Thus, townships may tend to maximize net revenues to the government rather than maximizing the profits of the enterprises under their control. As Christine Wong argues, "local governments try to maximize net revenues, which consist of profits and taxes [and fees] paid by the firm. They would be willing to allow the survival of money-losing firms as long as sufficient tax revenues [and fees] were generated to offset the losses."[21]

Third, the township government's dual role as de facto enterprise owner and tax collector creates the potential for township officials to collude with TVEs in evading taxes. Township officials may employ discretion in the implementation of central tax policy in order to shift revenues from shared tax receipts to profit channels that the township alone controls. While the township has a relatively hard budget constraint and cannot legally engage in deficit financing, the potential for tax evasion implies a concomitant potential for softening the budget constraint.

Finally, the township leadership (specifically the party apparatus) exercises institutionalized political oversight over the nominally independent local bank and credit cooperative offices, thereby affording TVEs privileged access to credit resources.

Given these caveats, the township may be characterized as a diversified

---

19. Qiu Jicheng, "Xiangzhen qiye—shequ (zhengfu) guanli moshi de jiben xiansuo (Township and village enterprises—The basic threads of the community (government) management model)," *Fazhan yanjiu tongxun (Development Research)* no. 104 (December 1988): 748, 759.

20. The township shares budgetary tax receipts with higher levels of government through a revenue-sharing tax system. In general, under this system the county sets a minimum target for tax collection, which the township must meet. If the township exceeds this target, it receives a certain share of the above-target amount. However, the central government maintains the exclusive right to determine the scope and rate of taxation; each lower level of government is responsible only for collecting these taxes from the enterprises under its jurisdiction.

21. Christine Wong, "Between Plan and Market: The Role of the Local Sector in Post-Mao China," in Bruce Reynolds, ed., *Chinese Economic Reform: How Far, How Fast?* (Boston: Academic Press, 1988), 104. See also World Bank, *China: Revenue Mobilization and Tax Policy Issues and Options* (Washington, D.C.: World Bank, 1990).

corporation that is more likely to maximize output or revenue than to maximize profits and that has a less-than-hard budget constraint and preferential access to financing. As Song Lina and Du He note in their report for the World Bank,

> As chief owner of the assets of township enterprises, the township government, as part of its function, should oversee the operational behavior of the enterprise in the same way as boards of directors in Western countries do. . . . But close examination reveals that governments' duty to their enterprises is motivated by their own financial needs and by the pursuit of wider community goals.[22]

Subsequent sections examine contract incentives and market discipline to determine the extent to which these forces effectively constrain the behavior of township officials and enterprise managers.

Internal Contract Discipline

Township and village officials and enterprise managers are extremely sensitive to the terms of their contracts, since these terms directly influence their remuneration. This section outlines the content of contracts, demonstrating that performance is measured more in terms of output than profits. It explains this emphasis in terms of the structure of taxes. In addition, the discussion suggests that in the context of township and village enterprises positive incentives are more effective than negative incentives in eliciting the desired behavior on the part of managers.

In most cases, the county policy management office (under the county party committee) or the county economic commission is responsible for establishing the specific criteria (*kaohe zhibiao*) by which township party and government executives are to be evaluated and on which bases their remuneration will be determined. Although specific criteria vary by county, they are usually divided between economic and social targets. Economic indicators center around industry, and in many of the research sites total value of industrial output is most important, followed by sales, profits, and taxes.[23] Other economic indicators usually include output of agriculture and agricultural subsidiary products and in some cases include separate indicators for export-oriented performance, such as total value of exports and number of joint venture agreements signed. The scope of social targets ranges from education

---

22. Song Lina and Du He, "The Role of Township Governments in Rural Industrialization," in William A. Byrd and Qingsong Lin, eds., *China's Rural Industry: Structure, Development, and Reform,* (Oxford: Oxford University Press, published for the World Bank, 1990), 355.

23. Informants 66, 99, 126, 175, 191.

to family planning to public order. In Luhang Town (Shanghai), for example, of a total 100 points possible, 60 were assigned for economic indicators and 40 for social indicators.[24] Target levels appear to increase between 5 and 25 percent per year, depending on the locale and the macroeconomic situation.[25]

Industrial output value carries the most weight among performance indicators for township officials in many locales, and reports suggest that this prominence leads officials to focus on output value to the exclusion of other indicators that relate more directly to economic efficiency. A representative of Songyang Town (Shanghai) laments the emphasis on output: "Up to now leaders have only worried about output value, but that's not what counts. What counts is profit."[26] However, the prominence of output value as a performance indicator can be understood in the context of the structure of taxes.[27] Indirect taxes—specifically the product tax and the value-added tax—are paid at production and are then included in the sales price of a good. As table 5 shows, indirect taxes comprise a large and increasing share of tax revenues from TVEs. Thus, county officials—who share in the tax receipts but not the profits of TVEs—may try to ensure adequate performance on taxes by making the readily measurable indicator of output value a centerpiece of township executives' contracts. Although some county officials employ tax as a performance indicator as well, one county executive commented that he considers it unwise to push tax targets directly, because if county-level tax receipts are too high, the provincial level is likely to increase the minimum amount of taxes it expects the county to hand over.[28] By focusing incentives on output value, the county may hope to ensure adequate tax revenues, while leaving itself room to maneuver through the selective approval of tax breaks after the minimum level of tax receipts is met. The county must strike a delicate balance in setting performance targets. Revenues that enter tax channels reveal greater fiscal capacity to higher levels of government; at the same time, however, the county has only a limited capacity to tap into township revenue outside of regular fiscal channels.

The disproportionate emphasis on output value has caused a number of undesirable consequences that have begun to prompt a move away from output value toward sales and profits as the most important indicators of performance.[29] According to a study conducted in Jiangsu, the focus on output value has led townships to expand productive capacity without atten-

---

24. Informant 66.
25. Informants 84, 175.
26. Informant 99.
27. I am indebted to Christine Wong for making this relationship clear.
28. Informant 103.
29. Informants 98, 103.

**TABLE 5.   Taxes Owed and Paid by
Township- and Village-Run Enterprises**

Year	Total (billion yuan)	Income Tax (billion yuan)	Income Tax (% share)
Owed			
1985	10.86	3.27	30.1
1986	13.73	3.86	28.1
1987	16.94	4.44	26.2
1988	23.65	5.98	25.3
1989	27.25	6.09	22.3
1990	27.54	5.71	20.7
1991	33.38	6.81	20.4
Paid			
1988	17.65	3.81	21.6
1989	19.61	3.79	19.3
1990	20.32	3.55	17.5
1991	24.43	4.03	16.5

Sources: Same as table 1 and *Zhongguo tongji nianjian
1992* (Chinese statistical yearbook 1992).

tion to the efficiency of production or the salability of products.[30] The problem becomes particularly serious during recessionary periods, when unsold goods accumulate in inventory while production continues apace. For unsold goods, the burden of indirect taxes is borne by the producer rather than being passed on to the buyer.[31] In response, the new economic performance criteria drafted in 1992 by a county economic commission in Wuxi, for example, place much greater emphasis on sales,[32] while the criteria drafted in 1989 by a county government in Shanghai place greater emphasis on profits.[33]

30. He Baoshan et al., eds., *Jiangsu nongcun feinonghua fazhan yanjiu* (Research on the non-agricultural development of rural Jiangsu) (Shanghai: Shanghai renmin chubanshe, 1991), 121. For an account of similar problems at the enterprise level, see Shao Xinfu et al., "Jiadingxian xiangzhen qiye chengbaozhi de shijian (The experience with Jiading County's township and village enterprise contracting system)," in Jiadingxian nianjian bianji weiyuanhui, *Jiading nianjian 1988–1990* (Jiading yearbook 1988–1990) (Shanghai: Tongji daxue chubanshe, n.d), 185–87.

31. See note 27.

32. Informant 191.

33. "Jiaweifa (1989) #8: Zhonggong jiading xianwei jiadingxian renmin zhengfu guanyu wanshan 1989 nian xiangzhen dangzheng jiguan ganbu kaohe jiangli banfa de tongzhi (Jiading Party Document (1989) #8: Announcement of the Jiading County Party Committee and People's Government regarding the perfection of the 1989 methods for evaluation and reward of town(ship) cadres in party and government organs)," in *Jiading Yearbook 1988–1990* (Jiading, 1991), 44–45.

Social targets indirectly shape the incentives for economic behavior on the part of township leaders. Concerns about public order, for example, may lead township officials to prioritize employment above economic efficiency. Thus, it is common practice for the township to assign quotas to collective factories, indicating the number of jobs each must provide for local residents. These social targets also have another indirect effect on the economic behavior of township officials: the more revenues officials extract from TVEs, the more resources they can commit to educational programs, family planning campaigns, and so on.

Regardless of the performance indicators used, expectations regarding economic performance increased dramatically following the promulgation of Central Document #2 (1992), which ushered in the most recent fast-growth campaign and led to the ratcheting up of economic targets. The tremendous pressure to meet and surpass high targets has undesirable consequences as well. In some cases, township leaders have refused to make investments across township borders because the profits, taxes, and employment benefits generated would contribute to another township.[34] This problem has been resolved in some cases through the use of creative contract terms, but the conflict highlights the nature of the incentive structure under which township cadres function.

Like its counterpart at the county level, the township policy management office sets the *kaohe zhibiao* used to evaluate both village leaders and enterprise managers. At these levels as well, contracts emphasize output value, followed by sales, profits, and taxes.[35] The case of a party secretary in a village in Nantang Township (Shanghai) illustrates how contract incentives are structured. According to his contract for 1991, his starting salary was pegged (based on a step function) to the level of industrial output achieved in the village that year; because the village's total output value exceeded a 2 million yuan threshold, he received a starting salary of 5,100 yuan. (Less successful village leaders received lower starting salaries; the minimum possible starting salary was 2,800 yuan.) In addition, he received 50 yuan for every 10 thousand yuan of profit over and above the village's target level of 1.85 million yuan. Village enterprises produced total profits of 2.5 million yuan; therefore, he received a profit bonus of 3,250 yuan. These two items accounted for the lion's share (about 85 percent) of his income, which totalled 9,960 yuan.[36] Another example offers further evidence that remuneration varies with performance. One village in Luhang Town (Shanghai) that had been ranked third in terms of output value in 1989 had by 1991 fallen to ninth

---

34. Informant 37.
35. Informant 191.
36. Informant 126.

in the ranking of all villages in the town. Because he failed to meet his *kaohe zhibiao,* the village party secretary's income fell by several thousand yuan to 2,950 yuan in 1991, while party secretaries of higher-ranked villages earned over 6,000 yuan each in the same year.[37]

The contract terms for enterprise managers are similar in the essentials to those described for village leaders, although the income differentials appear to be higher. In Luhang Town (Shanghai) in 1991, the salary of the highest paid manager was 11,000 yuan, while that of the lowest paid was 4,000.[38] The differentials in the Shanghai suburban counties are small—dampening the incentive effect—relative to those in the Jiangsu and Zhejiang Province sites because of the relatively low ceilings placed on wages and enforced by the tax bureau in Shanghai.[39] Although wage ceilings exist elsewhere as well, laxer enforcement by tax officials enables accountants to cover higher wage bills by inflating other tax-deductible costs, allowing successful managers to garner much higher salaries. One Shanghai manager complained that if only he had been born in Zhejiang he would be making much more money.[40] Remuneration policies can differ greatly even in neighboring areas due in part to restrictions on labor mobility, to be discussed in the subsequent section. Similarly, joint ventures can employ incentives much more effectively since they are not subject to the same wage bill restrictions.

While there are clear positive incentives for good performance, bargaining over target levels is common, thus softening to some extent the discipline imposed by contracts.[41] Moreover, negative incentives for managers appear to be implemented less effectively than positive ones. Many managerial contracts contain penalties for performance that falls below target levels. For example, a penalty may entail a deduction from the manager's base salary or require the manager to make up for a shortfall in profits.[42] However, these negative incentives go unenforced in some cases, and this situation has produced the saying "*baoying bu baokui* (contract for profits but not for losses)."[43] As one Chinese professor of management science commented, both the township leaders and the managers they supervise are life-long members of the same rural community; thus there is a tendency not to penalize managers when their performance falls below contracted norms.[44] As a result, managers bear less risk than intended by contract designers.

---

37. Informant 62.
38. Informant 66.
39. Informant 105.
40. Informant 47.
41. Informant 105. See also Shao, "Experience with Contracting," 186.
42. Informant 129.
43. Informants 41, 42. See also Shao, "Experience with Contracting," 185.
44. Informant 41.

The focus here is on the contractual incentives operating on managers and township and village officials, with the assumption that these incentives will be passed on to their employees. Based on the findings of this and other studies, the assumption appears justified. For example, given the growing importance of sales performance, managers have devised numerous incentive schemes for sales agents, ranging from salaries based on a flat percentage of sales to price-linked bonus schemes, with the result that some sales agents earn more than do managers themselves.[45] With respect to shop floor employees, one study finds a strong "link between earnings and work," with basic wages accounting for only 50 percent of the wages received by workers in the TVEs surveyed, performance-based bonus pay accounting for an additional 30 percent, and overtime pay accounting for the remaining 20 percent.[46] However, the study also reports that "average wage[s] increased more rapidly than labor productivity (net enterprise income per worker), suggesting that townships and villages were more concerned about rural employment and income generation than profits."[47]

This section demonstrates that contracts do provide effective positive incentives for good performance, with pay and performance varying together. However, performance tends to be measured in terms of output rather than profits, although shifts toward sales and profits as performance indicators have occurred in certain locales. At the same time, township executives—as public officials—are also evaluated on the basis of social targets, which diverts attention away from purely economic considerations. In addition, negative incentives for poor performance appear to be less strictly enforced, thereby undermining contractual incentives for the weakest enterprise managers.

Labor Market Discipline

Labor markets provide discipline to the extent that there is competition for advancement, that advancement is a reward for good performance, and that there is a real possibility of being demoted or fired as a result of poor performance. Labor market discipline is a weaker influence on behavior than are contractual incentives, in large part because of the significant administrative barriers to the free movement of labor. TVE workers employed in their hometowns are subject to relatively weak discipline, while TVE employees from outside the local community (*waidiren*) are subject to a relatively high degree of labor market discipline. TVE managers compete for advancement

---

45. Du Haiyan, *Zhongguo nongcun gongyehua yanjiu* (Research on rural industrialization in China) (Hubei: Zhongguo wujia chubanshe, 1992), 93.
46. He et al., *Non-agricultural Development.*
47. Ibid., 165.

within a small, local talent pool, but anecdotal evidence suggests that the nature of their assignments and their tenure in office do reflect their performance records. Finally, township officials compete for advancement in a significantly larger talent pool and "rise or fall" on the basis of their economic performance.

Although complete data linking economic performance and career paths of township officials are not readily available, anecdotal evidence suggests that strong economic performance is the key to advancement. According to an official of the Shanghai Suburban Industry Management Bureau, which governs township- and village-run industry, county leaders appoint township executives and party secretaries with the intention that they will participate directly in decision making with respect to TVEs. As this official put it, they "rise or fall on the basis of economic success."[48] The official also pointed out that township leaders are appointed for three-year terms and that this creates a very short time horizon. As a result, township leaders tend to focus on short-term enterprise performance. Furthermore, rather than reinvesting in the enterprises under their jurisdiction, they may use these profits to build highly visible community projects so that their contributions to the community are well known before their terms expire.[49] According to Susan Shirk, "Under the post-1980 incentive structure, the political ambitions of individual local officials became closely identified with the economic accomplishments of their domains. . . . Whether officials aimed to climb the ladder of success to Beijing or to become leading figures on the local scene, their reputation was enhanced by industrial growth and local building projects."[50] Although Shirk's analysis refers to provincial-level officials, the same clearly holds true at the township level.

Unlike most TVE managers, township leaders are selected from a large, countywide pool.[51] Of ten township executives and party secretaries interviewed, six had served in similar capacities in other townships within the same county.[52] While many of these township leaders rose through local administrative hierarchies, others had diverse backgrounds in county-level government, school administration, and veterinary medicine.[53]

In contrast, competition for managerial positions in TVEs is often limited to a relatively small pool within the township, but for those who have

48. Informant 37.

49. Ibid.

50. Susan L. Shirk, *The Political Logic of Economic Reform in China* (Berkeley: University of California Press, 1993): 189–90.

51. In the Jiangnan region, encompassing Shanghai, southern Jiangsu, and Zhejiang, many counties have populations well over 1 million.

52. Informants 34, 64, 97, 134, 144, 196.

53. Informants 64, 66, 143.

become managers, career paths—particularly the length of tenure and the importance to the local community of the enterprise to which one is posted—do reflect performance to some extent. Two separate studies of TVE managers in Jiangsu Province show that approximately 95 percent are selected from within the township or village where the enterprise is located.[54] Moreover, managers tend to be selected from among those with experience as cadres. Interviews conducted in Nantang Township (Shanghai) reveal a characteristic career pattern among TVE managers, who rose from team leader to village (brigade) accountant or village party secretary to a position in the township (commune) government before assuming the position of TVE manager. Similarly, a survey of 200 rural industrial enterprises shows that over 50 percent of managers had previously served as local government cadres.[55] The reason for the large share of former cadres among TVE managers may be as much for their political reliability (*"shifou 'kaodezhu'"*) as for their managerial experience.[56]

Indeed, studies indicate that, in general, managerial career patterns reflect managers' abilities to achieve the goals of township leaders. As noted previously with respect to rural industry, local officials are concerned about the ability of firms both to provide income and employment for local residents and to provide revenue to the local government. According to one study, "Once those responsible for the enterprise become unable to satisfy community interests, the community government uses the most severe measures—dismissing the leader or replacing the leadership group."[57] Over 60 percent of the enterprises surveyed had undergone a change of leadership since founding—with more than two leadership changes on average, while the average tenure for an enterprise manager was approximately 4.5 years.[58] Among managers, the perception is that good managers enjoy longer tenures.[59] However, unsuccessful managers are usually transferred—to smaller firms or to administrative rather than productive units, for example—rather than being fired or demoted to the rank of worker.[60] In cases where the posts of manager and party secretary are held separately, the post of party secretary is often the

---

54. He et al., *Non-agricultural Development*, 184; and Meng Xin, "The Rural Labor Market," in William A. Byrd and Qingsong Lin, eds., *China's Rural Industry: Structure, Development, and Reform* (Oxford: Oxford University Press, published for the World Bank, 1990), 299–322, esp. 302–3. The latter shows that while 93 percent of managers are hired locally in Wuxi County (Jiangsu), the figures are 78 percent for Jieshou County (Anhui); 74 percent for Shangrao County (Guangxi); and 54 percent for Nanhai County (Guangdong).
55. Qiu, "Basic Threads," 758.
56. Du, *Rural Industrialization*, 119; Qiu, "Basic Threads," 758–59.
57. Qiu, "Basic Threads," 759.
58. Ibid.
59. Informants 50, 77.
60. Informants 49, 129.

less responsible position. In these cases, a transfer from a managerial position to the position of party secretary may be considered a demotion.[61]

With respect to shop floor employees, labor market discipline for those who are local residents and for those who are outsiders must be examined separately. Virtually none of the local TVE employees in any of the research sites investigated faced any possibility of losing their jobs because of poor performance or even because of redundancy. It is "virtually impossible to fire a local worker (even a redundant one), except in cases of the most egregious violations of labor discipline—such as causing injury to another worker—and then only through a long and drawn-out process."[62] Moreover, "obstacles to firing or laying off workers became more serious after Tiananmen Square raised concerns about political stability and unemployment in the countryside."[63] Township officials complain that in this regard TVEs have become like state enterprises and that local workers have no sense of the threat of job loss.[64] As noted in the previous section, TVE managers in some townships are given targets regarding how many jobs they must provide for local residents (particularly recent school graduates) each year.[65] As a result, the majority of TVE managers interviewed reported that the total number of workers in the firm was too large. These conditions suggest that the labor market provides little discipline for local TVE employees.

By contrast, TVE managers can hire and fire employees from outside the locale at their own discretion. As the manager of one village-run factory in Shanghai commented, "This factory has a few workers from Anhui, and I would like more because I can fire them if they're bad. If they're from my own village, I'm stuck with the bad workers; I can't fire them."[66] This anecdotal evidence is consistent with the priority that officials and managers place on local employment, and suggests that labor market discipline is significantly stronger for those working outside their own villages or townships. Furthermore, the number of outside workers appears to be increasing, particularly in the rapidly developing coastal region. Estimates of the share of TVE workers hired from outside the township, county, or province range from about 6 to 20 percent for various sites in Jiangsu Province during the late 1980s.[67] For TVEs overall, it appears that once a certain threshold level of employment for local residents has been reached, then on the margin labor

61. Informant 49.
62. Informant 76.
63. Whiting, "Comfort of the Collective."
64. Informant 97.
65. Informants 96, 102.
66. Informant 126.
67. Du, *Rural Industrialization,* 109–10; He et al., *Non-agricultural Development,* 183; and Meng, "Rural Labor Market," 302–3.

can be hired and fired relatively freely. However, outside workers still tend to be clustered in less desirable jobs, and in some cases they are paid on a lower scale than are local workers. At the same time, enterprises still bear the burden of employing less-disciplined but better-paid local labor in the majority of shop floor jobs.

The perpetuation of barriers to the free movement of labor, combined with a preference for full employment motivated by the desire on the part of township officials for social and political stability, undermines the potential for strong labor market discipline on the shop floor. TVE managers also face very limited competition on the labor market, since most are selected from a small pool of local candidates. Nevertheless, the particular post a manager fills and the length of time he or she fills it do reflect the manager's ability to achieve the goals set by township leaders. Similarly, township officials, while selected from a larger, countywide pool, succeed or fail based on their ability to promote rapid economic growth and community welfare. Labor market forces may be a powerful influence on township officials, but contract incentives seem to have a more powerful influence on local managers and workers than do labor market forces, and in these cases incomes more clearly reflect performance than do career patterns.

Capital Market Discipline

This section examines the extent to which the capital market disciplines collective enterprise managers in the rural industrial sector. One of the most prominent characteristics of the TVE sector is its ready access to capital, and this characteristic accounts in large part for the rapid growth of these firms. The ample supply of capital stems, on the one hand, from the increasing rural savings rate and, on the other, from the role that township government plays in credit allocation. As a result of increased savings deposits, the local offices of the Agriculture Bank and the Rural Credit Cooperatives, which depend mainly on local deposits for loan funds, are able to increase lending to TVEs. These lenders have developed a set of loan criteria intended to channel funds to the most creditworthy customers. At the same time, the township government uses various means at its disposal to reduce both the cost and risk of borrowing for TVEs and to reduce the risk of lending for local financial institutions. Achievement of its goals is paramount for the township government and, as discussed in the preceding sections, these goals include guaranteeing employment for local residents, increasing TVE output to meet performance criteria, and increasing the revenues accruing to the government. In addition to intervening to reduce the risk of lending to TVEs, the township government also uses its political influence over local lenders to induce them to make loans furthering these government goals—goals that are not necessarily shared by the lenders. This behavior on the part of the township government weakens the discipline imposed by the capital market.

The first part of this section describes the institutional framework by which rural household savings are converted into TVE loans. The second part examines township government interference in the allocation of bank loans. The third part describes the role played by the township government in securing alternative sources of capital for TVEs. The final part reexamines the notion of the hard budget constraint at the township level.

The Bank and Credit Cooperative System

Although the Chinese banking system has undergone significant reforms allowing competition among lenders with previously distinct bailiwicks, the majority of banking transactions in the rural sector are still conducted through the Agriculture Bank or the Rural Credit Cooperatives. This section focuses on the lending activity of these institutions, referring to the lending activity of other commercial banks as required. Often the only bank represented by an office at the township level is the Agriculture Bank; the township-level office is not an independent accounting unit, but rather is under the direction of the county-level branch office. Rural Credit Cooperatives, by contrast, have nominal autonomy. They were created in the 1950s using the combined assets of township residents; they are independent accounting units and have the status of independent legal entities (*faren*). In reality, however, rural credit cooperatives often share the same staff and leadership as the township Agriculture Bank office, and in practice their funds are combined, although credit cooperatives maintain separate account books.[68]

The Agriculture Bank and the Rural Credit Cooperatives depend mainly on local deposits for loan funds, and the growing supply of capital available for loans to TVEs derives from rapid increases in savings fueled by rising rural incomes. As the right-hand side of table 6 shows, household savings deposits in the Agriculture Bank have increased dramatically since 1979, doubling about every two years. Similarly, household deposits in the Rural Credit Cooperatives have also increased rapidly from a somewhat larger base.

The scale of the township-level Agriculture Bank's total loans outstanding is controlled by binding targets (also described as mandatory plans [*zhilingxing jihua*] sent down by the county bank branch.[69] Bank officials interviewed report that these are strict ceilings that the township-level office

---

68. Informants 57, 99, 177, 198.

69. According to the bank officials interviewed at each site, binding targets were instituted with the beginning of the economic rectification campaign. The campaign was initiated in late 1988 and continued through 1991. In general, there are a number of instruments by which the

cannot exceed by so much as one penny (*fen*), even though these ceilings often represent only a fraction of deposits. Indeed, in the townships where interviews were conducted, the bank office did not technically exceed these targets.[70] In general, target levels reflect central evaluations of the macroeconomic situation, and targets were a major tool of macroeconomic control during the economic rectification campaign of late 1988–91. Central policy stipulated that total loans to rural enterprises would not increase at all during 1989,[71] and that rather draconian policy was relaxed only slightly for the remainder of the rectification campaign.[72] The central office of the Agriculture Bank attempted to guarantee implementation by stipulating that adherence to the binding targets would be an important element of the performance evaluations of local bank branch executives.[73] Loans for fixed-asset

---

central bank (the People's Bank of China) can, in theory, exercise indirect monetary control: most importantly by (1) increasing the interest rate on central bank lending to the Agriculture Bank and the other commercial banks, (2) restricting central bank lending to the commercial banks, and (3) increasing the reserve requirements for the commercial banks. See Zhou Xiaochuan and Zhu Li, "China's Banking System: Current Status, Perspective on Reform," *Journal of Comparative Economics* no. 11 (1987): 401. Nevertheless, these indirect controls have proven ineffective in maintaining macroeconomic balance, forcing the central bank to intervene directly in the operation of the commercial banks, using administrative measures such as loan ceilings in order to bring about monetary control.

70. Informants 159, 198.

71. See Agriculture Bank President Ma Yongwei's speech to the meeting of Agriculture Bank branch presidents on January 21, 1989, abstracted in Ma Yongwei, "Jianchi guanche sanzhong quanhui de zhidao fangzhen nuli zuohao jinnian de nongcun jinrong gongzuo (Persist in implementing the guiding principles of the Third Plenum, conscientiously pursue this year's rural financial work," *Zhongguo nongcun jinrong (China's Rural Finance)* no. 3 (1989): 8–12. The reference is to the Third Plenum of the Thirteenth Central Committee, the party meeting at which economic rectification was initiated. As Barry Naughton has highlighted with respect to previous rectification campaigns, the expansionary atmosphere "would be altered only by the adoption by the central political leadership of contractionary policies as a major point of the current political line." See Barry Naughton, "Macroeconomic Management and System Reform in China," in Gordon White, ed., *The Chinese State in the Era of Economic Reform: The Road to Crisis* (New York: M. E. Sharpe, 1991), 66.

72. The relaxation of the loan policy was a result of its severe impact on rural enterprises, many of which closed—at least temporarily—throwing rural residents out of work. Rural unemployment heightened concerns about political stability in the countryside. One bank official commented that at that time loans were intended to guarantee employment and that therefore the evaluation of loan guarantors (discussed on pp. 91–93) existed in form only. His implication was that the evaluation has since become more rigorous. (Informant 158.) On general policy at that time, see Ma Yongwei, "Jianchi guanche zhili zhengdun shenhua gaige de fangzhen zhichi nongcun jingji chixu wending xietiao de fazhan (Persist in implementing the principles of rectification and deepening reform, support the continued stable and coordinated development of the rural economy)," *Zhongguo nongcun jinrong (China's Rural Finance)* no. 3 (1990): 9–15.

73. See Ma Yongwei's speech of November 7, 1988, abstracted in Ma Yongwei, "Ma yongwei tongzhi zai zhongguo nongye yinhang fenhang hangzhang huiyishang de jianghua

investment were even more tightly controlled during the period of rectification. Township-level offices did not have the authority to approve any loans in
this category; rather, decisions regarding fixed-asset loans were made by the
county branch. National statistics on loans to rural enterprises by the Agricultural Bank show that loan growth did contract sharply in 1989 and remain
below average during economic rectification, although it was not held to zero.
(See table 6.)

In contrast to the local offices of the Agriculture Bank, credit cooperatives are more flexible, because although the county-level branch of the Agriculture Bank also issues targets for loans outstanding to the cooperatives,
these targets appear to be guidance targets (*zhidaoxing*) and are thus nonbind-
ing.[74] Credit cooperatives make loans based on the level of deposits (*duocun
duodai*) and on the special reserve requirements set for cooperatives by the
central bank.[75] (See tables 7–8.) Loans made by credit cooperatives have
increased rapidly even through the period of economic rectification. Table 6
shows that, between 1987 and 1991, credit cooperative loans increased by
154 percent, while Agriculture Bank loans increased by only 52 percent, even
though savings deposits in the Agriculture Bank were growing much more
rapidly (increasing by 184 percent compared to 83 percent for credit cooperatives during the same period). The fewer constraints on the credit cooperatives
have allowed them to lend more aggressively to TVEs.

Control by targets imparts a campaign mentality to local bank officials.
The Agriculture Bank office in Songyang Town (Shanghai) reportedly did not
fund a single new project during the entire three-year course of economic
rectification.[76] As a result, local officials want to take advantage of the relaxed
policies in place since early 1992 by making up for lost time.[77] One local
official commented that the town government was planning ten new projects
funded by bank loans and that he would consider it a success even if three
failed, because the important point was to acquire as many fixed assets as
possible while credit policy was loose.[78] Sharp increases in cadre performance targets (*kaohe zhibiao*) encourage this mentality. The official noted that

(Comrade Ma Yongwei's speech to the meeting of branch presidents of the Agriculture Bank of
China)," *Zhongguo nongcun jinrong (China's Rural Finance)* no. 23 (1988): 4–7.

74. One article in the journal *Shanghai Finance* refers to 1988 binding targets to control
the scale of loans made by credit cooperatives "in some places." See Jin Chunpin, "Nongcun
xinyong de kuisun xianxiang zhide zhongshi (It is worth taking seriously the phenomenon of
losses on the part of rural credit cooperatives)," *Shanghai Jinrong (Shanghai Finance)* no. 2
(1990): 38. Nevertheless, bank officials interviewed for this project emphasized the flexibility of
credit cooperatives with respect to loans. (Informant 198.)

75. Informant 57.

76. Informant 96.

77. Informant 97.

78. Informant 84.

TABLE 6. Loans and Savings Deposits

Year	Total Loans (billion yuan)	Total Loans (percentage increase)	Year	Household Deposits (billion yuan)	Household Deposits (percentage increase)
Agriculture Bank Loans to TVEs			Agriculture Bank Rural Household Savings Deposits		
1979	2.99		1979	2.12	
1980	5.30	77.3	1980	3.22	51.9
1981	6.21	17.3	1981	4.26	32.2
1982	7.34	18.1	1982	5.38	26.3
1983	8.00	9.1	1983	6.70	24.6
1984	15.77	97.1	1984	10.05	50.1
1985	18.80	19.2	1985	15.53	54.5
1986	28.79	53.2	1986	25.77	65.9
1987	35.01	21.6	1987	42.62	65.4
1988	40.77	16.5	1988	59.37	39.3
1989	42.06	3.2	1989	84.85	42.9
1990	46.22	9.9	1990	121.21	42.9
1991	53.11	14.9	1991	157.76	30.2
Credit Cooperative Loans to TVEs			Credit Cooperative Rural Household Savings Deposits		
1979	1.41		1979	7.85	
1980	2.74	94.6	1980	11.69	49.0
1981	3.55	28.9	1981	16.94	44.9
1982	4.23	19.3	1982	22.79	34.5
1983	6.00	42.0	1983	31.96	40.3
1984	13.50	124.8	1984	43.79	37.0
1985	16.44	21.8	1985	56.48	29.0
1986	26.58	61.7	1986	76.61	35.6
1987	35.93	35.2	1987	100.57	31.3
1988	44.02	22.5	1988	114.23	13.6
1989	54.02	22.7	1989	140.68	23.2
1990	70.07	29.7	1990	184.16	30.9
1991	91.27	30.3	1991	231.67	25.8

Sources: Zhongguo nongcun jinrong tongji 1979–89 (China's rural financial statistics 1979–89) (Beijing: State Statistical Bureau); *Zhongguo nongcun jingrong tongji nianjian 1991* (China's rural finance statistical yearbook 1991) (Beijing: State Statistical Bureau); *Zhongguo xiangzhen qiye tongji zhaiyao 1992* (China's township and village enterprise statistical abstract 1992) (Beijing: State Statistical Bureau); *Zhongguo tongji nianjian 1992* (China's statistical yearbook 1992) (Beijing: State Statistical Bureau).

it was easier to meet rapid increases in the target for output value by building new enterprises than by improving the performance of existing ones.[79] Similarly, in order to meet the target for the number of foreign joint venture contracts signed, the town's industrial corporation served as the guarantor for

79. Ibid.

TABLE 7.   Credit Cooperative Liabilities and Assets

Item	1987 (billion yuan)	1988	1989	1990	1991
Liabilities					
Total	161.9	191.1	231.0	299.9	368.9
Deposits	122.5	140.0	166.3	214.5	270.9
Collective	21.9	25.7	25.7	30.3	39.3
Household	100.6	114.2	140.7	184.2	231.6
Interbank loans to coops	3.8	3.6	3.8	4.2	5.1
Other liabilities	35.6	47.5	60.9	81.3	92.9
Assets					
Total	161.9	191.1	231.0	299.9	368.9
Loans	77.1	90.9	109.1	141.3	180.8
Collective agriculture	6.5	8.0	10.6	13.4	17.0
Rural enterprises	35.9	44.0	54.0	70.1	91.0
Rural households	34.0	37.2	41.4	51.8	63.1
Other loans	0.8	1.6	3.0	6.0	9.7
Deposits with Ag. Bank	55.2	58.0	65.6	77.2	91.6
Deposits with Central Bank[a]	4.7	4.9	3.7	5.3	9.1
Other assets	24.8	37.4	52.6	76.1	87.4

Sources: Zhongguo nongcun jingrong tongji nianjian 1991 (China's rural finance statistical yearbook 1991) (Beijing: State Statistical Bureau).

[a]Special reserve requirements.

a foreign partner to secure bank loans locally (without adequate information about the partner's creditworthiness). When the venture fell through, the bank, and the town as guarantor, were left with the debt burden. In response to this type of behavior by town leaders, a bank official at the county level was already—as of 1992—anticipating the need for yet another economic rectification campaign to counterbalance the fast-growth campaign initiated by Deng Xiaoping in February 1992.[80]

The Township Government and Implementation of Credit Policy

While increasing rural savings have fueled the growth of loans to TVEs, political interference on the part of the township government has distorted to varying extents the ways in which these loans have been allocated. The following paragraphs examine the implementation of loan criteria, including the use of enterprise credit ratings, the practice of requiring the borrower to provide loan matching funds from the borrower's own re-

---

80. Ibid.

TABLE 8. Agriculture Bank Liabilities and Assets

Item	1987 (billion yuan)	1988	1989	1990	1991
Liabilities					
Total	273.7	314.3	373.2	473.6	578.6
Deposits	148.7	171.4	205.5	264.1	331.9
Enterprise	30.5	35.1	36.9	43.8	54.6
Agriculture	65.7	67.2	72.3	85.4	102.8
Household	42.6	59.4	84.9	121.2	157.7
Other deposits	9.9	9.6	11.5	13.6	16.8
Central bank loans to Ag. Bank	83.5	99.4	118.3	143.9	175.0
Interbank loans to Ag. Bank	5.5	8.8	16.0	27.6	30.1
Other liabilities	36.0	34.8	33.3	38.1	41.5
Assets					
Total		314.3	373.2	473.6	578.6
Loans		263.2	305.8	377.4	457.8
State industry		15.4	18.9	25.0	30.8
State commerce		156.9	187.4	235.9	286.9
Rural industry		40.8	42.1	46.2	49.8
Fixed-asset loans		5.8	6.6	7.6	9.9
Credit coops		3.4	3.4	3.7	4.1
Other loans		40.9	47.5	58.9	76.3
Required reserves		20.2	25.9	34.0	43.1
Deposits with central bank		13.3	25.0	38.8	42.8
Interbank loans		12.7	10.5	16.8	27.8
Other assets		4.9	6.0	6.6	7.1

Sources: Zhongguo nongcun jinrong tongji nianjian 1991 (China's rural finance statistical yearbook 1991) (Beijing: State Statistical Bureau); *Zhongguo nongcun tongji nianjian 1991* (China's rural statistical yearbook 1991) (Beijing: State Statistical Bureau).

sources (*ziyou zijin*), and the practice of requiring a loan guarantor or collateral.[81]

The practice of rating enterprises (*xinyong pinggu*) represents an important source of enterprise discipline; however, political interference can still override this and other principles of credit allocation. The exact criteria by which enterprises are rated and the precise weighting of those criteria are unclear, but they include economic results (*jingji xiaoyi*), development trends (*fazhan qushi*), and potential sales performance (*chanpin*

---

81. The discussion of these loan criteria will treat the Agriculture Bank and the Rural Credit Cooperatives together, because, as noted previously, their funds are often combined in practice. Other loan criteria include the stipulation that credit allocation must reflect national industrial development priorities, with, for example, no new loans going to firms in overcrowded processing industries. However, a full discussion of the implementation of national industrial policy via credit allocation is beyond the scope of this chapter.

xiaolu).[82] Specifically, township-level bank offices tend to focus on an enterprise's output value, sales, and profit, and ratings are reviewed twice a year.[83] The records of the Dongtan Town Agriculture Bank in Wuxi show that as of June 1992, top-rated enterprises had received 68 percent of all loans, while second-rate enterprises had received 11 percent, third-rate enterprises 5 percent, and unrated enterprises 16 percent.[84] Unrated enterprises include, among others, those that are profitable but rank poorly in terms of output value. Loans to third-rate enterprises were slated to decrease by 70 thousand yuan in 1992, but the change was to be negligible—equivalent to less than 1 percent of total loans. In fact, in Songyang Town (Shanghai), bank officials reported that third-rate enterprises could count on receiving at least the same amount in loans—even if they were losing money.[85] A bank official from the neighboring township of Daqiao reported that in 1991 nearly half the township- and village-run enterprises there were losing money and that the local office of the Agriculture Bank had granted them loans in order to pay wages at year-end.[86] Nevertheless, low-rated enterprises do forfeit certain benefits; in Hualing Town (Wenzhou), top-rated enterprises enjoy preferential interest rates, for example.[87] Overall, these data suggest that lower-rated enterprises are only very slowly beginning to face some discipline in the capital market, while the continuation of loans to poorly rated firms suggests a political concern for the maintenance of employment levels and employee welfare.

Moreover, credit ratings themselves may be distorted. According to a commentator in the journal *Shanghai Finance,* in the process of rating enterprises, banks "are unable to avoid inappropriate local administrative interference. Some local governments and bureaus, in order to ensure that the enterprises under their jurisdiction receive a high rating, have no qualms about intervening personally."[88] Interference is even more common in bank decision

---

82. Shen Sandu, "Dui xinyong pinggu gongzuo de jidian sikao (Several thoughts on credit rating work)," *Shanghai Jinrong (Shanghai Finance)* no. 2 (1990): 40.

83. Informant 57.

84. Other townships' bank/credit cooperative accounts reveal similar breakdowns. (Informant 99.) In the text, "top-rated" is used as a shorthand to represent three categories—special-rate (*teji*), high-rate (*youji*), and first-rate (*yiji*). Few townships boast any special-rate enterprises. Township bank officials combined high-rate and first-rate categories in reporting loan percentages, and it appears that these two categories of enterprises receive similar treatment from the bank.

85. Informant 96.

86. Informant 101. See also Li Chu'en, Shi Shoujiang, and Zhu Lifiang, "Xiangzhen qiye yuqi daizhi daikuan xintan (A new discussion of township and village enterprises' delinquent and unrecoverable loans)," *Zhongguo nongcun jinrong (China's Rural Finance)* no. 5 (1990): 57, which also discuss the use of loans to pay wages.

87. Informant 159.

88. Shen, "Credit Rating Work," 40.

making regarding new projects. According to a township government official in Dongtan Town (Wuxi),

> There is government interference in the allocation of bank loans. Successful enterprises can get loans directly—and this is most enterprises. But especially for new enterprises, if the bank doesn't want to support them, the party secretary will go in person with the enterprise manager and accountant to the bank—but this is the minority. Of course, for less-developed townships, government interference is even greater. Still, the bank is already gradually beginning to operate by economic laws; it already considers its own economic results (*jingji xiaoyi*).[89]

Similar interference is well documented for state enterprises.[90]

This ad hoc interference is facilitated by institutionalized relationships. Although township bank officials are appointed within the Agriculture Bank system by their county-level superiors, the leaders of the township party-government apparatus must approve the appointments. Moreover, the party affairs of township bank officials are governed at the township level. Thus, township leaders have authority over township bank officials via party channels.[91] Interviews confirm not only the institutional potential for, but also the actual exercise of local party authority over banks. Institutionalized control goes beyond party channels in some cases. In Dongtan Town (Wuxi), a bank official reported that "the vice-general manager of the [town government's] industrial corporation is concurrently the manager of the credit cooperative; so the interests of the industrial corporation are attended to and borrowing money is convenient."[92] Political interference may not undermine capital market discipline if enterprises are then disciplined to be efficient through political channels; but given the apparently low priority accorded efficiency considerations among township leaders' goals, such political discipline is unlikely to be forthcoming under the current set of incentives. The discussion will return to this issue later.

Banks attempt to restrict the availability of "soft" credit by requiring that borrowers demonstrate the existence of a certain percentage of matching

89. Informant 196.

90. See Huang Yasheng, "Web of Interests and Patterns of Behavior of Chinese Local Economic Bureaucracies and Enterprises during Reforms," *The China Quarterly* no. 123 (September 1990): 431–58; Andrew Walder, "Local Bargaining Relationships and Urban Industrial Finance," in Kenneth Lieberthal and David Lampton, eds., *Bureaucracy, Politics, and Decision-Making in Post-Mao China* (Berkeley: University of California Press, 1992), 308–33; and Gordon White and Paul Bowles, *Towards a Capital Market? Reforms in the Chinese Banking System: Transcript of a Research Trip*, Research Report No. 6 (Sussex: Institute of Development Studies China, 1987).

91. Informants 57, 63, 136, 159, 163, 177, 198.

92. Informant 198.

funds from the borrower's own resources (*ziyou zijin*). According to Agriculture Bank regulations, working capital loans require *ziyou zijin* equivalent to 30 percent of the loan amount, while fixed-asset loans require 50 percent.[93] In principle, *ziyou zijin* derives from an enterprise's retained profits, as well as from certain officially mandated funds set aside from pretax profits and other sources of nondebt investment funds.[94] For a variety of reasons to be discussed, enterprises often lack sufficient *ziyou zijin* to meet bank requirements.

Township bank officials, on one hand, may simply waive the requirement in light of political pressure. On the other hand, enterprises, with the support of the township government, may evade *ziyou zijin* requirements by taking advantage of loopholes in the banking system. While reforms in the banking system allow commercial banks to compete for accounts, disclosure practices are still based on the assumption that enterprises have accounts at only one bank. Enterprises then exploit this loophole by using funds from an undisclosed loan at one bank for *ziyou zijin* at another.[95] In this way, enterprises can reach high levels of indebtedness without the lenders' knowledge. In some cases, enterprises employ this strategy in defiance of local Agriculture Bank officials—when they need more credit but are unable to secure new loans or to pay back old loans at home banks.[96] In other cases, the township offices of the Agriculture Bank collude in this practice, as a result of political pressure, shared local interests, or personal connections.[97] For example, in Luhang Town (Shanghai), a new enterprise was established in 1991 with a total investment of 1.59 million yuan, including 0.5 million in loans from the town office of the Agriculture Bank, 0.49 million in loans from the Construction Bank, 0.5 million in loans from the Bank of China (the latter two both located

---

93. Informant 96.

94. See Yu Chiqian and Huang Haiguang, eds., *Dangdai zhongguo de xiangzhen qiye (China today: Village and township enterprises)* (Beijing: Dangdai zhongguo chubanshe, 1991), 438–41, 447–50.

95. This phenomenon, referred to as *duotou kaihu*, has received extensive coverage in Chinese journals. See, for example, Shu Hengchang, Wei Deyong, and Wang Canwen, "Qingli duotou kaihu jiaqiang zhanghu guanli (Clear up multiple accounts, strengthen account management)," *Shanghai Jinrong (Shanghai Finance)* no. 12 (1990): 41–42; Cai Xiongwei (Agriculture Bank, Suzhou Branch), "Xiangzhen qiye de 'zhaiwulian' weihe nanyi jiekai (Why the township and village enterprise 'debt chain' is hard to break)," *Shanghai Jinrong (Shanghai Finance)* no. 12 (1990): 35–37; Bi Honglin and Yan Xiu, "Duotou kaihu duotou daikuan de biduan ji duice (The harmful practice of multiple accounts and multiple loans and countermeasures)," *Zhongguo nongcun jinrong (China's Rural Finance)* no. 8 (1990): 56; Luo Xianfu, Deng Heren, and Liu Zhonglong, "Qingli zhengdun qiye duotou kaihu (Sort out and rectify multiple enterprise accounts)," *Zhongguo Jinrong (China's Finance)* no. 4 (1991): 28–29; Mao Rongfang, "Qiye duotou kaihu de biduan yu guanli duice (The harmful practice of multiple enterprise accounts and managerial countermeasures)," *Shanghai Jinrong (Shanghai Finance)* no. 5 (1991): 21–22.

96. Bi and Yan, "Harmful Practice," 56.

97. Informant 96.

outside the town) and 0.1 million yuan in old equipment transferred from another factory. According to an informant, the loans were taken out in the name of another enterprise and were guaranteed by the township industrial corporation. The informant noted that the town's Agriculture Bank office, is, in terms of party relations, under the leadership of the town party committee and that, in addition, the bank officials are all local residents and friends with the party leaders. In this way, he explained, the enterprise could borrow money from the local Agriculture Bank and, with the bank's knowledge, use these funds as *ziyou zijin* in order to secure loans at other banks.[98] This phenomenon highlights the ways in which township governments and their enterprises can exploit incomplete reforms in the transitional banking system, undermining discipline in the capital market.

In response to this problem, only one site of the five investigated, the county in Wenzhou, has passed regulations requiring that each enterprise license state the name of the home bank at which the enterprise has its accounts (*kaihu yinhang*). According to an official at the township office of the Industrial and Commercial Bank,[99] the regulation was motivated by the severity of indebtedness (*fuzhai jingying*) in collective enterprises.[100] This action suggests that a more complete regulatory framework can reinforce the discipline imposed by the capital market. Indeed, some Chinese analysts have called for the drafting of a more complete set of regulations nationwide.[101] Others, however, have called for a return (at least temporarily) to the pre-reform banking structure in which the Agriculture Bank (including credit cooperatives) had sole responsibility for loans in the rural industrial sector.[102]

Another element of discipline is the requirement that borrowers provide either guarantors or collateral for loans, but in this case as in others, the disciplinary function of the requirement is undermined in practice.[103] According to regulations, the guarantor must be an "economic entity" (*jingji shiti*) with its

---

98. Informant 48.

99. Hualing Town (Wenzhou) is the only township investigated with an Industrial and Commercial Bank office at the township level.

100. Informant 158.

101. See, for example, Shu, Wei, and Wang, "Clear Up Multiple Accounts," 42.

102. Mao, "Harmful Practice and Managerial Countermeasures," 21.

103. This requirement does not apply to working-capital loans within the quota (*dinge*) planned for each township-run enterprise by the township office of the Agriculture Bank. Any loan funds above the planned amount or loan funds for new projects, however, would be subject to this requirement. (Top-ranked enterprises are exempt in many cases.) Only the township Agriculture Bank, which is the "home bank" for township-run enterprises, has a plan quota for loans to these enterprises. The home bank need not rely on loan guarantors for planned loans because it handles accounts receivable for township-run enterprises; therefore, the bank can deduct loan payments directly from payments received from the enterprise's clients. (Informant 56.) The ability to deduct loan payments directly from enterprise accounts, when used, is a powerful constraint on enterprise reliance on "soft" credit. However, this constraint depends on the existence of paying clients.

own independent source of income. In addition, it must be recognized as a legal entity (*faren*), and it must not be a government organ (*guojia jiguan*).[104] Although the township industrial corporation (*gongye gongsi*) is a government office with official functions, it is simultaneously an economic and legal entity.[105] Thus, in most cases the township industrial corporation serves as guarantor for township-run enterprises, while the village industrial and commercial company (*shiye gongsi*)—the economic arm of the village governance structure—serves as guarantor for village-run enterprises.[106] Nevertheless, the industrial corporation is frequently referred to as an "empty" guarantor (*kong danbao*), because it seldom uses funds from its own economic resources to fulfill its obligations.[107] It frequently places levies on the retained profits of the successful enterprises under its jurisdiction in order to repay delinquent loans of enterprises that are performing poorly (*tongshou huandai*).[108] In addition, it may request that the bank extend the loan period (in some cases with the industrial corporation making the interest payments)[109], or it may seek to borrow money from another source to cover the loan.[110] For example, a factory in Meilin Town (Shanghai) was unable to repay a 100 thousand yuan loan from the township Agriculture Bank because of its inability to collect accounts receivable. The industrial corporation took out loans at interest from a number of diverse sources, including the Chinese YMCA (headquartered in Shanghai), in order to repay the bank. The factory remained in debt to the industrial corporation, which, in turn, was in debt to a number of sources.[111]

For cases in which the township industrial corporation or the village company is unable or unwilling to serve as guarantor, the township public finance office (*caizhengsuo*) frequently serves as guarantor, although informants acknowledge that this is a violation of the regulations.[112] Moreover, when a firm defaults on a loan guaranteed by the public finance office, paying off the loan from finance office funds is a last resort. First, the public finance office may encourage the bank to roll over the loan account, or it may borrow money from other cash-flush government bureaus to pay off the loan.[113] The bank is often willing to roll over the loan account as long as the enterprise is

---

104. Xu Heping, "Zhongshi danbao shencha que bao zhaiquan luoshi (Take seriously the investigation of guarantors, ensure the fulfillment of creditors' rights)," *Shanghai Nongcun Jinrong (Shanghai Rural Finance)* no. 1 (1992): 42–43.

105. Informant 46.

106. Informants 57, 198.

107. Informants 96, 177. This type of guarantor is also referred to as a guarantor in form (but not substance) (*xingshi danbao*). See Xu, "Investigation of Guarantors," 42–43.

108. Informants 53, 83, 106, 177, 198.

109. Informant 83.

110. Informants 68, 198.

111. Informant 68.

112. Informants 56, 68, 70.

113. Informants 56, 70.

still paying interest.[114] In some places, the public finance office assists enterprises by making the interest payments for them.[115]

The local government—whether via the industrial corporation or the public finance bureau—performs an important function in guaranteeing enterprise loans. It ostensibly reduces the risk borne by the banks, thereby encouraging them to make loans to relatively small-scale rural enterprises, which face formidable obstacles to development. At the same time, by reducing the risk to the enterprise, it encourages the firm to undertake ambitious projects and fosters firm development. However, in many cases the township government, as loan guarantor, contributes to the availability of "easy" credit for marginal enterprises, rather than increasing pressure on enterprises to perform. Moreover, by subsidizing the cost of capital through the payment of interest or the repayment of principal, the township government encourages excessive use of credit resources and investment in capital-intensive rather than labor-intensive processes, particularly where the limited supply of local labor does not reflect the national labor surplus.

Loans backed up by collateral (*diya danbao*) are most difficult to collect once they go into default, because the burden of collection falls to the bank. Banks come under tremendous pressure not to collect because the practice of repossessing and auctioning property is not well developed in social or legal terms.[116] The township office and county branch of the Agriculture Bank in the Wenzhou site reported that, as of mid-1992, they had attempted and failed to collect several delinquent loans guaranteed by collateral (usually buildings or equipment). The property had not been auctioned because the courts were unwilling to pursue the case vigorously.[117] At another research site, problems occurred because, although the value of the loan collateral had—at least nominally—been verified by a notary (*gongzheng*), when the enterprise defaulted on the loan and the Agriculture Bank attempted to collect, the collateral was found to be essentially worthless.[118] Like the weakness of the regulatory framework described with regard to disclosure practices, the unwillingness of the courts to enforce loan contracts undermines the discipline imposed by the banking system.

The record of banks in pursuing delinquent loans is mixed. As noted earlier, the absence of legal recourse has hindered banks in their efforts to collect loans. In light of this constraint, two approaches appear most common: first, bank officials report the willingness to grant additional loans to enter-

---

114. Informant 127.
115. Informants 97, 135.
116. See, for example, the discussion in Zhou Qiren and Hu Zhuangjun, "'Fuzhai jingying' de hongguan xiaoying (The macro effects of 'chronic indebtedness,'" *Fazhan Yanjiu Tongxun (Development Research)* no. 54 (May 1987): 312.
117. Informants 159, 163.
118. Informant 177.

prises that are behind in loan payments—even if the firms are losing money—as long as the firms appear able to develop some kind of marketable product.[119] Second, bank officials report relying on the township industrial corporation to repay loans through the practice of *tongshou huandai* (i.e., placing a levy on the profits of successful enterprises to pay off the debts of weaker enterprises). In cases in which the industrial corporation is unable or unwilling to pay the debts, the bank may have no choice but to consider the loan unrecoverable. Among the township-level Agriculture Bank offices investigated for which comparable data are available, the share of unrecoverable (*daizhi/daizhang*) loans for 1991 ranged from 1.4 percent of total loans outstanding in Dongtan Town (Wuxi) to 4.4 percent in Hualing Town (Wenzhou) to 4.8 percent in Songyang Town (Shanghai).[120] As reflected in the discussion, many problematic loans never fall into this category; thus these figures represent only a small part of the picture.

The heavy reliance on bank loans is not only facilitated but also in no small part caused by the practices of the township government. Collective enterprises retain only a fraction of their gross profits; in general, these firms pay, in addition to taxes, a variety of legally mandated fees and illegal exactions before paying an often sizable share of the remaining profits to the local government. Indeed, managers of both township- and village-run collectives complain that local leaders take money from enterprises as they please,[121] and bank officials complain that local governments treat enterprises like "money trees," which undermines firms' financial health.[122] According to the Songyang Town official, enterprises retain only about 12 percent of gross profits on average.[123] This limits the ability of enterprises both to repay loans and to provide for their own capital needs. The situation is exacerbated by the common practice of exacting levies on profitable enterprises to pay off the debts of weaker enterprises for which the township industrial corporation serves as loan guarantor. It is also exacerbated by the less common practice of forfeiting enterprise depreciation funds to the local government for other uses.[124]

---

119. Informants 96, 101, 158.

120. These figures do not include overdue loans (*yuqi daikuan*), which are in arrears for less than two years.

121. Informants 71, 85, 126.

122. Cai, "'Debt Chain'," 35–37. In Luhang Town (Shanghai) as of 1991, the town industrial corporation was still engaged in a *tongshou tongzhi* relationship with its enterprises. *Tongshou tongzhi* refers to a situation in which enterprises hand over all profits to the local government and look to the government for all major expenditures. This issue is discussed at greater length in Whiting, "Comfort of the Collective."

123. Informant 97. It is not clear whether this estimate includes illegal exactions or the profits handed over to the local government.

124. Informants 70, 121.

As a recent World Bank study shows, the share of profits remitted by TVEs to the township government that are used for productive investment in enterprises has been declining. Rather, remitted profits are increasingly spent on township and village construction and on cultural, educational, and welfare-related projects as well as on the salaries of the growing number of local cadres who are not on the official state payroll.[125] These spending priorities are consistent with the kinds of achievements that result in promotions for township leaders, as discussed in the previous section. However, as the author of the World Bank study points out, "The declining proportion of reinvestment in industry is making [TVEs] increasingly dependent on credit financing."[126] Not only are new enterprises more highly leveraged, but with reinvestment from the township government not forthcoming and bank loans for fixed-asset investment tightly restricted, existing enterprises commonly use working capital funds (whether bank loans or *ziyou zijin*) for fixed-asset investment.[127] These enterprises then turn again to the banking system, anticipating easy access to additional working capital loans.

The experience of Songyang Town (Shanghai) demonstrates the extent of reliance on bank loans. According to the report of a town government official, from 1986 to 1989 debt increased an average of 25 percent per year, while net profits of town-run industrial enterprises decreased 5 percent per year, on average.[128] Interest payments alone were becoming a burden, and by 1989 interest payments equalled net profits, which averaged less than 75 thousand yuan per enterprise. Debt as a share of total assets increased from 15 percent in 1980 to 40 percent in 1989, and by 1989 it was commonly 80 percent or more for new enterprises.

The ability of enterprises to repay their debts is further reduced by the declining profitability of investments. In Songyang Town's town-run industrial enterprises, for example, the profits and taxes produced by 100 yuan of fixed assets (*zichan lishui lu*) declined from 37 yuan in 1980 to 21 yuan in 1989.[129] A town government official attributed this decline to excessive investments in nonproductive assets (e.g., buildings), failed investment deci-

---

125. Wang, "Capital Formation and Utilization," 229.

126. Ibid.

127. Informants 48, 59, 177, 198. See also Li, Shi, and Zhu, "Delinquent and Unrecoverable Loans," 57.

128. Informant 97. This trend appears to be widely felt across economic indicators. According to a survey of 200 large-scale rural industrial enterprises, from 1975–1985 the output value produced by each ten thousand yuan of investment decreased 6.5 percent per year on average. Income from sales decreased 5.6 percent per year on average; gross profits decreased 8.3 percent; net profits decreased 8.8 percent; and enterprise-retained profits decreased 9.4 percent. Zhou and Hu, "Macro-effects," 318.

129. Informant 97. If Songyang followed countywide trends, the figure declined again in 1990. Informant 108.

sions, increasing raw material and wage costs, unsalable products accumulating in inventory, mounting unpaid accounts receivable, and high interest payments, in addition to burdensome taxes and fees.[130] While the declining profitability stemming from these problems is an alarming trend, Barry Naughton points out that the decline may, at least in part, result from the dissipation, through increasing entry and competition, of the monopoly rents available to earlier entrants.[131]

From another perspective, information problems make it difficult for banks to make wise loan decisions. Because of a shortage of well-trained personnel, banks often rely on self-reporting by enterprises of production levels and profitability without independent verification.[132] Furthermore, bank managers complain that they lack both the personnel and the skills to evaluate new loan requests. The manager of the Agriculture Bank in Songyang Town (Shanghai) commented that it was impossible for his staff to conduct a feasibility study to assess the market potential of a proposed project. Instead, the staff relied on the opinions of the town's political leaders and the enterprise manager. As a result, the bank has repeatedly granted loans for products that ultimately were unsalable. In many of these cases, firms in the same metropolitan area (Greater Shanghai) producing the same products had already saturated the market.[133]

The expanding geographic scope of bank lending activity poses other informational difficulties. While banks seek higher returns and lower risks, in an information-poor environment, they are unable to identify the best return with the lowest risk. Nevertheless, some local governments have been instrumental in arranging loans from outside the home locale. In one Wuxi county, total loans outstanding for TVEs totalled about 2.1 billion yuan in 1991, only about 0.3 billion of which was from the county Agriculture Bank system and only about 0.5 billion of which was from all of the county's specialized banks combined.[134] The county party committee assisted the town in securing loans from banks and other institutions outside the area,[135] and as one government official commented, the interest rate charged by the outside banks depended on the quality of the personal connections.[136] Although some governments in

130. Informant 97. A recent article based on 1991 data echoes these themes. See Wang Guangyi and Li Jingbai, "Jingti: xindai zijin yingyunzhong de 'heidong' (Warning: The black hole in which credit funds operate)," *Shanghai Jinrong (Shanghai Finance)* no. 11 (1992): 18–19.

131. Barry Naughton, "Implications of the State Monopoly Over Industry and Its Relaxation," *Modern China* 18, no. 1 (January 1992): 14–41. The World Bank study on rural industry also raises this point. See Byrd and Zhu, "Market Interactions and Industrial Structure," 90–91.

132. Shen, "Credit Rating Work," 40.

133. Informant 96.

134. Informant 191.

135. Informant 198.

136. Informant 191.

less-developed regions try to use administrative measures to prohibit the outward flow of capital, Dongtan Town (Wuxi) has obtained loans from banks in both Anhui and Xinjiang provinces.[137] This practice suggests that, despite political barriers, capital is beginning to flow toward more profitable—if not necessarily the most profitable—uses.

Clearly, financial institutions operate under severe constraints. Despite these constraints, capital market discipline is gradually beginning to have some bite. Most loans flow to highly rated enterprises.

However, there remains a significant undisciplined element in bank lending. Weak firms are supported through bank loans because such support is consistent with the desire of local government officials to maintain employment and maximize revenue. As outlined above, these goals are defined by the incentive structure under which local government officials operate, and officials act on these goals through their positions as (*a*) de facto owners of local enterprises, and (*b*) holders of political power in a highly politicized economic system.

Other Sources of Capital

Even in light of continued political interference and an underdeveloped legal framework, access to easy credit through the banking system is gradually diminishing. As a result, townships and their enterprises are increasingly turning to sources of capital outside the banking system. One group of Chinese analysts identified this trend as early as 1985; it found, based on a survey of 200 large-scale rural industrial enterprises, that while short-term bank loans themselves increased over 20 percent compared to the first half of that year, the share of bank loans in total working capital debt nevertheless fell from 46 to 37 percent.[138] Loans from nonbank sources accounted for over 60 percent of working capital loans and over 30 percent of fixed-asset loans in 1985.[139] Table 9 shows that the officially reported share of bank loans in fixed-asset investment by township- and village-run industrial enterprises declined from nearly 50 percent in 1987 to about 35 percent in 1990.[140] Similarly, the

---

137. Informant 196.

138. Zhou and Hu, "Macro Effects," 309.

139. See the results from the same enterprise survey published in Zhou, Qiu, and Hu, "Foundation of the Credit System," 493.

140. The table probably understates the actual proportion of loans. Item 2, *ziyou zijin*, may have a large component of loans—whether through the exploitation of loopholes in bank disclosure rules (as shown in the previous discussion) or through loans from other sources. Imported capital (item 3) refers to funds from domestic or foreign joint ventures. This form of capital is becoming increasingly important as townships rush to sign agreements with both state (and other domestic) enterprises and foreign firms to bring in additional capital and to meet performance

share of bank loans in working capital funds declined from about 50 percent to 44 percent during the same period. However, the figures reflect only those loans made by the Agriculture Bank and the Rural Credit Cooperatives; loans made by other banks, such as the Industrial and Commercial Bank, are not included. Nevertheless, much of the remainder of these funds derives from nonbank sources. These nonbank sources of capital include government bureaus, enterprises (via loans, accounts payable, etc.), and local residents (via internal bond issues to enterprise employees, etc.).

Among government bureaus, the largest provider of loans to rural collectives appears to be the public finance bureau, although no official data are available to confirm this. In addition to serving as loan guarantors for some enterprises, public finance bureaus at both the township and county levels also make loans at interest from their circulating funds (*zhouzhuanjin*) directly to enterprises.[141] Although the exact magnitude of these loans is unclear, in the townships investigated, they have rarely exceeded several million yuan. The ways in which these loans are allocated circumvent the discipline inherent in the loan criteria employed—at least in principle—by the Agriculture Bank. According to public finance officials interviewed, these loans are used primarily for loss-making or troubled enterprises that have been denied bank loans.[142] Not only do public finance office loan practices undermine the principle of allocating loans based on credit ratings, they also undermine the implementation of industrial policy priorities. One enterprise in Luhang Town (Shanghai), for example, was denied a loan to develop a metal processing workshop because of a bank regulation prohibiting new loans to processing

---

targets (*kaohezhibiao*). Item 4, grants from the bureau in charge—usually the township industrial corporation—are in many cases themselves bank loans taken out in the name of the industrial corporation. (Informant 46.) Funds collected from local residents (item 5) may take the form of loans with interest rates higher than those offered by banks in order to encourage residents to contribute to local industrial development. (Informant 126.) Finally, item 6, the "national support fund" (*guojia fuchi jijin*), is a kind of preferential tax policy. Enterprises exceeding their tax quotas receive a certain percentage of the above-quota tax payment as a refund, which becomes the "support fund." According to one public finance official, one rationale for this policy is to help viable enterprises that are nevertheless faced with chronic indebtedness to repay their loans. (Informant 135.) Overall, while the table shows declining reliance on bank loans for fixed-asset investment, the data probably hide a sizable proportion of both bank loans and other sources of capital.

141. Informants 53, 70, 112, 181. Public finance officials do not use the terms *loan* or *interest* in order to distinguish these concepts from those used in the banking domain. Rather, loans are called *credits* (*caizheng xinyong*) and interest charges are referred to as *use fees* (*caizheng zijin zhanyong fei*). Various public finance officials report that the rates charged are slightly lower than, roughly equal to, or slightly higher than the interest rates charged by banks. (Informants 112, 125, 181.) The circulating funds used for loans to TVEs apparently derive from the accumulation of annual surpluses of extrabudgetary income. (Informant 70.)

142. Informants 112, 181.

TABLE 9.   Sources of Fixed-Asset Investment and Working Capital for Township- and Village-Run Industrial Enterprises

	1987	1988	1989	1990	1991
	(billion current yuan)				
Fixed Asset Investment					
Total	24.32	n/a	25.15	23.05	37.55
Bank loans	11.77	n/a	9.41	7.96	15.20
Own funds (*ziyou zijin*)	5.30	n/a	5.89	5.66	11.13
Imported capital	1.65	n/a	3.06	4.74	3.74
Bureau grants	1.72	n/a	1.99	1.53	2.09
Residents' funds	1.14	n/a	1.20	0.66	1.27
National support fund	0.87	n/a	0.97	0.72	1.05
Other	1.87	n/a	2.64	1.79	3.07
	1987	1988	1989	1990	1991
	(percentage share)				
Total	100.0	n/a	100.0	100.0	100.0
Bank loans	48.4	n/a	37.4	34.5	40.5
Own funds (*ziyou zijin*)	21.8	n/a	23.4	24.5	29.6
Imported capital	6.8	n/a	12.1	20.6	9.9
Bureau grants	7.1	n/a	7.9	6.6	5.6
Residents' funds	4.7	n/a	4.8	2.9	3.4
National support fund	3.6	n/a	3.8	3.1	2.8
Other	7.7	n/a	10.5	7.7	8.2
	1987	1988	1989	1990	1991
	(billion current yuan)				
Working Capital					
Total	93.48		159.82	195.89	257.49
Bank loans	47.99	58.03	69.23	86.21	
Other	45.49		90.59	109.68	
	1987	1988	1989	1990	1991
	(percentage share)				
Total	100.0		100.0	100.0	
Bank loans	51.3		43.3	44.0	
Other	48.7		56.7	56.0	

Sources: Zhongguo xiangzhen giye nianjian 1978–87, 1989, 1990, 1991 (China's township and village enterprise yearbook 1978–87, 1989, 1990, 1991) (Beijing: State Statistical Bureau); *Zhongguo nongcun jingrong tongji nianjian 1991* (China's rural finance statistical yearbook 1991) (Beijing: State Statistical Bureau).

industries. It was granted a loan for the same project by the county public finance bureau.[143]

It appears that virtually any government bureau that has funds at its disposal uses them to make loans to enterprises either directly or through the public

---

143. Informant 49.

finance office. Indeed, in some places government bureaus are assigned to assist specific enterprises by the local government. The legal fees received by legal services offices and the trademark fees received by industrial and commercial bureaus, for example, have, at times, been used to provide loan funds to local collectives.[144] According to one tax official, it is also common practice for the tax bureau to allow rural collectives to be in arrears in paying their taxes. Enterprises then use these funds to supplement their working capital.[145]

When enterprises need funds, the local government often "builds bridges" to other enterprises for short-term loans.[146] One enterprise in Nantang Township (Shanghai), for example, had 8.4 million yuan in bank loans outstanding as of 1991, while profits had fallen from a high of 2.3 million yuan in 1989 to 100 thousand yuan in 1991. As a result, the enterprise borrowed 500 thousand yuan from other rural enterprises in 1991 in order to keep up with loan payments.[147] At least within a given locality, interenterprise loans are often made not on the basis of profitability, but rather on the basis of directives from the township government.

An even more prevalent form of interenterprise debt—one that crosses territorial boundaries and ownership categories—is the growing problem of mounting accounts payable and accounts receivable. The seriousness of this problem is reflected in the fact that the economic rectification campaign of late 1988–1991 was followed—not surprisingly—by a campaign to eliminate so-called triangular debts (*sanjiaozhai*), that is, unpaid accounts among enterprises. According to the survey of 200 large-scale rural industrial enterprises cited above, as of 1985, accounts payable was second only to bank loans in its share of total enterprise liabilities. In 1985, bank loans (including both working capital and fixed-asset loans) accounted for 43 percent of total liabilities, while accounts payable made up 32 percent.[148] The same study shows that the share of accounts payable in total liabilities was growing rapidly during the mid-1980s, increasing ten percentage points between December 1984 and June 1986. As one factory manager on the receiving end of this problem put

144. Informant 112.

145. Informant 194. Enterprises in difficulty can also receive tax breaks at the discretion of local government officials, even when conditions do not accord with centrally defined tax policies. This phenomenon is discussed in detail in Whiting, "Comfort of the Collective." See also the treatment in World Bank, *China: Revenue Mobilization and Tax Policy.* Kornai identifies the consequences of such practices in terms of softening enterprise budget constraints in J. Kornai, "Resource-Constrained versus Demand-Constrained Systems," *Econometrica* 47, no. 4 (July 1979): 801–19. This kind of tax practice does not reduce the enterprise's overall burden if the same funds are tapped through alternative local government levies. Tax evasion is addressed from the perspective of the township government in the following discussion of the township government's hard budget constraint.

146. Informants 46, 83, 125, 198.

147. Informant 125.

148. Zhou and Hu, "Macro Effects," 300.

it, "Contracts here don't mean anything. Other units owe us a lot of money."[149] Moreover, enterprises have little recourse when clients fail to pay. Localism is so pervasive that when one county or township government sends court, police, or enterprise representatives to another locality to collect payment, the resident court and police personnel are often unwilling to act against the interests of the offending local enterprise.[150] Although enterprises are likely to be constrained by poor reputations in the long run, mounting accounts payable have become a short-term means of softening the budget constraint for a growing number of enterprises.

Like other capital sources, contributions from local residents also take many forms, from prerequisites for employment to informal contributions at interest to bond issues to enterprise employees and more formal public bond issues. Interest-bearing loans from residents often pay higher interest rates than banks, thereby adding to the burdensome interest payments owed by debt-laden rural collectives. One enterprise in Nantang Town (Shanghai) borrowed 125 thousand yuan from workers for use as working capital funds at nearly twice the interest rate charged by the credit cooperative.[151] In addition, the township as a whole collected approximately 4 million yuan from local workers and farmers at twice the interest rate offered on savings accounts by the bank. In the latter instance, government cadres were assigned quotas governing the amounts each was to collect from various target groups in the township. It is not clear how or when interest payments were to be made or whether local residents could withdraw their funds. Thus, it appears that this source of capital imposes little discipline on managerial behavior.

A more formal means of soliciting funds from local residents is through the issue of enterprise bonds. In Dongtan Town (Wuxi), nine enterprises had issued bonds as of mid-1992, six publicly and three internally. According to a township government official, one-, two-, and three-year bonds were available with annual interest rates ranging from 9.1 to 10 percent.[152] These bond issues, approved by the county branch of the People's Bank of China, most likely impose greater discipline on the enterprise than the less formal and perhaps more compulsory approaches to collecting funds from the local population.

The Hard Budget Constraint at the Township Level

Up to this point, this section has focused primarily on the enterprise as the unit of analysis—an approach driven, in part, by the nature of the data on credit and credit policy. The data suggest that easy credit in a variety of forms

---

149. Informant 123.
150. Zhang Weiguo (formerly of the *Shanghai World Economic Herald*), lecture, University of Michigan, Center for Chinese Studies, Ann Arbor, April 13, 1993.
151. Informants 126, 134.
152. Informant 198.

TABLE 10.   Losses of Township- and Village-Run Enterprises, National-Level Data

Year	Total Number of Firms (mil)	Number Loss- Making Firms (mil)	Total Amount of Losses (bil Y)	Increase in Loss- Making Firms (%)	Increase in Amt. of Losses (%)	Share Loss- Making Firms (%)	Losses as Share of Net Profits (%)
1985	1.850	0.065	0.849			3.5	5.0
1986	1.728	0.076	1.449	16.2	70.7	4.4	9.0
1987	1.583	0.074	1.834	−2.3	26.6	4.7	9.7
1988	1.590	0.063	1.850	−14.8	0.9	4.0	7.1
1989	1.536	0.079	3.790	25.6	104.9	5.1	15.8
1990	1.454	0.086	4.740	8.9	25.1	5.9	20.4
1991	1.442	0.067	4.270	−22.1	−9.9	4.6	15.0

Sources: Same as table 1.

contributes to a soft budget constraint for rural collectives. However, even if enterprises have softened budget constraints, the township as a whole ostensibly has a hard budget constraint, because township governments cannot in principle run budget deficits. What do the available data suggest about constraints on the economic behavior of the township as a whole?

As noted previously, townships engage in cross subsidization of enterprise losses through the practice of *tongshou huandai,* but what is the extent of losses, and how persistent are they? The national statistics presented in tables 10 through 12 show that between 1985 and 1991, the number of loss-making township- and village-run enterprises has consistently hovered between 3.5 and 6 percent of the total but that the amount of the losses has increased over 5 times—from 850 million yuan in 1985 to nearly 4.3 billion yuan in 1991. The rate of increase in the amount of losses appears to coincide with campaign cycles in the economy, with the highest increases in losses occurring following the onset of contractionary policies in 1985 and late 1988.[153]

The data available for several research sites appear to coincide with national trends. A 1992 midyear report on one Wuxi county states that as of April 1992, losses to industrial TVEs were up 10.1 percent over the same period during the previous year, reaching 39.35 million yuan.[154] As table 11 shows, in 1990, losses to TVEs in the Shanghai county where Songyang Town is located increased 20 percent to reach 15.2 million yuan, while the number of loss-making firms increased 13.6 percent over the 1989 figure. In 1991 the number of loss makers decreased 10.7 percent to 209 enterprises—

153. For a discussion of the cyclical nature of macroeconomic policy, see Naughton, "Macroeconomic Management."

154. Informant 192.

TABLE 11. Losses of Township- and Village-Run Enterprises, County-Level Data, Site of Songyang Town, Shanghai

Year	Total Number of Firms	Number Loss-Making Firms	Total Amount of Losses (mil Y)	Increase in Loss-Making Firms (%)	Increase in Amt. of Losses (%)	Share Loss-Making Firms (%)	Losses as Share of Net Profits (%)
1989	2251	206	12.65			9.2	15.9
1990	2278	234	15.18	13.6	20.0	10.3	17.5
1991	2332	209	12.98	−10.7	−14.5	9.0	10.9

Source: Interview data.

still above the 1989 number of 206. Similarly, the amount of losses in 1991 decreased 14.5 percent to 13 million yuan—again higher than the 1989 amount of 12.7 million. Losses represented 15.9 percent of net profits in 1989, 17.5 percent in 1990, and 10.9 percent in 1991. Statistics on Songyang Town (Shanghai), shown in table 12, reflect better performance than do the county- and national-level aggregate figures. In 1991 as in 1989, there were eight loss-making enterprises, but the amount of losses in 1991 fell dramatically, to below the 1989 level. Overall, townships appear to sustain a relatively stable number of loss-making enterprises, while the amount of losses has tended to increase over time.

The extent of losses suggests that although townships cannot in principle run deficits, there may be elements of the financial situation that townships can use to soften the budget constraint. Here, the focus is on the ability of the township government to soften the budget constraint by evading taxes. Under the revenue-sharing tax system, most townships must meet a minimum target for tax collection set by the county; beyond that, townships receive a certain percentage of the above-target amount. To varying extents, townships seek to

TABLE 12. Losses of Township- and Village-Run Enterprises, Township-Level Data, Songyang Town, Shanghai

Year	Total Number of Firms	Number Loss-Making Firms	Total Amount of Losses (mil Y)	Increase in Loss-Making Firms (%)	Increase in Amt. of Losses (%)	Share Loss-Making Firms (%)	Losses as Share of Net Profits (%)
1989	199	8	0.48			4.0	5.3
1990	207	11	0.59	37.5	22.9	5.3	6.2
1991	218	8	0.29	−27.3	−50.8	3.7	3.1

Source: Interview data.

limit the amount by which they exceed their targets.[155] In many cases, townships collude with collective enterprises to grant fraudulent or loosely interpreted tax breaks;[156] the township government can then tap these funds through remitted profits and other levies or leave them in enterprises for use there. This enables townships to retain 100 percent of the funds that did not enter into tax channels, rather than retaining only a portion of these funds through the above-target sharing of taxes.[157] Indeed, in Dongtan Town (Wuxi) a tax official commented that "the tax law became irrelevant after the implementation of the revenue-sharing tax system (*caizheng baogan yihou, bu yao shuifa*)."[158] A government official in the same town reported that the entire county paid only 20 million yuan in income tax, although it is one of the wealthiest counties in the entire country. He said, referring to the 20 million, "That is very little, and it's getting smaller and smaller. It's ridiculous! (*Bu xianghua le!*)."[159] Without complete information about the extent of legitimate tax exemptions and reductions, it is impossible to interpret definitively, but it is interesting to note that for TVEs nationwide, income tax payments increased only 1.4 percent between 1988 and 1991, while gross profits increased 6 percent per year on average over the same period. (See Table 5.) It is unlikely that tax breaks on such a scale are all valid from the perspective of the central government.[160] The township government's position as both de

---

155. Informants 83, 177, 196.

156. The fraudulent practices under discussion here are distinct from official preferential policies, which, for example, allow certain enterprises to repay bank loans from a certain portion of *pretax* profits.

157. Even townships that, according to the revenue-sharing contract, would retain 100 percent of above-target revenues engage in this practice in order to avoid the ratcheting up of base target levels in future contracts with the county.

158. Informant 194.

159. Informant 196. This discussion draws on Whiting, "Comfort of the Collective."

160. For central government efforts to combat this problem see: "Guojia shuiwuju guanyu yange jianshui mianshui guanli de guiding (State administration of taxation regulations regarding strict management of tax reductions and exemptions, August 18, 1988)," in *Zhili zhengdun shenhua gaige zhengce fagui xuanbian (Selected policies and laws on rectification and deepening of reform)* (Beijing: Zhongguo caizheng jingji chubanshe, 1990), 155–56; "Guowuyuan bangongting zhuanfa guojia shuiwuju guanyu qingli zhengdun he yange kongzhi jianshui mianshui jijian de tongzhi (State Council Office notice of transmission of State Administration of Taxation opinion regarding rectification and control of tax reductions and exemptions, November 30, 1988)," *Guowuyuan Gongbao (State Council Bulletin)* no. 1 (February 1989): 23–25; "Guojia shuiwuju guanyu qingli zhengdun he yange kongzhi jianshui mianshui de juti shishi yijian (State Administration of Taxation opinion regarding specific measures to rectify and strictly control tax reductions and exemptions, March 9, 1989)," in *Selected Policies and Laws on Rectification,* 168–72; "Guowuyuan pizhuan guojia shuiwuju guanyu jinyibu tuijin yifa zhishui jiaqiang shuishou guanli baogao de tongzhi (State Council notice of approval and transmission of State Administration of Taxation report regarding further advancing administration of taxes according to law [and] strengthening tax management, October 11, 1991)," *Guowuyuan Gongbao (State Council Bulletin)* no. 43 (January 1992): 1496–1501.

facto enterprise owner and tax collector creates the incentive and the means for it to siphon off central tax revenues for its own use, thereby softening its budget constraint to some extent.[161]

Product Market Discipline

Vigorous competition in product markets appears to function as a very important source of discipline for TVEs and suggests that, for these product markets, reform has wrought major changes in the excess demand characteristic of prereform centrally planned economies. Moreover, of the various types of market discipline examined here, product market discipline appears to be the least subject to manipulation by township cadres.

TVE managers report the need continually to expand the market area for their products in the face of extreme competition. A majority of the TVE managers questioned for the World Bank study on rural industry characterized competition as either "relatively," "very," or "extremely fierce," and, as a result of this kind of competition, markets for many TVE products exhibit falling prices.[162] The 1986 survey of 200 large-scale rural industrial enterprises reveals that over 35 percent of the products produced by these firms were sold in other provinces.[163] Similarly, the World Bank reports that the majority of the firms it investigated "sell at least 40 percent of their output outside the home province."[164] The increasing sales radius has been accompanied by a growing number of enterprise employees involved in sales, and intensified price competition has been accompanied by various forms of nonprice competition, ranging from increasingly lavish entertainment of potential buyers to kickbacks.[165]

There have been some reports of protectionism by local governments. According to Christine Wong, in the early 1980s "protectionist tactics ranged from excluding outside products from local markets to threatening local enterprises with cutoffs of funds and bank loans, supplies of fuel, etc. should they dare to buy the products of competitors."[166] This form of protectionism may have declined over time. Nevertheless, in the 1990s township cadres in

---

161. Christine Wong discusses the perpetuation of soft budget constraints at both the enterprise and local government levels. See Wong, "Role of the Local Sector," 106.

162. Byrd and Zhu, "Market Interactions and Industrial Structure," 90–92. See also Du, *Research on Rural Industrialization,* 90.

163. Du Yan, "Xiangzhen gongye qiye jingying de shichang huanjing (The market environment in which rural industrial enterprises operate)," *Development Research* no. 49 (February 28, 1987): 272–73.

164. Byrd and Zhu, "Market Interactions and Industrial Structure," 91. See also Du, *Research on Rural Industrialization,* 90.

165. Du, "The Market Environment," 272–73.

166. Wong, "Role of the Local Sector," 104.

Shanghai and Wuxi, where collective ownership predominates, still seek to protect their collective enterprises by prohibiting the establishment of private firms—at least in sectors in which collective ones already exist.[167]

Despite these efforts, in general, managers report decreasing turnover rates on product inventories. According to the 200-enterprise survey cited above, inventory turnover rates decreased from 7.78 in 1984 to 6.9 in 1985 to 1.97 in the first half of 1986.[168] This situation has forced managers to sell products at lower prices, and many still report a growing number of unsalable goods. Over 53 percent of the 200 enterprises surveyed reported difficulty in marketing their products. In response to questions about why they had difficulty selling their products, 41 percent of the managers reported "too much production of similar products," while 48 percent reported having competitors in the same locale.[169] Respondents described their competitors as large in number but relatively small in scale.

The World Bank study sheds some light on this problem by identifying the patterns of competition characteristic of TVEs—most notably, imitative competition. "A resourceful entrepreneur finds out about a new product or process that has been successful elsewhere and earns high profits at first. But since entry is easy, a host of imitators soon spring up, and prices and profits decline sharply."[170] According to the study, sixteen aluminum extrusion and processing plants were established in Wuxi in the mid-1980s. However, because of intense competition, the majority of these firms were forced to operate well below capacity.[171] "According to [Wuxi] county government reports, the principal problems confronting [TVEs] were caused by intensified market competition and the increased rate of failure of capital investments. Some enterprises with capital investments of more than Y1 million began suffering from overstocks of products just one year after going into production."[172] Indeed, township cadres in Nantang Township (Shanghai) related a similar experience with an unsuccessful investment. Having received a tip that latex rubber gloves were extremely profitable in light of the AIDS epidemic, the township acted quickly to invest to develop its productive capacity. However, the township discovered that it could not sell the products; the firm ceased production without recouping the investment and was unable to apply

167. Whiting, "Comfort of the Collective," 25–26.
168. Du, "Market Environment," 273. These declines may be related in part to larger macroeconomic cycles in the economy.
169. Ibid.
170. Byrd and Zhu, "Market Interactions and Industrial Structure," 92.
171. Wang, "Capital Formation and Utilization," 241.
172. Luo Xiaopeng, "Ownership and Status Stratification," in William A. Byrd and Lin Qingsong, eds., *China's Rural Industry: Structure, Development, and Reform* (Oxford: Oxford University Press, published for the World Bank, 1990), 134–71, esp. 158.

the equipment to alternative uses.[173] The official policy of rural industrialization, referred to as "leaving the farm but not the countryside" (*litu bulixiang*), exacerbates the problem by encouraging "small production scales and dispersed location patterns."[174]

Exposure to this market environment is mitigated for some TVEs by direct or indirect inclusion in the state plan. Particularly in the rural areas surrounding the major industrial center of Shanghai, many TVEs have long-term contracts with state enterprises that guarantee purchase of 100 percent of the TVEs' output. Most of these contracts are secured through domestic joint ventures between state enterprises and TVEs. According to the Shanghai Municipal Agriculture Committee, as of 1991, 45 percent of TVE output in Shanghai was produced in state-TVE joint ventures; 20 percent of this output was governed by binding state plans, with another 50 percent governed by guidance planning.[175] Until recently, some older TVEs were included in state plans even without having established joint ventures with state enterprises. For example, until 1989, the output of one Shanghai TVE was guaranteed purchase by the state-run Shanghai Electrical Equipment Company, but in that year plans for the firm's products were abolished, leaving the firm responsible for its own sales.[176] According to the 200-enterprise survey cited earlier, over 23 percent of the goods produced by these firms in 1985 were purchased by foreign trade or material bureaus or were guaranteed purchase (*baoxiao*) by state-run industrial or commercial enterprises.[177] However, as demonstrated by the previous example, the number of products governed by the state plan has decreased; thus, a growing number of TVE products face the discipline of the marketplace. Still, inclusion in binding plans is desirable because, although profits may be lower, the market is more stable. For this reason, the World Bank reports that some local authorities seek to ensure the stability of sales "by *increasing* the proportion of product orders covered by state planning . . . ."[178]

TVE products face perhaps even greater competition on world markets where, managers report, prices are often lower than domestic prices. Although some managers reject participation in the world market, others continue to export for a number of reasons. First, export performance is linked to managerial bonuses in some managers' contracts. Second, some managers

---

173. Informant 131. See also "Shijiao sifenzhisan rujiao shoutao shengchangxian tingchan (Three quarters of the production lines for latex rubber gloves in suburban Shanghai cease production)," *Shanghai gongye jingji bao (Shanghai Industrial Economy)*, June 15, 1989, 1.

174. Wang, "Capital Formation and Utilization," 239.

175. Informant 39.

176. Informant 44.

177. Du, "Market Environment," 273.

178. Luo, "Ownership and Status Stratification," 159, emphasis added.

report that demand for their products is more stable on the world market in light of repeated economic rectification campaigns at home. Third, by exporting, managers can gain access to foreign exchange with which they can import more advanced equipment. Participation on the world market, no matter the motivation, may impose another element of discipline on the behavior of TVE managers. (However, without more complete data, it is impossible to determine the extent to which foreign trade corporations subsidize TVE exports, if at all.)

Overall, TVEs face extreme competition both at home and abroad; thus, product markets likely provide the most powerful source of discipline over the behavior of township leaders and enterprise managers.

Conclusion

This chapter has examined the ways in which contract incentives and market discipline constrain the behavior of township officials and enterprise managers. The discussion of internal contracts demonstrates that contract incentives are effective but that the content of contracts differs in orientation from what one would expect to find in a profit-maximizing corporation. Rather, performance indicators—both those designed by county officials to evaluate township leaders and those designed by township leaders to evaluate managers—are more consonant with the political roles of local officials than with their entrepreneurial roles.

Similarly, with respect to labor market forces, the discipline imposed by the market is limited by the politically motivated desire for full employment and the administrative restrictions on labor mobility; thus, local township residents employed by TVEs are subject to very weak labor market discipline. Managers of TVEs face limited competition in the labor market and are more likely to be transferred than to be fired for poor performance. Nonetheless, the position a manager holds within the township is a direct reflection of his or her ability to achieve township goals. Likewise, township officials rise or fall based on their ability to promote rapid economic growth and community welfare.

Discipline in the capital market is improving; most loans flow to highly rated enterprises. However, township officials are still capable of intervening to pursue their immediate goals of increasing local incomes, maintaining employment, and increasing government revenues at the expense of responsible credit policy; as a result, banks continue to support weak firms with loans. Other problems undermining capital market discipline include the lack of adequate market information and the absence of a complete legal/regulatory framework with full disclosure requirements and contract enforcement.

Some economists have argued that the high degree to which TVEs are leveraged is not problematic in light of the similar characteristics of successful firms in other East Asian countries—notably Japan and South Korea.[179] However, the Chinese case differs in certain key respects. TVEs are not "national champions"—that is, elite firms cultivated by the national state to compete successfully in world markets—but rather "township champions." Because township officials are overwhelmingly oriented toward the development and welfare of their own townships, they pursue policies that, viewed from a national perspective, unnecessarily duplicate productive capacity and waste scarce capital resources. Because of the power of local officials stemming from their multiple roles as de facto enterprise owners, tax collectors, and bank overseers, TVEs are only weakly regulated by central fiscal and monetary policies. Neither the market nor the state consistently disciplines the use of capital.

Product markets, which are characterized in general by vigorous competition, impose the strongest discipline on TVEs. Although some TVE products still fall under the state plan, the scope of the plan is already extremely narrow and the ability of township governments to protect product markets is quite limited. However, discipline in product markets must be accompanied by discipline in capital and labor markets in order to alter fundamentally the behavior of township officials and TVE managers. In the absence of effective capital market discipline, for example, the potential constraining influence of the product market on enterprise behavior is dissipated; some inefficient managers continue to gain access to loan capital despite failure to perform well in the highly competitive product market.

The Chinese economy is in a period of transition during which some elements of softness remain in the constraints facing enterprises, but, as this chapter demonstrates, efficiency concerns are already increasingly making themselves felt by township officials and enterprise managers alike. Profit and sales targets are beginning to receive more prominence in the contracts of both local officials and managers. In terms of the labor market, the growing number of TVE employees who are hired from outside the local community face relatively strict discipline, suggesting that labor market discipline is becoming more effective on the margin. Banks are becoming more concerned with their own profitability and better able to resist the demands of township officials, while bank officials in some areas are already pushing for better disclosure rules and stronger enforcement of loan contracts. These and other elements of the Chinese system under reform will elicit increasingly efficient performance in the dynamic rural industrial sector. In particular, since the Fourteenth Party Congress held in November 1993, the central leadership has made the over-

---

179. Barry Naughton, personal communication.

haul of the fiscal and banking systems the centerpiece of current reform efforts. Progress in these two key areas will contribute to hardening the budget constraint faced by township leaders and TVE managers. Nevertheless, wholly effective market discipline will continue to be thwarted as long as township officials have the power and the incentives to bend markets to parochial political ends.

CHAPTER 5

Institutions, Social Ties, and Commitment in China's Corporatist Transformation

Victor Nee and Sijin Su

This chapter analyzes the institutional framework that accounts for improved economic performance in China. The foundations of a market economy are only partially instituted, while China's industrial economy remains in an uncharted zone between state and market coordination of the economy. Yet parts of China, especially the coastal provinces, have reported the fastest growing market-driven economies in the world. Why has China's partial reform resulted in rapid and sustained gains in economic performance? When the Chinese state permitted profit sharing with local governments and firms, it initiated a period of institutional innovation. The crucial factors leading to improvements in economic performance were reforms that brought about fiscal decentralization; local governments playing a new partnership relationship with profit-oriented firms; and a progressive informal privatization. These institutional innovations have proven remarkably effective in promoting economic growth.

We draw on arguments from new institutionalist theory in economics and sociology to explain economic growth in China. New institutionalist economics has concentrated on the importance of political and economic institutions in shaping economic performance (Eggertsson 1990). North (1981) focused on the role of the state in specifying and enforcing rules governing rights to property and of economic institutions, principally the firm and the market.[1] To explain economic growth, North asks whether rules governing

The research for this chapter was funded by a grant from the National Science Foundation #SES-9309651, the College of Arts & Sciences at Cornell, and the LT Lam South China fund. We wish to thank Bonnie Chen and Robert Merton.

1. North and Weingast (1989), for example, examine the evolution of English political institutions after the Glorious Revolution of 1688 and argue that limitations on the confiscatory power of government resulted in more secure property rights and changes in political institutions strengthening Parliament and the courts, and made credible the government's commitment to honoring its agreements. They contend that these changes in political institutions help explain

property rights provide incentives for productive activity and examines the extent to which political actors make a credible commitment to upholding these rules. Because the state plays a key role in monitoring and enforcing property rights, political actors as well as economic actors require appropriate incentives. Otherwise, if political actors lack the incentives to abide by the rules, they will not be self-enforcing, especially in the case of rules limiting the ruler's ability to expropriate economic surplus. In North and Weingast's (1989) view, the more rulers alter property rights for their own benefit, the less the incentive for producers to engage in productive activity and for firms to invest. Institutional change that limits the state's ability to extract surplus and increases the security of private property is therefore critical to establishing conditions favorable to sustained economic growth. Such change fundamentally entails providing incentives to political actors to make credible a government's commitment to upholding its agreements.

In explaining China's relative success in market reform, Weingast (1993) argued that political reforms implemented in the early years of reform gave rise to a market-preserving federalism in which local governments provide a counterbalance to the power of the central state, limiting its ability to expropriate economic surplus. The market-preserving federalist argument assumes the existence of a market economy in which labor and capital are fully mobile. As long as capital and labor are mobile, their exit power constrains the rent-seeking behavior of local government. However, applied to China, this assumption does not hold, especially in the earlier years of reform when the socialist state controlled the movement of both labor and capital. The federalist framework is unable to specify the institutional constraints that limit the predatory power of local government in the nonmarket institutional environment that characterized the early stages of reform. State-centered arguments focusing on the entrepreneurial role of local state officials also do not address the dilemma posed by unconstrained local state power (Oi 1992; Walder 1995). If the local state is unrestrained in its capacity to intervene and appropriate economic surplus, then what accounts for the improvement in the incentives at the level of the firm that give rise to rapid gains in productivity? To be sure, fiscal decentralization improved incentives for local state officials, but an adequate explanation of gains in productivity must specify the institutional changes that lead to improving incentives for economic actors and account for political actors making credible commitments to agreements that provide more favorable terms of exchange than under unreformed state socialism.

---

how it was that economic development continued in England and faltered in France. Their analysis assumes that the key explanatory variables are the "political factors underpinning economic growth and the development of markets—not simply the rules governing economic exchange, but also the institutions governing how these rules are enforced and how they may be changed" (803).

The state-centered approach emphasizes the importance of formal institutions in promoting credible commitment; yet formal rules are seldom effective without the backing of informal institutional constraints (North 1990). Economic sociologists have demonstrated in a wide array of institutional contexts the manner in which networks of personal relations structure economic exchange by fostering trust and serving as a conduit of reliable information (Granovetter 1985; Powell and Smith-Doerr 1994). Thus far, however, studies of how institutions and social structure shape economic action have fallen into parallel, but separate, literatures in economics and sociology.

Recent work in economic sociology has sought to integrate new institutional economics with its focus on choice within institutional constraints and the embeddedness perspective of economic sociology (Nee and Ingram, forthcoming). Our analysis extends this framework to argue that the sources of long-term economic performance are more fully explained by reference to the role of social institutions in combination with political and economic institutions. First, transaction costs are lower in institutional settings where trust and cooperation flow from informal norms and established social relationships. Second, institutional arrangements that promote repeated social exchanges foster credible commitment. Lastly, political institutions that promote growth are backed by social institutions that limit free riding.

Our analysis focuses on institutional innovations—profit sharing and informal privatization—in the rise of local corporatism. By local corporatism, we refer to a loosely coupled coalition between local government, financial institutions, and firms (collective and state-owned) aimed at promoting market-oriented growth.[2] Local corporatism involves political and economic actors in an interorganizational field in which long-standing social ties based on frequent face-to-face interactions foster local solidarity, often against the encroachment of the central state. It is loosely coupled because although local corporatism is based on mutual dependency between the government and firm, firms seek to retain a greater share of profits while local governments strive to maximize revenues, giving rise to a conflict of interest. Corporatist arrangements involve both market and nonmarket allocation of labor, capital, and land (Lin 1995). They often involve different levels of government, across regions, in profit-oriented joint ventures and are based on formal own-

---

2. Our definition differs from Oi's 1992 conception of "corporatism." Oi conceives of the relationship between local government and firm as *intra*organizational. While we conceive of corporatism as encompassing an *inter*-organizational field made up of government, financial institutions, and firms. Our definition takes into account a partitioning of rights between local government, financial institutions, and firms. It allows a greater scope for politics, defined as gaming over the control of resources, in the analysis of the relationship between local government and industry. It also emphasizes the importance of social institutions and network ties as the cement that binds corporatist arrangements. In these respects it is similar to Lin's (1995) conception of "local market socialism."

ership of industrial enterprises by local government. The rise of local corporatism has been accompanied by a gradual, though partial, privatization of collective and, to a lesser extent, state-owned enterprises. Most of this privatization has been informal. Informal privatization refers to a social transfer of rights over public property to private individuals that is not constitutionally recognized and therefore not backed by legal ownership.

The Chinese state has opposed large-scale formal privatization, but the growth of new markets and the increasing value of marketized state and collective firms and land have nevertheless heightened interest in privatizing public property in China. As Demsetz (1967) has argued, property rights develop to internalize externalities when the gains from exclusive rights become larger than the cost of acquiring them. Blocked from embarking on formal privatization of collective and state-owned enterprises, economic actors have instead pursued informal strategies of privatization. Their activities have given rise to a new partitioning of property rights in the Chinese industrial economy.

Informal privatization is based mainly on social recognition of rights to the use of resources. It relies on the existence of established, ongoing social relationships. Informal property rights are, in essence, norms (or rules) governing the use of resources. As such, the monitoring and enforcement of informal property claims are endogenous to social exchange. Informal rights are embedded in a broader framework of norms and customary practices. They are claims on the use of resources contingent on compliance with ancillary norms of the group. As in a family, these rights are defined through mutual agreement and understanding, monitored by members of the group, and enforced through social sanctions. Violations of informal property rights provoke spontaneous sanctions, ranging from social disapproval to ostracism and conflict. Informal rights are often implicit in the mutual understanding of parties to a transaction or members of a social group. Only when challenged are explicit statements of rights declared. The more stable the social network in which informal rights are embedded, the less likely that rights will be contested and the more secure the right. For these reasons, strategies of informal privatization increase the incentive to invest in the stability of social ties buttressing economic exchange.

Lacking legal backing, claims to exclusive rights remain vulnerable to contestation. When contested, informal rights involve higher transaction costs than formal rights to exclusive use. Informal rights are characteristically ambiguous and therefore difficult to partition in the case of multiple and competing claims. Rights over assets cannot be readily transferred, whether through inheritance or negotiated market transactions. However, as with squatter's rights, claims over the use of public property established informally tend to harden with time, as usage becomes customary and backed by social norms. Thus, conversion of public property to private use begins informally through social practice but, importantly, informal rights may lay the basis for claims to formal ownership rights in the future. An example of informal privatization is seen in the transfer of communal land to peasant households through responsibility contracts during the decollectivization of agriculture. Over time peasants come to view land assigned to their household as private property. Although the ownership of land remains formally public, it is doubtful that, despite efforts by the state to retain public property rights over land, such efforts can weaken informal property claims over agricultural land (Christiansen 1987). Yet private markets in land are illegal, and transfer of land-use rights involves a substantially lower price structure than if formal ownership rights were being traded.

The dependence of informal property claims on mutual local understandings and agreements, and their vulnerability to contestation result in a dilution of rights to exclusive use by an individual claimant. As with rights among family members, there is a tendency toward communal sharing of rights. This is reflected in China by the rapid increase in bonus payments and nonwage benefits to workers in marketized firms, and in the cases of formal privatization, in the distribution to employees of rights to acquire equity shares in the firm. However, compared to the prereform structure of incentives, which provided incentives to free ride, informal privatization paves the way for a redefinition of interests and rules favoring productivity gains and reductions in transaction costs.

In the following pages, we first review briefly the institutional environment of partial reform after 1978, with special emphasis on the fiscal reform that resulted in the institutional innovations of profit sharing and local corporatism. We then focus on the characteristic features of local corporatism by describing the new roles of local government as investor, allocator of factor resources, and economic coordinator. We describe the institutional framework that promotes cooperation between firms and local government and sustains the ongoing personal ties that provide the social cement of local corporatism. Next, we provide case studies documenting informal privatization in state-owned firms, joint ventures, and nonstate collective firms. Our data are based on field research conducted separately by us from September 1990 to January 1991 and in July 1992.[3] The field research sites were in the southeast coastal city of Xiamen, one of the earliest Special Economic Zones, and the suburban townships of Wuxi in the Jiangnan region. During the reform period, Xiamen

---

3. Su's field research includes 57 interviews with managers of Chinese firms in Hong Kong and Xiamen, a survey of 60 firms in Xiamen City, and a sample of contracts used by firms. Nee's field research involves interviews with 20 factory managers and local officials in Wuxi, Shaoxing, and Xiamen in July 1992.

has attracted many foreign investors and experienced a rapid increase in the population of joint ventures, and Wuxi, closely associated with the Sunan model, has experienced the fastest rate of growth in township industries.

The Institutional Foundation of Local Corporatism

The centerpiece of industrial reform in China after 1978 was the implementation of the responsibility contract system. The aim of this reform measure was to reduce the central government's fiscal burden, render local government and firms fiscally independent, and provide them with incentives to pursue market-oriented growth (Oi 1992). The reform resulted in the shift of fiscal redistributive power from the central government to local governments. Under the new decentralized fiscal system, local governments and firms were required to assume responsibility for their profits and losses, while the central government gradually reduced its level of fiscal responsibility in the provinces.[4]

In the new system, the firm shares its profits with local government according to a formula fixed ex ante. Profits made over and above the stipulated amount are retained by the firm.[5] The new industrial responsibility system is formally backed by legally binding contracts signed by the firm and local government or, in the case of state-owned enterprises, negotiated between local government and the central state. An unintended outcome of fiscal reform was the redefinition of property rights as regards the central government, the local government, and the firm. Through fiscal reform, the central

---

4. Following the implementation of fiscal decentralization and profit sharing, an increasing proportion of economic activity, including that of many state-owned firms, fell outside of the central plan and became increasingly dependent on market institutions. For example, the key raw material sector of the industrial economy has gradually shifted to market allocation. Currently, only 72 categories of raw materials are still allocated by central planning, dramatically declining from 837 in the early 1980s. In 1992, 86.2 percent of materials purchased by economic enterprises were obtained from market channels. This percentage is higher in the southeastern coastal provinces, where 90 percent of input materials are procured through market transactions. Nationwide, there now are over 60,000 retail and wholesale centers that specialize in buying and selling raw materials and serve as a national marketing network (Renmin Ribao, December 21, 1992, 1). According to the Yearbook on Economic Reform (1991), rural industries now mostly rely on markets to procure supplies and to distribute their products. The growth of markets has been rapid and is accelerating in velocity. Although local firms still rely on local governments to help them gain access to needed resources still allocated by central planning, such dependence on non-market channels is rapidly declining as specialized factor markets replace the plan. In addition, firms increasingly acquire new technologies and investment capital from market sources, both domestic and foreign.

5. Profit sharing encourages managers to redistribute surplus in the firm among employees and report only modest profits. Reports of larger than expected profits might result in efforts by local government to renegotiate the terms of the contract.

state transferred rights to economic surplus to local governments. Profit sharing arrangements between local governments and firms, in turn, endowed firms with greater fiscal autonomy and rights over the distribution of economic surplus. Table 1 documents the rapid increase in retained profits in state-owned industrial firms within the state budget.

Profit sharing is, in our view, the key institutional change that opened the way for informal privatization. By agreeing to a fixed share of the profit specified in a binding contract, local government, in effect, tacitly limits its property claim over the firm. Profit sharing establishes the basis for a partitioning of rights, thereby lowering the transaction costs between government and firm. Rather than government being compelled to directly monitor firms and their employees, profit sharing establishes the economic basis for increased firm-level autonomy. It specifies the terms for a new distribution of economic surplus favoring direct producers and managers by limiting the power of government to expropriate surplus generated by the firm. It encourages management to improve incentives for achieving productivity gains in the firm. Informal privatization should be viewed as a by-product of profit sharing, in part via the manager responsibility contract. As long as the firm provides a reliable revenue stream to local government, the manager can expect to retain his or her post and any informal rights over the use of the firm's resources established through mutual understanding. The sentiment of even a partial claim to rights of use increases the incentive to allocate resources more efficiently. However, informal privatization is an arrangement that also enables local government to retain formal property rights over the firm. If a manager or entrepreneur fails to meet the performance standards of local government, his or her informal rights can be withdrawn.

Thus, the institutional innovations of profit sharing and informal privatization structure incentives in a manner that favors the growth of productive activities, while they fiscally constrain the past emphasis on socialist redistribution. Managers and entrepreneurs have greater incentives to perform when they have a claim, albeit informal, to partial ownership of the firm. Like squatters, they sense that their informal rights might result in a privileged claim for formal ownership rights in any future government-sponsored program of privatization. Because local governments depend on industry's profitability as their primary means to increase their revenue, they have a strong incentive for achieving gains in relative economic performance in an increasingly competitive market environment. As profit rates decline under competitive pressure (Naughton 1992), local governments are compelled to extract less from industry in order to optimize industry's competitiveness and chances for survival. Hence, under conditions of competitive markets, local governments face hard constraints on the extent to which they can expropriate surplus from local industry.

TABLE 1. Retained Profits of State-Owned Industrial Firms (within state budget), 1978–88, in Hundred Million Yuan

Profits	1978	1979	1980	1981	1982	1983	1984	1985	1986	1987	1988
Total	460.4	513.0	551.3	521.2	519.3	571.3	614.6	622.0	571.5	608.9	702.1
Retained	7.8	40.6	69.2	84.9	112.0	138.9	160.1	204.4	214.3	233.7	285.9
Retained per capita (yuan)	31.2	156.0	254.2	300.0	376.2	456.6	536.4	665.0	674.1	716.6	847.0
Percentage retained out of total	1.69	7.91	12.55	16.29	21.57	24.31	26.05	32.86	37.50	40.89	40.72

Source: The First Decade of Enterprise Reform in China (Bejing: Reform Press, 1990), 646.

The change in the structure of property rights brought about by profit sharing and informal privatization increases the autonomy of the firm. Profit sharing imposes limitations on rent seeking; it is in essence a tax on profits. In exchange for a share of the profit, government provides a host of services to local industry. Over time, as informal rights pass on to managers and entrepreneurs, local government becomes progressively disengaged from active micromanagement of the firm. Local government instead selectively interprets, monitors, and enforces the fundamental rules of cooperation and competition specified by the central state, while it constructs and maintains institutional arrangements aimed at promoting local economic development as a means to increase its revenues.

In sum, the institutional basis of local corporatism is not simply fiscal decentralization, but also the institutional innovation of profit sharing. Under profit-sharing arrangements, both local government and firms have greater incentive to pursue productive activity. Local government depends almost entirely on profitable firms for its source of revenues. The more profitable the firms in its jurisdiction and the higher the rate of economic growth, the larger its revenue from profit sharing and the larger its revenue base. Profit sharing provides local government with an interest in improving infrastructure (roads, transportation, communication, power, and education) and maintaining a stable regulatory environment. Fundamentally, it entails an exchange of services for revenue.

The Role of Government in Corporatist Regions

The role of political institutions in China has changed incrementally during the transition from a state socialist redistributive economy to a hybrid market economy. Change in the terms of relationship between industry and government continues to redefine the role of political institutions as they shift emphasis from socialist redistribution to market-oriented growth. In the past, local governments served as lower-level redistributive agencies collecting goods from the periphery to move to the center and distributing goods channeled down from central redistributive bureaus. Following fiscal decentralization, however, local governments must generate extrabudgetary revenue to support their activities. Because loss-making firms impose a net drain on local government budgets, fiscal decentralization created incentives for political actors to agree to contracts favorable to economic actors, in order to improve incentives and thereby increase revenues by achieving a higher rate of economic growth.

The corporatist relationship between local government and industry emerged from local adaptations to problems associated with partial reform. In an institutional environment characterized by weak market structures, poorly specified property rights, and pervasive institutional uncertainty, corporatist governments serve as third-party enforcers of agreements and contracts between parties to an exchange. In addition, local governments assist firms to secure reliable access to needed factor resources, especially those in short supply in the marketplace or those whose prices are subsidized. They play a middleman role in obtaining credit capital for firms. They fix prices as a means of subsidizing start-up firms on key factor resources. They oversee the recruitment of new managers. They approve and coordinate local economic development by allocating investment capital in a manner that promotes the competitiveness of local industry, whether by vertical or horizontal integration or by attracting new capital and technology. They redistribute revenues from industry to invest in infrastructure such as education, roads, public transportation, and other services. They invest directly in new profit-making ventures; they seek new sources of investment capital for local projects; they allocate factor resources, especially land and labor, to promote local economic growth; and they coordinate profit-sharing ventures with firms. In short, corporatist cooperation between local government and industry provides industry with the backing and resources needed by entrepreneurs and managers to compete in a socialist mixed economy in which market forces remain subordinate to still-dominant redistributive institutions.

Direct investment in business ventures by local government usually takes the form of joint ventures, partnerships, and joint-stock companies. In Xiamen, for example, the city government established the Sanjiang Company, an investment firm, in partnership with three state-owned firms in the city, as part of an effort to develop an export-oriented industrial base there. The city government contributed 60 percent of the investment capital, with the remaining 40 percent contributed by the three state-owned firms. The terms of this joint-stock company specified risk sharing and profit sharing according to the share each party had contributed. The city government appointed Sanjiang's general manager. After the first year of operation, the firm was contracted by the manager in a leaselike arrangement. The city government is satisfied if Sanjiang succeeds in promoting export-oriented investment and growth.

Corporatist local governments also invest in business projects to improve their revenue base. The amount local governments invest varies from project to project, ranging from 10 percent to, occasionally, 100 percent of the total capital required. The start-up capital often includes not only land and physical plant, but also the cost of developing new product lines and acquiring new technologies. In the Sunan and South China area (Fujian and Guangdong), township enterprises are primarily owned by local governments, although some are joint ventures involving coinvestment by urban firms and township governments. Township enterprises are increasingly contracted out to private entrepreneurs through profit-sharing responsibility contracts. In the Fushan area in South China, for example, more than 80 percent of township and village firms have been contracted out to private individuals.

From the point of view of local government, contracting out enterprises it owns is designed to ensure a stable source of revenue. Rather than simply acting as revenue collectors, corporatist governments become revenue generators. For the entrepreneur, contracting a firm is a means of acquiring rights of usage in order to engage in profit-making activities. The contract governance structure provides a formal framework that limits the government's claim to economic surplus and therefore lays the basis for entrepreneurs to secure informal property claims.

A direct result of fiscal reform was to impose greater responsibility on local governments in the investment of capital for local economic development, especially for capital construction projects that were in the past allocated through central planning. Local development funds come mainly from the profits and taxes gained from local firms. However, in cases requiring large-scale development funds, local governments seek new sources of investment capital, from either domestic or international sources. Because domestic banks can only issue loans equal to the total amount of deposits in their area, local governments have increasingly sought to invite government units and firms outside of their administrative area to invest in local projects. The role played by local governments in negotiating loans or investment capital on behalf of local firms is to serve as guarantor that the terms of the loan or investment will be honored. Investment capital for many infrastructure projects, including airports, harbors, and highways, is borrowed from international and domestic capital markets. There are no geographical restrictions on local governments in their efforts to locate new sources of investment capital to finance local economic development. In South China, for example, local governments cultivate overseas Chinese connections as a source of investment capital for local business ventures. When international sources of capital are not available, as in the Sunan area, local governments may coordinate joint investment with state-owned urban enterprises outside of their administrative area. Coinvestment usually involves setting up joint ventures with investors from inland areas seeking to profit from the economic boom of the southeastern coastal provinces. In Xiamen, for example, the city government has negotiated joint-venture projects with Sichuan, Jiangxi, Gansu, Hunan, and Hubei, as well as with government units and firms in other coastal provinces. These domestic joint ventures had resulted in the founding of 1,090 firms by 1990.

The Huaxia Electric Group illustrates the diverse array of funding sources mobilized by the Xiamen city government. To raise the capital needed to establish this export-oriented electronic firm in 1987, the city government negotiated with five domestic joint-venture firms and four sino-foreign joint-venture firms in the city, and with the Electronic Ministry in Beijing, the Bank of China in Hong Kong, the International Bank Group Limited in Xiamen, two Chinese investment firms in Hong Kong, the Jiangxi provincial government, the Zhengjiang provincial government, two firms in Sichuan, and six research institutes. One of the largest firms in Xiamen, the Huaxia Electronic Group has become one of the largest exporters of Chinese electronic products and is a major source of revenue for the city government.

The role of local governments in nonmarket allocation of factor resources is most clearly revealed by the way in which they make loans selectively available to local firms. Following the fiscal reform implemented in the late 1970s, firms no longer obtain funds to finance capital projects through the state. Instead they rely increasingly on bank loans to meet their capital needs. Here local governments play an important role in manipulating local banks to make scarce investment capital available to favored firms. They push industrial development. And in South China local governments selectively fund business ventures that seek international markets for their projects, in order to encourage export-oriented growth. Priority is also given to projects that have greater potential for profit; these are more likely to receive local government support in obtaining loans from local banks. Managers and entrepreneurs indicate that when their firms have incurred financial losses, they have had greater difficulty in getting loans. Some have said that loans to them were suspended after they reported financial losses. Since local governments depend on profits from firms in their area for their revenue base, there is a careful calculation in the allocation of scarce local capital to favor profit-making firms and to avoid loans to firms that have a record of financial losses. Banks have also become more selective in issuing loans, and may resist efforts by local government to manipulate their loan-making activities. After the banking reform of 1985, banks are now permitted to invest in business ventures under the profit-sharing contract governance system. Thus, domestic banks increasingly issue loans to firms in order to share in their profits.

Local governments also play an important role in the allocation of factor resources in the field of real estate. In South China, local governments contribute land to joint-venture projects with local firms. The 1983 joint-venture law explicitly specified that land could be counted as capital contribution in sino-foreign joint-venture projects. This practice quickly spread to domestic joint-venture deals, and resulted in the rapid commercialization of land.

Under the contract governance structure, the firm has the autonomy to determine its employment policy. There are still no well-established labor markets that allow for the free movement of labor as in a market economy, but especially in township firms, employees work on a contractual basis. Unlike employees in state-owned enterprises, they are not permanent workers. They can be hired and fired according to the labor needs of the nonstate firm. For example, in the Sunan area some firm managers report that they experience pressure from local government to hire more workers than they need, but that they increasingly resist pressure to do so. Contracting firms have an incentive to economize on their wage bill. Similarly, insofar as local governments have an interest in the profitability of the firm through profit sharing, they are less likely to impose more workers on the firm than are needed. Overall, the nonmarket allocative role of government has increasingly been shaped by profit-making incentives. This has resulted in a significant but gradual decline in the redistributive role of government (Nee 1989; Nee 1996).

A subtle indicator of the extent of nonmarket allocation in China is the level of reliance on vertical ties between the firm and government to obtain needed factor resources. Here the picture is mixed, depending on the extent of marketization across regions and economic sectors. *Guanxi* ties (social connections) with redistributors in government agencies are becoming more important in obtaining some key supplies (such as iron and steel, electricity, fuel, and other commodities controlled under planning) whose shortages have been aggravated by the rapid pace of economic growth. To secure reliable amounts of such inputs, firms seek to cultivate connections, or *guanxi,* with redistributors and with local government to gain a priority ranking from them. For other firms, *guanxi* ties to secure supplies have become less important. Firms that provide a major source of revenue for local governments, for example, do not need to cultivate *guanxi* ties with local government officials. Since local governments depend on them as a major source of their revenue, officials are eager to privilege these firms by providing them with key factor resources at below-market prices. In such cases there is a pattern of close corporatist cooperation between firm and government.

Still other firms are indifferent to *guanxi* ties with local government because they are entirely market-dependent for their input and output. These are the most market-oriented publicly-owned firms, and are especially found among the export-oriented, joint-venture firms with brand-name products that rely on labor-intensive production technology and whose raw materials are readily available in the marketplace. Sino-foreign joint-venture firms are especially indifferent to maintaining *guanxi* ties with local government, since their input materials are usually imported and their products exported. Rather than the firm seeking to cultivate *guanxi* ties with local government, it is local government that seeks to cultivate *guanxi* ties with the firm's management. For these firms are not only important sources of revenue, but they also provide a source of investment capital for new business ventures.

Whether the firm or government takes the lead in cultivating *guanxi* ties, a characteristic feature of local corporatism is a heavy reliance on personal ties in coordination of interests shared by government and industry. The level of government and industry coordination varies from firm to firm, and from area to area. Local governments provide coordination in helping entrepreneurs find business partners; developing ideas for new business ventures; overseeing negotiations between foreign investors and local firms in setting up joint-venture projects; and participating in dispute resolutions between parties to business transactions. Many firm managers we interviewed reported that the support of local government was important to their business, especially in negotiations involving transactions with overseas investors and firms from outside the locality. Many of these outside investors are overseas Chinese. Business deals often cannot be consummated without the backing of local government, owing to pervasive uncertainties stemming from the institutional environment of only partial reform. Corporatist ties between government and industry reduce the level of red tape involved in doing business, and provide greater assurances in the monitoring and enforcement of contracts involving both foreign and domestic business partners. At the same time, local governments strive to create environments that favor business in order to compete for investment capital and to increase their revenue base.

Hybrid Organizational Forms and Informal Privatization

The transition economy has given birth to a new diversity of organizational forms and a plurality of property rights, forming an intermediate economy regulated by redistributive and market mechanisms (Nee 1992). Socialist hybrids such as the marketized collective and state-owned firm have been shaped by a rapidly changing institutional environment in which market forces incrementally replace the state socialist redistributive mechanism. Hybrids are characterized by their bilateral dependence on resources and governance structures from more than one existing organization, sometimes across geographical and administrative boundaries (Borys and Jemison 1989; Pfeffer and Nowak 1976). Hybrid forms include sino-foreign joint ventures, domestic joint ventures, and mixed property forms involving various combinations of state, collective, and private ownership. Underneath the organizational labels of collective and state-ownership, a vast movement toward privatizing the ownership of industrial firms is taking place across sectors and regions, and within the firms themselves (Su 1993; Su 1994). The new mixed economy in China thus spans the continuum from formal and hierarchical state-owned enterprises to small informal private businesses, with a large intermediate economy composed of hybrid organizational forms.

The most common hybrid organizational forms in the Chinese industrial economy are joint ventures, contracting arrangements, and partnerships (or joint-stock). Joint ventures include sino-sino ventures, usually involving domestic firms of different ownership types, such as state-owned and nonstate firms, and also sino-foreign joint ventures. The purpose of these hybrid forms is to pool resources and technologies to gain competitive advantage in the marketplace, both domestic and international. In sino-foreign joint ventures, for example, the terms of exchange involve the combination of new technologies and capital with Chinese factor resources (e.g., cheap labor, land, raw material) and market access.

Arrangements for contracting state and collective enterprises—as a whole or in part—to a private entrepreneur or management group vary greatly. Methods include collective contracting, joint-stock contracting, manager-responsibility contracting, and individual contracting. In collective contracting, the employees of a firm organize to sign a contract with their local government; then the contract is in turn subcontracted to individual entrepreneurs. In joint-stock contracting, several people organize a management team to subcontract a profit-sharing contract. The terms of the contract usually require the commitment of an amount of floating capital, which determines the basis of profit sharing and fiscal responsibility for the venture. Contracts are for a specified period of time, and their terms bind the entrepreneur or management group to a percentage of profit or a rent. Contractors can be domestic or foreign in origin. The managers we interviewed reported that contracting led to substantial changes in management practices and organizational behavior. While the formal ownership classification remained unchanged, firm and subfirm contracting resulted in a mixture of ownership forms within the firm. In many state-owned firms, for example, a new hierarchy based upon multiple layers of individual contracting and subcontracting emerged. Such arrangements partition rights of use within the firm in a manner that mimics private property rights (Stark 1989). Implicit in the right to write subcontracts are claims of exclusive use over resources.

As in joint ventures, partnerships (or joint-stock arrangements) can include an array of economic and political actors, from government units, at various levels and across administrative boundaries, to firms and private investors—domestic and foreign. In partnership arrangements, responsibilities for profits and losses are shared according to the value of capital, land, or technologies contributed by the partners.

Table 2 reports the rapid growth of hybrid organizational forms in Xiamen City from 1982 to 1990. The numbers of collectively owned firms decline as many are converted to hybrid forms. The most rapidly growing categories were sino-foreign joint ventures and exclusively foreign-owned firms. Table 3 reports the increase in the relative industrial output value of hybrid forms in the Xiamen economy. By 1990, state-owned enterprises fell to 32 percent of total industrial output, from 76 percent in 1982. Joint ventures involving a private investor increased to 31 percent and sino-foreign and foreign-owned firms grew to 24 percent of the total industrial output of Xiamen City. In fact, tables 2 and 3 understate the extent to which hybrids have

TABLE 2. Number of Industrial Firms by Ownership in Xiaman City, by Number of Firms

Item	1982	1983	1984	1985	1986	1987	1988	1989	1990
Total	776	767	766	616	624	678	737	824	914
1. State-owned	181	181	180	187	191	202	206	211	205
2. Collectively owned	594	585	579	381	352	357	372	377	378
3. Joint ventures between items 1 and 2	—	—	1	19	27	32	38	37	41
4. Joint venture between item 1 and privately owned	—	—	3	7	11	26	43	65	83
5. Joint ventures between item 2 and privately owned	—	—	—	4	13	13	15	18	17
6. Shan-zi enterprises	1	1	3	14	23	42	60	109	188
7. Other	—	—	—	4	7	6	3	—	6

Sources: Fen Jin De Xiamen (Xiamen in rapid development) (Xiamen: Statistics Bureau, 1990), 67, 75; and *Yearbook of Xiamen Special Economic Zone* (Xiamen: Statistics Bureau, 1990), for 1990, 173; for 1991, 256.

TABLE 3. Total Amount of Industrial Output by Ownership in Xiamen City, in Million Yuan

Item	1982	1984	1985	1986	1987	1988	1989	1990
Total	113.18	150.32	218.52	246.86	328.57	481.57	551.00	662.12
	(100.00)	(100.00)	(100.00)	(100.00)	(100.00)	(100.00)	(100.00)	(100.00)
1. State-owned	86.44	110.45	130.65	150.24	169.06	189.04	209.63	212.08
	(76.37)	(76.25)	(59.79)	(60.86)	(51.45)	(39.26)	(38.05)	(32.03)
2. Collectively owned	25.29	32.06	40.75	40.28	46.29	65.77	54.53	55.69
	(22.35)	(21.33)	(18.65)	(16.32)	(14.09)	(13.66)	(9.90)	(8.41)
3. Joint ventures between items 1 and 2	—	0.21	4.90	9.29	10.40	13.21	12.67	14.19
	—	(0.14)	(2.24)	(3.76)	(3.16)	(2.74)	(2.30)	(2.14)
4. Joint ventures between item 1 and privately owned	—	1.56	29.60	20.37	58.31	138.04	162.10	206.96
	—	(0.10)	(13.54)	(8.25)	(17.75)	(28.66)	(29.42)	(31.26)
5. Joint ventures between item 2 and privately owned	—	—	—	2.88	2.37	2.25	2.88	4.09
	—	—	—	(1.17)	(0.72)	(0.47)	(0.52)	(0.62)
6. Shan-zhi enterprises	1.41	5.98	10.29	20.15	36.36	66.04	104.05	162.17
	(1.25)	(3.98)	(4.71)	(8.16)	(11.07)	(13.71)	(18.88)	(24.49)
7. Other	0.04	0.06	1.76	3.66	5.77	7.22	5.14	6.93
	(0.04)	(0.40)	(0.81)	(1.48)	(1.76)	(1.50)	(0.93)	(1.05)

Sources: Fen Jin De Xiamen (Xiamen in rapid development) (Xiamen: Statistics Bureau, 1990), 67, 75; and *Yearbook of Xiamen Special Economic Zone* (Xiamen: Statistics Bureau, 1990), for 1990, 173; for 1991, 256.

Note: In parenthesis are percentages of the total. Shan-zhi enterprises consist of: Sino-foreign joint ventures and foreign solely owned enterprises.

become the dominant organizational form in the Xiamen economy. This results from state-owned enterprises still being required to register as "state-owned," despite changes in their organizational practices deriving from the implementation of contract arrangements.

Indeed, many hybrid forms are still classified as "state-owned" even though they have undergone substantive changes stemming from informal privatization—changes including the way in which capital is formed, the way in which business is conducted, the way in which profits are shared. Fundamentally, the calculation of cost and benefit in hybrid forms conforms more to the behavior of firms disciplined by the market environment than to the bargaining behavior of state socialist redistributive economies. The organizational behavior of socialist hybrids reflects a redefinition of property rights and the gradual conversion of public property forms to private forms of ownership. Thus, the hybrid forms have led to a blurring of ownership forms in which the official classification of the firm does not match the actual nature of the firm. For example, some firms are still registered as "state-owned" when in fact the main component of the firm has merged with foreign partners in a joint-venture project. Many managers we interviewed did not know how to categorize the ownership form of the firm. They described organizational cultures that they associate with firms in capitalist economies, that combined partners representing different ownership forms, yet that were still classified as state-owned. Some firms, though still classified as "collective ownership," were in fact run by private entrepreneurs or overseas Chinese businessmen.[6]

The process of informal privatization in the Xiamen Food Company exemplifies the way in which new property rights emerge in response to the willingness of involved parties to adjust to new cost-benefit possibilities (Demsetz 1967). That state-owned firm converted a department into a subsidiary, the Food Trading Company, as a profit center responsible for its financial losses. The contract set profit sharing at a fixed ratio, with the main state-owned firm claiming 90 percent of earned profits. The subsidiary was then contracted out to three employees of the original department. These entrepreneurs quickly expanded the product line of their trading company beyond that of the parent company, so that it became the wholesaler and retailer for a number of firms, not only from the Xiamen area, but also from outside the region (including foreign products). Eventually the value of the business involving products from other firms grew to be six or seven times larger than

---

6. The blurring of property forms is not incompatible with a partitioning of property rights within the firm. This is because coinvestors in joint ventures and joint-stock companies maintain careful accounts of assets each side has contributed to the venture, especially when foreign partners are involved. In Xiamen City, for example, many municipal districts have set up asset management bureaus since 1986, following a surge in the founding of joint ventures. Stricter accounting procedures also allow for monitoring the flow of assets of joint ventures.

the value of the parent company's products. This development led the three entrepreneurs to request the right to purchase the assets of the original department of the parent company. The entrepreneurs lobbied to have their contract voided on the grounds that their business had changed, and that the original terms no longer applied. The Xiamen Food Company eventually realized that it could no longer impose control over its subsidiary, and it agreed to sell the entrepreneurs the assets used to start up the subsidiary at a fair market price. Those original assets were worth considerably less than the business that the entrepreneurs had developed themselves.

Another example illustrates the stages of informal privatization in a domestic joint-venture project. The Light Industrial Product Import and Export Corporation in Fuzhou, a large state-owned trading company, formed a joint venture with a private entrepreneur in the nearby city of Putian. The state enterprise put up 70 percent of the start-up capital. Within a short period of time the Fuzhou firm established 27 joint-venture businesses, both foreign and domestic. The rapid expansion overloaded the capacity of the firm to manage all of its joint ventures and it therefore decided to sell out its share in less lucrative ventures. The company sold its original investment in the joint venture with the Putian entrepreneur at market price. Soon after this transaction, the entrepreneur formed a joint venture with a Taiwanese firm. The spin-off of the joint venture to the private entrepreneur did not terminate business relationships between the two companies, however. Following the sale of its 70 percent interest, the Fuzhou firm continued to do business with the Putian entrepreneur, albeit through market transactions. Thus, this represented a shift from hierarchy to market governance structures motivated by transaction cost economizing (Williamson 1975). Joint ventures involve transaction costs inasmuch as they demand a great deal of management.

The privatization process involving nonstate collective firms conforms to a similar pattern. The privatization process is gradual, usually beginning with the contracting out of the village or township firm to a private entrepreneur. Although the formal property right remains collective, local leaders recognize the entrepreneur's claim to informal property rights over the use of the firm's resources. For example, Lin was a construction worker in Longhai county in Fujian province and in 1987, at the age of 52, he became the firm manager. In that same year, the Lin family signed a responsibility contract with the township government in which they agreed to pay a fixed percentage of their profits. According to the terms of their contract, the township leaders agreed to allocate village land for the Lins' use and to help them secure a bank loan. In 1991 and 1992, the Lins obtained a 200,000 and 400,000 yuan loan from a local construction bank with their help. The only requirement imposed on the Lin family was to pay the township government the amount specified by their contract; the family otherwise was free to pursue their business interests. In 1991 the family business paid the township government about 400,000 yuan in profit sharing and management fees. The Lins regarded the business as their own, and hired family members in all of the management positions: manager, deputy manager, and accountant. The officials of the township government similarly regarded the business as belonging to the Lin family, and were content to receive a steady source of revenue from them. In 1992 the firm hired more than 600 employees, including engineers, managers, and technicians, with assets valued at 2 million yuan.

The Fuzhou Electronic Manufacturing Company (FEMC) is a medium-sized state-owned firm. In its effort to develop oversea markets for its products, FEMC contracted its marketing department to a Hong Kong businessman. Within FEMC, the contracted marketing subunit was still viewed as a department of the firm, but outside the firm it was viewed as an independent business. According to the contract signed with the Hong Kong businessman, profit sharing was based on a seven to three ratio, with FEMC getting 70 percent of the profits. After contracting the marketing department for two years, the Hong Kong businessman purchased the subunit and formally registered it as an independent business. FEMC used the proceeds of the sale to acquire 20 percent of the stock of this newly registered private business. Today the firm is the major trading company in Fuzhou marketing local electronics products in international markets. These case studies illustrate the change in the structure of property rights that accounts for the dramatic economic growth experienced in the coastal provinces of China.

Figure 1 outlines the informal privatization of a village enterprise in the suburbs of Wuxi in Jiangsu province. The village leaders decided to build a modern four-story hotel on village land. They put up part of the start-up capital and a loan secured from the agricultural bank and mobilized villagers to build the hotel through the production brigade organization. But without previous experience in hotel management, the village leaders floundered once the hotel was opened. During the first years of operation, the hotel lost money and the village couldn't pay the mortgage. Eventually the agricultural bank took over the hotel and purchased the several acres of land surrounding the hotel site. Noticing that one of the village's production team leaders had entrepreneurial talent, the bank manager decided to contract the hotel to him, while retaining him as an employee of the bank. Working together with the bank, Wang launched an ambitious program of expansion. He secured an additional loan to build a new wing of the hotel, developed a new hotel supply business to service the rapidly growing hospitality industry in Wuxi, and started an electrical supply business. The hotel business continued to lose money, but Wang's new lines of business proved to be very profitable. Wang began negotiations with the largest hotel group in Shanghai to acquire new technology to construct a laundry plant, which he sensed could profitably service the Wuxi hospitality industry.

Although he is formally a bank employee, Wang works entirely from his

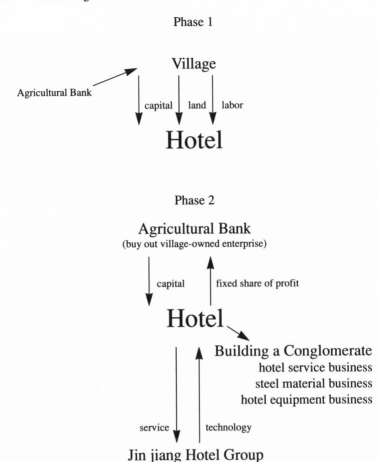

Fig. 1. Informal privatization in a hybrid firm. Example is from a sub-urban village in Wuxi.

office in the hotel complex. He sees himself as an independent businessman, not an employee of the bank (from which he does not now draw a salary). He maintains operational control of his business and makes his own strategic decisions in his diversification plans. He views his relationship to the bank as a mortgage payer, with his obligation to the bank limited to paying the mortgages in a timely manner. He is otherwise a free agent. Bank officials are satisfied with Wang's performance in servicing the loan, since they could not have managed the hotel and the construction of the new wing themselves. Because the hotel continues to lose money, they realize that without Wang's new lines of business, they would be faced with bad loans.

Village leaders now complain bitterly about losing the hotel as they see the new wing under construction and hear about the lucrative businesses that Wang started. They would like to take the hotel back from the bank. But Wang is independent of the village. The bank provides him with legitimacy and so he feels free to hire employees who are not fellow villagers. He knows the bank officials well, has worked with them since the mid-1980s, and is comfortable with the understanding he has with them. Although legally the bank owns the land and hotel, its officers have an informal understanding with Wang that the business belongs to him. In the absence of legal rights, the recognition of property claims is entirely social. Both parties understand the importance of a long-term business association for their mutual interests, and have strong incentives to invest in the stability of their social connection. Wang feels reasonably secure in his informal ownership claim.

Conclusion

Economic performance in China's industrial economy has improved because institutional innovations have combined to change the structure of incentives for both local government and industry. Analyses that emphasize only the role of local government in promoting market-oriented economic growth overlook the importance of getting incentives right at the level of the firm. To be sure, fiscal reform provided positive incentives to local government to promote conditions favorable to economic growth, but local officials in Maoist China also sought rapid and sustained economic development. Differentiating the post-Maoist era from the past are institutional innovations that are incrementally changing the relationship between local government and the firm. These innovations have led to a reallocation of control rights over economic surplus to managers, who divert cash flow to themselves and to workers in industrial firms (Qian 1994). Profit sharing redefined interests by setting limits on the extent surplus could be expropriated by government and by creating residual claims that economic actors could secure in the firm through strategies of informal privatization. This partitioning of property rights proved effective in creating positive incentives for both political and economic actors to promote market-oriented economic growth.

The rise of local corporatism has led analysts to highlight the economic role of political institutions (Weingast 1993; McMillan and Naughton 1992; Oi 1992; Walder 1995). Yet without reference to the economic role of social institutions, an explanation of the success of Chinese reforms in stimulating productivity gains in the firm would be incomplete. Institutions that maintain stable social ties between local officials, managers, and entrepreneurs not only lower the cost of bargaining between diverse interest groups, but also enhance credible commitment since reputation matters under conditions of repeated social exchange. Similarly, given the constraints on formal privatization, progressive informal privatization is crucial in changing the structure of incentives at the level of the firm. Informal property rights are in essence social norms, and as such their monitoring and enforcement are endogenous to social exchange. The comparative advantage of local corporatism under conditions of partial reform is precisely that the close cooperation between government and industry in market and nonmarket contexts significantly lowers transaction costs relative to alternative governance structures.

As the market grows, improvement in the relative gains from productive activity incrementally corresponds with a decline in the significance of redistributive power (Nee 1989; Nee 1996). This is reflected in the turn toward market-oriented activities, not only among private entrepreneurs, but among cadre entrepreneurs as well. The defining feature of entrepreneurs, whether cadre or noncadre, resides in their deriving profit from market exchange. To be sure, the redistributive power of cadre entrepreneurs contributes to substantially higher returns on market-oriented activity under partial reform when combined redistributive and market power remain a source of advantage. But as market transaction thickens and barriers to entry are lowered, competitive pressures from private firms are likely to reduce the comparative advantages of local corporatism (Nee 1992). Just as redistributive power has declined significantly at the national level, so, we believe, will there be incremental decline in the significance of local redistributive power. This process is likely to be gradual, if only because constructing the institutional foundations of a market economy takes place over a long time, as indicated by the transitions from state socialism in China, Eastern Europe, and the former Soviet Union. Even under corporatist arrangements, however, a decline in the significance of redistributive power should be evidenced by the growing relative returns of technocrats, managers, entrepreneurs, and workers in the marketized sector, compared with returns to officials and staff in the public nonprofit sectors of the economy (e.g., government, schools, universities, hospitals).

Rather than viewing local government as the engine of change and development, we maintain that corporatist arrangements encompass an interorganizational field of local officials, managers, and entrepreneurs who seek market-oriented economic growth. The extensive and progressive informal privatization in Chinese industry is consistent with new institutionalist theory, which argues that private property rights provide more effective incentives under market conditions than public property forms. A state-centered focus on formal property rights misses the critical dimension of institutional change that has occurred in China. Our analysis highlights the importance of the economic role of *social institutions:* the informal rules of the game or social norms that back private property claims in collective and state-owned enterprises, and institutional arrangements that promote repeated social exchange and hence foster trust and cooperation. When there is a high degree of institutional uncertainty, as in partial reform, credible commitment stems from social institutions. The dynamism behind local corporatism is rooted both in the interest of government to increase the size of its revenue base and in the self-interest of economic actors—managers, entrepreneurs, workers—in the firm in increasing their share of the surplus. In this respect, local corporatism in China does not greatly differ from corporatist arrangements in advanced capitalist economies.

REFERENCES

Borys, Bryan, and David B. Jemison. 1989. "Hybrid Arrangements as Strategic Alliances: Theoretical Issues in Organizational Combinations." *Academy of Management Review* 14:234–49.

Christiansen, Flemming. 1987. "Private Land in China? Some Aspects of the Development of Socialist Land Ownership in Post-Mao China." *Journal of Communist Studies* 3:55–70.

Demsetz, Harold. 1967. "Toward a Theory of Property Rights." *American Economic Review* 57:347–59.

Eggertsson, Thrainn. 1990. *Economic Behavior and Institutions.* Cambridge: Cambridge University Press.

Granovetter, Mark. 1985. "Economic Action and Social Structure: The Problem of Embeddedness." *American Journal of Sociology* 91:481–510.

Homans, George C. 1974. *Social Behavior: Its Elementary Forms.* New York: Harcourt Brace Jovanovich.

Lin, Nan. 1995. "Local Market Socialism: Local Corporatism in Action in Rural China." *Theory and Society* 24:301–54.

McMillan, John, and Barry Naughton. 1992. "How to Reform a Planned Economy: Lessons from China." *Oxford Review of Economic Policy* 8:130–40.

Naughton, Barry. 1992. "Implications of the State Monopoly over Industry and Its Relaxation." *Modern China* 18:14–41.

Nee, Victor. 1989. "A Theory of Market Transition: From Redistribution to Markets in State Socialism." *American Sociological Review* 54:663–81.

———. 1992. "Organizational Dynamics of Market Transition: Hybrid Forms, Property Rights, and Mixed Economy in China." *Administrative Science Quarterly* 37:1–27.

———. 1996. "The Emergence of a Market Society: Changing Mechanisms of Stratification in China." *American Journal of Sociology* 101:908–49.

Nee, Victor, and Paul Ingram. "Embeddedness and Beyond: Institutions, Exchange, and Social Structure." In *The New Institutionalism in Economic Sociology,* ed. M. Brinton and V. Nee. New York: Russell Sage Foundation. Forthcoming.

North, Douglass C. 1981. *Structure and Change in Economic History.* New York: Norton.

———. 1990. *Institutions, Institutional Change, and Economic Performance.* Cambridge: Cambridge University Press.

North, Douglass C., and Barry Weingast. 1989. "Constitutions and Commitment: The Evolution of Institutions Governing Public Choice in Seventeenth-Century England." *The Journal of Economic History* 49:803–32.

Oi, Jean C. 1990. "The Fate of the Collective after the Commune." In *Chinese Society on the Eve of Tiananmen: The Impact of Reform,* ed. D. Davis and E. Vogel, 15–30. Cambridge: Council of East Asian Studies.

———. 1992. "Fiscal Reform and the Economic Foundations of Local State Corporatism in China." *World Politics* 45:99–126.

Pfeffer, Jeffrey, and Phillip Nowak. 1976. "Joint Ventures and Interorganizational Dependence." *Administrative Science Quarterly* 21:398–418.

Powell, Walter W., and Laurel Smith-Doerr. 1994. "Networks and Economic Life." In *The Handbook of Economic Sociology,* ed. N. Smelser and R. Swedberg, 368–403. New York: Russell Sage Foundation.

Qian, Yingyi. 1994. "Issues of Enterprise Reform in China." Department of Economics, Stanford University.

Stark, David. 1989. "Coexisting Organizational Forms in Hungary's Emerging Mixed Economy." In *Remaking the Economic Institutions of Socialism: China and Eastern Europe,* ed. V. Nee and D. Stark, 136–68. Stanford, CA: Stanford University Press.

Su, Sijin. 1993. "Institutional Change and Dynamics of Market Growth in Chinese Firms." Ph.D. diss., Department of Sociology, Cornell University.

———. 1994. "Hybrid Organizational Forms in South China: 'One Firm, Two Systems.'" In *The Economic Transformation of South China: Reform and Development in the Post-Mao Era,* ed. T. Lyons and V. Nee, 199–214. Ithaca, NY: Cornell East Asia Series.

Walder, Andrew. 1995. "Local Government as Industrial Firms: Organizational Analysis of China's Transitional Economy." *American Journal of Sociology* 101:263–301.

Weingast, Barry R. 1993. "The Economic Role of Political Institutions." Working Papers on the Transitions from State Socialism. #93.8, Mario Einaudi Center for International Studies, Cornell University, Ithaca, NY.

Williamson, Oliver E. 1975. *Markets and Hierarchies: Analysis and Antitrust Implications.* New York: Free Press.

CHAPTER 6

Private Entrepreneurship in the Nascent Market Economy of Vietnam: Markets and Linkages

Per Ronnås

This chapter examines the development of markets for inputs and outputs in particular, but also factor markets, as they show up in a comprehensive survey of nonstate enterprises in Vietnam in 1991.[1] In order to put the analysis in perspective, the chapter also highlights some other general features of small nonstate enterprises in Vietnam, as they appeared in the survey.

As a point of departure, it deserves to be noted that the private sector in Vietnam is neither new nor insignificant. By 1989, it accounted for 29.3 percent of all employment in the country, versus only 14.5 percent in the state sector. In urban areas, 39.2 percent of the labor force worked in the private sector, compared to 46.9 percent in the state sector.[2] If we confine ourselves to the manufacturing sector, we find that the private sector was a more important source of employment (44.3 percent) than the state sector (36.8 percent). The residual 18.4 percent was accounted for by cooperatives. Since then, the private sector has grown by leaps and bounds. By 1992, the share of state enterprises in total manufacturing employment had fallen to a mere 20.5 percent. The private sector accounted for approximately half of the labor force in manufacturing, while approximately 30 percent worked in cooperative enterprises.[3]

---

1. The survey was a collaborative effort between the Asian Regional Team for Employment Promotion of the International Labour Organisation (ILO-ARTEP), the Swedish International Developmemt Authority (SIDA), and the Institute of Labour Science and Social Affairs of the Ministry of Labour, Invalids, and Social Affairs in Vietnam. The main fundings have been published in Per Ronnåas, *Employment Generation Through Private Entrepreneurships in Vietnam* (New Delhi: SIDA / ILO-ARTEP, 1993). The present chapter draws largely on the material published in this volume.

2. *Vietnam Population Census 1989: Completed Census Results* (Hanoi: Central Census Steering Committee, 1991), 4:434–61.

3. *So lieu thong ke lao dong va xa hoi 1992* (Hanoi: Bo lao dong-thuong binh va xa hoi, Trung tam thong tin khoa hoc lao dong va xa hoi, 1993), 23. Comparisons over time are difficult, as the figures refer to different sources. While the fall in the share of the state sector in manufac-

The Survey and General Enterprise Characteristics

The survey included some 1,000 enterprises, altogether, equally divided between the north and the south of the country and between urban and rural areas.[4] In order to capture the whole gamut of types of enterprises, a stratified sampling technique was used to ensure an adequate number of household, private, partnership, and cooperative enterprises in the sample.[5] The focus was on the manufacturing sector. Thus, 90 percent of the urban enterprises in the sample had manufacturing as their main activity. However, in the rural survey this restriction was relaxed in view of the scarcity of genuine manufacturing enterprises in the countryside. Altogether 64 percent of the surveyed rural enterprises had manufacturing as their main activity. Of these, 42 percent were engaged in agro-processing. An additional 11 percent were repair shops. Restaurants, cafes, and other trading enterprises made up 8 percent of the sample and various other and mixed categories 17 percent.

In 1990 the average urban private enterprise provided employment for 13.7 persons and produced a total value added of 12,600 U.S. dollars (USD), or 813 USD per worker. Total assets per enterprise averaged slightly more than 30,000 USD. The average urban household enterprise, which by definition is smaller, employed 4.8 persons, 3.7 of whom were unpaid household members, and generated a value added of 3,600 USD, or 648 USD per capita (table 1). Partnership enterprises have roughly the same average size as private enterprises. Cooperatives tend to be considerably larger than private and partnership enterprises, particularly in terms of employment, but have lower labor productivity. Because of the skewed size distribution—with a small number of very large enterprises—the median size of the enterprises is much smaller than the average size. Thus, half of the private and partnership enterprises in the three main cities produced a total value added of less than 5,400 USD and a value added per worker of less than 500 USD in 1990. The majority of the household enterprises are very small. In urban

---

turing employment is beyond doubt, the distinction between the private and the cooperative sector appears to vary from one source to another.

4. The urban survey was carried out in Ho Chi Minh City, Hanoi, and Haiphong. The rural survey took place in the provinces of Ha Son Binh, Vinh Phu, and Quang Ninh in the north and Long An and Cuu Long in the south. For further details, see Per Ronnåas, *Employment Generation*, 10–15.

5. The distinction between these four types of nonstate enterprises is in reality somewhat ambiguous. Household enterprises are by definition small and rely primarily on their own labor. Private enterprises are distinguished from household enterprises primarily by a greater reliance on wage labor. Partnership enterprises differ from private enterprises in that they have two or more owners. The distinction between partnership and cooperative enterprises is sometimes unclear.

TABLE 1.   Main Economic Characteristics of Private and Household Enterprises in Rural and Urban Areas, 1990

	Household Enterprises		Private Enterprises	
	Urban	Rural	Urban	Rural
Income	11,586	4,127	48,456	27,693
Value added	3,592	1,216	12,591	6,299
Assets	8,451	1,847	30,273	5,679
Debts	196	33	2,549	347
No. of employees	4.77	3.53	13.63	10.40
No. of wage workers	0.95	0.37	11.06	7.53
Value added per worker	648	356	813	773
Assets per worker	1,501	538	2,188	709
Average wage	344	233	402	322

Note: Monetary values based on an average exchange rate of 5,100 Dong per USD in 1990.

areas, half of the household enterprises produced a total value added below 1,610 USD in 1990 and had less than 2,590 USD in total assets. The capital/labor ratio and labor productivity in these enterprises at the bottom of the scale is very low. Half of the urban enterprises had less than 623 USD in total assets per worker in 1990 and produced a value added of less than 380 USD per worker.

The differences in size and economic performance between the nonstate enterprises in Ho Chi Minh City on the one hand and Hanoi and Haiphong on the other hand are very large. Value added per worker as well as total value added is on average 2.5 to 3 times larger in Ho Chi Minh City than in the two northern cities. To some extent this is explained by the higher capital/labor ratio in Ho Chi Minh City, but a more important explanation would seem to be that urban enterprises in the south are more efficient in terms of their utilization of both labor and capital than are those in the north. In addition, economies of scale may explain some of the differences.

Virtually all urban nonstate enterprises use electricity and the vast majority also make use of power-operated machinery, although the degree of mechanization is higher in the south than in the north. Even among the household enterprises, two-thirds use some power-operated machinery and only 17 percent rely exclusively on hand tools.

Rural nonstate enterprises are much smaller and more undercapitalized than urban, irrespective of the type of ownership. Average total capital in rural enterprises is only one-fifth of that in urban enterprises, while the difference in the average capital/labor ratio is on the order of one to three (table 1). This is also reflected in the much lower level of mechanization in rural areas. Almost half of the rural enterprises covered by the survey use hand tools only. An additional 15.5 percent use manually operated machinery, while 39.4 percent use power operated machinery. A full 42 percent are not even connected to the electric grid. Undercapitalization and primitive methods of production inevitably result in low productivity. The value added per worker in the rural household enterprises is only 55 percent of that in the urban household enterprises. Almost half of the rural household enterprises produced a value added per worker of less than 200 USD in 1990, and less than a quarter of the enterprises produced a value added per worker in excess of 500 USD. A large number of rural household enterprises are clearly best described as distress industries, with little capital and primitive modes of operation, and yielding an income much below subsistence level.

Although many enterprises are recently established, it is noteworthy that a large number of the nonstate enterprises have a history that goes well beyond the introduction of renovation (*doi moi*). No less than 60.5 percent of the urban enterprises covered by the survey were established prior to 1988 and 24.5 percent were more than ten years old. The age structure varies regionally, as well as between the different ownership forms. Hanoi and Haiphong have a large number of both old and very new enterprises. It would appear that enterprises in these cities were established at a slow but rather even pace over the years until 1988. The introduction of *doi moi* had an immediate effect on entrepreneurship, and in the past few years the number of enterprises has mushroomed. In Ho Chi Minh City, on the other hand, virtually all enterprises have been established since the liberation, but the impact of *doi moi* has been much less. Less than one-fifth of the enterprises in this city were established in 1989–90, compared to 37 percent in the two northern cities.

In rural areas the agrarian reforms introduced in 1987 acted as a catalyst on entrepreneurship. As a consequence, most rural enterprises are very young. Some 59 percent were established in 1988–90. The relative youth of the rural enterprises is further emphasized by the fact that while 36.5 percent of the urban enterprises had previously existed in some other form, virtually all rural enterprises were established from scratch.

Factor Markets and Access to Capital, Labor, and Land

Availability of own capital determines who becomes an entrepreneur and who does not. It also determines, to a large extent, the scale of the enterprise. In household and private enterprises, own capital and interest-free loans from friends make up over 95 percent of the total invested capital at the time of the establishment of the enterprise in urban areas. For rural enterprises this share is marginally lower. Bank loans and other forms of credit play a totally insignificant role as a source of capital. Loans from private persons made up on average 5.4 percent of the starting capital in rural areas, but only 1.6 percent in urban areas. Workers' contributions, on the other hand, were a frequent and significant source of initial capital in urban areas, but hardly featured at all in rural areas, largely reflecting the lack of cooperative and partnership enterprises in rural areas (table 2) The glaring absence of the formal sector as a source of capital is true for both the north and the south. There were only minor differences in the importance of formal credits to total capital formation between the three cities and between the five provinces covered by the survey. Similarly, the differences between the smaller household enterprises and the generally larger private and partnership enterprises were marginal in this regard.

The average starting capital thus varies according to possibility rather than need. In Hanoi half of the enterprises started with less than 1,500 USD in capital, while in Ho Chi Minh City the median was 4,260 USD (table 3). Differences in access to capital also determine who sets up a household enterprise and who can establish a private enterprise. Half of the private enterprises in the three large cities started with more than 6,380 USD in capital, while less than half of the household enterprises had a starting capital in excess of 900 USD. The much more limited access to capital in rural areas is reflected in much smaller initial investments in enterprises. Half of the rural household enterprises started with less than 300 USD and half of the private enterprises were established with less than 1,000 USD in capital. The regional differences in the rural areas were at least as pronounced as those between the three cities. In the Red River basin (Ha Son Binh and Vinh Phu) the median initial capital was less than 200 USD, while in Cuu Long, in the Mekong Delta, it was no less than 1,700 USD and in Long An, outside Ho Chi Minh City, it was over 500 USD.

Shortage of capital stands out as by far the most frequently stated severe

TABLE 2. Sources of Capital at the Time of Establishment of Urban and Rural Enterprises

	Urban		Rural	
	Percentage[a]	Average[b]	Percentage[a]	Average[b]
Own capital	86.4	75.9	92.7	82.0
Interest-free loans	12.8	5.9	17.5	7.5
Bank loan	1.9	0.6	1.3	0.8
Credit cooperative	0.2	0.1	1.3	0.5
Local authority	0.5	0.1	0.3	0.1
Worker's contributions	22.5	13.5	0.5	0.3
Loan from private person	5.4	1.6	10.8	5.4
Advance against sales	0.2	0.1	1.5	0.6
Other source	3.3	2.3	2.3	1.8

[a]percentage of enterprises that utilized this source of capital
[b]average contribution to total capital formation for all enterprises

TABLE 3.   Total Investments at the Time of Establishment of Urban and Rural Enterprises, in U.S. Dollars

	Mean	Median	25%	75%	90%
Urban areas	12,850	4,040	2,880	11,320	28,090
Hanoi	6,000	1,450	380	4,430	10,680
Haiphong	15,830	5,618	1,020	22,560	42,180
Ho Chi Minh City	15,240	4,260	1,830	12,770	26,810
Household	3,190	890	170	2,940	7,320
Private	12,940	6,380	2,130	17,020	35,280
Partnership	8,680	4,090	1,530	12,600	25,450
Cooperatives	32,000	7,190	2,470	21,280	67,880
Rural areas	1,449	477	170	1,668	3,405
Ha Son Binh	556	192	89	683	1,915
Quang Ninh	1,318	468	128	936	2,882
Vinh Phu	721	196	85	656	1,756
Long An	1,048	511	213	1,362	2,639
Cuu Long	1,982	1,702	638	3,405	8,512
Household enterprises	912	298	98	851	2,125
Private enterprises	2,153	1,021	387	2,226	5,219

Notes: Values in U.S. dollars recalculated from tael gold. One tael of gold equals 37.5 grams, which equals 425.6 USD at present price of USD 353 per troy ounce (31.1 grams) of gold.

constraint at the time of the establishment of enterprises in both urban and rural areas (table 4). Although it is perhaps to be expected that entrepreneurs and managers would like to have more capital at their disposal and perceive shortage of capital as a constraint, it seems safe to conclude that the lack of a functioning capital market has had severe repercussions on the establishment of nonstate enterprises.

It deserves to be noted that the lack of a land and real estate market was also frequently stated as a major impediment, particularly in urban areas. The situation would appear to be particularly severe in Hanoi, where 18 percent of the enterprise managers stated that lack of suitable premises had been a main constraint at the time of the establishment of the enterprise. Not surprisingly, lack of premises had been a more frequent problem for the larger private and partnership enterprises than for the household enterprises.

By contrast, lack of skilled labor was seldom stated as a constraint at the time of the establishment of the enterprise, despite the virtual absence of formal labor markets. Personal contacts and recommendations by friends and relatives are by far the most important modes of recruiting labor, not only in rural but also in urban areas. More than 90 percent of both the urban and rural

TABLE 4. Severe Difficulties Experienced at the Time of Establishment, by Percentage of Enterprises

	Urban	Rural
Lack of		
Capital	39.4	43.6
Raw material	8.7	2.5
Market outlet	6.7	8.8
Technical know-how	3.8	3.0
Suitable machinery	5.1	2.3
Suitable premises	14.3	1.5
Skilled labor	0.4	0.8
Government regulations	2.7	3.0
Attitude of officials	0.7	0.8

enterprises stated that they relied on these methods for recruiting labor. Only 5.5 percent of the surveyed urban enterprises claimed to have difficulty in recruiting labor with appropriate skills and for only 5.2 percent was lack of skilled workers stated to be a major constraint to the development of the enterprise. The comparatively high overall level of education of the labor force is clearly a major advantage. The mean number of years of formal education among the labor force in the enterprises covered by the survey was more than eight years, with only very minor variations between types of enterprises and areas.[6] The high level of education is not only an advantage per se, but no doubt also facilitates on-the-job skill formation. On the demand side, it is reasonable to assume that a generally low level of technology reduces the need for specific skills. It is noteworthy that among the comparatively larger private enterprises in urban areas, 9.2 percent experienced difficulties in recruiting skilled labor. Among the small-scale state enterprises covered by the survey this percentage was 17.6, probably reflecting the use of more sophisticated technology, as well as less competitive wages in the state sector.

After establishment, the urban nonstate enterprises operate in a cash economy par excellence. Credit is neither received nor given. Over 90 percent usually pay for raw materials and other inputs on receipt and only a negligible 0.6 percent purchase on credit as a rule. Indeed, advance payment appears to be a more frequent mode of payment than credit, as 4.1 percent of the enterprises usually pay for their inputs in advance. Similarly, the vast majority of the enterprises sell for cash on delivery. Only 5.7 percent of the enterprises

---

6. It should be noted, however, that the educational level is, on the whole, higher in the north than in the south of the country.

sell occasionally on credit and 2.0 percent do so as a rule. Some enterprises resort to advance payment as a way of meeting the need for short-term capital. However, the overwhelming majority of transactions are clearly made on a "cash on delivery" basis. This is all the more remarkable in view of the often close relationship between buyer and seller.

Rural enterprises, too, carry out their transactions strictly on a cash basis. Virtually all enterprises, 98.6 percent, pay in cash as a rule upon receipt of goods. Purchase on credit features hardly at all. Less than 1 percent of the surveyed enterprises ever receive credit from suppliers. On the other hand, 13 percent of the enterprises pay, at least occasionally, in advance for raw materials and other inputs.

The urban nonstate enterprises rely primarily on their own capital for their operation. At the time of the survey only 26.9 percent of the enterprises stated that they had any external debts (table 5). Loans from friends and relatives were the most common source of external capital. Some 10.5 percent of the enterprises had raised capital in this way. The insignificance of the formal capital market as a source of capital is clearly reflected in the fact that only 6.5 percent of the enterprises had bank loans and an additional 1.9 percent had borrowed money from credit cooperatives. Private money lenders are almost as frequently resorted to as banks for capital, although the amounts borrowed from private lenders tend to be small.[7] Even among the enterprises with access to external capital the level of indebtedness is low, both in absolute and relative terms. Their median ratio of debt to total capital was only 0.20 and the median size of the debt was a mere 15 million dong (1,695 USD).

The infrequent and small reliance on external capital reflects an absolute lack of access to external capital rather than a high price of capital. Except for a few cases of clearly exorbitant interest rates paid by the surveyed urban enterprises, the rates of interest seem to generally be reasonable, irrespective of the source of the loan. Bank loans are generally at a standard rate of 4.5 percent per month, (that is, approximately 70 percent per year), which in 1990 was barely above the level of inflation. Loans from private money lenders would seem to carry only marginally higher interest rates.[8] Interestingly, loans from private and state enterprises more often than not do not carry any interest.[9] It would appear that in the few cases where credit was extended, it was often done free of charge. Loans from friends and relatives carried interest in 36 percent of the cases. Although the loans from the formal sector

---

7. The median amount borrowed from private lenders was only 9.5 million dong (1,073 USD), compared to 47.5 million dong (5,367 USD) from banks.

8. The median rate was 5 percent per month.

9. Six out of nine loans did not carry any interest.

TABLE 5. Frequency, Magnitude and Sources of External Credit for Urban Enterprises

	Hanoi	Haiphong	Ho Chi Minh	Total	Household	Private	Partnership	Coop
Percentage with external debts	25.0	42.2	22.1	26.9	12.6	28.9	31.6	34.4
Percentage with loans from								
Banks	3.0	16.6	4.4	6.5	0.0	6.3	6.2	13.0
Credit coops	0.0	5.5	1.7	1.9	0.9	0.8	2.7	4.4
Private moneylender	8.4	6.7	2.7	5.1	0.9	7.1	3.6	8.7
Employees	4.5	1.1	1.7	2.5	0.0	0.8	1.8	8.7
Private enterprises	0.0	2.2	2.2	1.5	0.0	1.6	2.6	2.2
State enterprises	2.3	1.1	0.0	1.1	0.0	0.0	2.6	2.2
Friends and relatives	8.3	18.9	8.4	10.5	8.9	14.1	9.7	7.6
Other sources	3.1	1.1	1.8	1.9	1.8	2.3	1.8	1.1
Median debt (1,000 dong)	9,800	32,000	10,660	15,000	3,000	25,975	16,500	19,000
Median debt/capital ratio	0.25	0.21	0.20	0.20	0.20	0.24	0.09	0.22

Note: Figures on median debt and median debt/capital ratio refer to enterprises with external debts only. 1 USD = 8.850 dong.

carry interest rates that in real terms are fairly low, it may still be noted that the nonstate enterprises are discriminated against by banks both with regard to access to loans and with regard to the terms of loans. State enterprises not only have privileged access to bank loans, but also benefit from subsidized interest rates. The standard rate of interest charged by banks to state enterprises in 1990 was only 2.5 percent per month, well below the level of inflation.

Most loans are short-term. The median term is only six months. Loans from friends and relatives and from workers are generally on a longer term than other loans. It is notable that bank loans, too, tend to be short-term; the median term is four months.

Very few rural enterprises rely on, or for that matter have access to, external capital in the form of loans or credit except on a very short-term basis. Out of 404 rural enterprises in the survey, 58 had liabilities in the form of loans or credits received. Twenty-two of these were interenterprise credits. Ten enterprises had taken loans from private money lenders, while only 3 had managed to obtain a bank loan and an additional 5 had borrowed money from credit cooperatives. Most of the rest were various short-term credits. The loans were almost all small and short-term. Some 44 percent of the loans were in amounts of less than a million dong (113 USD) and only ten percent were over ten million dong (1,130 USD). Only two of the loans were for a period exceeding one month. In contrast to the picture in the urban areas, the terms of the loans vary greatly; from 1 to 24 percent per month.

Markets for Inputs and Backward Linkages

Backward linkages with suppliers of raw materials and other inputs tend to be localized and rather personal. Thus, 35 percent of the urban nonstate enterprises have identified their suppliers of raw materials through personal contacts. In 84 percent of the cases some kind of search process preceded the choice of supplier and in only 6 percent of the cases was the choice of supplier an effect of any marketing effort on the part of the supplier. No less than 14 percent of the enterprises have received assistance from a government agency in linking up with a supplier. Differences between the three cities and between the various ownership forms in the mode of identification of suppliers do not seem to be very large, except that government agencies play a more active role as intermediaries in the north than in the south. It therefore comes as no surprise to find that the vast majority of enterprises depend on local suppliers. Some 72.7 percent of the enterprises rely exclusively on local suppliers, 6.9 percent of the enterprises depend to some extent on suppliers in other towns, and 6.9 percent procure inputs from suppliers in rural areas (table 6).

Individual households are the most important suppliers of raw material to

TABLE 6. Sources of Raw Material by Type and Location of Supplier for Urban Enterprises, by Percentage Share of Total Procurement

	0	1–24	25–49	50–74	75–99	100	Mean
Type of supplier							
Household	49.5	11.6	5.4	6.2	5.6	21.7	33.4
Nonstate enterprise	55.8	10.4	5.8	8.2	7.1	12.7	26.9
State enterprise	63.0	8.0	7.5	6.0	7.3	8.2	21.9
Other state agency	89.6	2.4	2.9	1.6	1.9	1.6	5.6
Collective farms	98.9	0.6	0.2	0.2	0.0	0.0	0.3
Other sources	91.4	1.5	0.8	1.3	1.3	4.0	6.3
Location of supplier							
Same town	8.6	3.8	4.3	2.3	8.3	72.7	83.4
Other town	93.1	2.2	0.6	1.3	1.6	1.1	3.8
Rural areas	93.1	2.2	0.6	1.3	1.6	1.1	3.8
Elsewhere	95.3	0.9	0.7	1.3	0.6	1.1	2.7

the urban nonstate enterprises. More than half of the enterprises procure at least some of their inputs, and 21.7 percent get all their inputs, from individual households (table 6). On average, it would seem that approximately a third of the inputs are procured from individual households. Other nonstate enterprises form the second most important group of suppliers of inputs. Approximately 27 percent of all inputs are procured from such enterprises and about 20 percent of the enterprises rely on other nonstate enterprises for 75 percent

TABLE 7. Sources of Raw Material by Type and Location of Supplier for Rural Enterprises, by Percentage Share of Total Procurement

	0	1–24	25–49	50–74	75–99	100	Mean
Type of supplier							
Individual persons	60.0	7.9	2.5	2.2	1.5	26.1	30.5
Private enterprises	33.2	2.9	2.1	6.8	11.1	43.9	58.5
State enterprises	86.8	2.5	3.2	1.7	1.6	3.9	8.0
State trading companies	98.6	0.0	0.0	0.8	0.0	0.4	1.1
Collective farms	98.9	0.4	0.4	0.0	0.0	0.4	0.5
Elsewhere	97.5	0.4	0.0	0.4	0.4	1.4	2.0
Location of supplier							
Same village	91.7	6.4	2.0	0.0	0.5	1.4	3.1
Same commune	71.9	5.5	3.7	3.7	4.7	10.6	19.0
Nearby town	53.5	4.6	5.1	7.3	3.2	25.3	34.8
Large city	61.8	5.0	2.3	3.2	5.9	21.7	30.3
Elsewhere	80.2	3.8	2.3	3.7	9.3	4.1	12.7

or more of their inputs. On the other hand, 56 percent of the enterprises do not procure any inputs from other nonstate enterprises. State enterprises and other state agencies figure rather prominently as suppliers to nonstate enterprises. Some 37 percent of the enterprises get some inputs from state enterprises and 10.4 percent of them procure inputs from other state agencies. Combined, these sources would seem to account for about 27.5 percent of the inputs. Almost 21 percent of the enterprises rely exclusively on state enterprises and agencies for their inputs.

An undesirable effect of the localized and personalized backward linkages is various inadequacies in the supply of raw materials. Almost one-third of the enterprises (31.7 percent) stated that the needed raw materials were not always available in sufficient quantities. This problem would seem to be greater in Hanoi (37.8 percent) and for the larger types of nonstate enterprises. Only 22 percent of the household enterprises claimed that this was a problem, as compared to over a third of the other three types of enterprises.

Difficulties in obtaining raw materials of sufficient quality is also perceived as a problem by almost one-third of the enterprises. This problem was most frequently registered in Haiphong (42.2 percent) and among private and collective enterprises.

The identification of suppliers and establishment of backward linkages necessarily poses greater difficulty for enterprises located in rural areas than for those in the large cities, as the availability and choice of local suppliers is more limited. Yet, the methods of identifying suppliers are rather similar for the urban and rural enterprises. Some 37.3 percent of the enterprises covered in the rural survey had identified their suppliers mainly through personal contacts. The majority, 59.1 percent, had undertaken some kind of search process beyond the network of personal contacts, but only 3.7 percent had identified the supplier(s) as a result of a marketing effort on behalf of the supplier. For 7.8 percent of the enterprises assistance by local authorities has been instrumental in identifying supplier(s). As in the urban areas, the insignificance of marketing efforts by suppliers implies that the purchasing enterprise has to rely on personal contacts and own search efforts to establish the necessary backward linkages. This puts small enterprises and those located in backward areas at a disadvantage. The differences in methods of identifying suppliers between the two main types of rural enterprises—household and private—seem on the whole to be insignificant and within the margin of error.

The much smaller importance of local suppliers for rural than for urban enterprises is clearly reflected in table 7. Altogether for the surveyed enterprises, only 22.1 percent of the inputs are procured locally, that is, from the same village or commune. The variations between household and private enterprises in this regard are insignificant. Less than 10 percent of the enterprises procure any inputs from the same village, while slightly more than a quarter of them procure inputs outside the village but within the same commune. About 12 percent of the enterprises depend exclusively on local suppliers.

Most inputs used in rural enterprises are of urban origin. Roughly 35 percent is obtained from local towns and an additional 30 percent is procured from large cities. Only 38.2 percent of the enterprises do not procure any inputs from large cities, indicating that the majority of enterprises depend, at least to some extent, on rather distant sources of supply. However, the fact that most enterprises procure some inputs from large cities should not distract attention from the role of small towns as suppliers of inputs to non-agricultural rural enterprises. Almost half of the enterprises procure some inputs from nearby towns and a quarter of them procure all their inputs from nearby towns. If the definition of the local economy is expanded to include local towns, which from most points of view seems reasonable, then it can be seen that well over half of the inputs are procured locally. This implies the existence of considerable local multiplier effects, although they go to small towns rather than to the purely rural areas.

On average, approximately 30 percent of the inputs used by the rural enterprises in the survey derive from individual households. Most of the rest is procured from other nonstate enterprises (58.5 percent). Backward linkages with the state sector are much weaker than is the case in urban areas. On average, only about 9 percent of the inputs are procured from state enterprises and agencies, versus 27.5 percent for the nonstate enterprises in the urban areas. This difference between rural and urban nonstate enterprises is noteworthy, not least considering that much of the inputs in rural enterprises are in fact procured from urban areas. Another interesting feature is the total insignificance of cooperative farms as sources of supply of inputs to rural nonstate enterprises. Although the role of cooperative farms has changed dramatically in the past few years, the fact that what until recently, at least in the north, was the most important economic institution in rural areas today plays no role at all as a supplier of inputs to other local firms is remarkable.

Problems with securing adequate quantities of inputs are, on the whole, more frequent in rural than in urban areas. About 39 percent of the rural enterprises in the survey experience such problems, compared to 32 percent of the urban enterprises. Among the rural manufacturing enterprises as many as 43.2 percent experience problems with securing adequate supplies of inputs, while only 22.6 percent of the agro-processing industries face this problem. The local level of economic development would seem to have a strong bearing on the ease with which adequate inputs are secured, and quantitative supply problems are much more frequent in the north than in the south. Only 15 percent of the enterprises in Cuu Long and 26.6 percent in Long An experience any difficulties in this regard, compared to 44.6 percent in Ha Son Binh and 61.9 percent in Vinh Phu.

Difficulties in obtaining satisfactory quality of inputs are, on the other hand, much less frequent in rural areas than in urban areas, but this is likely to have more to do with the type of products produced and inputs needed than anything else. In fact, in the rural areas it is mainly catering enterprises, such as restaurants and cafes, that experience problems with poor quality of inputs (25 percent).

Sales, Marketing and Forward Linkages

Urban Enterprises

Sale of goods is by far the most important source of revenue for the urban enterprises included in the survey, reflecting the focus of the survey on manufacturing enterprises. It accounted, on average, for approximately 92 percent of their total revenue in 1990. Only 7.3 percent of the enterprises had no revenue from sale of goods in 1990, while 88.4 percent received more than 50 percent of their revenues from this source. Services provided the second-most important source of revenue, on average 5.9 percent of total revenue. Some 14.1 percent of the enterprises received some income from services, and for 4.8 percent of them services provided the sole source of income. However, it should be stressed that these figures are not representative of urban nonstate enterprises as a whole, as the sample was biased toward manufacturing enterprises.

Forward linkages in the form of sales of goods display a broadly similar pattern to that of the backward linkages. Generally speaking, individual persons form the most important category of customers. Half of the enterprises sell at least part of their produce to individuals, and for 26.3 percent of the enterprises they form the sole category of customers (table 8). On the whole, it would seem that smaller enterprises are more oriented toward the individual consumer market than larger ones are. Approximately 56 percent of the production of household enterprises is sold to individuals, as against 38.2 percent for private enterprises, 27.8 percent for partnership enterprises and 12.9 percent for cooperatives. Some 45.7 percent of the household enterprises sell exclusively to individuals and only 28.3 percent of them do not cater at all to this category of customers. By contrast, only half of the private and partnership enterprises and a quarter of the cooperative enterprises sell to individual persons. In an imperfectly developed market like the Vietnamese, small enterprises are clearly in comparatively good position to cater to the individualized and atomized demand of individual consumers by virtue of their flexibility and proximity to the market.

The second main category of customers for household enterprises are

TABLE 8. Destination of Sales by Category of Buyer and Type of Urban Enterprise, by Percentage Share of Total Sales of Main Product

	0	1–24	25–49	50–74	75–99	100	Mean
Total urban							
Individual persons	50.0	12.4	4.5	4.8	2.1	26.3	34.3
Private enterprises	62.1	6.6	7.6	7.8	3.8	12.1	23.8
State enterprises	69.4	2.3	3.6	5.5	4.1	12.1	23.8
State trading companies	82.9	2.9	3.1	2.7	1.5	7.1	11.4
Local authorities	98.7	0.6	0.0	0.6	0.0	0.3	0.6
Export	95.5	0.9	0.6	0.3	0.6	2.5	3.5
Household enterprises							
Individual persons	28.3	10.8	6.6	5.4	3.3	45.7	55.7
Private enterprises	56.5	3.3	5.4	12.0	6.6	16.3	32.2
State enterprises	91.3	2.2	2.2	2.2	1.1	1.1	4.1
State trading companies	90.2	3.3	2.2	1.1	1.1	2.2	4.7
Local authorities	100.0	0.0	0.0	0.0	0.0	0.0	0.0
Export	100.0	0.0	0.0	0.0	0.0	0.0	0.0
Private enterprises							
Individual persons	47.1	10.0	4.2	8.3	0.8	30.3	38.2
Private enterprises	64.7	4.2	7.6	7.5	2.5	13.4	23.1
State enterprises	72.0	2.6	5.1	6.7	6.0	7.6	18.8
State trading companies	80.7	2.5	5.9	2.5	2.5	7.6	12.1
Local authorities	97.5	1.6	0.0	0.8	0.0	0.0	0.7
Export	93.3	1.6	0.0	0.8	0.8	3.4	4.9
Partnership enterprises							
Individual persons	52.9	15.7	5.9	4.9	2.0	18.6	27.8
Private enterprises	57.8	10.8	10.8	7.9	3.9	8.8	22.4
State enterprises	56.3	1.0	2.0	9.7	12.6	16.5	35.2
State trading companies	86.4	2.9	1.0	2.0	2.9	4.9	9.1
Local authorities	99.0	0.0	0.0	1.0	0.0	0.0	0.5
Export	98.0	0.0	1.0	0.0	0.0	1.0	1.4
Cooperatives							
Individual persons	75.3	13.5	0.0	0.0	2.4	8.6	12.9
Private enterprises	70.4	8.6	5.4	2.2	2.2	8.6	16.8
State enterprises	58.0	3.6	2.4	2.4	7.4	25.9	35.1
State trading companies	72.8	2.4	2.5	5.1	1.2	14.8	21.0
Local authorities	98.8	0.0	0.0	0.0	0.0	1.2	1.2
Export	90.1	1.2	1.2	0.0	1.2	6.2	8.0

other nonstate enterprises. Some 43.5 percent of the household enterprises sell at least partly to private enterprises and over 16 percent of them sell exclusively to such enterprises. Household enterprises can apparently be divided into two broad categories; one producing mainly for final consumers and another producing inputs for other nonstate enterprises. The virtual absence of forward linkages from household enterprises to the state sector is remarkable.

Household enterprises producing inputs for other enterprises often have a close and regular relationship with the customer. Some 16.8 percent of them have a subcontracting arrangement with another, in most cases private, enterprise (table 9).

The other types of enterprises have more varied forward linkages as groups, and links with the state sector are much more frequent than for household enterprises. Approximately one-third of the production of private enterprises and 45 percent of the production of partnership enterprises goes to the state sector. The state sector provides the sole customer for 15.2 percent of the private enterprises and 21.4 percent of the partnership enterprises. The state sector is by far the most important market for the cooperatives. Some 57.3 percent of their production is sold to the state sector and 41.9 percent of the cooperatives produce exclusively for the state sector. It is notable that the cooperatives as a whole depend much more on the state sector than on the private sector for their sales.

An important implication of these sales patterns is that while the development of household enterprises is closely linked to the development of the purchasing power of the population at large and, to a lesser extent, to the development of private enterprises, the fate of many, if not most, of the cooperative enterprises is closely linked to the development of the state sector. Private and partnership enterprises occupy an intermediate position. Although they sell more to the private than to the state sector, their dependence on the state sector as a market is far from negligible.

As might be expected, links between the urban nonstate enterprises and the state sector are stronger in the north than in the south. Approximately 40 percent of all sales of nonstate enterprises in Hanoi go to the state sector, compared to a third of the sales in Ho Chi Minh City. There is also a difference between the two cities in the nature of the links with the state sector. State trading companies account for about half of the sales to the state sector in Ho Chi Minh City, but for only a quarter of the sales in Hanoi.

Urban nonstate enterprises producing intermediary goods for sale to other enterprises often have a close relationship with, and one might add dependency on, the purchasing enterprise. Production on advance order is very common. Almost 39 percent of the private enterprises, 47.6 percent of the partnership, and 56.5 percent of the cooperatives produce "almost always" on advance order (table 9).

Subcontracting arrangements are rather frequent (table 9). For partnership and cooperative enterprises such arrangements are more common with state than with nonstate enterprises, while for private enterprises these proportions are equal. Apart from regular production on advance order, these arrangements often also involve assistance in the procurement of raw material

TABLE 9. Mode of Selling and Incidence of Subcontracting Among Urban Enterprises, in Percentage

	Hanoi	Haiphong	Ho Chi Minh	Total	Household	Private	Partnership	Coop
Produce on advance order?								
Never	25.2	11.6	33.3	26.6	45.1	24.1	23.8	10.6
Sometimes	27.0	25.6	31.9	29.3	29.4	33.6	23.8	30.6
Almost always	45.9	61.6	30.0	41.0	23.5	38.8	47.6	56.5
Subcontracting	21.8	10.4	28.0	22.8	16.8	15.0	26.2	36.0
Counterpart								
private enterprise	34.5	28.6	46.7	41.6	52.9	47.1	37.0	38.2
state enterprise	55.1	71.4	45.0	50.0	29.4	47.1	59.3	52.9
foreign company	3.4	0.0	3.3	3.1	0.0	0.0	0.0	8.8
other enterprise	6.9	0.0	6.9	5.2	17.6	0.0	3.7	0.0

TABLE 10. Place of Destination of Sales of Urban Enterprises by Form of Ownership, by Percentage Share of Total Sales of Main Product

	0	1–24	25–49	50–74	75–99	100	Mean
Total urban							
Same town	7.4	5.8	7.9	11.8	6.3	60.8	76.9
Other town	80.3	6.8	5.3	3.4	1.8	2.4	8.9
Rural areas	84.0	4.2	3.2	4.7	2.3	1.6	7.9
Elsewhere	93.2	1.3	0.8	1.6	1.4	2.1	4.6
Household enterprises							
Same town	2.3	5.6	3.3	7.8	3.4	78.4	87.7
Other town	88.6	6.8	2.2	1.1	1.1	0.0	3.5
Rural areas	86.4	2.2	2.3	3.3	4.5	1.1	7.5
Elsewhere	100.0	0.0	0.0	0.0	0.0	0.0	0.0
Private enterprises							
Same town	8.0	5.4	8.0	11.6	8.0	58.9	76.1
Other town	77.7	8.0	6.3	4.5	0.0	2.7	9.5
Rural areas	83.2	7.1	2.7	4.5	0.9	1.8	7.5
Elsewhere	90.2	2.7	0.9	0.9	1.8	3.6	6.5
Partnership enterprises							
Same town	7.0	3.0	9.0	17.0	9.0	55.0	76.2
Other town	78.0	6.0	6.0	5.0	2.0	3.0	10.8
Rural areas	84.0	5.0	3.0	6.0	1.0	1.0	7.0
Elsewhere	93.0	2.0	0.0	4.0	1.0	0.0	3.7
Cooperatives							
Same town	13.0	10.4	10.4	11.7	3.9	50.6	66.7
Other town	76.9	6.4	6.4	2.6	3.9	3.8	12.0
Rural areas	82.1	1.3	5.1	5.1	3.9	2.6	10.5
Elsewhere	89.7	0.0	1.3	1.3	2.6	5.1	8.6

and other inputs. In 9.2 percent of the cases the subcontracted enterprise also receives some assistance in raising capital and/or credits. Other forms of assistance are much less common, although in almost 5 percent of the cases some kind of technological transfer or assistance takes place.

As in the case of procurement of inputs (table 6), the poorly developed marketing and distribution channels result in geographic market fragmentation and highly localized sales patterns. More than three-quarters of the produce is sold locally, and 60.8 percent of the enterprises do not sell anything beyond the local market. Household enterprises, in particular, tend to confine their sales to the local market, and only few sell the bulk of their goods outside the local market. However, private and partnership enterprises, too, depend overwhelmingly on the local market (table 10). Some 57 percent of these enterprises sell exclusively locally and only 20 percent of them sell primarily elsewhere. Cooperative enterprises display a geographically some-what more dispersed sales pattern, with one-third of their sales outside the local market.

Almost half of the urban nonstate enterprises consider themselves subject to "severe" competition from other nonstate enterprises (table 11) and an additional 29.6 percent of them consider such competition to be "moderate." Severe competition from state enterprises is much less frequent (12.9 percent) and 60.1 percent of the enterprises consider the competition from state enter-prises to be insignificant.

However, the perception of competition varies considerably, both be-tween cities and between different types of ownership. Severe competition is much more frequently felt among enterprises in Ho Chi Minh City than in the two northern cities, not only from other nonstate enterprises, but also from state enterprises and, not least, from legal and illegal imports, which hardly figure at all as a source of competition in the north. These regional differences are hardly surprising in view of the much more developed market economy in the south. Another noteworthy feature is that household enterprises would seem to be more frequently exposed to competition from other nonstate enter-prises than private enterprises are. Some 52.3 percent of the household enter-prises perceive competition from other nonstate enterprises to be "severe," while only 16.2 percent consider it to be insignificant. The corresponding percentages for private enterprises are 35.9 and 34.4, respectively. Coopera-tives differ from the other types of nonstate enterprises in that they are rela-tively more exposed to competition from state enterprises. Only 48.4 percent of the cooperatives claim that competition from state enterprises is insignifi-cant, compared to approximately two-thirds of the other enterprises.

Tough market conditions are also reflected in frequent cases of accumula-tion of inventories of unsalable goods. Altogether 37.3 percent of the urban nonstate enterprises have accumulated stocks that are difficult to sell (table 12). This percentage is roughly the same across types of enterprises and for Hanoi and Ho Chi Minh City. It must be regarded as quite high, in particular considering that a large number of enterprises produce almost exclusively on advance order. Indeed, if one considers that 56.5 percent of the cooperatives produce "almost always" on advance order, the fact that 38.2 percent of them have accumulated stocks of unsalable goods is both surprising and somewhat alarming.

Excess supply on the market is the most frequently cited main reason behind the accumulation of unsalable goods. More noteworthy, however, is that 23.1 percent of the enterprises state that poor sales channels are the main reason behind the accumulated stocks of goods. This supports the conclusion that poorly developed distribution and marketing channels not only result in

TABLE 11. Percentage Urban Enterprises Experiencing "Severe" Competition

Source of Competition	Hanoi	Haiphong	Ho Chi Minh	Total	Household	Private	Partnership	Coop
Private enterprises	37.9	44.4	52.2	46.5	52.3	35.9	54.4	44.1
State enterprises	12.9	10.0	14.2	12.9	10.8	10.9	13.2	17.2
Legal imports	8.3	8.9	12.4	10.5	9.9	11.7	12.3	7.5
Illegal imports	1.5	1.1	8.0	4.7	5.4	2.3	6.1	5.4
Others	4.5	2.2	0.9	2.2	0.9	2.3	3.5	2.2

TABLE 12. Main Reasons That Urban Enterprises Have Accumulated Unsalable Inventories of Goods, in Percentages

Main Reason	Hanoi	Haiphong	Ho Chi Minh	Total	Household	Private	Partnership	Coop
	32.3	51.9	34.6	37.3	34.7	37.5	37.9	38.2
Market oversupplied	45.2	38.5	35.1	38.5	42.1	45.5	27.5	40.6
Low quality	4.8	7.7	8.1	7.1	2.6	4.5	7.5	15.6
Poor sales channels	21.4	17.9	27.0	23.1	36.8	22.7	22.5	9.4
Transport problems	4.8	0.0	2.7	2.6	2.6	0.0	2.5	3.1
Price too high	4.8	5.1	9.5	7.1	5.3	0.0	15.0	9.4
Other reasons	19.0	30.8	17.6	21.8	10.5	27.0	25.0	21.9

TABLE 13. Perception of Market Situation, Urban Enterprises, in Percentages

	Hanoi	Haiphong	Ho Chi Minh	Total	Household	Private	Partnership	Coop
Too many enterprises	48.8	45.5	55.4	51.6	60.4	41.8	51.8	53.3
Neither too few nor too many	37.8	34.1	30.6	34.2	28.8	40.2	30.4	37.8
Too few	10.2	14.8	10.4	11.2	6.3	14.8	15.2	7.8
No competitors	2.4	5.7	1.8	2.7	3.6	3.3	2.7	1.1

fragmented markets and localized sales patterns, but also affect overall sales performance and act as a constraint to the growth of individual enterprises. Significantly, household enterprises blame the accumulation of unsalable goods on poor sales channels much more frequently than private, partnership, or, for that matter, cooperative enterprises do (table 12). Small enterprises have fewer means to overcome the problems of poor distribution and marketing channels than large enterprises do. It also deserves to be noted that, except for cooperatives, low quality is, rightly or wrongly, seldom thought to be the main reason behind the accumulation of unsalable goods.

With the above in view, it comes as no surprise that most urban nonstate enterprises think that there are too many enterprises operating in their area of activity (table 13). This perception is most frequent among household enterprises (60.4 percent) and in Ho Chi Minh City (55.4 percent). Only 2.7 percent of the enterprises seem to enjoy a local monopoly position; this is rather more so in Haiphong than in the other cities.

An obvious response to competition is innovation, the introduction of new products and improvements in existing products. Altogether 37.4 percent of the enterprises established prior to 1989 have introduced new products in the past two years, and a similar percentage (38.0) say that they have made major improvements in existing products during this period. The introduction of new products has been somewhat more frequent in Ho Chi Minh City (41.8 percent) than in Hanoi (32.5 percent) or Haiphong (30.4 percent). Similarly, improvements in existing products have been more frequently resorted to in Ho Chi Minh City than in the two northern cities, although the differences are not very large. It is noteworthy that product development has taken place much more frequently in private, partnership, and cooperative enterprises than in household enterprises. Between 41.4 and 43.5 percent of the former types of enterprises have introduced a new product in the past two years, as against only 20.8 percent of the household enterprises. Similarly, 41.4 percent of the private and 44.8 percent of the partnership enterprises made major improvements in existing products, as against only 28.6 percent of the household enterprises.

Rural Enterprises

The structure of the revenues of the rural enterprises reflects their diverse nature. On average, some 73.4 percent of the total revenues of the rural enterprises covered by the survey were derived from sale of goods in 1990, while most of the rest, 20.4 percent, came from sale of services. Various other revenues made up the rest. Two-thirds of the enterprises had some revenue from sale of goods and 44.6 percent had revenues from sale of services. A handful of enterprises received income from capital in the form of interest, but the amounts gained in this manner were universally small.

Despite their smaller size, rural enterprises tend to have a larger number of customers and fewer close and durable forward linkages than their urban counterparts. Only 1 percent of the surveyed rural enterprises sell to a single customer, 20.6 percent have between two and ten customers, while the vast majority (78.4 percent) have more than ten customers. Similarly, production on advance order occurs much less frequently among rural than urban enterprises. More than half of the rural enterprises stated that they never produce on advance order, while a quarter almost always do. This should be compared with the urban nonstate enterprises, where only 26.6 percent never produce on advance order, while 41.0 percent do so as a rule.

Subcontracting arrangements, too, occur less frequently among rural enterprises than among urban. Some 14.3 percent of the manufacturing enterprises in rural areas, but only 1.0 percent of the agro-processing enterprises produce under a subcontracting arrangement with another enterprise. For all the enterprises included in the rural survey the figure is 5.9 percent. Only in Ha Son Binh does subcontracting play a major role. In this province some 26.7 percent of all the enterprises covered by the survey have a subcontracting arrangement. The enterprises in this province also have a relatively small number of customers. Two-thirds of them have ten customers or less.

Another notable difference is that subcontracting arrangements with state enterprises—which account for half of the cases in urban areas—virtually never occur in rural areas. This can probably be explained by the very localized patterns of subcontracting. About three-fourths of the subcontracting arrangements with private enterprises were with enterprises in the same district. This points to highly personal and geographically poorly developed channels between enterprises.

Individual persons are the main customers for rural enterprises. On average, 57.7 percent of the sales of the main product are to individuals. About three-fourths of the rural enterprises sell at least part of their main product to individuals, and for 43.8 percent this group accounts for all of the sales of the main product (table 14). Thus, individuals account for a significantly higher share of the sales for rural than for urban nonstate enterprises. One reason

TABLE 14. Destination of Sales by Category of Buyers and Type of Rural Enterprise, by Percentage Share of Total Sales of Main Product

Destination	0	1–24	25–49	50–74	75–99	100	Mean
Individual persons	25.6	9.6	6.1	9.6	5.3	43.8	57.7
Private enterprises	56.9	3.2	4.7	6.1	8.2	21.0	33.6
State enterprises	88.6	3.6	2.5	1.8	1.1	2.5	5.8
State trading companies	96.4	1.1	0.4	1.1	0.8	0.4	2.0
Local authorities	96.4	2.5	0.8	0.4	0.0	0.0	0.8
Export	98.9	0.4	0.0	0.0	0.4	0.4	0.8

may be the higher prevalence of repair shops in the rural sample of enterprises.

Private enterprises provide the second-most important group of customers, accounting for 33.6 percent of the sales, while state enterprises and agencies absorb only 7.8 percent of the sales. Less than 1 percent of the sales go to export, compared to 3.5 percent for the urban nonstate enterprises. Household and private enterprises present virtually identical sales patterns with regard to types of customers. The very low share of sales to state enterprises and agencies is noteworthy, and provides a stark contrast to the situation for the urban nonstate enterprises, where this category of buyers accounts for 35 percent of the sales. Clearly, the forward linkages to the state sector are much weaker for rural than for urban nonstate enterprises. Thus, while the demand for goods from urban nonstate enterprises on the whole depends rather heavily on the prosperity and development of state enterprises, this dependency is much weaker for the rural enterprises.

Rural enterprises primarily serve the local market. Approximately two-thirds of the sales are within the same district, 21 percent are within the same commune, and 12 percent are within the same village (table 15). The variations between the smaller household enterprises and the usually larger private enterprises in this regard are on the whole negligible. Agro-processing industries depend on nearby rural areas for three-quarters of their sales. For manufacturing enterprises the picture is somewhat more mixed. The strong reliance on the local market is in line with the large share of sales to households. However, this reliance implies that the development of most rural enterprises is highly dependent on local purchasing power. Furthermore, what may initially appear as a comfortable and secure home market may soon become a straitjacket to development as enterprises try to grow beyond the size of the local market. This market fragmentation is inefficient, as it hampers both specialization and competition.

Although a large share of the input of rural enterprises is procured from nearby towns, the forward linkages to these towns in the form of sales by rural enterprises are very weak. On average, only 5.8 percent of the sales go to nearby towns. By contrast, forward linkages with large cities are quite important. No less than 18.8 percent of the sales of the rural enterprises covered by the survey go to large cities. For the rural manufacturing and agro-processing enterprises, the percentages are higher: 22.6 and 20.2, respectively. Among both of these types of enterprises, approximately 18 percent sell exclusively to large cities. Scale seems to be of little consequence in this regard. Indeed, the percentage of sales to large cities is higher among the household than the private rural enterprises. As can be seen from table 15, enterprises that sell to large cities are quite distinct from those that serve the local market. While 16 percent sell exclusively to large cities, 78.7 percent do not sell at all to large cities. Thus, very few sell on both the local and the urban market. The enterprises that depend on large cities for their

TABLE 15. Destination of Sales, Rural Enterprises by Category, by Percentage Share of Total Sales of Main Product

	0	1–24	25–49	50–74	75–99	100	Mean
Total rural enterprises							
Same village	74.1	8.4	5.6	5.7	1.9	4.2	12.3
Same commune	62.7	6.5	8.8	9.1	3.1	9.9	21.3
Same district	55.5	4.2	5.4	11.4	3.8	19.8	32.1
Nearby towns	89.0	3.5	1.6	3.1	0.0	3.0	5.8
Large cities	78.7	1.2	1.2	1.2	1.9	16.0	18.8
Elsewhere	83.3	1.5	0.8	4.6	1.2	8.7	12.8
Household enterprises							
Same village	70.1	8.2	8.2	8.9	1.4	3.0	13.4
Same commune	61.2	3.7	14.1	10.9	0.7	9.0	20.9
Same district	51.5	5.2	7.4	12.7	0.7	22.4	33.9
Nearby towns	94.0	2.9	0.7	1.4	0.0	0.7	2.4
Large cities	76.1	1.4	2.2	2.2	2.2	17.9	21.2
Elsewhere	88.8	0.7	0.0	3.7	2.2	4.5	8.8
Private enterprises							
Same village	81.9	8.7	2.9	2.0	2.0	2.9	8.1
Same commune	63.8	9.6	3.8	5.8	6.8	10.5	21.7
Same district	57.1	1.0	3.9	10.5	8.6	19.0	33.8
Nearby towns	82.9	4.8	1.0	5.7	0.0	5.7	10.0
Large cities	81.9	0.0	2.0	0.0	2.0	14.3	16.6
Elsewhere	80.0	1.9	1.9	4.8	0.0	11.4	14.9
Manufacturing enterprises							
Same village	80.3	5.5	4.0	3.9	3.2	3.1	10.2
Same commune	70.9	6.2	8.7	6.3	3.2	4.7	14.4
Same district	54.3	4.0	7.1	12.5	4.7	17.3	31.5
Nearby towns	86.6	6.3	0.8	4.7	0.0	1.6	5.5
Large cities	73.2	1.6	2.4	1.6	3.2	18.1	22.6
Elsewhere	75.6	2.4	1.6	8.7	1.6	10.2	17.4
Agro-processing enterprises							
Same village	76.8	8.5	4.8	7.3	0.0	2.4	10.2
Same commune	53.7	6.1	4.9	10.9	4.9	19.5	32.1
Same district	61.0	1.2	3.6	10.8	3.6	23.2	32.0
Nearby towns	92.7	0.0	1.2	1.2	0.0	4.9	6.0
Large cities	79.3	0.0	0.0	1.2	1.2	18.3	20.2
Elsewhere	96.3	0.0	0.0	0.0	0.0	3.7	3.7

sales obviously already compete with urban enterprises for their market. From this point of view the rather high proportion of enterprises selling primarily to large cities may be seen as encouraging, as a sustained and dynamic development of the rural nonagricultural sectors can only be achieved if rural enterprises manage to also stay competitive with enterprises from other areas and cities. At the present, however, most rural enterprises competing on urban markets are clearly at a disadvantage. Compared to urban enterprises they suffer from a small capital base, low productivity and, often also, primitive production methods, as well as from location in an environment with poor infrastructure at some distance from the market.

TABLE 16. Destination of Sales, Rural Enterprises by Province, by Percentage Share of Total Sales of Main Product

	0	1–24	25–49	50–74	75–99	100	Mean
Ha Son Binh							
Same village	82.4	3.0	1.5	4.4	3.0	5.9	11.5
Same commune	77.9	1.5	4.4	4.4	1.5	10.3	15.5
Same district	73.5	3.0	3.0	8.8	1.5	10.3	17.7
Nearby towns	89.7	4.5	3.0	0.0	0.0	2.9	4.5
Large cities	57.4	3.0	1.5	1.5	0.0	36.8	38.6
Elsewhere	80.9	1.5	1.5	7.3	0.0	8.8	13.5
Quang Ninh							
Same village	46.5	18.7	18.6	16.3	0.0	0.0	20.2
Same commune	39.5	4.7	25.6	23.2	0.0	7.0	29.1
Same district	51.2	9.4	14.0	18.7	0.0	7.0	24.2
Nearby towns	97.7	0.0	0.0	0.0	0.0	2.3	2.3
Large cities	97.7	0.0	0.0	0.0	2.3	0.0	1.9
Elsewhere	72.1	2.3	0.0	7.0	2.3	16.3	23.0
Vinh Phu							
Same village	64.5	6.4	12.9	9.7	6.5	0.0	15.2
Same commune	51.6	9.7	9.6	19.4	3.2	6.5	24.0
Same district	35.5	9.7	9.7	16.2	0.0	29.0	43.2
Nearby towns	83.9	6.5	0.0	6.5	3.2	0.0	6.5
Large cities	90.3	0.0	6.4	0.0	3.2	0.0	4.7
Elsewhere	87.1	0.0	0.0	6.4	6.5	0.0	9.4
Long An							
Same village	80.0	5.4	0.0	1.8	0.0	12.7	14.1
Same commune	74.5	3.6	9.1	3.6	0.0	9.1	14.8
Same district	60.0	1.8	3.6	7.2	1.8	25.5	32.7
Nearby towns	87.3	0.0	1.8	7.2	0.0	3.6	8.4
Large cities	76.4	1.8	0.0	1.8	0.0	8.9	21.1
Elsewhere	80.0	1.8	0.0	1.8	0.0	7.3	17.5
Cuu Long							
Same village	83.1	10.8	3.0	1.5	1.5	0.0	5.2
Same commune	56.9	12.3	3.1	4.7	9.3	13.8	26.7
Same district	46.2	1.5	1.5	10.8	12.3	27.7	45.5
Nearby towns	87.7	6.1	1.5	1.5	0.0	3.1	5.5
Large cities	84.5	0.0	0.0	1.5	4.5	9.2	14.2
Elsewhere	93.8	1.5	1.5	1.5	0.0	1.5	3.1

There are very large differences in the geographical sales structure between the five provinces covered by the survey (table 16). The average proportion of sales on the local market, that is, within the district, varies from 44.7 percent in Ha Son Binh to 82.4 percent in Vinh Phu. Except for Ha Son Binh, the average proportion of sales going to the local market exceeds 60 percent in all of the provinces. The pattern of specialization of enterprises on production either for the local market or for more distant urban markets comes out very clearly in table 16. For example, in Cuu Long 13.7 percent of the enterprises sell at least 75 percent of their main product to large cities (Ho Chi Minh City), 84.5 percent do not sell at all to large cities, while a mere 1.5 percent sell between 1 and 74 percent of their main product to large cities. A rather similar picture is found in the other provinces. Thus, in Ha Son Binh 36.8 percent of the enterprises sell all of their main product to large cities (Hanoi), while 57.4 percent do not sell at all to large cities and 6 percent sell partly to large cities. The share of sales to large cities is inversely related to distance. Hence, enterprises in Long An, which is close to Ho Chi Minh City, sell more frequently to this city than enterprises in the more distant Cuu Long do, although enterprises in the latter province on average are much larger. Similarly, enterprises in Quang Ninh, the most remote of the five regions, virtually never sell to large cities. However, other factors, such as local traditions, historic ties, and so forth, clearly also matter. Thus, Ha Son Binh which is close to Hanoi, has a strong local tradition in certain types of handicraft and manufacturing and well-established ties with the market in Hanoi. In this province 42.6 percent of the enterprises sell at least part of their main product in Hanoi and 36.8 percent sell exclusively in Hanoi. Vinh Phu, too, is adjacent to Hanoi, but lacks a strong tradition in small-scale manufacturing, as well as entrenched commercial ties with Hanoi. In this province, less than 10 percent of the enterprises sell at least part of their main product in Hanoi and none of the enterprises covered by the survey in this province sell exclusively there.

The competitive environment in the rural areas is much weaker than in the large cities. Only 22.8 percent of the rural enterprises and 25.6 percent of the rural manufacturing enterprises covered by the survey think that they are subject to severe competition from other private enterprises (table 17), versus 46.5 percent of the urban nonstate enterprises. Some 38.4 percent of the rural enterprises think that competition from other private enterprises is "moderate," while 25.5 percent think it is "insignificant." For the rural manufacturing enterprises the corresponding percentages are 38.3 and 19.5. Competition from sources other than private enterprises appears on the whole to be negligible in rural areas. Thus, only 1.6 percent of the rural enterprises think that competition from state enterprises is "severe," while 90.1 percent stated that there was no competition at all from state enterprises. Neither do imports figure as a source of competition in rural areas. Only 2.2 percent of the enterprises think that this is a source of severe competition. By comparison, 12.9 percent of the nonstate enterprises in the urban areas experience "severe" competition from state enterprises and about 15 percent from imports.

The rather low level of competition in rural areas is even more starkly expressed in the fact that 47.9 percent of the enterprises in the rural survey state that they enjoy a local monopoly situation (table 18). In three of the provinces (Quang Ninh, Vinh Phu, and Long An) this figure is well above 50 percent. Agro-processing enterprises in particular benefit from a monopoly position (54.7 percent), but even among the rural manufacturing enterprises the percentage is as high as 35. This is in sharp contrast to the situation in the three cities covered by the survey, where only 2.7 percent (in Ho Chi Minh City 1.8 percent) of the enterprises state that they have no local competitors. Approximately one-third of the rural enterprises think that there are "too many" enterprises in their field in the area. This percentage varies sharply between the provinces, from 10.3 percent in Quang Ninh to 53.7 percent in Ha Son Binh. The high incidence of small-scale cottage and manufacturing enterprises producing rather similar types of goods for the same market no doubt explains the high figure for Ha Son Binh. However, the existence of pockets of fierce competition should not detract attention from the fact that because of the poorly developed, highly fragmented, and localized market structure in rural areas, most enterprises in most areas still enjoy a situation of little or no competition. Although this may be explained by the still very early stage of development of rural enterprises, it is hardly encouraging. The local monopoly positions imply that even rather inefficient enterprises can survive, provide few incentives for greater efficiency and product development, and put the individual customer at a disadvantage. Furthermore, this situation suggests that a good many rural enterprises may not face up to competition as markets are gradually opened up, and will have to shut down.

Only 21.8 percent of the rural enterprises had accumulated unsalable inventories of goods at the time of the survey (table 19). This is a considerably lower percentage than in the urban areas, where 37.3 percent of the enterprises had unsalable inventories of goods. This difference can be partly explained by the fact that relatively more rural than urban enterprises in the survey deal exclusively in services. Thus, among the rural manufacturing enterprises, 36.8 percent had unsalable inventories of goods, but for the agro-processing enterprises the figure was only 17.3 percent. The very large differences between the provinces can also partly, but far from entirely, be explained by differences in the industrial structure of the enterprises. Almost half of the enterprises in Ha Son Binh had accumulated unsalable inventories of stock, as against 10.5 percent in Quang Ninh and 15 to 20 percent in the other provinces (table 19). Manufacturing enterprises would seem to be particularly affected. These figures should be seen against the fact that enterprises in Ha Son Binh are generally more exposed to competitive markets than

TABLE 17. Percentage of Rural Enterprises Experiencing "Severe" Competition

Source of Competition	Ha Son Binh	Quang Ninh	Vinh Phu	Long An	Cuu Long	Total	House-hold	Private	Manu-facturing[a]	Agro-processing
Private enterprises	21.7	22.8	12.1	27.2	15.6	22.8	22.3	21.8	25.6	15.3
State enterprises	1.7	3.5	3.0	0.0	1.0	1.6	2.3	0.7	3.0	1.0
Legal imports	0.0	0.0	1.5	7.6	0.0	2.2	0.5	4.8	1.5	6.1
Illegal imports	0.0	0.0	0.0	1.1	0.0	0.3	0.5	0.7	0.0	0.0
Other sources	16.7	1.8	0.0	1.1	0.0	3.2	3.3	2.0	7.5	1.0

[a]excluding agro-processing.

TABLE 18. Perception of Market Situation Among Rural Enterprises

	Ha Son Binh	Quang Ninh	Vinh Phu	Long An	Cuu Long	Total	House-hold	Private	Manu-facturing[a]	Agro-processing
Too many enterprises	53.7	10.3	35.0	37.9	20.0	32.2	34.3	27.9	38.2	22.1
Neither too few nor too many	3.7	3.4	0.0	2.3	5.3	3.1	2.8	3.6	4.1	2.3
Too few	9.3	31.0	10.0	6.9	30.5	16.9	15.7	22.8	22.8	20.9
No competitors	33.3	55.2	55.0	52.9	44.2	47.9	47.2	50.0	35.0	54.7

[a]excluding agro-processing.

TABLE 19. Main Reasons That Rural Enterprises Have Accumulated Unsalable Inventories of Goods, in Percentages

Main Reason	Ha Son Binh	Quang Ninh	Vinh Phu	Long An	Cuu Long	Total	House-hold	Private	Manu-facturing[a]	Agro-processing
	48.3	10.5	19.7	17.4	17.7	21.8	20.9	22.4	36.8	17.3
Market over-supplied	24.0	50.0	41.7	33.3	17.6	28.2	23.1	34.5	26.7	23.1
Low quality	8.0	0.0	16.7	0.0	0.0	5.6	2.6	6.9	6.7	0.0
Poor sales channels	32.0	50.0	25.0	20.0	58.8	35.2	46.2	24.1	37.8	46.2
Transport problems	0.0	0.0	8.3	20.0	17.6	9.9	7.7	13.8	8.9	15.4
Price too high	0.0	0.0	0.0	6.7	5.9	2.8	2.6	3.4	2.2	0.0
Other reasons	36.0	0.0	8.3	20.0	0.0	18.3	17.9	17.2	17.8	15.4

[a]excluding agro-processing.

enterprises in the other four provinces. As noted, a large proportion of the enterprises in Ha Son Binh produce for the market in Hanoi, and there are relatively fewer enterprises producing under monopoly conditions for the local market than in the other provinces (table 16).

"Poor sales channels" is the most frequently quoted reason for accumulation of unsalable inventories (table 19). The second most quoted reason is "oversupply on the market." Problems of quality are apparently much less frequent in the eyes of the enterprise managers. It is interesting to note that poor sales channels are perceived to be by far the most frequent reason for unsalable inventories for household enterprises, while the larger private enterprises stated oversupply on the market to be the most frequent reason for unsalable stocks. The disadvantaged position of rural manufacturing enterprises in terms of access to markets is clearly suggested by the fact that unsalable inventories of goods are attributed to poor sales channels by 37.8 percent of the managers of manufacturing enterprises in rural areas, but by only 23.1 percent of their urban counterparts, who tend to blame oversupply on the market (38.5 percent). Among the agro-processing enterprises in rural areas, almost half blame unsalable inventories of goods on poor sales channels.

The lower level of competition is also reflected in a lower incidence of innovations and product change among enterprises in rural areas than in the urban areas. Some 15.3 percent of the rural enterprises established prior to 1988 introduced a new product/service in the past two years, while 21.4 percent made major improvements in existing products/services. This is considerably below the figures for the urban areas (37.4 and 38.0 percent respectively). Competition and requests from customers are the main motives behind changes and improvements in the product mix. Some 25 percent of the enterprises that introduced new products or made improvements in existing ones did so in response to increased competition. For 26.7 percent of these enterprises, requests from customers were the main reason, and for 20 percent difficulties in selling the existing goods were the main motive. The close link between competition and product development is also clear from the variation in the incidence of product development between the provinces. Thus, more than three times as many enterprises in Ha Son Binh introduced a new product or service in the past two years as in any of the other four provinces. The difference between Ha Son Binh and Vinh Phu in this regard was more than ten to one. Similarly, well over half of the enterprises in Ha Son Binh made major improvements in existing products in the past two years, versus 14 percent in Long An, 10 to 12 percent in Cuu Long and Vinh Phu, and a mere 4 percent in Quang Ninh. The links between exposure to competition and product development could hardly be clearer than this. In most cases the product change/improvement was said to have been successful.

Concluding Remarks

The study confirms the experience of other ex-socialist countries (not least in East Central Europe) that factor markets develop slowly and require considerable institutional underpinnings. Very few private enterprises—irrespective of size and location—have access to capital from formal financial institutions at the time of establishment. Loans against interest from nonformal sources do not make up for this deficiency, and instead entrepreneurs overwhelmingly depend on own capital and contributions from relatives, friends, and workers for the establishment of the enterprise. As going concerns, endogenous accumulation still remains the supreme source of capital for the nonstate enterprises. Bank loans are seldom obtained, and tend in any case to be on very short terms and in small amounts. Against this backdrop, it is not surprising to find that 54.9 percent of the urban and 65.7 percent of the rural nonstate enterprise managers state that shortage of capital is a main constraint to growth (table 20). At the national level, the failure to open up the formal financial markets to the private sector carries considerable costs. The survey results show that capital acts as a complement to labor rather than as a substitute, and that both labor productivity and wages are highly correlated with the capital/labor ratio of the enterprise. Furthermore, as the capital/labor ratio is 14 to 17 times higher in the small state enterprises than in the urban household and private enterprises—although wages tend to be higher in the latter than in the former category— the private sector is clearly a much more efficient vehicle for employment generation in a situation of capital scarcity than the state sector is.

As noted previously, the nonstate enterprises act in a pronounced cash

TABLE 20. Main Constraints to the Growth of the Enterprise, in Percentages

Constraint	Urban	Rural
Shortage of capital	54.9	65.7
Cannot afford to hire wage labor	3.8	2.2
Lack of skilled workers	3.6	2.2
Lack of technical know-how	7.3	4.5
Limited demand for current products	23.1	23.6
Too much competition	16.0	13.2
Lack of marketing/transport facilities	27.8	19.2
Lack of raw material	14.0	4.2
Lack of energy	17.1	7.2
Too much interference by local officials	0.7	3.7
Government policies uncertain	10.7	9.5

Note: The enterprise managers were requested to list a maximum of three main constraints.

economy, where credit is neither given nor received. Although the rudimentary financial sector provides a very ineffectual means for expediting payments, a more fundamental reason behind the predominance of cash transactions is no doubt the high transaction cost resulting from the lack of effective means of contract enforcement. Even though the legislative framework is gradually coming into place, the judiciary system remains very poorly equipped to uphold the rules of the game in the market place. As a consequence, credits and loans carry high risks.

The very poorly developed labor market is as yet not perceived as a major problem by the nonstate enterprises. However, this should provide little ground for complacency, as it is likely to reflect the small size and rather rudimentary production methods of most of the enterprises, rather than the efficiency of the highly informal and personal modes of labor recruitment. As enterprises grow and become more sophisticated, the need for efficient intermediation of labor will grow.

The absence of a land market and, more importantly, failure to incorporate the needs of small-scale enterprises in urban physical planning in the past present the urban enterprises with a problem. The situation is especially acute in Hanoi, where lack of adequate physical premises comes up as a frequent constraint, both to establishment and to expansion of existing enterprises. In rural areas the problem is rather one of poor infrastructure, in particular with regard to electrification.

The vast majority of the nonstate enterprises in both urban and rural areas do not sell beyond the local market. Lack of distribution and marketing channels, lack of information about consumer preferences and market potentials elsewhere, and, when such information is available, an absence of means of penetrating more distant markets are the main reasons behind the fragmented or cellular markets. This type of market structure breeds inefficiency and dwarfs the growth of otherwise competitive enterprises. It is inefficient because it hampers competition and provides a breeding ground for local monopolies. It is also a constraint to the growth of enterprises, as the size of the local market imposes a ceiling on the size of the enterprise. While it may be argued that the largeness of the markets in the main cities mitigates this problem, this is clearly not the situation in the rural areas and in small towns. It is significant that "limited demand for current products" and "lack of marketing and transport facilities" are much more frequently cited constraints to the growth of the enterprise than "too much competition" (table 20). The problems of poor marketing and distribution channels and marketing fragmentation are more severe in the north than in the south, and much more severe in rural than in urban areas. As noted, market fragmentation has resulted in two fundamentally different types of enterprises in rural areas; those serving the local market and those producing for the market in large cities. The former often enjoy monopoly positions, yet they are small and have limited growth potentials under present conditions. The latter face no absolute demand constraints, but are often subject to intense competition.

Fragmented and poorly functioning markets can be regarded as teething troubles in the nascent markets economy, which may be expected to abate with time. However, the pattern of the evolution of markets and market institutions is likely to have a bearing on the economic structure for a long time to come. The Chinese experience provides a good illustration of this point. The launching of comprehensive market-oriented reforms in rural areas at a time when the urban economy remained largely unreformed gave the development of rural enterprises a head start, and the initially fragmented markets provided for an almost classic case of infant industry development.[10] By the time markets began to open up, the rural industrial sector was firmly in place. Other fortuitous factors, such as an administrative system that provided a conducive institutional setting for the development of non-agricultural enterprises, a captive labor force, and a sharp discrete increase in agricultural incomes were also important. By contrast, the almost simultaneous reforms across the board in Vietnam imply that rural nonstate enterprises in Vietnam start from a much more disadvantaged position. There is already a vigorous and quite well developed private sector in the urban areas. The initial development of enterprises does not take place in a shortage economy with guaranteed and seemingly insatiable markets, but under conditions of stiff competition. As and if (which seems to be the case) factor markets, marketing channels, and market institutions develop in the large cities first and only gradually spread down the hierarchy of settlements, there is a severe risk that the development of non-agricultural enterprises in rural areas will be dwarfed in its cradle with familiar patterns of large-scale urban-bound migration, and an increasing rural-urban development gap will result.

---

10. Per Ronnås, "Economic Diversification and Growth in Rural China: The Anatomy of a Socialist Success Story," *Journal of Communist Studies* 9, no. 3 (September 1993).

CHAPTER 7

Reforming China's State-Owned Firms

John McMillan and Barry Naughton

China's economic reforms have been spectacularly succesful. Annual growth rates averaged nearly 10 percent per capita between 1982 and 1988, among the fastest growth rates in the world. Growth slowed sharply in 1988–90 with the political crisis around Tiananmen, but picked up to more than 10 percent in 1992–93.

China's state-owned firms are notoriously inefficient; press reports commonly describe them as "dinosaurs" and "terminally ill." But empirical studies show they are significantly less inefficient than they used to be. State firms contributed to China's economic growth by increasing their productivity. Before the reforms, industrial productivity had been almost stagnant: total factor productivity grew at an annual rate of only 0.4 percent between 1957 and 1978 (Chen et al. 1988). This changed after the reforms began: for the state firms in our sample, between 1980 and 1989 total factor productivity rose at an average annual rate of 4.5 percent.[1]

These productivity improvements are due in part to changes in the way the industrial bureaus controlled the state-owned firms, and to changes in the firms' internal organization, as will be described in this chapter. But the productivity gains are also due in part to another change that occurred early in China's reforms. According to the model of Gates, Milgrom, and Roberts (in this volume), an increase in competition is complementary with strengthening managerial incentives, in the sense that the effects of the managerial incentives will be greater if the firm's environment is competitive than if it is not. China's state-owned firms were faced with competition from nonstate firms, competition that had not existed before 1980.

---

1. Production-function estimates from other data sets show similar increases in state firms' productivity. Chen et al. (1988) estimated that between 1978 and 1985 industrial productivity grew at an annual rate of 4.8 percent. Gordon and Li 1989 estimated, using a sample of 400 state enterprises, that productivity rose by 4.6 percent annually over 1983–87. Dollar 1990 estimated, using a sample of 20 state enterprises, that productivity rose by 4.7 percent annually over 1978–82. Woo, Hai, and Jin 1993, however, find a contrary result: there seems to have been little productivity growth in the state firms in their sample from 1984–88.

167

China's most dynamic sector, far more dynamic than the state sector that is the subject of this chapter, has been non-state-owned industrial firms. These firms, mostly located in rural areas, have a range of formal organizational structures, but they are primarily profit-seeking firms (Whiting, in this volume; Nee, in this volume). The nonstate sector has grown since 1978 at an annual rate of 17.6 percent, such that in 1990 it accounted for a striking 45 percent of total industrial output. Some of these nonstate firms produce the same outputs as state firms, and thus impose competitive pressure on the state firms. According to Gates, Milgrom, and Roberts (in this volume), therefore, the reform that permitted nonstate industrial firms to operate intensified the effects of the reforms that were specifically directed at the state-owned firms.

The data we use to study the effects of reforms on China's state-owned enterprises come from surveys conducted by the Institute of Economics, Chinese Academy of Social Science (CASS), in consultation with us as well as with economists from the University of Michigan and Oxford University. Annual data for 1980–89 for 769 enterprises in four provinces (Sichuan, Jiangsu, Jilin, and Shanxi) give details of the firms' internal incentives, the firms' cost and revenue accounts, and the nature of the relationship between the firms and the state. The questionnaires were sent out by the provincial System Reform Commissions (which are responsible for assessing and implementing reform measures) to 800 enterprises, and 769 valid questionnaires were returned. The System Reform Commission does not directly supervise enterprise activity, but it is an official government body with which the enterprise has regular interactions, which may account for the high response rate. The questionnaire had two parts. The first part, directed specifically to the factory manager, asked 70 questions, mostly qualitative, relating to the firm's incentive system and its relation to governmental supervisors. The second part, designed to be answered by the enterprise accountant, asked 321 quantitative questions covering almost every aspect of enterprise activity during the years 1980 through 1989.

All the firms sampled are state-owned, and large firms are overrepresented in comparison to state-owned firms in general. The sample therefore covers the core of the traditional state-run economy, the set of enterprises for which it is generally held that progress in reforms has been modest, compared to the small-scale, nonstate sector. The sample appears reasonably representative of state-run industry as a whole in dimensions other than enterprise size. Output per employee in 1980, the first year of the sample, was 11,329 yuan, 6 percent below the national average; by 1989, output per employee had increased to 18, 891 yuan (in constant 1980 prices), and was now 3 percent above the national average. Between 1980 and 1989, output per employee increased 67 percent in the CASS sample, slightly better than the 52 percent increase recorded for state-run industry as a whole.[2]

The Dual-Price System

China partially reformed the prices facing state-owned enterprises, by introducing a dual-track system. China did not undertake comprehensive price reform. But gradual marketization accompanied by sustained entry of new producers caused a realignment of prices. Before the reforms, state-owned enterprises were required to sell all their output to the state at state-fixed prices. Under the reforms, these firms have been allowed to sell some of their output on free markets: in 1989, according to the CASS survey, on average 38 percent of a state-owned firm's outputs were directly sold on markets, and for some state firms market sales were 100 percent of output. Similarly, an increasingly large fraction of state firms' inputs have been purchased on free markets, rather than being allocated by the state: in 1989, on average, 56 percent of state-owned firms' inputs were procured through market purchases, and for some state firms, 100 percent of inputs were market-procured. There is a dual price system, with the market price usually being substantially above the official price. From the viewpoint of economic incentives, the key point is that, at the margin, decisions are made in the face of market prices. The fact that the price received from the state is less than the price received from the market merely means that the firm is paying a lump-sum tax. For a firm's decisions on how much to produce, what inputs to use, and what kind of investment to undertake, the state-imposed output quota is irrelevant, as long as that quota is smaller than the total output. What matters for such decisions is the price that will be received for any extra output, which is the free-market price (Byrd 1987; McMillan and Naughton 1993).

Evidence that most industries' prices have been effectively reformed comes from data on profit rates. With the erratic pricing of the centrally planned economy, prices bear little relation to costs. In 1980, profit rates in industry ranged from 7 percent to 98 percent. By 1989, prices had become more uniformly related to costs: in most industries profit rates were between 8 percent and 23 percent (Naughton 1995). Further evidence on China's progressive marketization comes from calculation of marginal products. In a textbook-perfect market economy, the free operation of the price system

---

2. What follows draws on, and summarizes, our work on the CASS data set with Theodore Groves and Yongmiao Hong (Groves et al. 1993, 1994, 1995) and with Gang Lin (McMillan, Naughton, and Lin 1993), as well as work reported in McMillan and Naughton 1992 and 1993.

would ensure that the marginal product of labor became the same in all firms; and similarly for the marginal product of capital. Wide variations among marginal products indicate, on the other hand, that the economy is using its valuable resources of labor and capital inefficiently. Recent research finds that the variation in marginal products of both capital and labor has shrunk as China's reforms have progressed (Jefferson and Xu 1991; Jefferson, Rawski, and Zheng, 1992).

Dual pricing forced state-owned firms to compete, both with other state-owned firms and with nonstate firms. In order to sell on free markets, state-owned firms had to please their customers; thus they were forced to produce at a higher quality than when they had the government as a guaranteed buyer.

Contracts with the State and Internal Incentives

Beginning in 1978 and continuing throughout the 1980s, China reformed the contracts between state-owned industrial firms and the state. Enterprises that had been largely controlled by the state were given some market or market-like incentives (though by the end of the decade, 12 years into the reforms, they were still a long way from looking like capitalist firms). State-owned enterprises were allowed to keep some fraction of their profits, where before all profits had been remitted to the state; enterprises began to sell some of their output and buy some of their input in free markets, rather than selling and procuring everything at state-controlled prices; managers were given monetary rewards explicitly based on their firm's performance; workers began to be paid bonuses, and some workers were hired on temporary or fixed-term contracts; and the right to decide what to produce, how much to produce, and how to produce it was shifted from the state to the enterprise.

Different firms had vastly different experiences with reform policies. The date at which a firm received the right to make its own output decisions varied throughout the decade: some had output autonomy in 1980, some still did not have it in 1989. Marginal profit retention rates grew through the decade, from a mean of 24 percent in 1980 to a mean of 63 percent in 1989. Again, however, individual firms' experiences were highly diverse. Some firms in 1980 were still required to deliver most of their profits to the government. Others had a contract that required them to deliver a fixed amount of profit to the government and retain all profits beyond that. Such a contract, offering 100 percent marginal incentives—that is, giving the firm full rights to residual earnings—has effects that are very close to those of ownership (except that these rights are attenuated in time: the contract lasts for three to five years).

This commercialization has resulted in improved productivity. Under the system of enterprise contracting, state firms are required to deliver a certain fixed amount of profit to the government, and are allowed to retain a substantial fraction of any profits they generate beyond this fixed amount.The data show that, when firms' autonomy increased (when either the firm's profit-retention rate was increased, or the responsibility for deciding output levels was shifted down from the state to the firm), managers responded by strengthening the discipline imposed on workers: they increased the proportion of the workers' income paid in the form of bonuses and they increased the fraction of workers whom, being on fixed-term contracts, it was, in principle, possible to fire. The new incentives were effective: productivity increased significantly following the strengthening of worker incentives. The increase in autonomy raised workers' (but not managers') incomes and investment in the enterprise. It raised total profits, but tended not to raise remittances to the state or to lower subsidies from the state (Groves et al. 1994).

Managers of state-owned firms are now paid according to their firms' performance: the data show a clear link between a top manager's pay, on the one hand, and his firm's sales and profits, on the other hand. In addition to these direct monetary incentives, managers can be demoted for subpar performance by their firms and promoted for unusually good performance. The data show that the careers of the managers of China's state-owned firms are in fact affected by how well or badly their firms do, so the prospect of promotion or demotion does work as an incentive (Groves et al. 1995).

Manager Auctions

One of the most intriguing of the reforms imposed on China's state firms was that of managerial jobs being put up for auction. This reform was experimental and not widely used—the auctions occurred in about one-seventh of the firms in the CASS sample—and thus it was not important in the overall scheme of reforms. But it is a good example of an imaginative reform that has some useful effects, and it warrants some investigation.

In the manager auctions, potential managers bid for the right to be the firm's top manager for a specified period of time—typically three to five years. Each bid consists of a promise of the amount of profits the firm will deliver to the government in each year of the contract. Bids are made meaningful by requiring the successful bidder to post a security deposit—on average about 50 percent of the manager's annual income—to be forfeited in whole or part if the promised profits are not forthcoming. The winning bidder is chosen not only by how much profit he offers, but also by an evaluation of his competence, his plans for the firm, and so on. The new manager receives a contract that makes his pay vary with the firm's financial performance. The bidders often include the firm's current top manager, lower-level employees of the firm, officials from the ministry that regulates the firm, and outsiders who believe they can do a better job than the incumbent. Before the bidding, the firm's accounts are opened to anyone who might decide to bid. The winner is often the previous manager: in the CASS survey the incumbent won 55 percent of the auctions. It is not surprising that the incumbent has an advantage in the bidding and often wins; what is noteworthy is that this is not an overwhelming advantage, and the incumbent loses almost half of the time. Thus, the auctions produce considerable turnover of management.

In a market economy, long-term observation of performance in mid-level managerial positions provides information about a potential manager's abilities. In the transition economy, observed performance is suspect, as it was not attained in a genuine market setting. Anecdotal evidence has it that the bidding process has served to identify competent managers who were previously unknown to the industrial bureau; thus the auctions have succeeded in putting better people into management jobs.

The auctions also reveal information about the firm's potentialities. Postauction productivity, according to the same study (Groves et al. 1995), significantly exceeds preauction productivity. And the increase is larger when the incumbent manager wins the auction than when someone else wins. This may seem paradoxical, but it reflects the information-revealing role of the auctions. Suppose a firm's performance is only partly under the control of the manager; a firm may simply inherently be either a good or a poor performer. The incumbent manager of a firm that is performing poorly, having inside information, knows how much scope there is for improving its performance. Outside bidders cannot infer from the information available to them whether the firm's poor performance is the result of its inherently low productivity or of slack management. Outside bidders therefore submit moderately high bids, to allow for the possibility that the firm may have either a high or a low potential. The incumbent manager will bid high if the firm has a good potential and low if it has a poor potential. Thus, incumbent managers tend to win the bidding for those firms that have good potential but have been underperforming; outside bidders tend to win those firms that have poor potential. Given that the postauction managerial incentives are stronger than preauction managerial incentives, all firms do better after the auction. But the biggest improvements will come in the firms with the highest potential, and these tend to be won by incumbent managers. Hence, we observe that productivity increases most in those firms that incumbent managers win. The auction, therefore, reveals information about the firm's inherent productivity. The Chinese manager auctions promoted more effective regulation by revealing information about the inherent productivity of the firm and by identifying hitherto unrecognized competent managers.

The Political Economy of Enterprise Reform

By introducing some elementary incentives that fall short of privatization, China's reformers have elicited significant productivity improvements from the state-owned firms. As Jeffrey Sachs has said: "The Asian experience does suggest . . . that successful development might be helped as much by raising the quality of public sector management as by privatizing public enterprises or by liberalizing markets" (Sachs 1987, 294).

What induced China's bureacrats to regulate for firm efficiency? The increased competition squeezed state-owned firms' profits, and this meant that state firms' remittances to the government fell. State firms were the main source of government revenue. To slow the drop in government revenue, the state was impelled in the mid- to late 1980s to spur the state firms to become more profitable. Firms had been given some profit incentives at the beginning of the 1980s. But during the late 1980s, driven by their need for revenue, state officials increasingly made profit remittances the primary obligation of firms. Financial discipline was tightened, so that firms faced not only greater financial risk, but also steeper compensation schedules and stronger incentives. The need for increased financial discipline was created by the increased product-market discipline that resulted from entry and competition; financial discipline then reinforced the effects of the product-market discipline.

REFERENCES

Byrd, William A. 1987. "The Impact of the Two-Tier Plan/Market System in Chinese Industry." *Journal of Comparative Economics* 11:295–308.
Chen, Kuan; Jefferson, Gary; Rawski, Thomas; Wang, Hongchang; and Zheng, Yuxin. 1988. "Productivity Change in Chinese Industry: 1953–1985." *Journal of Comparative Economics* 12:570–91.
Dollar, David. 1990. "Economic Reform and Allocative Efficiency in China's State-Owned Industry." *Economic Development and Cultural Change* 34:89–105.
Gordon, Roger, and Li, Wei. 1990. "The Change in Productivity of Chinese State Enterprises, 1983–1988: Preliminary Results." University of Michigan, Mimeographed.
Groves, Theodore; Hong, Yongmiao; McMillan, John; and Naughton, Barry. 1993. "Productivity Growth in China's State-Run Industry." University of California, San Diego, Mimeographed.
Groves, Theodore; Hong, Yongmiao; McMillan, John; and Naughton, Barry. 1994. "Autonomy and Incentives in Chinese State Enterprises." *Quarterly Journal of Economics* 109, no. 1:183–209.
Groves, Theodore; Hong, Yongmiao; McMillan, John; and Naughton, Barry. 1995.

"China's Managerial Labor Market." *Journal of Political Economy* 103, no. 4:873–92.

Jefferson, Gary H.; Chen, Kang; and Singh, Inderjit. 1992. "Lessons from China's Economic Reform." *Journal of Comparative Economics* 16, no. 2:201–25.

Jefferson, Gary H.; Rawski, Thomas; and Zheng, Yuxin. 1992. "Growth, Efficiency and Convergence in China's State and Collective Industry." *Economic Development and Cultural Change,* 40, no. 2:239–66.

Jefferson, Gary H., and Xu, Wenyi. 1991. "The Impact of Reform on Socialist Enterprises in Transition: Structure, Conduct, and Performance in Chinese Industry." *Journal of Comparative Economics* 15:45–64.

McMillan, John, and Naughton, Barry. 1992. "How to Reform a Planned Economy: Lessons from China." *Oxford Review of Economic Policy* 8:130–43.

McMillan, John, and Naughton, Barry. 1993. "Evaluating the Dual-Track System." Unpublished, University of California, San Diego.

McMillan, John; Naughton, Barry; and Lin, Gang. 1993. "Contracts between Firm and State." Unpublished, University of California, San Diego.

Naughton, Barry. 1995. *Growing out of the Plan: Chinese Economic Reform, 1978–93.* Cambridge: Cambridge University Press.

Sachs, Jeffrey. 1987. "Trade and Exchange Rate Policies in Growth Oriented Adjustment Programmes." In V. Corbo, M. Goldstein, and M. Khan, eds., *Growth Oriented Adjustment Programmes.* Washington DC: World Bank.

Woo, Wing Tye; Hai, Wen; and Jin, Yibiao. 1994. "How Successful Has Chinese Enterprise Reform Been?" *Journal of Comparative Economics* 18, no. 3:410–38.

CHAPTER 8

Institutional Innovations and the Role of Local Government in Transition Economies: The Case of Guangdong Province of China

Yingyi Qian and Joseph Stiglitz

China's economic reforms since 1979 have led to rapid economic growth: the average growth rate of GNP was about 9 percent for the fifteen years between 1979 and 1993, and reached 12.8 percent in 1992 and 13.4 percent in 1993.[1] It appears that China will soon become the next East Asian country to enter the stage of economic takeoff, following the successful experience of Japan, Singapore, Hong Kong, Taiwan, South Korea, Thailand, Malaysia, and Indonesia.

This chapter contains main findings from the case study of the Pearl River Delta in Guangdong Province near Hong Kong and Macao, one of the fastest growing regions in China.[2] At the focus are the five municipalities in the area: Shenzhen, Guangzhou, Shunde, Zhongshan, and Zhuhai. Two of them, Shenzhen and Zhuhai, were designated as Special Economic Zones (SEZs) by the central government in 1980, and the remaining three are known as "coastal economically open cities," which enjoy several forms of preferential treatment and have gained considerable autonomy from the central government. Shunde and Zhongshan are also known as two of the "Four Little Tigers" within Guangdong (the other two are Dongguan and Nanhai), and Guangzhou is the capital city of the province.

This chapter is about institutional innovations and the role of local government in Guangdong in its economic development and transition toward a

This chapter is based on our work for the World Bank project "The East Asian Miracle: Economic Growth and Public Policy." The authors would like to thank John McMillan, Barry Naughton, and Jan Svejnar for comments. Views expressed here are not necessarily those of the World Bank or the Chinese government.

1. Data source: various issues of *Statistical Yearbook of China* and *Statistical Yearbook of Guangdong.* (Beijing: State Statistical Bureau.)

2. Evidence presented here is drawn from interviews with local government officials and enterprise managers in Guangdong between December 11 and December 18, 1992.

market economy. Because we focus only on the Pearl River Delta and on the time period of 1992, the observations presented here should not be generalized, without qualification, to the rest of China, although the national tendency is clearly in the same direction.

The chapter is organized as follows. First we provide an overview of the area in which the case study was conducted. Then we discuss the changing role of local government in the process of development and reform. Next we address ownership issues of enterprise, discuss the development of entrepreneurship and learning to use the market in the transition process, and examine innovations in financial institutions and markets. Finally we discuss the new approaches to local public finance.

An Overview of Guangdong Province and the Pearl River Delta

Guangdong Province is one of the fastest growing provinces in China. With a population of 64 million, more than South Korea and Taiwan combined, the average annual growth rate of GDP in Guangdong Province was 12.6 percent between 1979 and 1991, and 19.5 percent in 1992. Guangdong already ranked number one in terms of GDP in 1990 among all thirty provinces, moving up from its number four position in 1985. Export in Guangdong grew even faster, at an annual rate of 19.3 percent between 1979 and 1991. Guangdong accounted for about 20 percent of total national export in 1991, and this figure was estimated to jump to about 25 percent in 1992.

Most of the growth in Guangdong Province is concentrated in the Pearl River Delta. Adjacent to Hong Kong and Macao and with a population of 20 million, the Pearl River Delta has about one-third of the population of Guangdong Province and is about the size of Taiwan. The Pearl River Delta accounts for about two-thirds of the GDP and about three-quarters of the exports of Guangdong. The growth rate in the area is also much higher than that of other regions in the province.[3]

The economic development goal for Guangdong Province is to catch up to the "Four Little Dragons" of East Asia (mainly South Korea and Taiwan) in twenty years in terms of per capita GDP in purchasing power parity. A twenty-year provincial development plan is under preparation. According to their calculations, assuming the Taiwanese economy grows at an average annual rate of 5.7 percent for the next twenty years, in order to catch up with Taiwan,

---

3. In this region there are no visible, clustered, very poor people and the lower tail of the distribution appears to be small. Most of the very poor are from outside the region and live in temporary shelters; they are temporary construction workers and vegetable growers. The lack of the very poor is, perhaps, due to the socialist legacy of egalitarianism.

Guangdong needs to grow at an annual rate of 12.9 percent if the exchange rate USD1 = RMB2.8 is used (the official rate is USD1 = RMB5.7; USD = U.S. dollars). This is not entirely impossible, given Guangdong's past record of an annual growth rate of 12.6 percent between 1979 and 1991. To achieve this goal, the Pearl River Delta must grow even faster, another expectation that may not be entirely unreasonable. For example, Shunde municipality, with a population of about 930,000, plans to grow at an annual rate of 15–16 percent for the next twenty years. The goal set by Zhongshan Municipality, with a population of 1.2 million, is to catch up to the Four Little Dragons within 15 years, five years earlier than the province as a whole.

The Role of Local Government

Consensus on the Role of Government in the Market

In other East Asian economies, the main resource allocation mechanism has been a market based on private property. The question of the role of government is a question of how the government should selectively intervene to correct market failures or to facilitate the creation or functioning of market institutions. In China, economic development in the past fifteen years has been situated in an environment of transition from a centrally planned economy to a market economy. The question of the role of government is discussed here in a different way. The focus is on how to reduce the role of the government in China. From different perspectives and approaches, China and other East Asian countries are asking what the appropriate balance should be between government and the market. There seems to be a consensus that either extreme view is inappropriate.

One of the major purposes of reforms in China is to shift from central planning to the market as a means of resource allocation. Guangdong is in the vanguard in this respect: the traditional type of planning has faded away very quickly in the past few years. For example, 95 percent of retail prices in the provinces are liberalized, and among all agricultural products, the provincial government regulates only the prices of silk and tobacco. Investment used to be tightly controlled by the government, but not anymore: in 1991, less than 4 percent of investment in Guangdong was made within the central government budget and less than 7 percent within the provincial budget.

A constant theme that came up during our discussions with government officials was "transforming the role and functioning of the government," meaning the government should no longer play the role of planner, as in the past, but rather should be a "regulator" of the market. Mainly because of the legacy of central planning, even lower level government officials show considerable consciousness of the role of government in economic development.

This should not be a surprise, because those same officials have struggled for decades, searching for the right role and function for the government in the economy. The failures of the past provide lessons for the future.

What is interesting is the general consensus on the role of the government at different levels and different locations, and the similarity between these views and the views of the governments in other East Asian countries, where conditions are quite different. We raised the same question on the role of government to officials from different municipalities, and they gave similar, but slightly different answers. In one municipality, the role of government was summarized as follows: to create and enforce market institutions; to maintain macroeconomic stability; to implement industrial policies; and to ensure equality and social justice. In another, we were told that the role of government is to create conditions for market competition (e.g., regulation) and to correct market failures (e.g., to provide public goods and ensure against environmental degradation).

Multilayers of Government:
Vertical and Horizontal Interactions

The organizational structure of China's economy as well as its political system can be characterized as one of "M-form" hierarchy, that is, a multilayer, multiregional organization with multilayer structure along vertical lines and multiregional structure along horizontal lines (Qian and Xu 1993). Along the vertical lines, there are six layers: central, provincial, prefecture, county, township, and village.[4] Government at each level has considerable authority in formulating economic policies, and in particular, it controls enterprises.

The first question regarding the role of government in China is which level of government one refers to. It is true that in the fast-growing area of the southern part of China, especially in Guangdong, the role of the *central* government is diminishing. However, it would be wrong to conclude, as some people seem to have, that the diminishing role of government is the reason for Guangdong's success. We have contacted local government officials at the provincial, municipal, county, and township levels. Two things have changed since the reforms: the local government is more important than the central government; and it tends to intervene by using indirect rather than direct methods, which is an important part of the changing function of the government.

Two further features are worth mentioning. The first is the shared governance structure along vertical lines. In terms of industrial policy, for example,

---

4. A municipality can be province-level, prefecture-level, or country-level. Unlike in the United States, a municipality in China is usually a larger unit than a county.

the central government sets national policy and the provincial government sets provincial policy, and so on. The dialogue and communication between different levels of government remains strong, despite autonomy gained at the local level. This is partly due to the fact that the party and governmental hierarchies have not collapsed. Guangdong Province is viewed as an extreme example of a strong local government that often ignores central government's instructions. Even there, we found both vertical and horizontal communication between the governments. For example, when we were in Zhuhai, the deputy director of the State System Reform Commission, accompanied by the director of Guangdong Provincial System Reform Commission, whom we met in Guangzhou a few days before, visited the area for a general inspection concerning financial sector development.

The second feature is the horizontal communication and competition among regions. Competition among the two Special Economic Zones (Shenzhen and Zhuhai) and other municipalities is intense. Each municipality government is well informed about the development strategy of the others and feels the pressure thus generated. For example, in Shenzhen, the most publicized Special Economic Zone in China, government officials openly admitted that the region enjoyed favorable conditions not so much from, say, preferential tax treatment as from the reduction in bureaucratic paperwork and the facilitation of the requisite approvals. Now other municipalities not in the special economic zones have followed suit, so Shenzhen no longer has these advantages, but they must work even harder to create a better environment to attract more investment.

Partly due to this decentralized structure of government, many government officials, such as mayors and directors of functioning departments, have turned out to be quite entrepreneurial. Competition between regions constantly calls for innovative ideas from lower-level government to relax constraints imposed by the upper-level government. In the old planning system, bargaining with the superior official was almost the only way for one region to get ahead of another. Now, with much more freedom, entrepreneurship in the government is a critical factor in the competition between regions.

Functioning of the Government

Many important decisions are made by the "coordinating meeting of the governor" at the provincial level or "coordinating meeting of the mayor" at the municipality level, which include executive officials in different government departments who coordinate activities. Most policies are still determined by the regional (province, municipality, or county) Standing Committee of the Communist Party, which usually has seven to ten members. In a typical meeting, many people from different branches of government, like the finance

bureau, banks, the industrial bureaus, and even enterprise managers, participate.

Unlike the Communist Party in Eastern Europe and the former Soviet
Union, the Chinese Communist Party has a tradition of being able to adapt to
changing environments. In the past, cadres have been screened and trained to
adapt to political movements, like the Great Leap Forward and Cultural
Revolution. Now they adapt quickly to another environment: fast growth in
the market economy. This explains why in Eastern Europe and Russia, party
cadres and bureaucrats were always viewed as a conservative force that re-
sisted reforms, but in China, with the exception of a few departments like
propaganda, most government and party officials either became entrepreneurs
themselves, or showed strong entrepreneurship in their posts as governors,
mayors, or country sheriffs.

There is often duplication of functions between the party and the government. In most enterprises, one of them has primary responsibility, while the
other serves as a check. Who has the primary responsibility is determined
more by personality and connection than by rules.

Many government activities have been transferred from bureaus to newly
established companies whose managers were former government officials
(and some of them still are). For example, the development project of reclaimed farm land from the sea in Zhongshan was the job of the Zhongshan
Municipal Agricultural Commission in the past. A few years ago, a new
company, owned by the municipal government, was formed to carry out this
priority project. Now this company runs many businesses in addition to the
project of reclaimed farm land, such as retailing and real estate, as well as
industry. The government provided the company with incentives for other
activities as well and helped the firm in a variety of ways, such as providing
land, facilitating the acquiring of licenses, and providing subsidies through
tax instruments. During the transition, there remains an ambiguity between
the government and business.

Development Strategies and Industrial Policies

Each level of government determines industrial priorities according to its own
economic conditions and under the general guidelines of the higher level of
government. In general, technology, infrastructure, and energy are high priority industries in this area. In terms of implementation, each level of government may reduce a certain amount of taxes. For example, if a particular high-
tech project receives tax benefits from the central government, another high-
tech project may receive tax benefits from the provincial government.

Another instrument is the allocation of credit. In this area, there is
generally no compulsory command issued by the government to banks. The

banks are aware of government priorities, and when credit is rationed consideration is first given to priority industries, if they meet the profitability tests. In some cases, government may exchange favors for particular projects, for example, to allow more import or export quotas. However, the role of explicit subsidies from the government to priority industries is limited. This seems to be consistent with the practice of other East Asian countries. There are some exceptions when there is an effect such as a direct subsidy: the project of reclaimed farm land from the sea in Zhongshan, for example, received interest subsidies from the finance bureau of the municipal government.

Industrial policies and development strategies result from cooperation between the government and enterprises. In Zhuhai, a Special Economic Zone, the initial development strategy that focused on tourism was not successful. In 1985, there was a citywide discussion of development strategy and industrial policy that included government departments, enterprises, and academic experts, as well as experts from outside the region and the country. A consensus was reached: Zhuhai should set priorities on foreign investment, products for export, technology-intensive industries, and high-tech industries for an outward-oriented economy. Rather than the government setting the development strategy and industrial policy, they are set by cooperation and communication among government, enterprises, and experts in order to achieve better outcome and coordination.

Another feature is worth mentioning. Perhaps because there are no formal organized interest groups in China, there seems to be a less serious "capture" problem from interest groups, such as plagued most Western democracies once the government was involved in setting industrial policies.

Relationship between Local Government and Business

Because most enterprises are owned or controlled by some level of government, the problem of government/business cooperation—as viewed in most capitalist economies—does not arise. The natural relationship between government and business, perhaps facilitated by the party as described above, is one of cooperation. There is a strong tendency in the Pearl River Delta for the local government, when faced with interference from, say, the central government, to collude with local enterprises to help hide profits, bargain with the central government, and so on. For that matter, the provincial government also colludes with the municipal government. The same is repeated between the municipal government and county government when facing the provincial government. One of the main incentives for collusion is the tremendous pressure of competition among different regions to grow fast and get rich quickly.

An example of cooperation between government and business is the government-arranged industrial grouping where well-run firms take over or merge with loss-making firms, a practice similar to one sometimes observed in the American banking industry. In Zhongshan Municipality, the government (mainly the finance bureau) provides incentives for well-run firms to take over loss-making firms (e.g., land will be provided to the merged firm, tax benefits will be extended, and bad debts will be written off). This not only reduces the subsidies to the firm but also turns capacity to productive use.[5]

Ownership and Enterprises

The Varieties of Public Ownership

In Guangdong Province, state-owned enterprises (SOEs) became less and less important as the share of nonstate ownership in industrial output value increased to about 60 percent in 1990 (at the time the national figure was 45 percent). Nonstate enterprises have a variety of forms of ownership, such as collective, cooperative, joint-venture, joint-stock, township and village, foreign venture, and private. The majority of them are still considered "public ownership."

Several interesting points deserve attention. There is a continuous spectrum of ownership ranging from state-owned under central government control to private ownership in its pure form. Even within the state sector, state-owned firms run by municipality and county governments differ considerably from state-owned firms affiliated with the central or provincial governments. They are more like collective firms of a municipality or a county. They are not subject to planning and are less subject to direct government interventions. The state-owned firms of Zhongshan Municipality perform relatively well and seem to behave much like private firms.

Two observations about incentives of managers (as well as government officials) are noted. First, the ratio of managerial salaries to workers is much lower than that in the United States, or even Japan. Second, most managers and government officials (as opposed to private businessmen) are not given assets, but may instead receive dinners, luxury cars, cellular phones, and other work-related luxuries. We saw Lexus and Mercedes-Benz automobiles and Motorola cellular phones everywhere, and a dinner tab is often expensive, even by American standards. There are perhaps some incentive effects of not giving assets: one has to keep working hard; otherwise one will lose everything. As one official said: "We can take away cars, but not cash."

---

5. This is the case that we were told about. Conceivably, there may be other unsuccessful cases with money lost after government-led mergers.

Joint Ventures

Looking closely into joint ventures we found interesting structures. The well-run Zhongshan Polyester Fibre Plant Co. Ltd. is a Sino-Hong Kong joint venture in which the Chinese have a 75 percent share and the remaining 25 percent is owned by a Hong Kong company (25 percent is the minimum share required to be qualified as a foreign joint venture), with a total investment of 140 million yuan. There are several interesting aspects about the ownership structure. First, although a 75 percent share is publicly owned, there are three "owners" under control by different jurisdictions. The three domestic partners are China Silk Import and Export Corp. (which is affiliated with the Ministry of Foreign Economic Relations and Trade of the central government), Guangdong Provincial Silk Import and Export Corp. (a provincial corporation), and Zhongshan Trading Development Company (a municipality company), which contributed land. Second, the Hong Kong partner initially provided ideas for types of technology to import (from France and Germany), and then ceased to be active in managerial decisions. The board meeting is held twice a year and decides profit targets and shares to go to wages, welfare, and reinvestment. Third, the executive managers, who used to be factory directors of the state-owned chemical firms, were selected by the municipal government.

By the official definition of China's statistical bureau, this firm is no longer regarded as a state-owned firm. It falls into the category of "Sino-foreign joint ventures." However, because 75 percent of its shares are publicly owned, it would be regarded as a firm in the public sector in the West. Nevertheless, from an economic perspective, the firm is run like a private for-profit firm. We see several roles played by the Hong Kong partner. First, it serves as a commitment by the government that this firm will be run on business principles only, without the kind of government intervention that occurs in state-owned firms; second, it provided initial information (and capital, which is less important) about what technology to import (because its product was for import substitution, information concerning the foreign market was less important); and third, it serves the role of overseer of the local manager.

This type of joint venture is not exceptional. Another example is Zhuhai's Asia Simulation & Control System Engineering Co. Ltd., a highly successful high-tech firm that we visited. It also has 75 percent of its shares owned by the Chinese and three different public partners, but the 25 percent Hong Kong shares are actually owned by a Hong Kong firm owned by the Chinese government. This 100 percent publicly owned firm runs just like a private corporation, and its chief executives have a strong sense of being accountable to shareholders. Although all four institutional partners represent the public, they have different interests and the only thing they can agree on is the maximization of profits.

Township-Village Enterprises (TVEs)

The most successful enterprises in the region we visited are not private firms in a pure form. What can township, village, or other partnerships do that individuals can't? One answer is the mobilization of large amounts of capital and labor in a short time period. If everything is privatized first, not only is organizational capital lost, but considerable energy goes into solving coordination problems under asymmetric information, and possibly also into rent-seeking. Furthermore, problems with new equity issues and with private owners may also arise. Before market-monitoring institutions became well-established, the public was more afraid of its wealth being "stolen" (misappropriated) by a private firm than by a public firm. In a township or a village, the immediate question facing the community is how to make more profit and what technology to use. The ownership problem is postponed to be solved later.

Shunde, with a population of 930,000, is famous for its township enterprises. In 1991, total industrial output in Shunde was 10.66 billion yuan, of which 3.19 billion came from municipality enterprises (1.5 billion from state-owned and the rest from collectives), 6.4 billion from township enterprises, and 1.05 billion from village and private enterprises. In Shunde, we visited Rongqi Township, with a population of about 50,000. The township has more than 200 industrial enterprises, with a total industrial output of 1.5 billion yuan in 1991. Rongqi Township is expected to reach 4 billion yuan in industrial output in 1995. We visited one township enterprise in Rongqi Township—the Pearl River Refrigerator Factory. It produced 30,000 refrigerators in 1985 and captured about 2 percent of the market share in China. In 1991, it produced 500,000 refrigerators, or about 10 percent of the market share in China. The factory now has about 700 sales agencies in all thirty provinces in China, and its products have received state high quality products prizes.

In the past, community members did not leave the community. But more recently that has changed. As mobility increases and people are tempted to leave a region for jobs elsewhere, it may become necessary to make each community member an explicit shareholder. To this end, there is some experimenting with "joint-stock cooperatives" in some counties in the region (e.g., Tianhe District of Guangzhou).

Comparative analysis of China's township and village enterprises and other modes of organization provides interesting insights into their success. The township and village enterprises differ dramatically from Yugoslav worker-managed firms. The population size of a Chinese township or village is fixed; it is not a decision variable. The community raises capital from its members and borrows from rural credit cooperatives and state banks. It first hires its own labor from the community and then hires workers from other regions. The hired workers are treated as labor, a cost to production. In Yugoslavia, worker-managed firms maximize per-worker income, so there is an incentive not to hire workers. Also, because shares can't be redeemed when workers leave the firm, capital tends to be depleted. In contrast, township-village enterprises in China seem to maximize revenue as long as there is surplus labor in the community, and then maximize profit afterward.

Another significant difference between Yugoslav firms and Chinese township-village enterprises is that inside the community, the free-rider problem is solved by incentive schemes. In most cases, workers are paid by piece rate, imposed by the factory director. This is possible because inside the firm, workers do not participate in managerial decisions. One legacy from the past is that the union is strictly under the party's control and is restricted to focusing on workers' welfare.

On the other hand, the difference between SOEs and TVEs is that in the latter, workers can be fired, but in the former, they cannot. Managerial pecuniary incentives are not very different; typically, top managers' monetary income is about 2–3 times the average workers' income. Most incentives are seen as perks, like luxury cars, fancy dinners, trips abroad, corporate cards, and the like. A second difference between SOEs and TVEs is the perceived different option value to buying future shares of the firm if it becomes a joint-stock company.

Finally, there are at least three reasons why the community mode of production didn't work in agriculture but township and village enterprises did work in industrial production: (1) workers in TVEs are not participatory in managerial decisions; (2) the supervision technology allows piece rate incentive schemes to work in industrial production; and (3) there is an option value to buying future shares.

Entrepreneurship and Learning

Development of Entrepreneurship

In many less-developed countries, the key factor that seems to be in short supply is "entrepreneurship," the ability and willingness to bring together capital, labor, and technology to produce goods in an efficient way, to find and develop markets, and, ultimately, to bear risks. One of the most striking and impressive phenomena we observed during our visit was the fast development of entrepreneurship on a mass scale. How can we explain it?

We have identified several ingredients in this remarkable success. The first two have to do with initial conditions: (1) the multilayer, multiregional organizational structure, to which we referred earlier, resulted in a number of well-developed institutions with a certain degree of autonomy, which could form the basis of the *new* enterprises; and (2) the web of connections between this region and Hong Kong provided a natural flow of information about technology, markets, and, most importantly, entrepreneurship. Entrepreneurial behavior is, like other forms of behavior, learned behavior. It is a form of behavior that will be imitated if it seems likely to be "successful." The evident success of entrepreneurship in Hong Kong and Taiwan clearly provided strong evidence that there were large returns to entrepreneurship. Strong role models were provided (and the similarity of certain behaviors, such as the extensive use of cellular phones, is probably more than a coincidence).

But as important as these conditions were, even more so was the role of public policy. Government seems to have done several things that had the effect of promoting entrepreneurship, besides providing an infrastructure that allowed it to flourish. First, it structured the transition process in such a way as to take advantage of the existing organizational capital. We see the process of transition in China as a process of *restructuring* the existing institutions to create new wealth, rather than destroying the old set of institutions and building a whole new set from scratch, as seems to be the focus of the transition strategy in Eastern Europe and Russia. Making use of existing organizations has the advantage of reducing uncertainty and not losing existing organizational capital. China can do this in a less costly way because the organizational hierarchy was in a decentralized multilayer, multiregional form even before 1979.

Second, as we discuss more extensively in the following, China structured the reforms in such a way as to provide enterprises with the ability to learn about entrepreneurship. It not only avoided the problems of "information overload," but it also appeared to reduce the risks associated with investment and entrepreneurial activity (and allowed those risks to be more widely shared, e.g., by the local community). Given the limitations on equity markets in the early stages of development, this facility for risk sharing may be quite important.

Third, government *encouraged* entrepreneurship within virtually all of its subunits, as we discuss more extensively later in the chapter.

Finally, government itself created institutions to undertake entrepreneurship and, in effect, became an entrepreneur itself. The example of creating a corporation to reclaim land from the sea in Zhongshan is but one of many.

The Role of Hong Kong in the Pearl River Delta

The role of Hong Kong in the Pearl River Delta is more evident if we compare it with another fast-growing area in China: southern Jiangsu, adjacent to Shanghai. In 1992, the combined economies of three municipalities of southern Jiangsu (Suzhou, Wuxi, and Changzhou) surpassed that of Shanghai. The role of Shanghai has been critical in the rapid growth in southern Jiangsu. Even though southern Jiangsu developed earlier and had a better foundation than the Pearl River Delta, because Shanghai is not as advanced as Hong Kong in terms of technology, information, and market institutions, the general level of technology used and products produced in southern Jiangsu lag behind the Pearl River Delta.

Another unique feature of the Pearl River Delta is the concentration of families of overseas Chinese. One out of every six Hong Kong residents originated from Dongguan Municipality near Guangzhou (which we didn't visit). About 600,000 overseas Chinese originated from the region of Zhongshan, with a population of 1.2 million. In addition to the foreign capital and technology that the overseas Chinese bring into the region, there are also invisible, but invaluable, assets of "trusts." Most joint ventures with Hong Kong in the Pearl River Delta are started through family ties or local connections and maintained by trust bonds, so that many problems of adverse selection and moral hazard associated with foreign joint ventures have been minimized.

Sequencing of Reforms and Structured Learning

China's economic reforms featured a particular sequence: agricultural reforms preceded industrial reforms; the two-tier price system was introduced before prices were fully liberalized; incentive contracting systems were instituted before ownership and property rights issues were addressed; discretion and autonomy of managers of state-owned enterprises were gradually increased, and so on. This sequencing may not have come from intentional planning or strategies, but rather as an outcome of complex political processes.

We found the observed sequencing of China's reforms—marketization first and property rights issues second—interesting from the perspective of learning during transition. Transition from a planned economy to a market economy is a process of learning to use the market, and of learning to invent and select market institutions. Learning by experimentation is an important feature of China's reforms. The particular sequencing of China's transition seems to suggest that a structured learning procedure may have an advantage in avoiding information overload. At the individual level, people learn, first, what the market prices are; second, where the profit opportunities are; third, how to maximize profits, given the constraints; and fourth, how to increase profits by relaxing constraints. At the institutional level, the government learns, first, what kinds of decisions can be decentralized without disruptive costs; second, who should carry out what types of experiments; and third, what new institutions should be selected and promoted.

By putting the issues of redistribution of *existing* wealth aside at the beginning of reforms, the focus was put on establishing *new* firms, employing *new* technology, creating *new* wealth, and above all, developing entrepreneurship on a mass scale. Marketization in China is seen mainly as a process of learning how to create new wealth in a decentralized environment. In contrast, although the property rights issue is fundamental, it is also a tough political issue with a strong flavor of redistribution, and so it will likely be difficult to reach a consensus. There is no doubt that China must eventually address the property rights issue, but we are suggesting that an appropriate sequencing may have important implications for the efficiency of the transition.

The philosophy behind gradualism and sequencing of China's reforms is very much like the philosophy of treating patients in traditional Chinese medicine: instead of having an operation to remove, say, a cancer right away, the treatment emphasizes regaining the vigor of the body by adjusting diet, exercising, and learning to control oneself at the initial stage. Only at a later stage will the cancer be treated, not by operation, but by "digestion."

Innovations in Financial Institutions and Markets

The Pearl River Delta is one of the fastest growing areas in China and it attracts vast savings deposits from both inside and outside the region. There are several reasons why deposits are very high: (1) internal savings are high due to a high level of income and growth of income; (2) overseas Chinese donations and investment is concentrated in the area; (3) investment by inland provinces and firms, which use the area as a window to the outside world, are high; and (4) inland enterprises take advantage of loose restrictions on the use of money they deposit in the area; for example, the bonus fund is strictly monitored by the banks in other regions but is less so in this area (an extreme example is Hainan Province, where many inland enterprises deposit money in order to simply cash out for bonuses, because there appears to be no effective restriction on the island).

Within the region, the credit limits imposed on state banks by the Central Bank appear as a major constraint, though credit availability does increase with deposits. China's banking system is still not much reformed; the main control instrument of the Central Bank remains direct credit limits by quotas. With more deposits and then resources available for lending in the region, various innovations are being tried to increase financial resources channeled to the firms without explicitly violating the credit quotas. Local branches of state banks use the following means to meet the increasing needs for credit in the region: (1) borrowing credit quotas from other provinces where there are unused quotas due to low deposits; this is typically done through interbank loans; for example, banks in Zhongshan borrowed about 2.1 billion yuan through interbank loans from other regions; (2) arranging loans for local enterprises directly from inland enterprises to circumvent the banking system; therefore no credit quotas are used; (3) using bank-affiliated trust investment corporations to channel deposits to the firms; again, these are not regarded as bank loans; (4) using bank-affiliated urban and rural credit cooperatives to make more loans; unlike state banks, credit cooperatives are regulated by a lending-deposit ratio (which is about 80 percent) rather than by credit limits; and (5) banks issuing bonds and using the proceeds to lend to enterprises; this lending activity is again not counted as bank loans.

Enterprises are also innovative in raising capital by circumventing the strict credit limits. Large well-established firms issue bonds to the public (often other "public" firms), which are not counted toward credit limits. A more popular method for small or start-up firms is to raise capital from employees by either internal bonds (paying higher interest rates than bank deposits) or internal shares (preferred shares, in fact, which do not carry control rights). This is also seen as an incentive device to motivate workers. The informational advantage of issuing internal shares is that they avoid the "winner's curse" problem of new equity issues.

Most financial innovations make use of loopholes in central government regulations and fall in a gray area. From the point of view of the central government, many of these innovations are viewed as "gimmicks" to circumvent credit limits imposed by the Central Bank, which may cause macroeconomic imbalance in the economy (as in early 1993). This raises an interesting question concerning dynamic institutional changes. Should the local government and enterprises wait for changes (such as improved financial markets) brought about by the central government, or should they go ahead and push for change?

Both the lending rate and deposit rate of interest are regulated by the Central Bank. The lending rate is quite low, about 7.8 percent per year. There are several ways to increase the effective lending rate. The banks may require counterbalancing financing: the deposit rate for enterprise used to be extremely low, about 1.8 percent per annum (as opposed to about 9 percent for individuals). The banks also lend money through their own trust and investment corporations, in which the lending rate is more flexible. We were told that the "market rate" at the time of our visit was somewhere around 15 percent.

In Special Economic Zones, collateral is required for most lending.

Other regions have started to follow suit, but the dominant method for reducing default risk is the use of loan guarantees, typically by the parent company, but also sometimes by other enterprises in the industrial group, or by a supervising agency of the government.

At least in the Pearl River Delta, state banks consistently claim that the government does not force them to lend to priority industries. They approve loans based solely on a profitability test. If all projects pass this test, then they support priority industries. Of course, at such a low interest rate, there is an implicit subsidy. In a few exceptions, like agricultural projects or approved high-tech projects, the central or local governments provide explicit interest subsidies through the budget. The upper-level government has many other means to induce the lower-level government (and the banks) to support priorities; for example, a promise of more import quotas or export licenses. The government apparently has more instruments than other countries in implementing its industrial policy.

To accommodate the fast-growing foreign trade in the region, the foreign exchange swap market was organized by the local government and has been active for the past few years. In Zhongshan, the total transaction in the foreign exchange swap market was only USD5.05 million in 1988, but increased to USD52.17 million in 1991. Fifty percent of the total transaction is used for buying raw material and intermediate inputs, 15 percent for repayment of foreign debt, and 15 percent for achieving a balance of payment for foreign companies in the region.

Shenzhen is the location of one of the two stock markets in China. There are about a dozen stocks listed in Shenzhen that are classified as A shares (for Chinese) and B shares (for foreigners). Daily transaction is about 400 million yuan at the Shenzhen stock exchange. For those corporations listed on the stock market, only individual shares are traded, not institution shares, which account for about 60–70 percent of the total shares. Because all institution shares are owned by government agencies, institutions, or state-owned firms, for the time being, these publicly traded corporations would still be considered in the public sector in the West.

Innovations in Local Public Finance

Again, at the national level, the fiscal system as a whole has not yet undergone dramatic reform. An ad hoc fiscal system known as the "fiscal contracting system" has been in place for several years. Essentially, the central government contracts with each province for the revenue (including taxes and profits) to be submitted in the next three to five years according to a formula (a fixed quota or a sharing rule). The same process is repeated at all six layers of the government. This, for the time being, provides incentives for local governments to raise revenue, while at the same time giving them flexibility in terms of reducing taxes for certain industries.

At the local level, there has been considerable innovation, in terms of dealing with the central authorities, in raising revenues, and in solving local expenditure problems. For instance, to avoid the ratchet effect, each level of government has a tendency to hide revenue from the upper level of government.[6] In this fast-growing area, a common practice is called "storing the money into enterprises," which means that the local government lowers taxes to reduce tax revenue, just fulfilling the quotas. In exchange for this favor, enterprises usually pick up tabs for certain expenditures of the government, for example, dinner costs. This is an example of explicit collusion between local government and enterprises, playing a trick on the central government. But they all seem to be going for the same goal: growth of the region.

Traditionally, in standard textbook discussions, infrastructure and utilities are thought to be financed from the government budget. However, we found this to be not quite true in the Pearl River Delta. There are many toll highways and roads and almost all bridges have toll booths. We were told that roads were built by municipality or county governments by issuing bonds to the public with slightly higher interest than bank deposits, and that they were supposed to be self-financing (through charging tolls). (As mentioned earlier, bond financing is not included in the total credit limit imposed by the Central Bank.) To facilitate this, the government imposed a constraint on the minimum length of road that could be constructed. Another interesting case is electricity. Because the provincial government allows the utility company to impose surcharges for the use of electricity, electric utilities are a profitable business; hence, no special policy is required to finance power generators.

Another widespread phenomena in the area (and in fact all over China), due to insufficient tax revenue to finance government operations, is that almost all government agencies and institutions (e.g., universities) are either directly engaged in profitable business, or charge fees for services (i.e., benefit taxes). The money earned is collected and distributed to individuals as bonuses and to the unit as welfare funds. Here are two examples we saw during our short visit. First, our translator was assigned by the Provincial Foreign Affairs Office, we were charged for the translating service, and the fees were distributed within his division. Second, the economics department

---

6. According to officials from Guangdong Provincial System Reform Commission, Guangdong Province was supposed to remit 1.8 billion in tax revenue to the central government in 1990, according to the original contract. It actually paid 3.8 billion. In 1991, it remitted 6.9 billion rather than the 2 billion originally agreed upon. But the central government does not agree on this interpretation, and claims that these figures are based on different methods of calculating the local government's revenue remittance. Apparently, the incompleteness of contract has created many conflicting claims between the central and local governments.

of Zhongshan University also has several businesses, such as running training sessions for the Provincial Finance Bureau and conducting research projects for Hong Kong. What is interesting is that most activities are conducted as small "collective" activities, partly for the reason that private licenses, a precondition to opening a bank account, are difficult to obtain. However, to reduce the free-rider problem, the group is usually small.

While there are obviously many drawbacks to this sort of activity, there is also a clear benefit: the promotion of entrepreneurship on a mass scale. The obvious question is how to deal with the adverse effects of corruption. All of these mechanisms, including discretion in the reduction of taxes, seem subject to corruption, collusion, and rent seeking. The big question, to which we don't quite know the answer, is why these problems do not seem to be serious enough to hamper growth, as seems to be the case in many Latin American countries. There seems to be an implicit consensus about what are acceptable norms of behavior and what are not. One check on unacceptable corruption is the party: duplication of the functions of government and the party sometimes serves as part of a system of checks and balances.

Although local governments can't determine the types of taxes and tax rates, they are able to determine reduction of taxes within some limits set by the central government. Taxes (usually profit tax, but sometimes indirect turnover taxes such as product tax, VAT, business tax and urban maintenance and construction tax) can be negotiated. There is a close relationship between government and firms on financial matters, even though nonstate firms are not subject to planning and state-owned firms have gained considerable autonomy. This relationship has both costs and benefits. On the cost side, distortions are introduced by one-to-one negotiations; on the benefit side, these practices encourage cooperation between government and enterprises and provide government with more leverage to accomplish its priorities.

A considerable number of discussions and experiments on social security are going on at county, municipality, and provincial levels. It appears likely that, within the Pearl River Delta, a system similar to the one in Singapore will eventually be established, wherein a compulsory deposit is made to an individual, fully funded account for use for retirement, health care, and housing purchase. Due to the current large population of older people, some mixed mechanism will be used during the transition period.

Concluding Remarks

A case study of Guangdong Province, focusing on institutional innovations and the role of local government in its remarkable economic development, is, of necessity, different in many essential respects from the other case studies in the East Asia Miracle project. This is for the obvious reason that the government in China used to embrace such a high proportion of all economic activity. Yet it is remarkable how many themes developed in these other studies are evidenced here: the importance of markets; the high degree of export orientation (particularly, if one takes as "exports" exports out of the province); the close collaboration between enterprises and government; and the success of growth without the extremes of inequality associated with earlier successful development efforts. Earlier studies, such as that of Amsden (1989) for Korea, described the role of government as the entrepreneurial state; others, such as that of Wade (1990) for Taiwan, described the role of government as "governing the market." In China, both of these roles are clearly in evidence. The government has encouraged entrepreneurship throughout the society, including within local governmental units. The government has governed the market and helped direct economic activity into areas that are most conducive to growth. But the role of the government has been far greater: the government has helped to create the markets, and the government has taken on the remarkable task of creating institutions that will eventually supplant much of its role in economic activity.

While the experiences of China have something to say to other developing countries, perhaps they have most to say to the former socialist economies that are in the process of making the transition to a market economy. The Chinese "model" is markedly different from that which many of the Eastern European countries seem to be using. It may provide important lessons on the role of the government, the creation of market institutions, and the sequencing of reforms in the transition process.

REFERENCES

Amsden, Alice H. 1989. *Asia's Next Giant: South Korea and Late Industrialization.* New York: Oxford Univresity Press.
Qian, Yingyi, and Chenggang Xu. 1993. "Why China's Economic Reforms Differ: The M-Form Hierarchy and Entry/Expansion of the Non-State Sector." *The Economics of Transition* 1, no. 2 (June): 135–70.
Wade, Robert. 1990. *Governing the Market: Economic Theory and the Role of Government in East Asian Industrialization.* Princeton, N.J.: Princeton University Press.

Part 3
Reforming Agriculture

CHAPTER 9

Gradual Reform and Institutional Development: The Keys to Success of China's Agricultural Reforms

Scott Rozelle

Following the article on the desirability and feasibility of slow reform by McMillan and Naughton (1991), a number of authors have concluded that the pace of China's reform was as critical to its success as the substance of any single policy (Perkins 1992; Harrold 1992; Gelb, Jefferson, and Singh 1993). The transition of a socialist economy to a more market-oriented one requires the creation of a number of institutions and the construction of new infrastructure. Gradual reform provides policy makers with the time and information they need to help manage this stage of development and avoid sharp, instability-creating shocks.

One common element in these studies on gradualism is the acknowledgment of the key role played by the agricultural sector in the early stages of China's reform process. Interestingly, other than commentary on the importance of the introduction of the household responsibility system in the early 1980s, there is little analysis of the overall approach taken by reformers to accomplish this initial step. Readers are left with the impression that in one great leap agricultural markets were liberalized and reforms completed. Some analysts have even conjectured that the growth in the rural sector has occurred primarily as a result of the sector's complete liberalization (Sachs 1993). Ironically, this has created the somewhat contradictory impression that China's first step to overall gradual reform was to decontrol agriculture with a big bang.

Most policy makers and academics charged with creating, implementing, and analyzing China's agricultural policies during the reform period, however, are puzzled by such observations. The ideological architects of the

The author would like to thank Loren Brandt, John McMillan, Barry Naughton, and Albert Park for providing comments on earlier drafts of this chapter. The support of the Ford Foundation in Beijing and the Agricultural Science Foundation of the Rockefeller Foundation is gratefully acknowledged.

agricultural reforms never intended to overthrow the planning system (Lardy and Lieberthal 1983). There was rapid change in the organization of agricultural production, but policy-makers were reluctant to allow resources in the sector to be allocated by market forces (ZGNYNJ 1985, 1988). Even during the drafting of the eighth five-year plan in 1990, agricultural officials were struggling over the pace of sectoral reform (Liu 1991). Reforms were allowed to proceed only on the condition that a steady supply of low-cost food and fiber flowed out of the rural sector. Although this strategy undoubtedly slowed the growth of agricultural incomes, it did insure stability. It was not until recently that more complete market liberalization was undertaken.

The goal of this chapter is to explore the process of agricultural reform in China. Specifically, the chapter examines the complexities of reform in the sector, demonstrating the limited scope of the early policies and the slow evolution of market liberalization over the past 15 years. Second, the agricultural reforms are demonstrated to display the same characteristics as those for the general economy (as described by McMillan and Naughton 1991): there was no original plan; the reforms have been purposely implemented in a slow manner to avoid instability and allow for the building of an institutional base; and policies have been self-reinforcing, in that once started, activities performed by the reformed portion of the economy have gradually been able to fulfill the role of the unliberalized sector, making further government control superfluous and thereby inducing a continuous liberalization process. Third, a programming model based on field data collected by the author in the mid-1980s and early 1990s is used to understand the microeconomic behavior of farm households that underlie the success of gradual reform.

China's Agricultural Reform Process

Nearly every major paper written recently on China's reform experience has noted the importance of the contribution of the agricultural sector. The initial agricultural reforms were seen by some to provide experimental grounds for exploring the power and limitations of the market system and learning how to control the economy through indirect means (Perkins 1992). Others claim that the productivity gains generated by the agricultural reforms created a large part of the initial surplus investment that was to fuel the rapid industrialization of the later reform period (Chen, Jefferson, and Singh 1992; Harrold 1992). The sector also provided the labor that was used in the rural industrialization push (McKinnon 1993). Agricultural reforms aided China's development by creating demand for the products of factories in the liberalized part of the economy (Qian and Xu 1993). McMillan and Naughton (1991) believe that the contribution of agriculture through its impact on rural industrialization had even more important downstream effects. The entry of profit-seeking firms in the robust rural nonstate sector has provided a source of competition for enterprises in the rest of the economy, stimulating subsequent reform efforts.

What has been neglected in the literature, or at least has been portrayed in an overly simplistic manner, is the complexity of the reforms, and the importance of the order and timing of the implementation of the liberalization measures within the agricultural sector. In nearly every reference to the agricultural reforms, they are described as being a set of policies implemented during the late 1970s and early 1980s in a sector that had been the focus of heavy investment in the prereform era (Stone 1988; ZGNYNJ 1988). All the sector lacked was an organizational form that provided incentives to make farmers work hard, allocate resources more effectively, and increase productivity (Harrold 1992). Decollectivization led to an upsurge in productivity, markets were liberalized, and the reforms in the sector were essentially complete.

Continuing Control and Policy Intervention in Agriculture

In fact, rural reform measures were not even centered on market liberalization in the early 1980s. Surprisingly, while reformers made several key fundamental modifications to policies in the late 1970s and early 1980s, some of the most rigid and interventionary prereform policies remained firmly in place. In the mid-1980s, markets were not the principal force guiding resource allocation in much of agriculture. Nearly 15 years passed after the initial set of reform measures had been implemented before more complete market-liberalizing reforms were finally adopted in widespread regions throughout the country. One of the most remarkable features of China's agricultural reform process, however, has been the nearly seamless, undisruptive manner in which new transitions have been realized. It is perhaps the very smoothness of these transitions in the last several years that has kept these fundamental changes out of the popular press and academic debates.

This is not to say that the early rural reforms did not represent a significant departure from earlier Maoist policies. In the early reform years, reformers removed regulations prohibiting the local marketing of many products. Agricultural prices were administratively raised. Most significantly, the household responsibility system (HRS) was implemented, changing the basic unit of decision making and profit retention from the production team to the household. These incentive policies were immensely successful in raising sectoral productivity (McMillan, Whalley, and Zhu 1989; Lin 1992). But the effectiveness of these reforms initially lay in harder working rural household members within a highly controlled economic environment, not in liberalizing markets. In the mid-1980s, surplus labor and capital created by these first reforms were allowed to move out of the cropping sector (Lin, Cai, and Li 1994), but factor and product markets in rural China have remained highly fragmented (except in such regions as South China in the 1980s and the Yangtse Delta in the early 1990s).

Reformers did eliminate some prohibitions on local and interregional trade. But in terms of letting market forces allocate resources and determine investment, the biggest changes were initially made in markets that did not threaten certain key elements of Chinese agricultural policy. The role of agriculture in China's economy had mainly been that of supplying cheap and stable quantities of food to China's urban areas and a steady supply of raw materials to certain industries (Zhao 1982; Eckstein 1975). In addition, agricultural policies had always been concerned with maintaining a minimum welfare level in rural areas (Lardy and Lieberthal 1983; Mao 1977). Although the reform-era policies were designed to increase the efficiency of producers in the agricultural sector (Lardy 1983), documents outlining the early reforms make it clear that in no way were these changes going to be allowed to impinge on the stability goals that had been the target of earlier agricultural policies (Hsu 1993).

In the prereform period, China's leaders had met these stability goals in several ways. Agricultural officials maintained a virtual monopoly over the procurement and input supply systems (Sicular 1988; Stone 1988). Although by the late 1980s all but six products (grain, oil, cotton, sugar, tobacco, and silk cocoons) had been substantially removed from the planning process, these six crops account for over 90 percent of sown area (ZGTJNJ 1990). Regional officials are still actively engaged in agricultural planning (Liu 1991). Increasing yields and maintaining agricultural productivity are important to local leaders since they have helped fulfill mandatory delivery targets (Rozelle 1994b). Meeting targets has often been considered more important than raising agricultural incomes, and market activity is frequently not allowed to take place until procurement obligations have been met. Until early 1993, farmers were encouraged to maintain agricultural productivity and sell their surplus to the state by incentive schemes that tied access to critical inputs to their performance (Park 1993).

Maintaining control over land allocation and planting decisions has provided the government with another way to ensure a stable supply of food and fiber. While land is nominally contracted out to farmers, local leaders are often able to indiscriminantly confiscate and reallocate land from farm households (Rozelle 1994a). The threat of the loss of land has been used to induce farmers to maintain high productivity and meet their obligations to the state (Rozelle and Liang 1992). By 1991, the planting and technology adoption decisions were still made by the collective in more than 50 percent of the villages in the coastal area, and more than 30 percent in other regions of China (Sicular 1991).

The government grain system also continued to play a dominant role in the procurement of agricultural staples and their distribution in consumption centers (Wu 1992). As late as 1991, huge parts of the central government's budget were dedicated to subsidizing large portions of the food budgets of urban residents. Key agricultural inputs, especially chemical fertilizer, remained totally monopolized by the state-run Agricultural Inputs Corporation (AIC) in the early 1990s.

As a result of these policies, even in the face of declining real prices, producers increased the area sown to grain throughout the late 1980s and early 1990s, leading the country to record levels of grain output in 1990 and yields in 1992 (ZGTJNJ 1991, 1993). Inputs were available in abundance, with few shortages being reported (Ye 1992). Food lines and shortages in urban and rural areas were nonexistent. Except for a spike in the price of grain in 1988 and 1989, prices have been low, with expenditures on food taking up an ever smaller proportion of the average urban resident's budget (Huang 1994).

Recent Liberalization Measures: Moving to Market Control

It has only been in the past several years, following this period of relative good performance, and as a result of general budgetary pressures, that the government has slowly but steadily begun to dismantle these product procurement and input allocation institutions (Park 1993a). The initial push began in the consumer sector. Grain subsidies were partially removed in 1991, and then fully eliminated in 1992 (Zhong 1993). Grain rationing stations are still being operated by the government grain system, but they have been contracted out and managers of local storefronts are now responsible for their profits and losses. These bureaucrats-turned-merchants still have access to government-run wholesale channels, but they are also free to buy from any other source.

On the production side, Guangdong Province took the lead, abolishing market surplus quotas to farmers in 1991 (Park 1993a). In the following year, the national grain planning system formally eliminated all planned interprovincial grain transfers. According to interviews with officials from the Ministry of Domestic Trade, a number of coastal provinces (Guangdong, Fujian, Zhejiang, Shanghai, Jiangsu, and Shandong) and Sichuan Province followed the "Guangdong plan." Other provinces maintained procurement quotas, but had to purchase the grain at prevailing market prices (Park 1993b). By the end of 1993, this policy had been completely implemented.

In the meantime, the grain procurement side of the grain system was also being radically reformed. In 1993, the Ministry of Domestic Trade virtually "privatized" the procurement arm of the grain bureau (Park 1993a). In return for control over the assets of the grain bureau in most rural counties, former bureau leaders have become managers of grain trading firms with little budgetary support from government sources. To survive, managers must operate profitable trading organizations. While these new grain enterprises enjoy certain advantages over their private competitors (e.g., in provinces that have maintained marketing quotas, the procurement price is typically set 2 to 3 percent below the market price), they are no longer guaranteed market access to traditional demand centers through planned purchases.

Relaxation of restrictions has also occurred in the vegetable oil, sugar, and fertilizer markets. Government officials are currently debating whether or not other crops, such as cotton and silk cocoons, should be demonopolized. For the first time since the mid-1980s (when fertilizer was decontrolled for a brief two-year period of time), the trading of agricultural inputs, including fertilizer, has been demonopolized (Ye 1991). In 1992, certain government organizations were allowed to buy and sell fertilizer and other farm inputs in competition with the AIC. Almost immediately, township-level agricultural technical stations, county experiment stations, seed companies, special county-level trading companies, and others also began to engage in the buying and selling of fertilizer and other inputs.

The Impact on Sectoral Performance

While much has been written about the impact of decollectivization on production, productivity, and sectoral income (McMillan, Whalley, and Zhu 1989; Fan 1991; Lin 1992), most empirical analyses have only looked at the early reform period. In contrast, no analytical effort has been made to separate the impact of the gradual market liberalization from that of the other changes. The stagnation of rural incomes in the late 1980s, however, has attracted the attention of Western researchers, and has been blamed, in part, on the gradual reforms. The state's pricing and procurement policies in the late 1980s have been associated with the flagging agricultural prices and stagnant incomes in many rural areas, especially those that depended heavily on cropping (Sicular 1991). Lack of land markets has been suggested to be the cause of falling investment. Labor market imperfections may have kept large parts of the population from access to wage-earning opportunities and held back growth (Rozelle 1994a).

While many other factors are also changing, it may be that the recent market liberalization moves are behind the recent upturn in rural incomes. After not rising between 1985 and 1990, real rural per capita income increases have become more widespread in the early 1990s (ZGTJNJ 1986–1993). In 1992, real income of rural residents rose by an average of 3 percent, and the growth was registered by all but two provinces. Hence, it appears as if the gradual reform strategy in agriculture has been associated with slow (or at least postponed) increases in aggregate income. However, the performance of

China's approach, even considering the stagnation of the late 1980s, is more encouraging than that of most central and Eastern European countries, where agricultural economies suffered sharp downturns in income and productivity after the introduction of liberalization policies (Tangermann 1994).

Unplanned, Slow, and Self-reinforcing

Markets for the exchange of agricultural products in urban areas developed throughout the 1980s (table 1, col. 1). From a level of 2,226 in 1980, the number of urban center markets expanded steadily at nearly 20 percent per year, and by 1990 had reached 13,106. During this same period, the size of each market increased dramatically, and the average value of transactions increased by more than ten times (col. 2).

Since the magnitude of these numbers is hard to comprehend on a national scale, columns 3 and 4 provide the same information for a single municipality, Beijing. In 1980, only 34 registered exchange markets existed in Beijing, transacting an average of 248,000 yuan in trade per year. During the early 1980s, if agricultural trade had been decontrolled, on average, over 300,000 Beijing residents would have had to share a single market site. Clearly, such a weak infrastructural base could never have served the city sufficiently. By the end of the decade, however, the number and size of markets had increased substantially. (In fact, according to interviews with the Ministry of Domestic Trade, the rate of expansion of urban markets has increased in the early 1990s, and is being supplemented by a rising number of

TABLE 1. Development of Food Markets in Urban Areas, 1980–90

	Number of Urban Market Sites and Capitalization Volumes				Number of Registered Traders (yuan)	Amount of Capital Used by Traders (yuan)
	National		Beijing			
Year	No. of Mkts.	Avg. Volume	No. of Mkts.	Avg. Volume		
1980	2,226	54,270	34	248,824		
1981	3,298	1,033,796	41	1,363,415	241,015	5,278
1982	3,591	1,152,097	41	1,474,146	349,987	5,319
1983	4,491	1,145,765	42	1,557,381	462,419	5,708
1984	6,144	1,566,543	65	902,615	849,966	8,747
1985	8,013	1,505,948	374	506,524	1,463,799	7,020
1986	9,701	2,519,403	423	1,010,426	2,295,055	7,324
1987	10,908	3,181,927	412	1,403,981	3,355,232	8,373
1988	12,181	4,476,830	460	2,382,717	5,845,026	9,446
1989	13,111	5,519,121	452	3,136,106	4,954,020	12,516
1990	13,106	6,392,654	495	3,731,737	5,224,672	12,019

Source: ZGGSXZGLTJ 1992.

more dispersed street vendors). While still probably not capable of supplying all of the nation's capital with food products, the 500 formally registered markets do currently supply a large part of the diet of most residents. From less than 1 yuan of business per capita in 1980, each resident in Beijing purchased an average of 180 yuan of products from these markets in 1990.[1]

The number of registered traders and the amount of their trading capital have also risen monotonically throughout the 1980s (columns 5 and 6). There were only 241,000 private and semiprivate trade enterprises registered with the State Marketing Bureau in 1980. By 1990, this number had risen to 5.2 million, over 20 times the level of a decade earlier. The average amount of capital used by these traders also expanded from about 5,000 yuan in 1980 to more than 12,000 yuan in 1990 (although this represents only a modest increase when measured in real terms). While the opportunity to make profits from trade does attract people from other occupations (and so as regulations relax, ceteris paribus, more people will engage in trade), it is equally true that the knowledge of trading and access to capital for buying and selling agricultural products does not instantaneously appear. Even if there had been sufficient market infrastructure in urban areas to handle large volumes of agricultural trade in the early 1980s, it is almost certain that the smooth flow of goods would have been inhibited by the lack of integrated networks of trading channels if the state had liberalized food markets completely at that time. Most likely it would have taken a number of years to build up the networks that exist in China today.

While no firm figures exist, it is almost certain that transportation bottlenecks have been among the most limiting constraints on the development of rural to urban food markets in the 1980s. Over 30 percent of the nation's grain is still moved by "primitive" means (e.g., by cart or pole-driven boat; Wu 1992). Railway transport, which at one time was virtually the only way to make interprovincial movements of grain, now accounts for the total volume. Sharp increases in the production of trucks and other motorized vehicles (ZGTJNJ 1992) have, in part, allowed the volume of agricultural products to expand to their current level. Truck transportation has become the most popular means of short- and medium-distance grain shipment, accounting for over 50 percent of the total transportation volume in the early 1990s (Wu 1992).

In summary, there has been a rapid buildup in the nonstate food marketing channels between urban centers and rural areas. But it is only after more than ten years that large portions of the urban diet are able to smoothly flow through these non-state-run markets. And even in the early 1990s, over half of the nation's urban grain supplies continue to utilize government wholesale and

---

1. All figures from the State Marketing Bureau are reported in nominal dollars.

distribution networks (Wu 1992). Until very recently these flows were still at least partly subject to a detailed, interprovincial planning process.

However, with this well-integrated network in place, it is easy to see why the transition to a more liberalized grain marketing framework proceeded so smoothly in recent years, as the reformers recentered their attention on further liberalization of the agricultural system. When state grain stores were contracted out to their managers, the stores became part of this competitive marketing system. These outlets, which had relied on making profits on rationed grain (which only they could supply), were suddenly forced to compete for their customers. They could not charge high monopoly prices, because their customers could always go to the local markets to purchase their rice, wheat, and other staples. Likewise, these newly liberalized grain stores helped make the government distribution network more competitive. If the municipal grain wholesaler was charging too high a price or supplying grain that was of too low a quality, outlet managers had the option of purchasing grain stocks from local wholesale markets or private grain merchants.

Transition without Institutional Development:
The Case of Fertilizer Market Reforms

It could be argued that more rapid reforms would have led to a similar system but in an earlier period, thereby avoiding inefficiencies during the interim. While claims based on counterfactuals are impossible to prove, an illustrative example can be found in the case of the fertilizer market liberalization in the mid-1980s. It is suggested that rapid decontrol of the sector's distribution functions, when the marketing infrastructure was not prepared to handle massive movements of non-state-controlled inputs, in part led to the subsequent chaos in many of China's fertilizer markets in 1986 and 1987.

In the mid-1980s, the fertilizer distribution system was organized almost exactly as it had been in the prereform era (Stone 1986). The allocation of nearly all fertilizer was decided by a planning process involving the regional agricultural, industrial, and planning departments and the ministries at the national level. The AIC, which was run by the Ministry of Commerce (now the Ministry of Domestic Trade), managed the distribution of nearly all agricultural inputs, including fertilizer, farm chemicals, plastic sheeting, diesel fuel, and simple farm tools.

Within this strictly controlled sector of the rural economy, two factors led to serious regional imbalances in the production and use of chemical fertilizers (Ye 1992). Chemical fertilizer allocation, even in the early 1980s, was in large part tied to agricultural crop marketing, biasing the distribution toward productive, surplus areas (Liu and Xie 1982). These patterns of consumption created a situation where application rates were extremely high (and the marginal response to fertilizer was low) in some of the most agriculturally well-endowed areas. At the same time, other areas found it impossible to gain access to adequate fertilizer supplies, despite high marginal returns.

These imbalances were reinforced by investment decisions in fertilizer production. Chemical fertilizer plant investment was small-scale and primarily followed consumption patterns (Stone 1986). There was little fertilizer flowing among regions. Only a small percentage of fertilizer was traded among the provinces, and much of that was part of the national distributive plan.

Hence, even though there was a basis for trade in the mid-1980s (i.e., widely varying marginal returns to inputs), only small amounts of planned and lesser amounts of black market volumes of chemical fertilizer moved among agricultural regions. But after the bumper harvests of 1984, Stone (1989) describes a chain of events that led to the relaxation of restrictions against free-market sales of chemical fertilizer in 1985 and 1986. In 1985, rural financial problems had peaked with the inability of the grain procurement system to pay for all of the crops farmers had delivered to the state at the end of 1984. Earlier expansion of local and regional fertilizer supply capacity resulted in rapid accumulation of local chemical fertilizer inventories. When the marginal price of grain dropped in 1985, a slackening of derived demand for fertilizer further exacerbated this surplus. As part of an emergency deal between Beijing and the localities, spurred in part by the inability to pay for the accumulating inventories of fertilizer, the AIC severely cut back on the amount of fertilizer they would purchase from factories. In return, the government provided an outlet for accumulating inventories by legalizing fertilizer trade and giving fertilizer plant managers the right to arrange for the sale of all extra-plan fertilizer. Individuals were also allowed to engage in the fertilizer trade. It was thought that in addition to easing the immediate financial crises, free-market fertilizer trade could also solve the long-standing imbalances among regions, leading to more efficient use of resources and higher grain production.

But instead of solving China's agricultural problem, the fertilizer wars of the late 1980s were unleashed (Lyons 1992). Prices soared in remote areas, and access to previously planned allocations suddenly disappeared in others (Stone 1989). Highjackings of fertilizer trucks were commonly reported in local and national newspapers. It was perceived that unscrupulous traders were taking advantage of unsophisticated farmers and local government officials. Fertilizer market breakdowns were reported in many regions of the country (Lyons 1992; Rozelle 1991; Ye 1991; Stone et al., forthcoming).

In October 1987, the government officially recentralized the sales of all fertilizers, declaring the attempt to free agricultural input markets to be a failure (ZGNYNJ 1988). The original system of fertilizer distribution was largely reinstituted (Ye 1991). While some have argued that the markets were working better than reported by the popular press and that the remonopolization of fertilizer trade was a ploy orchestrated by corrupt officials wanting to control this lucrative source of financial gain (Stone 1989), there undoubtedly were at least some substantive reasons for suspending the reforms.

The move to deregulate the fertilizer market was undertaken with little forethought, and was implemented with no prior experimentation or trial period. The main marketing channel came to be fertilizer factories selling to individuals, who carted their wares throughout the country. Since private communication and trade networks were not well developed, many regions were initially left out of the growing private trade. There were no safeguards assuring that sufficient minimum supplies were available to all areas, even to the point where some regions did not have enough fertilizer to meet their contractual needs for crops that had to be turned over to the state (as discovered during interviews by the author with grain and agricultural bureau officials in Hubei and Hunan provinces in 1988 and 1989). Being in scarce supply, the value at the margin for some groups of farmers was very high, leading to pricing practices that appeared exploitative. Since marketing channels had not had time to develop, the same sharp regional imbalances remained, and stability in some rural areas was threatened.

In 1992, after a seven-year hiatus, during which time China's domestic marketing capacity and import networks had developed substantially, a new round of fertilizer marketing reforms was quietly reintroduced (Ye and Rozelle 1994). The impetus for these reforms came from the elimination of the procurement quota at below-market prices. When the tax implicit in the mandatory procurement quota was eliminated, it gave the budget-conscious government an opportunity to eliminate the fertilizer subsidies that had been tied to those sales.

But this time the fertilizer market was not thrown open to unprepared private sellers under duress of a financial crisis. Instead, well before the 1992 crop season, it was announced that other government agencies (e.g., seed companies, supply cooperatives, county trading companies, and agricultural extension stations) were allowed to engage in the buying and selling of fertilizer and other farm inputs. Since many of these agencies themselves had been developing marketing channels in the previous years for their own products, there was a natural network through which the newly marketized fertilizer could be sold. Fertilizer prices have risen in the past two years, but this appears to be due more to inflation and the elimination of production subsidies than to imperfections in marketing networks. Interviews in late 1993 revealed that competition among the different rural organizations for the sales of fertilizer was fierce, and that profit margins were surprisingly small. Some units complained that the windfalls they had expected to receive never materialized.

Other traders found the market so competitive that they were unable to earn enough profits to remain in the agricultural inputs trade business.

The Dynamic of Reform: An Empirical Illustration

To illustrate some of the microeconomic dynamics underlying the success of China's agricultural reforms, a model of a representative rural household is developed. A series of environments are sequentially designed to simulate the different phases of the economy since reform (table 2). A fully restricted environment is set up to act as a baseline case for the rural household at the beginning of the reforms; individuals were operating in an economy with imperfectly operating factor and product markets, and made decisions subject to the requirements of the rigid procurement and subsidized input schemes described above (table 2, col. 1). The second scenario explores what would have occurred if the early reform policies had removed the state from agricultural product marketing and input provision even though markets had not yet had a chance to develop (table 2, col. 2).[2] In the third modeling exercise (col. 3), the objective is to examine the effect of the government's continued intervention in the procurement and input supply systems once markets have become more complete, and basic productive factors, such as labor and capital, have become more mobile. This situation corresponds to the early 1990s, when markets had developed in many regions for many products, but prior to the most recent push for liberalizing reforms. In the final scenario (col. 4), reforms policies are finally implemented in an unrestricted economy characterized by relatively complete markets. This simulation is intended to show the effects of the recent market liberalization measures.

A short description of the basic optimization model and the data used to create and calibrate the model are contained in appendix 1. The following section examines the results of the simulations.

Simulating the Effect of Agricultural Reforms in China's Developing Economy

Three series of simulation exercises examine the impact of reform measures on farmers' production behavior, as well as on household marketing and income performance. In particular, the investigation focuses on the impact of the removal of government policy interventions (especially crop procurement and fertilizer subsidy programs) in the presence and absence of complete

---

2. This exercise models, in part, the fertilizer market liberalization case examined above. The purpose of the discussion, however, is focused not on market breakdowns but on understanding farmer behavior and its impact on food production and income growth.

TABLE 2.   Summary of Simulations and Corresponding Events

Restrictions	Model 1: Fully Restricted	Model 2: Incomplete Market	Model 3: Policy-Restricted	Model 4: Unrestricted
Restrictions on procurement and input distribution activities	yes	no	yes	no
Incomplete markets and restrictions on labor and capital allocations	yes	yes	no	no
Corresponding time period in China's reforms	Pre-reform and early reform period (early to mid-1980s)	Simulates rapid liberalization in early reform period	Late reform period—after liberalization, before second stage of reforms (late 1980s, early 1990s)	Full liberalization policies in effect (mid-1990s)

factor markets (i.e., when there are restrictions on labor and capital markets and when there are not). While the model generates the results of a representative farm household, the concern here is on how these decisions would affect the goals of government policy makers. As seen in earlier sections of this chapter, sectoral leaders are concerned with maintaining agricultural productivity and the output of grain in order to assure the provision of stable and cheap supplies of food to urban residents. In a somewhat secondary manner, they are also concerned with maintaining and increasing farm income, which benefits households, increases rural demand for locally manufactured goods, and finances investment and input purchases that then feed back to increase agricultural production. Hence, attention will be paid primarily to the production decisions of the households that affect agricultural productivity, grain output, and agricultural incomes.

From an initial baseline case, designed to replicate household behavior in the early reform era, the first experiment investigates the effect of removing government procurement policies in the presence of factor market imperfections (table 2, cols. 1 and 2). This can be thought of as a "big bang approach," since reforms are assumed to be carried out immediately after the earlier liberalization measures (which are implied in the structure of the basic model—e.g., HRS reforms, price increases, etc.), but before factor and other markets have had time to develop.

Model 1 is "fully restricted" in that the representative farmer operates in an economy without well-defined factor markets, and the household's output, procurement, and marketing decisions are curtailed by government policies. The policy restrictions are:

1. A mandatory procurement quota constraint: the representative farmer is required to deliver 1,000 kg of rice, 123 kg of cotton, 315 kg of wheat, and 25 kg of rapeseed to the state at quota prices.
2. A "linked" fertilizer subsidy constraint: in return for fulfilling the procurement quotas, the farmer is entitled to purchase the following quantities of plan fertilizer at quota prices: 6 and 50 kg of urea for each 100 kg of grain and cotton, respectively, sold to the state under contract; and 225 kg each of ABC and single super phosphate (SSP) for every hectare of grain sown.
3. Minimum organic fertilizer and cash crop constraints: The farmer is required to apply a minimum of 34 tons of organic fertilizer to each hectares of sown rice and cannot plant more than 0.07 hectares of cash crops (e.g., mint).

The factor market restrictions that are imposed on the model are: the farmer has no access to off-farm employment of any kind; the farmer cannot hire in or hire out labor for farming; and there is no credit market and thus the farmer cannot borrow money. Model 2, the "incomplete market model," shows what happens when reforms remove the quotas and subsidies faced by farm households, but farmers still do not have free access to well-functioning labor and capital markets. In a modeling sense, this means that the policy restrictions have been removed but the factor market restrictions are still in place.

Columns 1 and 2 in table 3 present the results of this first policy experiment. The farmer in model 1 (the fully restricted model) applies 223 kilograms of fertilizer, over half of which comes from organic sources. The farmer is forced by policy and factor market restrictions to produce all eight crops, and applies high rates of fertilizer (from 300 to 435 kilograms per hectare) on each. The farmer produces 3,134 kilograms of grain on the representative farm, and earns an income of 2,599 yuan.

After the big bang reforms (that is, when procurement policies and subsidies are removed even before markets have had a chance to develop), household incomes rise by over 40 percent to 3,873 yuan per year. Most of this gain comes from allocative efficiencies arising from the more profitable

TABLE 3. Comparison of Optimal Solutions in the Four Simulation Models

	Model 1: Fully Restricted	Model 2: Incomplete Market	Model 3: Policy Restricted	Model 4: Unrestricted
Fertilizer Consumption (nutrient weight, kg)				
Total nutrients	223	215	258	245
Chemical	84	103	236	245
N	64	78	144	154
P	19	25	92	91
Organic	139	112	22	0
Crop mix (ha)				
Hybrid rice	0.01	0.07	0.01	0.00
Indica rice	0.05	0.03	0.00	0.00
Japonica rice	0.25	0.14	0.37	0.47
Cotton	0.09	0.00	0.09	0.00
Wheat	0.07	0.07	0.46	0.47
Rapeseed	0.06	0.11	0.01	0.00
Barley	0.09	0.07	0.00	0.00
Mint	0.07	0.22	0.00	0.00
Land idle in the winter	0.18	0.00	0.00	0.00
Nutrient application rate (nutrient weight, kg/ha)				
Hybrid rice	435	375	375	
Indica rice	300	263		
Japonica rice	300	233	263	263
Cotton	390		390	
Wheat	360	263	263	263
Rapeseed	300	300	300	
Barley	330	330		
Mint	330	330		
Total grain production (kg)[a]	3,134	2,606	5,096	5,803
Net revenue (yuan)	2,599	3,873	4,163	5,368
Shadow price of (yuan)[b]				
Labor	4.74	6.23	23.49	23.49
Capital	0.10	0.26	0.10	0.10

[a]Total grain production is the total amount of grain harvested from the entire farm, which has 0.94 hectare.
[b]Shadow price of labor/capital is the imputed value of the constrained resource, or the potential gain in the objective function value if that resource was increased by one unit. Shadow price for labor is calculated for the entire peak season, in which the shadow price varies daily.

mix of crops produced on the farm, since the farmer is not required by policy to produce low-yielding, input-consuming crops like cotton, and can move more fully into profitable cash crops such as mint, which was the crop that generated the highest profits in the study area. Some of the gain is also a direct result of the lower implicit tax being shouldered by the farmer, who now does not have to sell low-priced grain to the state, but part of this gain is offset by the loss of the subsidy embodied in the state-allocated fertilizer.

While beneficial to rural residents, the new policies may lead to food shortages in the urban areas and other extrarural problems. The procurement and fertilizer subsidy policies apparently were quite effective when applied in an economy featuring few alternatives for labor and capital use. Farmers were required to plant large amounts of grain and cotton to meet their procurement quota. When removed, the application of fertilizer systematically falls, and the rate used on each of the individual crops is either lower or the same. While there are some gains from specialization, without an opportunity to hire in labor or use credit, the farmer is still balancing household labor across seven productive activities, trying to utilize his own family's resources as efficiently as possible. Overall, as a result of these actions, grain output falls by 17 percent, which equals over half of the marketed surplus rates in China's food economy in the early 1980s.

China did not take the big bang approach. Instead, a number of years passed after the initial reforms were implemented without pushing forward any new, radical measures. The government continued to use its procurement quota as a mechanism to ensure stable food supplies to the cities, while at the same time (except for the brief period in 1986 and 1987), they kept monopoly control over fertilizer distribution. But there was progress in the development of markets, as well as a movement of labor out of agriculture into the off-farm sector.

The effectiveness of China's institutional development approach can be seen by comparing models 1 and 3 (table 3). While it may have taken a number of years to be realized, all indicators favorable to society (both urban and rural) moved upward. Agricultural intensity rose, based on the increasing input use and more specialized crop selection. These decisions led to *both* higher grain output and higher incomes. Incomes have increased the most, however, due to the contribution of off-farm income sources. Rising income has also supplemented the effort to increase agricultural output, since the capital constraint has now been relieved. Hired labor was used to replace the family labor that moved out of agriculture. On the basis of this stylized example, the superiority of the slow reform approach is illustrated.

There is one further benefit to taking the institutional development approach. After markets have been developed, the policies that were originally kept in place to maintain grain and fiber output and marketings eventually lose their effectiveness and can be eliminated with no negative effect on either rural incomes or grain output. This is illustrated by comparing models 3 and

4. When farmers are fully free to make all decisions, and face complete markets, they choose to specialize in those crops that have the highest return. Households commit as much labor as possible to off-farm activities, but are able to increase grain output. Because there is no capital constraint, they can hire labor and can specialize in the production of high-quality rice and wheat. Once reformers have moved themselves to this last phase, they may find themselves in a win-win situation. By eliminating costly interventionary programs, both rural incomes and grain production can be increased.

Conclusions and Policy Implications

The importance of the role played by China's rural economy is readily recognized by analysts of reform. However, in their rush to explain their insights into China's general reform success, the transition of China's agricultural sector has frequently been over-simplified. The early reforms increased incentives, but left most actors working within an economy that was closely controlled by a government whose primary aim for the sector had changed little since the Mao era. China's leaders maintained those policies that they knew could provide a stable supply of food and fiber. Market allocation had little to do with resource allocation in the early years. Only after the successes of decollectivization had freed up enough capital and labor from the agricultural sector did the reformers begin to encourage investment in the noncropping sector. But just as in McMillan and Naughton's (1991) perception of the reforms, the first real market liberalization was allowed only on the periphery. This nonmainstream set of newly freed up producers soon developed a broader and more stable operating base of its own, and after steadily expanding for more than ten years, became a force of change in its own right.

The lesson for countries considering liberalization should be clear. If agriculture is one of the sectors to lead the way, it is important to understand the role the sector is supposed to play in the development of the economy. A strong food sector is critical in most economies to support industrial development and to promote stability. Incentives can be given to farm households and other rural dwellers without moving immediately to a system of market-directed resource allocation. Those policies that are considered to be most effective in making the agricultural sector move toward its goals should not be abandoned in the early stages of reform. If only a part of the rural economy is given the opportunity to develop marketing channels and communication networks, even if there are inefficiencies in the early period after reform, these should be considered part of the investment needed to build up a viable set of marketing institutions. However, the part that is freed up, while not wanting to be controlled, should be encouraged to develop, as it is precisely this subsector that may be able to provide the competitive pressure to push forward with the reforms and move toward true market liberalization.

TABLE A1.   Schematic Tableau of the Jiangsu Farming Systems Model

	Crop Production	Animal Production and Marketing	Labor Hire-in	Employment		Obligation Labor
				Hire-out	Off-Farm	
Objective Function		+		+	+	
Resource Constraints						
Land	1					
Labor	1	1	−1	1	1	1
Capital	1	1	1	−1	−1	
Balance Rows						
Nutrient	1					
Crop marketing	−1	1				
Consumption						
Policy Constraints						
Crop procurement						
Urea purchase						
ABC purchase	−1					
Minimum use of organic fertilizer	−1					1
Minimum obl. labor day						1
Labor Market Restrictions						
Hire-in			1			
Hire-out				1		
Off-farm job					1	
Credit market restriction						

(continued)

APPENDIX 1

The Empirical Model

An empirical model was built to represent the farming system, economic conditions, and policy environment in central Jiangsu Province, a region in China's fast-growing coastal zone.[3] Similar to other linear programming models, this representative household model consists of three components— an objective function, a set of productive activities, and a series of constraints. (Table A1 contains a schematic tableau of the farming system model.)

The objective function includes revenues from crop and animal production, agricultural labor activities, and off-farm employment. Costs of crop and

---

3. In this representative household model, the general equilibrium effects of price response are ignored. These may be important, especially in the simulations where factor and product markets have developed.

TABLE A1—*Continued*

Chem. Fert Quota	Mk1	Organic Fertilizer	Consumption		Crop Marketing		Financing		RHS
			Own	Buy	Quota	Mkt	Sav	Loan	
					+	+			MAX
									=L=
		1							=L=
1	1	1		1			−1	−1	=L=
									=G=
−1−1	−1	−1							=G=
			1		1	1			=G=
			1	1					=G=
					1				=G=
1					−1				=L=
1									=L=
									=G=
									=G=
									=E=0
									=E=0
									=E=0
								1	=E=0

animal production, fertilizer purchase, labor hiring, interest payments, and purchased crop consumption are included with negative signs. Leisure and returns to organic fertilizer application enter into the objective function with positive values.

The model contains cropping and animal husbandry enterprises; off-farm employment in both the nearby rural areas and distant urban cities; activities showing commitment to high agricultural productivity, such as the purchase and utilization of chemical fertilizer; and the preparation and application of organic fertilizers. The model also includes activities allowing for crop consumption, output marketing, and credit transactions. The model includes piecewise production functions (using 12 levels for each of two inputs and interaction terms) to approximate the nonlinear relationship between fertilizer application and crop yields (Hazell and Norton 1986). The production function coefficients are econometrically estimated by the authors using farm-level survey data on output and inputs (see Ye 1992; Ye and Rozelle 1994 for details).

The model also specifies a number of constraints that embody important policy measures and structural barriers faced by the farm household. One set of constraints is developed to simulate the situation where the representative farm faces mandatory crop procurement and subsidized fertilizer allocation restrictions. The farmer's access to subsidized fertilizer is linked to the crop delivery quota. Both crop marketing and fertilizer purchase decisions are made under a two-tier pricing system.

Because of the importance of off-farm employment in the local economy, a series of farm and off-farm labor constraints is included. Agricultural labor use is broken down by crop and by time period to capture seasonality of labor use for cultivating different crops. The farm household has a choice of participation in one of two off-farm employment contracts; one requires long-term migration to a remote urban center, whereas the other allows household members to be employed in a nearby township- or village-run enterprise. Wages are higher for the former than for the latter. Farmers employed in nearby rural enterprises can return to their farming activities throughout the season.

Data

Data used in the model are from household surveys and interviews with local officials conducted by the authors during seven site visits carried out between 1988 and 1992. A total of 115 farm households were selected randomly from four villages in two counties in central Jiangsu Province. The household survey, carried out during the initial 15 months of fieldwork in 1988 and 1989, consisted of three separate visits to the sample households. The survey collected data on production practices, labor allocation, off-farm employment activities, prices, and wages, as well as the quantities and labor requirements for all types of chemical and organic fertilizers. Enumerators also questioned the farmers closely about the nature of their mandatory crop procurement contracts and about the amount and sources of all subsidized fertilizer allocations. The authors also made trips to the villages in 1991 and 1992 to collect supplemental information and to conduct a series of intensive, follow-up interviews with farmers, local leaders, and agricultural officials regarding fertilizer use and policy.

The study sites are representative of a genre of rural areas in eastern and central China that have a well-developed agricultural infrastructure and a rapidly developing rural industrial base. Crop yields and per capita income in the survey area are above the national average. The growth rate of rural industry and its share in the rural economy, however, are similar to national averages. Over 80 percent of cropland was dedicated to grain in the prereform years. But area devoted to cash crops followed national trends and expanded to more than 30 percent by 1988 (Jiangsu Provincial Statistical Bureau 1990).

Application rates for chemical fertilizer are similar to the provincial average, but are 58 percent higher than the national average.

Model Validity and Performance

To test the validity of the farming systems model, the optimal solution of a baseline version of the model was compared with observed household data in the survey area. The "basic version" of the Jiangsu model simulates all policy restriction that a farmer faces in the survey area, including government policies on fertilizer subsidies, crop procurement, and various local rules and regulations. This version of the model also simulates labor market imperfections by not allowing the farm household to spend more than 50 days in the off-farm labor market and by restricting the number of days that farmers can rely on exchange labor (i.e., labor from neighboring farmers, for whom the farmer must also work) to no more than 5 days per peak production period. These parameters are based on the results of the household survey. The basic model is closest to the fully restricted model (model 1), but contains fewer restrictions on activities in the labor market.

Major activities of farm and off-farm operations in the model's solution were found to be similar to the observed data. Almost all important local crops as well as other commonly observed activities (such as hog raising, organic fertilizer application, and off-farm employment) were included in the final solution. Key variables in the model, such as labor use, fertilizer consumption, and profit levels, deviated from the sample's mean levels by 6, 7, and 29 percent, respectively (see Ye 1992, for details).

REFERENCES

Chen, K. G., Gary Jefferson, and I. Singh. 1992. "Lessons from China's Economic Reform." *Journal of Comparative Economics* 16:201–25.
Crook, Frederick. 1989. "China's Current Household Contract System (Part I)," *USDA CPE Agriculture Report* 2, no. 3: 26–30.
Eckstein, Alexander. 1975. *Chinese Economic Development.* Ann Arbor: University of Michigan Press.
Fan, Shengjen. 1991. "Effects of Technological Change and Institutional Reform on Production Growth in Chinese Agriculture." *American Journal of Agricultural Economics* 73:266–75.
Gelb, Alan, Gary Jefferson, and Inderjit Singh. 1993. "Can Communist Economics Transform Incrementally? The Experience of China." In National Bureau of Economic Research, ed., *Macroeconomics Annual 1993.* Cambridge, Mass: National Bureau of Economic Research.
Harrold, Peter. 1992. "China's Reform Experience to Date." World Bank Discussion

Papers, No. 180, China and Mongolia Department, World Bank, Washington, DC.

Hazell, Peter B. R., and Roger D. Norton. 1986. *Mathematical Programming for Economic Analysis in Agriculture*. New York: MacMillan Publishing Company.

Hsu, John. 1993. *Economic Theories of Modern Chinese Economists*. Berkeley: University of California Press.

Huang, Jikun. 1994. "Demand for Staple Food and Quality Rice in Rural China." Working paper, Department of Agricultural Economics, China National Rice Research Institute, Hangzhou.

Jiangsu Provincial Statistical Bureau. 1990. *Jiangsu Sheng Shi Xian Jingji 1990* (Jiangsu Province: City and county economy 1990). Beijing: China Statistical Publishing House.

Lardy, Nicholas. 1983. *Agriculture in China's Modern Economic Development*. Cambridge: Cambridge University Press.

Lardy, Nicholas, and Kenneth Lieberthal, eds. 1983. *Chen Yun's Strategy for China's Development: A Non-Maoist Alternative*. New York: M. S. Sharpe.

Liang, Heng, 1993. "The Contractual Agreements and Labor Incentives in Rural China in the Late 1980s," Unpublished Ph.D. Dissertation, Department of Agricultural Economics, Cornell University, Ithaca, NY.

Lin, Justin. 1992. "Rural Reforms and Agricultural Growth in China." *American Economic Review* 82, no. 1: 34–51.

Lin, Justin, Fang Cai, and Zhou Li. 1994. "Why China's Reforms Have Been Successful: Its Implications for Other Reforming Economies." Working paper, Department of Rural Economy, Development Research Center, Beijing.

Liu, Beiyang, and Hongli Xie. 1982. "Problems of Present Incentive Sale of Chemical Fertilizers for Agricultural Production." *Nongye Jingji Wenti* (Problems of the agricultural economy) 10:51–60.

Liu, Jiang. 1991. *Quanguo Nongcun Jingji Fazhan: Shinian Guihua he Dibage Wunian Jihua* (The nation's rural economic development: The 10-year plan and the eighth 5-year plan). Beijing: China Economic Press.

Lyons, Thomas. 1992. "Cautionary Tales of Market Reform." Working Paper, Department of Economics, Cornell University, Ithaca, NY.

McKinnon, Ronald. 1993. "Gradual versus Rapid Liberalization in Socialist Economies: Financial Policies and Macroeconomic Stability in China and Russia Compared." Paper presented at the World Bank's Annual Conference on Development Economics, World Bank, Washington, DC.

McMillan, John, and Barry Naughton. 1991. "How to Reform a Planned Economy: Lessons from China." *Oxford Review of Economic Policy* 8, no.1: 130–44.

McMillan, J., J. Whalley, and L. Zhu. 1989. "The Impact of China's Economic Reforms on Agricultural Productivity Growth." *Journal of Political Economy* 97:781–807.

Mao Tsetung. 1977. *On the Ten Major Relationships*. Beijing: Foreign Language Press.

NYJJS Editorial Board. 1984. *Nongye Jishu Jingji Shouce* (Agricultural technical and economic handbook). Beijing: Agricultural Publishing House.

Oi, Jean. 1986. *State and Peasant in Contemporary China: The Political Economy of Village Government*. Berkeley: University of California Press.

Park, Albert. 1993a. "Grain Market Liberalization in Shaanxi Province." *USDA Economic Research Service Asia and Pacific Rim Agriculture and Trade Notes*, November 1–12.

———. 1993b. "Do Grain Quotas Matter?" Working Paper, Food Research Institute, Stanford University, Stanford, CA.

Perkins, Dwight. 1992. "China's 'Gradual' Approach to Market Reforms." Paper presented at a conference on Comparative Experiences of Economic Reform and Post-Socialist Transformation, El Escorial, Spain.

Putterman, Louis. 1993. *Continuity and Change in China's Rural Development: Collectives and Reform Eras in Perspective*. New York: Oxford University Press.

Qian, Yingyi, and Chenggen Xu. 1993. "Why China's Economic Reforms Differ." CP No. 25, Working Paper of the Development Economics Research Program, London School of Economics, London, England.

Rozelle, Scott. 1991. "The Economic Behavior of Village Leaders in China's Reforming Economy." Ph.D. Diss., Department of Agricultural Economics, Cornell University, Ithaca, NY.

———. 1996. "Stagnation without Equity." *China Journal* 35:76–99.

———. 1994a. "Decision Making in China's Rural Economy: Defining a Framework for Understanding the Behavior of Village Leaders and Farm Households." *China Quarterly* 137:99–124.

———. 1994b. "Quantifying Chinese Village Leader's Multiple Objectives." *Journal of Comparative Economics* 18:25–45.

Rozelle, Scott, and Heng Liang. 1992. "Contracts and Choices: Decision Making in Post-Reform Rural China." Paper presented at the AAEA/CAEA Jointly Sponsored Conference on Chinese Agricultural Development in the 1990s, Beijing.

Sachs, Jeffrey. 1993. "Comment" (on Gelb, Alan, Gary Jefferson, and Inderjit Singh, "Can Communist Economies Transform Incrementally? The Experience of China"). In National Bureau of Economic Research, ed., *Macroeconomics Annual, 1993*, 137–47. Cambridge, Mass.: Bureau of Economic Research.

Sicular, Terry. 1988. "Agricultural Planning and Pricing in the Post-Mao Period." *China Quarterly* 116:671–703.

———. 1991. "China's Agricultural Policy during the Reform Period." In Joint Economic Committee Congress of the United States, ed., *China's Economic Dilemmas in the 1990s: The Problems of Reforms, Modernization and Interdependence*. Washington, DC: Government Printing Office.

Stone, Bruce. 1986. "Chinese Fertilizer Application in the 1980s and 1990s: Issues of Growth, Balance, Allocation, Efficiency and Response." In Joint Congressional Economic Committee, ed., *China's Economy Looks Toward the Year 2000*, Vol. 1, 453–96. Washington, D.C.: Government Publishing Office.

———. 1988. "Developments in Agricultural Technology." *China Quarterly* 116: 767–822.

———. 1989. "Fertilizer's Greener Pastures." *The China Business Review* (September–October): 46–55.

Stone, Bruce, Tong Zhong, Scott Rozelle, Yvonne Ying, Z. Xu, and Dehua Jiang. Forthcoming. "Income Growth and Rural Development in Poor Chinese Counties, 1978–1987." In J. von Braun, ed., *Commercialization and Development*. Baltimore, MD: John Hopkins Press.

Tangermann, Stefan. 1994. "EC Membership by the Year 2000: A Realistic Objective." Paper presented to the AgraEurope Conference, "Towards 200: Agriculture, Agribusiness and the Food Industry in Central and Eastern Europe," Budapest, Hungary, March 3–4.

Wu, Shuo. 1992. "Interprovincial Circulation of Grain and Wholesale Markets in China." Paper Presented at the joint meeting of the Chinese Agricultural Economics Association, Taiwan Rural Economic Society, and American Agricultural Economics Association, Beijing.

Ye, Qiaolun. 1991. "Small-scale Fertilizer Plants in China: Problems and Perspectives." Working Paper, Food Research Institute, Stanford University.

———. 1992. "Fertilizer Policy and Farm-level Fertilizer Utilization in Jiangsu Province, China." Ph.D. Diss., Stanford University, Stanford, CA.

Ye, Qiaolun, and Scott Rozelle. 1994. "Fertilizer Demand in China's Reforming Economy." *Canadian Journal of Agricultural Economics* 42(June): 101–25.

Zhao, Ziyang. 1982. "Report on the Sixth Five-Year Plan." *Beijing Review* 25, no.51: 10–35.

Zhong, Funing. 1993. "A Review of Recent Grain Reforms in Rural and Urban Areas." Working paper, Department of Agricultural Economics, Nanjing Agricultural University, Nanjing.

ZGGSXZGLTJ. 1992. *Zhongguo Gongshang Xingzheng Guanli Tongji Sishinian* (Forty Years of Statistics of China's Market Administration and Management). Beijing: State Statistical Bureau Press.

ZGNYNJ. 1988. *Zhongguo Nongye Nianjian* (China Agricultural Yearbook). Beijing: China Agricultural Press.

ZGTJNJ. 1991–1993. *Zhongguo Tongji Nianjian* (China Statistical Yearbook). Beijing: China Statistical Press.

CHAPTER 10

Providing Public Goods in Rural China Postreform

Charles S. Gitomer

Rural institutional innovation in China has been driven by changes in incentives and property rights at the grassroots level. Rural institutional transformation has largely been ad hoc and bottom up. Organizational forms that have developed in response to the changes are endogenous outcomes of the process of reform. Under the collective economic system there were institutions to supply public goods. Reforms first modified and then destroyed the institutional basis of the system of public goods provision. Only gradually, through experimentation and trial and error, did the Chinese build new organizations and incentive systems to provide these public goods. In theory the public goods problem is not difficult to solve. Economic theory provides many solutions, and many societies have found acceptable arrangements in practice. Nonetheless, in the experience of transitional economies, this is a serious problem. In practice—as was the case in rural China—the old system of public goods supply is dismantled before a new one is put in place. Within this institutional vacuum new means to solve the public goods problem must be found, for failure to do so—particularly for vital agricultural inputs—can be disastrous. Failure to provide these goods subject to market failure can lead to the collapse of agricultural production and consequent economic crisis. For example, we know that similar problems have occurred in the former Soviet Union, but have not been successfully resolved. Somehow the Chinese have muddled through. How has this happened?

We may think of three complementary problems: prices, property rights, and incentives. One means of affecting reform is to decontrol prices and assign property rights. This will then remove the incentive problem. But in

This chapter was prepared while the author was a Visiting Scholar at the Graduate School of International Relations and Pacific Studies of the University of California, San Diego. Support was provided by an International Predissertation Fellowship from the Social Science Research Council and the American Council of Learned Societies funded by the Ford Foundation. I am grateful to Barry Naughton and John McMillan for advice and encouragement, and to Roger Bohn, Scott Rozelle, and conference participants for comments. All mistakes are mine.

the case of markets with public goods, natural monopoly, or other market failures, these problems must be solved simultaneously—a practical impossibility. Instead, a more or less adequate process of institutional development by approximation through improvisation is needed.

The Chinese case of rural institutional development has followed a path of improvisation. First incentives were adjusted, followed by assignment of property rights. Last, perhaps, will come complete price decontrol, but as of 1993 this had not yet happened.

This chapter explores changes in incentives and organizational structure of firms producing commodities subject to market failure. Changes in provision of these goods in rural China have been a result of the rapidly changing institutional arrangements of economic reform. The new organizational forms adopted were not designed all at once; rather, they are unintended consequences of a search for sets of complementary policies suited to the rapidly changing institutional environment. If designed from scratch, it is unlikely that the present incentive systems and organizations would have their present form. Instead, Chinese policy makers looked to past organizations that had proven successful and invited experimentation to develop new ones. Successful reforms, the result of a torrent of bottom-up innovation caused by the deregulation of agricultural activities, diffused quickly and were adopted throughout the country.

Irrigation and health care were both collectively provided goods before reform, though neither strictly meet the definition of a public good.[1] Even so, both have some characteristics of public goods and are subject to market failure. Irrigation services are nonexcludable to the extent that monitoring costs for exclusion can be very high. In any irrigation system, monitoring every canal and every farmer within the system watershed can be quite costly. Any farmer with a bucket can take water from a canal. Irrigation services are nonrival to the extent that one farmer can use the return flows of another. Since irrigation has high fixed costs and relatively low marginal costs, it may be subject to market failure. Preventative health care has strong public good characteristics, according to Jamison et al. (1984). Acute care, on the other hand, can be privately supplied and insured. However, acute care is subject to market failure, since it must be provided in every market, whether profitable or not.

This chapter will examine the evolution of organizations and incentives for the provision of goods subject to market failure in rural China using the

---

1. A pure public good is nonrival and nonexcludable in consumption. Nonrival means that consumption by one agent does not preclude consumption by another agent. Nonexcludable means that no agent can be excluded from consumption.

cases of irrigation management and health care reform. The stimuli for that evolution are the shocks of reform: the implementation of the agricultural production responsibility system beginning in 1979 and the dissolution of the People's Communes by 1983. In one case, irrigation, the shocks seem to have induced a stable, sustainable organization and incentive system while in the other, health care, no such resolution has yet been obtained. This outcome is ironic. Irrigation provision has more public good characteristics than health care, yet it is for irrigation that the problem of supply has been resolved satisfactorily.

Institutional Changes and Reform

The institutional transformation of rural China is rooted in the initial institutional conditions—those of the People's Communes. The People's Communes, the basic political and economic unit in the Chinese countryside before reform, were at the top of a three-tiered hierarchy. The next level was the production brigade, with ten to fifteen brigades per commune. The lowest-level unit, and the production accounting unit, was the production team. Production teams were about the size of natural villages, with ten to twenty households.

As the basic unit of accounting, the production team was the unit of collective production. Team members worked together to produce for the team and received their income from the team. Income was provided in work points, supposedly a measure of effective labor, but more realistically a measure of work attendance. They were awarded daily. To determine the annual payment to each team member, all work points awarded in the course of the previous year were totaled and each assigned a value as a portion of the net product of the team. Payments in cash and kind were then distributed to team members according to the work points earned.

The People's Commune production incentive system, the awarding of work points, effectively manipulated individual incentives so that all tasks were of more or less equal value to peasants. The work point system, while inefficient from a production standpoint, successfully allocated sufficient labor to all activities. The goods we are studying were provided under this collective production system. Irrigation and health care workers at the team level were awarded work points for their labor. Few people worked very hard, but the allocation of labor among productive activities was not a problem.

The People's Commune's production planning system was bureaucratic by nature. At the top was the commune administration, which was the producers' go between with government input supply and output marketing enterprises. As such, farmers in production teams were dependent on the commune for mediating purchase of inputs such as fuel and fertilizer from the government, and for grain sales to the government. All commodities moved through such procurement channels. Many market transactions were illegal.

At the beginning of reform, two policies were of particular importance in the countryside. One was the agricultural production responsibility system, a package of several reforms that included distribution of communal land and decentralization of production decision making from the production team to families, and a general increase of about 50 percent in grain procurement prices. The other was a general retrenchment of investment. Central government investment in the countryside, particularly in capital construction, dropped dramatically. It was halved between 1979 and 1981, surpassing 1979 levels only in 1990.

Incompatibility of incentives between family farms and the communes became evident almost immediately. With the introduction of the production responsibility system, the communes had become at best superfluous. With the continued development of markets for inputs and output, the communes began to obstruct input and output flows rather than facilitate them. Since peasant income now depended upon farming output, little or no time was devoted to production of collective goods. Much infrastructure developed at great cost under the communes fell into disrepair.

Successful experiments with decommunization led to a general dismantling of all communes by the end of 1983.[2] One inconsistency between family farms and the rural institutional structure was removed, but another problem arose as the work point system of incentive manipulation was abolished. The disappearance of this labor allocation system, combined with powerful incentives given to farmers to produce agricultural products by the responsibility system, was a strong stimulus for institutional innovation in the provision of goods formerly supplied by the commune.

The new incentive system is the crucial link to understanding the erosion of old institutional solutions to the public goods problem. Complementarities within the old set of policies were weakened by the introduction of the responsibility system for agricultural production and destroyed by the loss of the labor allocation properties of the work point system caused by the dissolution of the communes. New complementary policies were sought to replace those rendered ineffective by reform. It is within the very different framework of family farms, developing markets, and new institutional arrangements that organizations and incentives to solve the public goods problem evolved.[3]

---

2. These experiments and the problems that led to them are described in Shue 1984.

3. The collective remains a strong presence in parts of China today. In other places this is not so. This chapter focuses on alternative arrangements that have evolved in response to the dismantling or weakening of collective production.

Irrigation

Irrigation has been an integral part of Chinese agricultural output growth for centuries. As a part of organizational reform in the 1950s, increased irrigated area was emphasized as China sought to rebuild agricultural capacity following decades of civil war. Even Mao Zedong recognized its importance when he said "Water control is the lifeblood of agriculture."

How have organizations and incentives in the irrigation management system evolved during the reform process? What are the incentives for entry and the problems of sustainability of irrigation firms? How did constraints on changes in consumer welfare affect the incentives and organizational form chosen for the firm? The reforms applied to irrigation are initially characterized as a reaction to shocks caused by other reforms in the rural areas. Later reforms are reactions to noncomplementarities revealed in the development process. The new irrigation management firms are analogous to regulated private utilities. These utilities provide irrigation services to farmers at regulated prices and in return are allowed to produce for protected markets using production factors from the irrigation project. The profits from these ventures serve as cross subsidies for irrigation services losses. Additional resources have been directed to the firms through the revival of peasant labor contributions. These labor contributions combined with payments for irrigation services can been seen as equivalent to a two-part pricing structure for farmers. No claim is made about the efficiency of these arrangements, only that they work.

Prereform Irrigation Management

Irrigation management before economic reform was bureaucratic. Management was coordinated by a county bureau of the Ministry of Water Resources. Below the county level, management was by a small number of professional technicians helped by labor allocated by the commune. The emphasis in water management was not on efficient or economical water use, but rather on expanding available supplies through capital construction. Between 1952 and 1978, about two-thirds of state spending on water was for capital construction, and only one-third was for operating expenses. However, the share going to current operating expenses increased slowly during the 1970s.[4] Most capital construction was carried out using farmers drafted to work during the winter agricultural slack season.

Irrigation was given a specific labor allocation in the communal production plan. Since it was in the plan, commune member irrigation workers were

---

4. *Nongye Shuili Guangai Gaikuang* (1980).

TABLE 1. Central Government Water Resources Capital Construction Investment, 1975–92

Year	Capital Construction Investment (in million yuan)	Capital Construction Investment as a Percentage of GDP	Year	Capital Construction Investment (in million yuan)	Capital Construction Investment as a Percentage of GDP
1975	2,566	0.89	1984	1,982	0.29
1976	2,817	1.01	1985	1,802	0.21
1977	2,847	0.94	1986	1,736	0.18
1978	3,468	0.97	1987	2,118	0.19
1979	3,496	0.87	1988	2,365	0.17
1980	2,653	0.59	1989	2,953	0.18
1981	1,313	0.27	1990	4,065	0.23
1982	1,774	0.34	1991	5,016	0.25
1983	2,109	0.36	1992	6,919	0.29

Source: Capital construction investment figures for 1975–85: *Guojia Tongjiju Guding Zichan Touzi Tongjisi* (1987), 71–75; 1986–87: *Guojia Tongjiju Guding Zichan Touzi Tongjisi* (1989), 77; 1988–89: *Guojia Tongjiju Guding Zichan Touzi Tongjisi* (1991), 67; 1990: *Zhongguo Tongjiju* (1991), 159; 1991: *Zhongguo Tongjiju* (1992), 161; and 1992: *Zhongguo Tongjiju* (1993), 161. GDP figures for 1975–77: *Guojia Tongjiju Guomin Jingji Pingheng Tongjisi* (1987), 10, adjusted. 1978–92: *Zhongguo Tongjiju* (1993), 31.

paid in work points. Professional managers received salaries from the county water resources bureau. Irrigation costs were allocated as a part of production costs. Those irrigation costs not covered by commune income were subsidized by the Ministry of Water Resources.[5]

Implementation of the production responsibility system and the concomitant reduction in rural investment hurt the irrigation sector badly. Individual incentives introduced by the responsibility system came into direct opposition with those for irrigation services provision. Peasants had to till their fields to earn income rather than simply engage in any productive activity to receive work points as before. They were no longer willing, nor was it possible to compel them, to contribute labor to irrigation work.

At the same time the level of investment in water resources capital construction dropped precipitously, as shown in table 1. Investment dropped almost 25 percent from 1979 to 1980 and more than 60 percent between 1979 and 1981 in absolute terms, and even more as a percent of GDP. Since this investment was an important component of the water resources strategy, the sector suffered greatly.

The introduction of the responsibility system had other, more insidious effects on irrigation. State Agricultural Commission Document 41 (*Guojia nongwei* 1981) noted that wells and canals had been filled in, that irrigation projects had been damaged, and that in some cases projects were divided up among individuals or sold piece by piece. Bai (1982) noted that at that time water resources project damage was severe and that "theft, grabbing, and seizure of water" happened all the time because there was no law or organized system to enforce order. A more severe problem was that there was no one to manage water resources projects.

In this generally chaotic atmosphere the significant and potentially serious incompatibilities between bureaucratically managed irrigation systems and family farms came to the fore. Coupled with the strict budgetary constraints on agriculture, great pressure was exerted for institutional innovation in irrigation water supply. Since a continuation of the high investment development strategy was no longer tenable under the new investment regime, management was seen as a reasonable substitute. Farmers, with incentives now based on the marginal value of output rather than work attendance, were also bound to demand higher quality irrigation services. This higher quality of service required more management input. To extract maximum benefits from existing irrigation projects, minimize the effect of reductions in capital construction investment, achieve higher levels of service quality, and be more

---

5. For treatment of irrigation management before reform, see Vermeer 1977; United Nations Economic and Social Commission for Asia and the Pacific 1979; Nickum 1981; and Gustafsson 1984.

responsive to peasant farmers' needs, irrigation management was intensified.[6] The change also recognized the need for efficient water use and increased capital utilization rates.

Despite rapid increases, farmers' incomes were still very low. In 1980 average annual per capita rural income was still less than 200 yuan. Even by 1985 it was less than 400 yuan, and since 1985 there has been no growth in rural incomes, on average. The proportion of income farmers could afford to spend on water remained low. In addition, since they contributed labor to the construction of irrigation systems, farmers felt entitled to water at low prices. A problem for irrigation managers was to provide water to farmers at a low, government-mandated price. They were still not required to operate in an economically efficient way; financing continued to come from the commune and the Ministry of Water Resources.

In part as a result of the incompatibility between bureaucratically managed irrigation systems and family farms, irrigated area slowly but surely began to fall.[7] This is shown in table 2. Since irrigation is a key input to agriculture, any substantial sustained decline in irrigated area, such as that seen from 1979 to 1985, would have serious effects on growth in agricultural output. To overcome the division and destruction of irrigation projects, to halt the decline in irrigated area, and to make irrigation management systems compatible with the rest of the reforms, the work post responsibility system was introduced from industry. This system introduced incentives within a bureaucratic framework by offering contracts calling for a base salary plus bonuses. Bonuses could be earned for performance of specified tasks or meeting specified production targets; penalties were assessed for failure to meet minimum standards. This attempt to introduce incentives to the bureaucratic management of irrigation projects was conservative and evolutionary, in that it did not change the organizational structure, but rather tried to introduce changes in incentives within irrigation organizations.

Individual incentives were weak and often had collective organizational performance components. Zhang and Yin (1983) report that the work post responsibility system's most common form was "five fixed and one reward or penalty." The state determined for each project the project personnel, the project tasks, the timing of completion of those tasks, a financial and materials budget, and the responsibilities of individual workers. Workers would

---

6. This was a topic of discussion by spring 1981. See Wang Jiaqian and Guan Jianzhong, "Farmland water resource projects should make management the priority," *Renmin Ribao*, 3 April 1981, 2. See also Luo's 1982 interview with the Minister of Water Resources, Qian Zhengying, and *Renmin Ribao* 1982.

7. Nickum (1990) notes that part of the decline in irrigated area represents the retirement of marginal land under poor irrigation and part is statistical adjustment or artifact. Even so, reports of destruction of irrigation infrastructure indicate that this was likely a significant problem that led to real decreases in irrigated area.

TABLE 2. Irrigated Area and Percentage Changes in China, 1978–91

Year	Irrigated Area (in million hectares)	Percentage Change over Previous Year	Percentage Change over 1978
1978	44.97		
1979	45.00	0.08	0.08
1980	44.89	−0.25	−0.17
1981	44.57	−0.70	−0.87
1982	44.18	−0.89	−1.75
1983	44.64	1.06	−0.71
1984	44.45	−0.43	−1.14
1985	44.04	−0.94	−2.07
1986	44.23	0.43	−1.64
1987	44.40	0.40	−1.25
1988	44.38	−0.05	−1.30
1989	44.92	1.20	−0.11
1990	47.40	5.53	5.42
1991	47.82	0.88	6.35

Source: Data from 1978, 1980–91: *Guojia Tongjiju Nongcun Shehui Jingji Tongjisi* (State statistical bureau rural socio-economic statistics department). *Zhongguo Nongcun Tongji Nianjian* (China rural statistical yearbook), 1985–92. Beijing: *Zhongguo Tongji Chubanshe* (China Statistics Press), 1985–92. Data from 1979 are from James E. Nickum, "Irrigated Area Statistics in the People's Republic of China." Mimeo, 1987.

receive bonuses of a portion of project retained profits for completing their tasks on time and on budget amounting to 20 to 40 percent of annual income, or else face penalties of up to 20 percent of the value of shortfalls of production. Another form evaluated performance annually, awarding 100 points of bonuses for perfect performance, with lesser amounts for lesser accomplishments. At one reservoir each point could be worth 1.5 yuan. The potential bonus was as much as half of the annual fixed salary.

On the practical side Nickum (1985) makes the following observation.

> The work post responsibility system, frequently cited as a bureaucratic counterpart to the production responsibility system, has a long and not very illustrious history. In the relatively limited number of cases described. . . , it seemed to be little more than an awarding of bonuses for good work attendance (or more precisely, a threat to withhold a small amount of nominally discretionary wages for poor attendance).

He also notes that water management was seen as a "dead end" occupation, since while irrigation managers had fairly high levels of technical training, their earning potential under this incentive system was quite limited.

The work post responsibility system was a step in the right direction, but in reality the complementarity between the work post responsibility system and the production responsibility system was weak. Properly implemented marginal incentives may have been effective in bringing about the desired level of effort on the part of irrigation managers within irrigation's bureaucratic context. But as Nickum notes, the implementation was hardly ideal. The system was successful to a degree, in that water was still supplied to farmers and agricultural output continued to grow. But the further adaptability of the system was rendered moot by more radical experimentation. The work post responsibility system now remains only in relatively few.[8]

Even before the communes were dissolved, experimentation with organizations and incentives at the grassroots level was well under way.[9] Some of these new organizations and incentives would be required to provide irrigation to family farms after the dissolution of the communes.[10]

The financing cushion provided to irrigation projects by the communes and by the Ministry of Water Resources disappeared with decommunization. Since local irrigation projects could no longer rely on operating subsidies from the communes, and since they were still required to maintain low water prices, they were forced to evaluate the profit potential of entry into markets for other products. This period saw a push to develop multiproduct firms so that "subsidiary" lines of production could subsidize irrigation services.[11] These multiproduct irrigation firms developed into private regulated utilities.

The firms are private in the sense that their managers are residual claimants of profit and of rights of control.[12] Irrigation managers who lease their project own the irrigation firms, in this sense. Property rights are divided

---

8. Those projects that still use the work post responsibility system are ones that are either large-scale projects that are considered strategic, and so must be under the control of the government, or are projects that no one is willing to lease because leasing such a project would be a money-losing proposition.

9. The State Agricultural Commission Document 41 (*Guojia nongwei* 1981) explicitly requested experimentation with different organizations at the local level to find suitable ones to solve the problem of irrigation supply.

10. The irrigation bureaucracy at the lowest levels did not disappear. At the township (formerly commune) level, the *shuilizhan* (water resources station) took over from the commune bureaucratic organ. At the county level the *shuiliju* (Water Resource Bureau) remained. The *shuiliju* is the representative of the Ministry of Water Resources at the county level and the *shuilizhan* is the representative of the ministry at the township level. While the *shuiliju* and *shuilizhan* no longer undertake day-to-day management of water projects, they still perform some coordination tasks. There are vertical linkages from the *shuilizhan* to the *shuiliju* all the way to the top of the Ministry of Water Resources hierarchy. There are also horizontal linkages between the *shuilizhan* and the township government and between the *shuiliju* and the county government. This is where the coordinating functions of the ministry organs comes in. In addition, if there is a need, the bureaucrats can take over the management of water projects in an emergency.

11. The principles to be followed and suggested product lines for diversified operations are found in Pan and Zuo 1984.

12. Grossman and Hart (1986) define ownership as residing in the party to a contract who has residual rights of control over assets.

between the leaseholder and the government. Lease arrangements reserve for the government rights over sale and transfer of production factors, rights to a certain proportion of project income as taxes or rent, rights to retake the project at the end of the lease period (or sooner if the managers renege on their contractual obligations), and the stipulation that irrigation service provision is to take priority over other lines of operation. Residual rights of control are reserved to the firm. The state retains a specific bundle of property rights and vests the residual with the firm managers.

Irrigation firms are regulated utilities. Irrigation is deemed to be a socially necessary service. In China, as almost everywhere, it is subject to price cap regulation, usually without regard to marginal cost. Firms providing irrigation services also tend to have increasing returns to scale due to large fixed-asset investments. Marginal cost is low relative to fixed cost. Such firms are natural monopolies. Under marginal cost pricing, profits will generally be negative. If these firms are to be efficient without subsidy or alternative production lines, they are not sustainable.

The key question for these firms is how to produce irrigation services under price regulation and at the same time be sustainable. The nature of the irrigation production process and of the irrigation firm provides several clues to the answers. First, irrigation firms control large amounts of relatively scarce physical capital, human capital, and natural resources. Second, the demand for irrigation is episodic throughout the agricultural calendar, so firm resources only need to be used part-time to meet demand. Third, the inputs used for irrigation production are not specific to irrigation. That is, the inputs can also be used to produce goods other than irrigation. Additionally, there are possibilities for joint production.[13] Since these inputs are used only part of the year for irrigation, and are not specific to the irrigation production process, their use in only irrigation is inefficient. To increase firm revenue and factor utilization rates, other productive activities must be found. As a result of these characteristics of the irrigation firm and its production factors, what appears to be a dominant, or at least preferred, organizational form has emerged.

Private irrigation firms were formed even before dissolution of the communes. A dramatic departure from bureaucratic irrigation management, they emerged in small- and medium-scale irrigation projects at the commune level and below. As the communes were dissolved and government operating subsidies to the agricultural sector dried up, additional stress was placed on sustainability of the firms. Irrigation projects were either sold or leased to

---

13. An example of nonspecificity of physical capital inputs is the potential use of pump motors to power millstones to process grain. Examples of the nonspecificity of human capital inputs are the use of engineering knowledge in design and construction of buildings or the use of agronomic knowledge in the production of specialty crops. An example of nonspecificity of natural resources is the use of water stored in reservoirs to raise fish. This last is also an example of a joint production possibility.

project managers, with the stipulation that they would be responsible for providing irrigation services to farmers. These managers also knew that no subsidies would be forthcoming from the government. This system has been described in operation as early as 1979 in Guangxi in the south and 1980 in Shanxi in the northwest.[14]

Irrigation firms such as these operate under price ceiling-quantity floor regulation. That is, they provide a minimum amount of water at some regulated price. This exacerbates the problem of negative profits from increasing returns.

If irrigation firms are to be regulated, what are the appropriate forms of regulation? There are three schemes generally used for price regulation of natural monopolies. They are marginal cost pricing with subsidy, multipart tariffs, and multiproduct firms with cross subsidies.

Marginal cost pricing accompanied by a subsidy to make the monopoly sustainable is a simple form of monopoly regulation. The monopoly firm sets its price at marginal cost and receives a subsidy to let it break even. Consumer surplus is maximized and production of the good is efficient. One factor prevents using this method in China: the subsidy. It is not forthcoming from the government due to budgetary constraints. It may be possible in richer villages, but in general, no organization other than the government has sufficient resources to provide such subsides. For all but the richest villages we can discard this possibility.

A two-part tariff, the simplest form of a nonlinear tariff, is composed of fixed and variable parts: a fixed fee for access and a per-unit charge for use of the product. Local telephone service is a good example of this. Service is sold in two parts: a fixed charge for monthly service and a per-call charge. This scheme is attractive because, with an appropriately chosen rate structure, it can extract surplus from consumers to make the firm sustainable. It is unattractive from the consumer's point of view precisely because it extracts surplus in favor of the firm. The single most difficult problem to overcome is measurement for the variable charge. With many farmers, each with several tiny plots, the cost of monitoring volumetric water use can quickly become huge. Only some places use volumetric charges. An alternative to volumetric pricing already in use is pricing by area watered. This makes the pricing schedule less costly to implement by using a readily verifiable price structure that is already in place in many areas.

The third scheme is a multiproduct firm with cross subsidies. The firm provides a socially necessary commodity at a loss and subsidizes production of that commodity with profits from other lines of production. Here regulators decide that a particular service is socially necessary and should be priced so that everyone can afford it. In return for providing this service at an artificially low price, the firm is allowed entry into protected markets for other goods or

---

14. *Qu Shuili Gongcheng Guanli Zongzhan* 1980 and Song and Guo 1981, respectively.

services in which it may make positive profits. A good example is again from telecommunications. Before deregulation, AT&T was given a monopoly in long-distance services in return for providing low-priced local telephone service. The monopoly profits from long-distance service were used to subsidize local service. From a welfare perspective, this scheme is appealing. Consumers receive a necessary service at low cost and producers are allowed to make excess profits in other markets. For irrigation firms this has more desirable characteristics. They have excess productive capacity that can be absorbed in diversified operations. The nature of the markets irrigation firms enter requires large fixed-capital investments that give them some protection from cream-skimming entrants.[15] The advantages of this regulatory system are that it allows firms to be sustainable while at the same time providing farmers with low-cost water for irrigation. The firms also increase factor utilization rates far above what they would be if used only for irrigation. This is a simple model of a large number of irrigation firms that have appeared in China since 1979.

Some potential problems like cream skimming are avoided by the nature of the firm. The resolution of other problems is unclear. We do not know whether legal enforcement of contracts and firm incentives is sufficiently strong to make firms undertake necessary irrigation provision activities instead of profitable subsidiary activities.[16] Incentives for maintenance of irrigation projects were not sufficient.

The implementation of a responsibility system for irrigation had at is heart attempts to make water resources policy complementary with agricultural production policy and to overcome the problems brought to light by the work post responsibility system. Wang Yinzhong (1983) discussed three

---

15. Cream-skimming entry is best described by example from Brock and Evans 1983.

A public utility provides two services. It charges $10 per unit for the first service and $5 per unit for the second service. It incurs a cost of $7 per unit for both services. It thereby earns a profit of $3 per unit on the first service and takes a loss of $2 per unit on the second service. Its profits on the first service offset the losses on the second service. A competing firm which incurs a cost of $8 per unit for the first service, and which is therefore less efficient than the public utility, but which has no obligation to provide the second service, could offer the first service for $9.50 and thereby capture the market for the first service. The competing firm is said to cream skim the public utility's markets.

16. The requirements for participation can be quite stringent. *Qu Shuili Gongcheng Guanli Zongzhan* (1980) presented two requirements. The first was that actual irrigated area was at least as great as that planned for the project. This may not be as easy as it may seem, since many irrigation projects' actual irrigated area fell short of their planned irrigated area. The second was that grain yields be greater than 7.5 metric tons per cultivated hectare. This implies that diversified operations could only be carried out after the second of a double-crop rotation had been harvested, since very few areas of China get such high yields from a single crop. In most areas of the country, the requirement was simply that irrigation work be completed before diversified operations could be undertaken.

reasons for implementing a water resources contract responsibility system.[17] The first makes clear the need for complementarity between irrigation management and the family farming system. The second specifically points to the need for fiscal complementarity to develop sustainable water resources enterprises. The third reason not only includes the above two reasons, but also notes the need for specialization to provide irrigation management suited to China's family farms.

Wang describes five forms of responsibility system for irrigation. One is a rehashing of the work post responsibility system, but the other four are true vesting of property rights and autonomy in irrigation managers. Those leasing projects perform their irrigation work and then use the idle capacity and nonspecific assets to earn additional income or cross subsidies where possible. In some very small scale projects the profits from irrigation alone are positive, so additional lines of production are not for cross subsidization, but purely for profit. Implementing these forms of responsibility system not only provided irrigation to farmers, but also increased water project revenue and project manager income for small- and medium-scale projects.[18]

Wang also notes problems that the water resources responsibility system is supposed to solve. This is part of the tacit recognition of the need to develop complementary policy packages. He recommends managing irrigation facilities as autonomous businesses. The most important recommendation is to

---

17. Many other articles have appeared suggesting various types of responsibility systems, but this one demonstrates by far the clearest understanding of the need for complementarity. Some other articles to see are Yang and Li 1985; Wang Yishi 1985; and *Hebeisheng Shuiliting Bangongshi* 1983.

18. The first type of lease is an individual lease for small-scale irrigation projects. By 1983, 855 wells and small irrigation stations in Mixian County had been leased by individuals. For example, farmer Shen Tianxi leased two wells in November 1981. He paid production costs and depreciation, and in return was granted autonomy in economic decision making. Irrigated area expanded and Shen's income increased.

A second type of lease is for households. The form is similar to that of individual leases but the scale of project that can be managed is larger. In Mixian County, more than 100 small-, medium-, and large-scale projects had been leased under this system. Liu Song, a commune member with 17 years of experience managing and repairing mechanical pumps, and his family of six people leased the operation of four mechanical pump wells. Gross income from irrigation work and subsidiary operations was more than 300 yuan per person.

A third type of lease is by specialized teams or irrigation firms. This form of lease is used for large-scale gravity-flow projects, lift irrigation stations, and wells serving large command areas. The management of these projects is given new incentives, including autonomy in decision making, and the organizational structure is formalized, with internal contracts between management levels.

A final form of responsibility system is for very small scale water sources like small springs and streams. Individuals develop and manage these microsources. Investment comes from family and friends and simple water-moving technology is used. Most of the water is used on the developer's own fields. Command area is usually less than one hectare.

diversify production to increase factor utilization rates and to increase irrigation project income.

Diversified operations have taken many forms, since irrigation projects are very different. Pan and Zuo (1984) suggest many different enterprises as candidates for diversified operations. Most of these have been successful in increasing project factor utilization rates and income. Many projects that had been money losers over the years have become profitable for the first time.[19]

We can see the profitability of diversified operations in several examples. *Qu Shuili Gongcheng Guanli Zongzhan* (1980) documents early instances of diversified operations under reform from two counties in Guangxi. In Yulin County all projects adopted diversified operations in 1979.[20] Total income from these sidelines was 1.3 million yuan for 19 county-managed projects. This income allowed the projects to return to profitability. In the same province, the Panlong turbine pump lift station in Beilu County derived 440,000 yuan, some 14 times the project water fees of about 30,000 yuan, from diversified operations.[21] Song and Guo (1981) discuss six irrigation districts in two counties in Shanxi Province that met their costs and had surplus revenue derived wholly from diversified operations.[22] These initial successes made further adoption and diffusion of diversified operations as a means to cross-subsidize irrigation all the more attractive. Later examples from 1984 and 1985 show similar success in projects of all sizes, from individually managed wells to projects with command areas of more than 1,000 hectares.[23]

---

19. Comprehensive operations projects they suggest are: cropping and agriculture, including afforestation, plant nurseries, horticultural crops, fruit trees, silkworms, and tea; animal husbandry, including fish and shellfish, river pearls, milk cows, and meat; light industrial production, including household goods, forestry products, woven goods, brewing and distilling products, agricultural implements, and prefabricated concrete; service industry projects, including hotel and restaurant services and photography studios; and travel and tourism using local scenic and historical areas to draw tourists.

20. These included cropping, fisheries, planting trees, generating hydropower, raising hogs, and brewing.

21. Panlong station in Beilu County produced prefabricated concrete slabs, generated electricity, raised hogs and fish, brewed alcoholic beverages, repaired machines, and used project machinery to mill grain and provide transportation.

22. Five irrigation districts in Gaoping County produced cement, repaired motor vehicles, and raised fish and crops. They met their costs for irrigation and had a small surplus for distribution to the project workers. In Licheng County the Yongjin irrigation district made more than 200,000 yuan, enough to cover production costs for irrigation and other operations, with a surplus left over for project maintenance and distribution to workers.

23. At Henan Province, Huangcheng County's Youshudian irrigation station, grain processing, fisheries, and machine repair brought income of 50,000 yuan in 1984 while cement products, horticultural products, construction, and marketing brought total station income for 1985 to 250,000 yuan (Pan 1985).

At Henan Province, Tanghe County's 4,300-hectare command area Hushan irrigation dis-

The development of the multiproduct irrigation utility provided a solution to the problem of incentives for irrigation services provision under reform in rural China. Trial and error was the means by which this organizational form was developed. The organization embodies incentives for managers to produce irrigation services despite their natural monopoly characteristics. At the same time, farmers are supplied water at low cost. Utilization rates of scarce rural capital are also increased.

This does not mean that the scheme has been a complete success. Since 1985, weaknesses in the capacity of these organizations to perform maintenance and renovation have come to the fore. These problems are being solved in different ways in different areas. One solution to the maintenance problem involves what at first glance seems to be a return to the Maoist strategy of mass mobilization. We will show that what appears to be a return to labor drafts to perform maintenance can best be understood as the implementation of a two-part pricing scheme for irrigation water.

Maintenance was supposed to be undertaken by contracting units, but clearly it was not. Large labor investments were needed to perform maintenance and renovation work, but water management units certainly were unable to afford them or had no incentive to do so. The government, in behavior completely consistent with past reforms, turned to a past institution to resolve the maintenance problem.[24] Labor mobilization was to be the solution. The call for labor mobilization for project maintenance went out in *Hongqi,* the party ideological journal, in February 1986. Jing Ping (1986) called for farmers to do capital construction to rehabilitate old projects. In 1989 the Minister of Water Resources commented that losses of irrigated area were serious, nearly one million hectares, and that 50 million people lacked adequate drinking water.[25] Progress was slow, and the amount of irrigated area did not recover 1978 levels until 1990 (see table 2), but the increase of irrigated area to historical highs in 1990 and 1991 indicate the eventual success of the policy.

The solution to the maintenance problem can be analyzed as a reform of

---

trict, irrigation was provided for rice. Yields averaged 7.5 metric tons per hectare. In addition, repair of more than 1,200 agricultural implements, processing of 1,000 metric tons of grain, production of more than 30,000 units of plastic products, generation of 140,000 kilowatts of electricity from hydropower, and eleven other projects generated 15,000 yuan in profits on a gross output value of 150,000 yuan (Wang Yishi 1985).

At the other end of the spectrum, peasant Sun Chuansen of Jiangsu Province leased well operations and also ground fodder and milled rice using the well pump motors, earning income of more than 400 yuan from diversified operations (*Shitun Shuilizhan* 1986).

24. See Oksenberg 1969 and Nickum 1974 about labor mobilization for irrigation construction in the past.

25. Minister comments on water protection, management (1989).

the regulated pricing structure of water. Since maintenance and renovation were not being done by the firm, we deduce that the firm's income was insufficient or that incentives to the firm were too weak for the firm to be able or willing to undertake such work. Reform of the price structure allowed this need to be met.

The form of regulation we see is a blending of multiproduct firm pricing and multipart tariffs. Mobilization of labor may be seen as the fixed charge of a two-part tariff. Water fees, fixed below marginal cost, are paid as the variable portion of the tariff. Irrigation firms may still engage in subsidiary lines of production to bolster profitability. This will keep irrigation managers from leaving their primary job altogether to engage in subsidiary production.

Mobilization of labor is the fixed part of a multipart tariff, but it is not the same as the collectivist labor accumulation schemes studied by Oksenberg (1969) or Nickum (1974). Why? The new mobilization system allows farmers a choice of contributing labor or paying the labor wage equivalent in cash or kind. Such a choice was not available under labor accumulation. The new price regulation scheme now seems to be functioning effectively. Water is provided at low cost to farmers, irrigation firms are sustainable, and government expenditure on small- and medium-scale irrigation projects is minimal.

We may explain irrigation management reform as a change in pricing schemes. Under the communes no one paid for irrigation. The initial focus of reform was improved technical efficiency. With the dissolution of the communes and the reduction in central government investment, the focus changed to economic efficiency. Irrigation firms were developed to sell water at a regulated price in return for the right to engage in subsidiary production. When this scheme proved to provide insufficient income or incentives for the firm to perform large-scale, high-cost maintenance, another pricing scheme, involving a blending of multipart tariffs and multiproduct, cross-subsidizing regulation was put in place.

Health Care

Health care provision is one of the successes of the Chinese socialist development strategy. Average life expectancy has increased from 32 years in 1949 to more than 69 years today (Jamison et al. 1984). Control or eradication of endemic diseases like cholera, plague, malaria, and tuberculosis have markedly increased the productive capacity of Chinese workers and peasants. Reduction of infant mortality from levels typical of those of the poorest countries to those of the industrialized countries has contributed greatly to the increased welfare of the Chinese people.

Under reform, however, health care in rural areas has not fared well. While irrigation management was an unsettled issue for several years, the problems generated for it by reform have generally been solved. In health care, on the other hand, the situation continues to be unsettled. The rural health care system had significant problems in the early 1980s but seemed stabilized by 1985. In some poorer and more backward areas the system collapsed, while in richer areas a combination of private and government intervention stabilized and supported a moderately well developed system of medical care. Appropriate arrangements have been very slow to develop but new forms of institutions and organizations are clearly in the works.

What are the problems encountered with the reforms that provided the impetus for institutional innovation? What is the new structure of rural health care? What are the new organizational forms developed to replace those of the commune? What are the new incentive systems for rural health care providers? What are the prospects for various systems? These questions are answered by examining the supply and demand for health care. We will explore new organizations at the village and township levels (formerly the production team and commune levels) and the problems facing rural doctors and we will examine funding problems and systems developed so far for overcoming them. In particular, we will examine two competing forms of health insurance.

To understand the successes of Chinese rural health care provision and the problems brought by reform, we will briefly describe the prereform health care delivery system. The prereform Chinese health care delivery system was organized in a three-tiered system. The point of entry to the rural health care network was at the production brigade level. At this level, health care was provided by barefoot doctors. Trained in the bare essentials of health care, they divided their time between agriculture and health care work and received work points whether they did medical work or field work. The next two levels, for more complicated cases, were at the commune and county levels. At these levels, hospitals were staffed by full-time medical workers with training equivalent to physician's assistant, registered nurse, and physician. These full time workers received salaries from the commune and county. Production teams also commonly had part-time midwives and health aids.

Funding of the brigade health station was partly through fee-for-service, cooperative health insurance,[26] and through the work points received by barefoot doctors. Jamison et al. (1984) estimate that in the early 1980s about one-third of commune hospitals received direct state funding. Presumably the other two-thirds were financed locally. County-level hospitals are owned by

---

26. Cooperative health insurance or cooperative health care (*hezuo yiliao baojian*) is a system of health care insurance much like mutual insurance. Residents of a township or county contribute a small sum every year and in return receive some health coverage. The limited size of the risk pool may cause some problems. In 1981 nearly half of the rural population was covered by cooperative health insurance.

the central government and funded through the state budget.[27] This system of health care successfully provided low-cost preventative and acute care to the vast majority of the rural Chinese population.

Reform in the countryside has had effects on health care similar to those on irrigation. The implementation of the agricultural production responsibility system adversely affected the lowest level of health care worker first. Barefoot doctors, no longer paid in work points, could either tend their crops and earn income or tend their patients and not. Some areas did not allow them to lease land and others limited the amount of land they could lease for fear that they would not perform their medical duties. But since pay for medical work was not as great as pay for agricultural production, this condition was difficult to enforce (Zheng 1988). The general reduction in government budgetary outlays in rural areas effectively introduced a hard budget constraint to the township and county levels. Medical workers there were unsure about remuneration. Many left the field of medicine and the others were left to fend for themselves. No real reforms were attempted since the bureaucratic structure of the communes could still prop up the imperiled health care system.

Following decommunization, many of the same forces at work in irrigation began to work in health care. Financial sources disappeared with the communes. For village health care stations the financing from the commune, village, and individuals dried up. There was no subsidy for township clinics from the township government since the township government itself had little income, and as real incomes fell with the reduction of subsidies for entitlements, people could afford less and less health care, further reducing clinic income (*Weishengbu Caizhengbu* 1992).

Health care workers were no longer sure where they could practice. Costs increased dramatically. Many health care enterprises simply disbanded. In Xiaoshan County, Zhejiang, 21 percent of village health stations closed. One-third of the stations closed for good reasons, for example, access to higher level medical care was just as convenient. Other reasons for closings were worrisome. Almost 20 percent closed because rural doctors left medicine to pursue more lucrative trades, and another third of the stations closed because the villages they served were too small to provide a living for their doctor (Song 1988).

Jamison et al. (1984) note problems of incompatibility between individual and collective incentives. They particularly note that cooperative health insurance was in dramatic decline. Nationally, 85 percent of the brigades used

---

27. State per capita expenditures for rural recurrent health care costs were 2.76 yuan in 1981, compared to 5.07 yuan from private sources and 1.81 yuan from other sources (presumably various insurance schemes). This compares poorly with urban per capita expenditures of 26.19 yuan by the state, 2.76 yuan from private sources, and 3.51 yuan from other sources. This is indicative of a strong urban bias in health care spending (Jamison et al. 1984).

the system in 1975, but by 1981 only 58 percent did. An extreme example, Kaiping County, Guangdong, shows the number of participating brigades fell from 100 percent in 1977 to only 10 percent in 1984 (*Kaipingxian* 1988). Many doctors left the cooperative system to set up private practice (*Hubeisheng Weishengting* 1987). With less insurance available to rural people, the burden of costs fell increasingly on their shoulders in the form of fee-for-service health care, effectively excluding up to 20 percent of those in need of heath care from access (Harbaugh and Bannister 1993). Reform had clearly undermined the rural health care network. Something had to be done quickly to assure people access to care. Many experiments with organizational and incentive forms were undertaken.

Health care can be a competitive industry in theory. With no real barriers to entry, no natural monopoly, and no increasing returns to scale, there is no apparent market imperfection. The only criterion for entry is whether a medical worker expects to make a profit in the market. Even so, from a policy perspective, it is desirable to have medical care available for everyone who needs it. From the supply perspective, if the market price of medical care is high enough, an entrant can be found for every market.

From the consumer's perspective, easy access and low cost of care are desirable. For acute care there are trade-offs between the two. If accessibility is to be assured, prices must be sufficiently high to induce entry into every market by practitioners. But if prices are high, then some demanders will be forced out of the market. Also, costs tend to be high but infrequent. Insurance provides a way of smoothing the costs of acute health care. Preventative care costs are lower and more smoothly distributed over time. For these two reasons we expect preventative care to be emphasized. Preventative care, however, has public goods characteristics, making it more difficult to supply.

The basic tension between health care provider and health care recipient, then, is that health care providers must expect to earn a living wage if they are to enter the industry while consumers must expect to receive treatment that is not too costly at any given time. To do this, various means of insurance must be introduced.

The initial problem of reform for rural health care was how to maintain the ranks of rural health care providers in the face of greater incentives in other work (Zheng 1988). Table 3 shows the decline in the number of village health care providers over time. The number of village-level health care providers at all levels of training declined steadily from 1980 to 1984. The halving of the ranks in 1985 is the result of a redefinition of rural doctor, health technician, and nurse, but thereafter the total number of health care providers stabilizes. The increase in the number of rural doctors from 1985 reflects increasing numbers of technicians passing rural doctor certification examinations.

The implication of declining numbers of rural health care providers for

TABLE 3. Village (brigade) Clinic Personnel Statistics, Selected Years and 1982–91

Year	Rural Doctors	Health Technicians	Rural Midwives
1975	1,559,214	3,282,481	615,184
1980	1,463,406	2,357,370	634,858
1982	1,348,784	1,647,825	549,659
1983	1,279,490	1,387,724	540,332
1984	1,251,204	1,158,123	523,697
1985	643,022	650,072	513,977
1986	694,718	585,217	507,538
1987	723,799	554,700	481,630
1988	731,653	515,392	466,974
1989	753,686	487,589	444,791
1990	776,859	454,651	470,982
1991	794,507	458,817	462,436

Source: *Zhongguo Weisheng Nianjian*, 1983–92 (China health yearbook, 1983–92).
Note: Prior to 1985 rural doctors included all barefoot doctors. The designation of rural doctor indicates a specific minimum level of training that not all barefoot doctors had. This change in designation led to significant downward revision of the number of rural doctors and health technicians from 1985 onward.

market coverage is bad. With fewer doctors and technicians, there are fewer markets that can be covered. Several incentive systems were tried in response to the decline in the supply of medical care givers. Here we will examine health care contract management systems and collective management systems.

Health care contract management systems are similar to production responsibility systems. Contracts are signed by individuals or groups of health workers with the village government for use of health care facilities. In return, individuals may provide fee-for-service care. Groups have several financing options. Joint lease groups are private group practices. They rely on fee-for-service and private insurance as their main funding mechanisms. Collective management by groups is much like a health maintenance organization. The group relies on a cooperative medical care system for funding.

Contracts commonly allow for local government provision of office space, funds for supplies, and a base salary for the doctor in return for fee-for-service or cooperative provision of acute and preventative care, family planning, health care for women and children, and partial reimbursement for hospital stays (Contracting public health agencies 1983; Liu, Zhang, and Deng 1988).

Collective management of existing health care units was stressed. Reforms sought to give these units limited management, financial, and personnel autonomy to increase efficiency (*Yanzhe Shier Da Zhiyin* 1984). Even so, village collective-managed clinics began to have trouble when collective contributions to health care decreased substantially because the government began to insist that collectives be profitable. Despite calls by the Ministry of Health for village committees, town and village enterprises, and collective economic organizations to contribute a portion of their profits to a public benefit fund or insurance fund to support rural health care organizations, contributions still decreased (*Weisheng Buzhang Cui Yueli* 1988). Health care bore some of the burden from this reduction in collective social service funding.

In Hebei Province in 1986, contract management predominated. There was more local government involvement in areas with greater income. This indicates that village governments had revenue to allocate to health care. Poorer area governments had less revenue, so private medical care was the norm. Even so, there was no connection between the type of management structure in place and the profitability of a health care enterprise. Both government-run and contracted-management clinics had profitable and loss-making forms. Group practices were more prevalent in richer areas because richer villages could support more doctors, while individual practice was more common in poorer areas. That the dominant practice is individual practice (91 percent to just 8 percent for group practices) indicates that rural China is not very wealthy. Wang Hanqing et al. (1987) confirm this. They also find that village population is a significant indicator of the form of management employed. There are more collectively managed clinics in villages with population of more than 1,000 than in villages with populations of fewer than 1,000. Individually managed clinics are more likely to be found in villages with smaller populations. Villages of different sizes can sustain differing numbers of health care providers. Clearly a smaller village can provide a living for fewer doctors than a larger village.

The proportion of villages served by a health care facility has remained stable at 86 to 88 percent between 1984 and 1991. The total number of village health care facilities grew rapidly immediately after decommunization, reaching a peak in 1989, followed by small declines since 1990. The proportion of government-run health care facilities declined dramatically from a high in 1984 of 51 percent to 32 percent in 1989. About one-third of government-managed village health care stations disbanded or changed management structure. Individually managed facilities, on the other hand, grew by 50 percent between 1984 and 1989. They increased from 32 percent of facilities in 1984 to 48 percent in 1989. It is likely that most of the government-managed units were turned over to individual managers under contract to provide medical care. This is shown in table 4.

Jointly managed group contracts also increased during this period, but by a lesser amount. By 1985, shortly after decommunization, the number of facilities under the contract management system overtook those under the government management system. After 1989 we see further change as the

TABLE 4. Village-level Health Organization Management Structure, 1984–91, by Percentage

Year	Total Facilities	Village Collective Managed	Rural Doctor or Health Technician Joint Managed	Individually Managed
1984	100	51	10	32
1985	100	39	11	42
1989	100	32	11	48
1990	100	33	11	47
1991	100	36	11	45

Source: Zhongguo Weisheng Nianjian 1985, 1991, 1992.

number of government-managed facilities increased at the expense of contract-managed facilities.

The primary reason for the recent trend away from private practice in favor of government-managed health facilities is to be found in the financing system. The government-managed system is funded primarily by cooperative medical insurance, while the private contract system relies on fee-for-service and health insurance for funding. An additional reason for adopting government-managed collective systems of health care provision was to combat fraudulent treatment, poor administration, and outright quackery. Government management made certification and regulation of health care providers easier.

Another reason for the return to government-managed systems is the difference between effort and activities of government and private doctors. Hillier and Xiang (1994) note that doctors working for collectives spend about 90 percent of their work time on health care while private doctors spend only 75 percent of their time in health care work. They also point out that collectively employed doctors are more likely to undertake preventative care than private doctors.

Funding mechanisms are an integral part of the incentive structure. They must be complementary to the management structure of an organization. The Chinese rural health care system has two main funding mechanisms. One, the cooperative health care system (*hezuo yiliao baojian zhidu*), is linked to government- and collectively managed enterprises. The other, health insurance (*jiankang baoxian*), is linked to privately managed enterprises.

The cooperative health care systems have a strong resemblance to health maintenance organizations. Limits are placed on the locations people can receive health care and the value of services they can use. All participants contribute to a fund for health care and those in need use it. Premiums are supplemented by contributions from the government public benefit accumulation fund and often by employer matching grants. The system is based at the village and township level, so the risk pool is somewhat limited. Participation is voluntary, but the annual cost is so low that few people do not participate where it is available. Cooperative medical care coverage varies over localities, but it generally provides basic outpatient services and limited hospital stays for little or no cost.

Cooperative health care was a very common funding mechanism before reform. After 1978 it quickly fell out of favor in rural areas. Kaiping County, Guangdong saw participation drop by two-thirds after the introduction of the production responsibility system, as shown in table 5. Such a large drop in subscription rates will adversely affect any mutual insurance scheme since those more likely to drop out of the risk pool are those with less risk.

In the late 1980s, the cooperative health care system began to revive. Dongtai County, Jiangsu is a good example of this. Dongtai's cooperative health care system was arranged through the 735 villages in the county in affiliation with township clinics. Funding was from participating individuals and was matched by village government public benefit funds. Each individual paid one yuan per year for coverage. Of this two yuan per person per year total, 70 percent remained in the village to be disbursed to the village health station to cover treatment and pharmaceutical costs. The remaining 30 percent was turned over to the township cooperative health care committee to cover the costs of people from the village treated at the affiliated township clinic. Each year an individual was eligible for 30 to 50 yuan of benefits for hospital stays. After this amount was used, the cooperative health care fund covered one-third of the cost, with the individual responsible for the rest (Zhu and Guo 1986).

Health insurance, complementary to privately run health care, is a new phenomenon in rural China. It was proposed as an alternative to the failing cooperative medical care system in 1985 (Huang 1985). Offered by government insurance companies, it was seen as a better way of spreading health care risk than the cooperative health care system due to the potentially much

TABLE 5. Cooperative Medical Care in Kaiping County, Guangdong, 1969–85

Year	Number of Brigades	Brigades with Cooperative Health Insurance	Percentage of Brigades with Cooperative Health Insurance	Population Participating in Health Insurance
1977	275	275	100	478,154
1978	280	274	98	475,948
1979	285	251	88	446,535
1980	285	251	88	434,570
1981	285	221	78	383,373
1982	286	102	36	173,247
1983	287	52	18	
1984	287	28	10	

Source: *Kaipingxian Weishengzhi Bianxiezu* (Kaiping county health annals editorial group) 1988, 166–67.

larger risk pool. It was seen as a reasonable funding solution in response to the rise of private practice by health care providers. Many different kinds of policies have developed, but it is unclear how successful it has been.

One example of private insurance comes from Guangdong Province. Purchase of health insurance was voluntary. An oversight group of leaders from local cocontributors set policy. The company signed legally binding contracts with those for whom it provided coverage. Funding of the plan was from individual premiums and collective and government subsidies. Different insurance plans covered different problems, including major medical coverage, preventative care, and perinatal care (*Nongcun jiankang baoxian* 1988).

It is not clear whether health insurance differs significantly from the cooperative health care system. Health insurance may just be a more sophisticated version of the older system. Some forms of insurance are simply prepayment plans, while others appear to be genuine. Some are mutual insurance schemes. Others may just be Ponzi schemes.

What is clear, at least according to the literature, is that the experiments with health insurance have not been satisfactory. Much attention has recently been devoted to ways to revive the cooperative health care system, as described in the example of Dongtai County.[28] Such a change back toward the cooperative system fits well with the trend to government and collectively managed medical care seen recently.

Organizations, incentives, and funding for medical care have been the subject of experimentation since the beginning of reform. As yet no dominant policy package has emerged. Privately provided health care has attractive incentive policies for suppliers but the demand-side funding is weak. Private health care providers have nearly full marginal incentives. Nonetheless, the health insurance system seems to have failed. Publicly provided health care has attractive funding policies on the demand side but weak incentives for suppliers. The cooperative health care system provides care at low costs. Health care providers in publicly managed clinics, however, have fixed salaries or small marginal incentives, and hence little incentive to produce high quality health care.

Summary

Rural reform in China solved many problems and brought many more. We have examined two examples of attempts to solve the public goods problem in the face of a changing institutional environment. Deregulation of agricultural activities is the engine driving innovation in organizational arrangements and incentive systems. The necessity of solving the public goods problem to avert

---

28. See, for example, *Zhongguo Weisheng Nianjian* 1991, 359; Qian and Zhang 1993.

disaster gives the search for new forms its urgency. It is important just to find a system that works.

The search for organizations and incentive systems that are complementary has been through trial and error and from the bottom up. Innovation has been at the grassroots level, with successful organizations and incentive systems being quickly diffused and adopted throughout the country. This is the case with irrigation. Where solutions are not forthcoming, experimentation continues until a set of organizations and incentives that fit are found. This is the case with health care.

Irrigation is the more successful of our two cases. The nature of the enterprise helps assure that sufficient incentives for providing irrigation services are possible. The nonspecific nature of some capital used in irrigation is the key to its successful provision. Since some capital is not specific to irrigation services, it may be used in the production of other goods and services to provide a cross subsidy for production of irrigation services. Additional resources are directed to the firm by the use of a two-part tariff for water pricing. Water users pay a fixed charge in labor, cash, or kind and a variable charge based on water use.

Health care is the less successful case. Health care facilities are operating in almost nine out of ten villages. Access is not the problem; financing is. The solutions from irrigation will not work. Experiments with insurance have not been successful. The alternative cooperative solution is beset by problems caused by too small a risk pool. If the scope of the cooperative health care system could be expanded to the county or the provincial level, that problem could be solved. The remaining problem of incentives to salaried health care providers, however, would still need to be resolved.

The Chinese record of success in providing goods subject to market failures in the post-Mao era is good. While some goods have been provided more successfully than others, they are all still provided. Further, the innovation of organizations and incentive systems has led to an adequate process of institutional development for their continued supply. The means of supply are not necessarily efficient, but the goods are supplied. The Chinese have managed to muddle through using experimentation to develop ad hoc solutions to the public goods problem.

REFERENCES

Bai Lizhi. 1982. *"Jinyibu wanshan shuili zerenzhi"* (Further improve the water resources responsibility system). *Zhongguo Shuili* (Chinese Water Resources) 2:48–49.

Brock, William A., and David S. Evans. 1983. "Cream skimming." In David S. Evans, ed., *Breaking Up Bell, Essays on Industrial Organization and Regulation.* New York: North Holland.

Commentator Stresses Water Conservation Projects. 1986. Beijing *Xinhua* Radio Domestic Service in Chinese 19 February reported in Foreign Broadcast Information Service (FBIS) 19 February , K1–2.

"Contracting public health agencies to barefoot doctors suggested," Beijing *Jiankang Bao* in Chinese 6 January 1983, 1, reported in Joint Publication Research Service (JPRS) 83145 28 March 1983, China Report Science and Technology No. 192, 51.

Cunji banyi xingshi de diaocha (A survey of village-level medical management forms). In *Zhongguo Weisheng Nianjian Bianji Weiyuanhui* (China Health Yearbook Editing Committee), ed., *Zhongguo Weisheng Nianjian 1988*, (China health yearbook 1988), 96–97. Beijing: *Renmin Weisheng Chubanshe* (People's Health Press).

Evans, David S., ed. 1983. *Breaking Up Bell, Essays on Industrial Organization and Regulation.* New York: North Holland.

Grossman, Sanford J., and Oliver D. Hart. 1986. "The costs and benefits of ownership: a theory of vertical and lateral integration." *Journal of Political Economy* 94 (August): 691–719.

Guojia nongwei pizhuan shuilibu "Guanyu zai quanguo jiaqiang nongtian shuili gongcheng zerenzhi de baogao" de tongzhi, guonong banzi (1981) 41 hao, 1981 nian 7 yue 3 hao (Memorandum of the State Agriculture Commission approving the Ministry of Water Resources' "Report on strengthening the farmland water resources project responsibility system in the entire nation," State Agriculture Commission document 1981, no. 41, July 3, 1981). 1985. In *Shuilidianlibu* (Ministry of Water Resources and Electric Power), ed., *Shuili Gongcheng Jingying Guanli Wenjian Xuanbian* (Selected documents on water resources operations and management). Beijing: *Shuilidianli Chubanshe* (Water Resources and Electric Power Press).

Guojia Tongjiju (State Statistical Bureau), ed. 1991. *Zhongguo Tongji Nianjian, 1991* (China statistical yearbook, 1991). Beijing: *Zhongguo Tongji Chubanshe* (China Statistics Press).

Guojia Tongjiju (State Statistical Bureau), ed. 1992. *Zhongguo Tongji Nianjian, 1992* (China statistical yearbook, 1992). Beijing: *Zhongguo Tongji Chubanshe* (China Statistics Press).

Guojia Tongjiju (State Statistical Bureau), ed. 1993. *Zhongguo Tongji Nianjian, 1993* (China statistical yearbook, 1993). Beijing: *Zhongguo Tongji Chubanshe* (China Statistics Press).

Guojia Tongjiju Guding Zichan Touzi Tongjisi (State Statistical Bureau Fixed Asset Investment Statistics Department), ed. 1987. *Zhongguo Guding Zichan Touzi Tongji Ziliao, 1950–1985* (Chinese fixed asset investment statistical data, 1950–1985). Beijing: *Zhongguo Tongji Chubanshe* (China Statistics Press).

Guojia Tongjiju Guding Zichan Touzi Tongjisi (State Statistical Bureau Fixed Asset Investment Statistics Department), ed. 1989. *Zhongguo Guding Zichan Touzi*

Tongji Ziliao, 1986-1987 (Chinese fixed asset investment statistical data, 1986–1987). Beijing: *Zhongguo Tongji Chubanshe* (China Statistics Press).

Guojia Tongjiju Guding Zichan Touzi Tongjisi (State Statistical Bureau Fixed Asset Investment Statistics Department), ed. 1991. *Zhongguo Guding Zichan Touzi Tongji Ziliao, 1988–1989* (Chinese fixed asset investment statistical data, 1988–1989). Beijing: *Zhongguo Tongji Chubanshe* (China Statistics Press).

Guojia Tongjiju Guomin Jingji Pingheng Tongjisi (State Statistical Bureau National Economy Equilibrium Statistics Office), ed. 1987. *Guomin Shouru Tongji Ziliao Huibian, 1949–1985* (A compilation of national income statistical material, 1949–1985). Beijing, *Tongji Chubanshe* (Statistics Press).

Gustafsson, Jan-Erik. 1984. *Water Resources Development in the People's Republic of China.* Stockholm: Department of Land Improvement and Drainage, Royal Institute of Technology.

Harbaugh, Christina Wu, and Judith Bannister. 1993. "China's aging population: implications for rural and urban areas." Paper presented at the 45th annual meeting of the Association for Asian Studies, Los Angeles, March 26.

Hebeisheng Shuiliting Bangongshi (Hebei Province Water Resources Bureau General Office). 1983. *"Shixing guanli zerenzhi dimao liangfeng bao anquan"* (Implementing the management responsibility system assures security through verdant dikes and abundant grain). *Zhongguo Shuili* (Chinese Water Resources) 3:18.

Hillier, Sheila, and Xiang Zheng. 1994. "Rural health care in China: past, present, and future." In Denis Dwyer, ed., *China: The Next Decades.* London: Longman Scientific and Technical.

Huang Fanzhang. 1985. "Medical and health work and the medical insurance system." *Renmin Ribao,* translated in FBIS 26 February, K13–15.

Hubeisheng Weishengting Yizhengchu (Hubei Province Health Department Medical Administration Office). 1987. *"Shiying nongcun xin xingshi zhengdun jianshe xiangcun weisheng zuzhi"* (To suit the new rural form rectify and establish rural health organizations). *Zhongguo Nongcun Weisheng Shiye Guanli* (Management of Health Enterprises in Rural China) 10: 26–28.

Jamison, Dean T., John R. Evans, Timothy King, Ian Porter, Nicholas Prescott, and Andre Prost. 1984. *China: The Health Sector. A World Bank Country Study.* Washington, DC: World Bank.

Jing Ping. 1986. *"Jiaqiang nongtian shuili jianshe, gaishan nongye shengchan tiaojian"* (Strengthen farmland water resources construction and improve agricultural production conditions). *Hongqi* (Red Flag) 2:26–27.

Kaipingxian Weishengzhi Bianxiezu (Kaiping County Health Annals Editorial Group), ed. 1988. *Kaipingxian Weishengzhi* (Kaiping County health annals). Kaiping County, Guangdong: n.p.

Liu Zhenfang, Zhang Chenxi, and Deng Tianfu. 1988. *"Luopingcun xiangcun yisheng yu nongmin qianding yiliao baojian hetong de diaocha"* (An investigation of a contract for medical care signed between a rural doctor and peasants at Luoping Village). *Zhongguo Nongcun Weisheng Shiye Guanli* (Management of Health Enterprises in Rural China) 6:44–45.

Luo Zicheng. 1982. "Strive to increase water resources project economic benefits."

Nongcun Gongzuo Tongxun (Rural work report) 5:16, reported in United States Joint Publications Research Service China Report Agriculture 219, August 6, 8–10.

Minister comments on water protection, management. 1989. Beijing *Xinhua* in English, 9 January, reported in FBIS-CHI-89-005, 54.

Nickum, James E. 1974. "A collective approach to water resource development: The Chinese commune system, 1962–1972." Ph.D. diss., University of California, Berkeley.

Nickum, James E. 1985. "Moor or loess? Yucheng County fights flooding, drought, and organizational change." Mimeo, draft, April, Cornell University.

Nickum, James E. 1990. "Volatile waters: Is China's irrigation in decline?" In T. C. Tso, ed., *Agricultural Reform and Development in China: Achievements, Current Status, and Future Outlook.* Beltsville, MD: IDEALS, Inc.

Nickum, James E., ed. 1981. *Water Management Organization in the People's Republic of China.* Armonk, NY: M. E. Sharpe.

"Nongcun jiankang baoxian yu gezhong yiliao baojian zhidu shixing qingkuang" (The implementation situation for rural health insurance and all kinds of medical treatment systems). 1988. In *Zhonguo Weisheng Nianjian Bianji Weiyuanhui* (China Health Yearbook Editing Committee), ed., *Zhongguo Weisheng Nianjian, 1988,* 97–99. Beijing: *Renmin Weisheng Chubanshe* (People's Health Press).

Nongye Shuili Guangai Gaikuang (The water control and irrigation situation). 1981.In He Kang, ed., *Zhongguo Nongye Nianjian, 1980* (China agricultural yearbook, 1980), 345. Beijing: *Nongye Chubanshe* (Agriculture Press).

Oksenberg, Michel. 1969. "Policy for accumulation in Communist China: The case of the mass irrigation campaign." Ph.D. diss., Columbia University, New York, NY.

Pan Shuyuan. 1985. *"Youshudian dianguanzhan zai gaige zhong qianjin"* (Youshudian electric irrigation station advances during reform). *Zhongguo Shuili* (Chinese Water Resources) 10:26.

Pan Zhinan and Zuo Yuanxian, eds. 1984. *Shuili Gongcheng de Zonghe Jingying* (Comprehensive operations of water resources projects). Beijing: *Shuilidianli Chubanshe* (Water Resources and Electric Power Press).

Qian Guishu and Zhang Xiyan. 1993. *"Huifu hezuo yiliao de kunnan yu jiejue banfa"* (Problems and means to resolve them in recovering the cooperative health care system). *Zhongguo Nongcun Weisheng Shiye Guanli* (Management of Rural Health Care Enterprises in China) 4:17–18.

Qian Zhengying on modernizing irrigation. 1986. Beijing *Xinhua* in English 1414 GMT 13 June, reported in FBIS 19 June, K15.

Qu Shuili Gongcheng Guanli Zongzhan (District Water Control Project Management General Station). 1980. *"Dali fazhan shuili gongcheng zonghe jingying"* (Vigorously develop water control project comprehensive management). *Sixiang Jiefang* (Liberated Thinking) 8:16–17.

Renmin Ribao. 1982. *"Guanhao yonghao xianyou nongtian shuili gongcheng"* (Manage well and use well existing water resources projects). 3 July, 2.

Shitun Shuilizhan, Tongshanxian, Jiangsusheng (Shitun water resources station,

Tongshan County, Jiangsu Province). 1986. *"Yige zhuanyehu banzhan de dianxing"* (A model of a specialized household managing a station). *Zhongguo Shuili* (Chinese Water Resources) 1:33.

Shue, Vivienne. 1984. "The fate of the commune." *Modern China* 10, no. 3:259–83.

Shuilidianlibu (Ministry of Water Resources and Electric Power), ed. 1985. *Shuili Gongcheng Jingying Guanli Wenjian Xuanbian* (Selected documents on water resources operations and management). Beijing: *Shuilidianli Chubanshe* (Water Resources and Electric Power Press).

Song Jiyang. 1988. *"168 ge cun baojianzhan tingban yuanyin fenxi"* (An analysis of the reasons for closing of 168 village health stations). *Zhongguo Nongcun Weisheng Shiye Guanli (*Management of Health Enterprises in Rural China) 4:31–33.

Song Lusheng and Guo Shaoyu. 1981. *Shuili jingying guanlishang de yixiang gaige— Jindongnan diqu shixing shuili guanli zerenzhi de diaocha* (A reform of water resources administration and management—a study of Jindongnan prefecture implementing the water resources responsibility system). *Nongye Jingji Wenti* (Problems of Agricultural Economics) 9:12–14.

United Nations. Economic and Social Commission for Asia and the Pacific. 1979. *Proceedings of the Workshop on Efficient Use and Maintenance of Irrigation Systems at the Farm Level in China.* Water Resources Series No. 51. Bangkok: UNESCAP.

Vermeer, Eduard B. 1977. *Water Conservancy and Irrigation in China: Social, Economic, and Agro-technical Aspects.* The Hague: Leiden University Press.

Wang Hanqing, Li Guang, Zhang Kewen, Wang Ling, and Shen Yulan. 1987. *"Chongyangxian cunji weisheng zuzhi xianzhuang diaocha"* (An investigation of the present conditions of village level health organizations in Chongyang County). *Zhongguo Nongcun Weisheng Shiye Guanli* (Management of Rural Health Care Enterprises in China) 6:45–47.

Wang Yinzhong. 1983. *"Luoshi shuili chengbao zerenzhi tuixing guangai qiyehua guanli"* (Implement the water resources contract responsibility system and carry out irrigation enterprise management). *Zhongguo Shuili* (Chinese Water Resources) 4:13–16.

Wang Yishi. 1985. *"Guanqu yao zhifu, yao zou gaige de lu"* (Irrigation districts that want to get rich should take the reform road). *Zhongguo Shuili (*Chinese Water Resources) 10:26.

Weishengbu Caizhengbu Lianhe Diaochazu (Ministry of Health and Ministry of Finance Joint Investigation Group). 1992. *"Nongcun weisheng jingji diaocha"* (Rural health economics survey). *Weisheng Jingji Yanjiu* (Health Economics Research) 5:5–11, 19.

Weisheng Buzhang Cui Yueli Zai Quanguo Weisheng Tingzhang Huiyi Shang de Zongjie Jianghua (1987.1.9) (The summary speech of Minister of Public Health Cui Yueli at the National Public Health Office head meeting, January 9,1987). 1988. In *Zhongguo Weisheng Nianjian Bianji Weiyuanhui* (China Health Yearbook Editing Committee), ed., *Zhongguo Weisheng Nianjian 1988* (China health yearbook, 1988), 1–12. Beijing: *Renmin Weisheng Chubanshe* (People's Health Press).

Yang Wu and Li Huaqi. 1985. *"Nongtian shuili gongcheng de gaige jianyi"* (A proposal for reform of water resources projects). *Zhongguo Shuili* (Chinese Water Resources) 6:10–11.

Yanzhe Shier da Zhiyin De Fangxiang Kaichuang Weisheng—Wang Wei Tongzhi Zai Quanguo Weisheng Tingjuzhang Huiyi Shang De Jianghua (1983 Nian 1 Yue 9 Ri) (Open up the guiding principle of the Twelfth Party Congress. Comrade Wang Wei's address to the national meeting of public health office and bureau heads). 1984. In *Zhongguo Weisheng Nianjian Bianji Weiyuanhui* (China Health Yearbook Editing Committee), ed., *Zhongguo Weisheng Nianjian, 1984,* 1–9. Beijing: *Renmin Weisheng Chubanshe* (People's Health Press).

Zhang Xianfu and Yin Zhiku. 1983. *"Quanmian jiaqiang shuiku guanli tigao shuili gongcheng jingji xiaoyi"* (Comprehensively strengthen reservoir management to increase water resources project economic benefits). *Shuili Gongcheng Jishu Guanli* (Water Resources Project Technical Management) 3:59–61.

Zheng Liqi. 1988. *"Xiangcun yisheng wenti chuyi"* (Opinions on the problems of rural doctors). *Zhongguo Nongcun Weisheng Shiye Guanli* (Management of Rural Health Care Enterprises in China) 4:34–35.

Zhongguo Weisheng Nianjian Bianji Weiyuanhui (China Health Yearbook Editing Committee), ed. 1983. *Zhongguo Weisheng Nianjian, 1983* (China health yearbook, 1983). Beijing: *Renmin Weisheng Chubanshe* (People's Health Press).

Zhongguo Weisheng Nianjian Bianji Weiyuanhui (China Health Yearbook Editing Committee), ed. 1984. *Zhongguo Weisheng Nianjian, 1984* (China health yearbook, 1985). Beijing: *Renmin Weisheng Chubanshe* (People's Health Press).

Zhongguo Weisheng Nianjian Bianji Weiyuanhui (China Health Yearbook Editing Committee), ed. 1985. *Zhongguo Weisheng Nianjian, 1985* (China health yearbook, 1985). Beijing: *Renmin Weisheng Chubanshe* (People's Health Press).

Zhongguo Weisheng Nianjian Bianji Weiyuanhui (China Health Yearbook Editing Committee), ed. 1986. *Zhongguo Weisheng Nianjian, 1986* (China health yearbook, 1986). Beijing: *Renmin Weisheng Chubanshe* (People's Health Press).

Zhongguo Weisheng Nianjian Bianji Weiyuanhui (China Health Yearbook Editing Committee), ed. 1987. *Zhongguo Weisheng Nianjian, 1987* (China health yearbook, 1987). Beijing: *Renmin Weisheng Chubanshe* (People's Health Press).

Zhongguo Weisheng Nianjian Bianji Weiyuanhui (China Health Yearbook Editing Committee), ed. 1988. *Zhongguo Weisheng Nianjian, 1988* (China health yearbook, 1988). Beijing: *Renmin Weisheng Chubanshe* (People's Health Press).

Zhongguo Weisheng Nianjian Bianji Weiyuanhui (China Health Yearbook Editing Committee), ed. 1989. *Zhongguo Weisheng Nianjian, 1989* (China health yearbook, 1989). Beijing: *Renmin Weisheng Chubanshe* (People's Health Press).

Zhongguo Weisheng Nianjian Bianji Weiyuanhui (China Health Yearbook Editing Committee), ed. 1990. *Zhongguo Weisheng Nianjian, 1990* (China health yearbook, 1990). Beijing: *Renmin Weisheng Chubanshe* (People's Health Press).

Zhongguo Weisheng Nianjian Bianji Weiyuanhui (China Health Yearbook Editing Committee), ed. 1991. *Zhongguo Weisheng Nianjian, 1991* (China health yearbook, 1991). Beijing: *Renmin Weisheng Chubanshe* (People's Health Press).

Zhongguo Weisheng Nianjian Bianji Weiyuanhui (China Health Yearbook Editing Committee), ed. 1992. *Zhongguo Weisheng Nianjian, 1992* (China health yearbook, 1992). Beijing: *Renmin Weisheng Chubanshe* (People's Health Press).

Zhu Jian and Guo Fan. 1986. *"Hezuo yiliao reng shi xianjieduan jiejue nongmin jiuyi wenti de yige hao zhidu"* (Cooperative health care is still a good system to resolve peasants' problems of demand for medical care in the present stage). *Nongmin Ribao* (Peasant Daily), July 30, 4.

CHAPTER 11

The Acquisition of Private Property Rights in Ukrainian Agriculture

Simon Johnson and Zanny Minton-Beddoes

There has been a great deal of discussion recently about whether parts of the former Soviet Union could follow the "Chinese path" of economic reform. The precise interpretation of this path varies between people and according to their political purposes, but everyone would agree that a key element must be the "reform" of agriculture, including a significant degree of de factor privatization.[1]

Given this context, it is not surprising that Leonid Kuchma, the Ukrainian prime minister, has emphasized the need to "privatize" agriculture. The underlying idea is that the liberalization of agriculture and the introduction of new nonstate forms of property rights, including private family farms, will improve incentives and increase production. This will increase the availability of food and should tend to improve living standards. Economic reform will therefore be likely to result in improved economic conditions (as it has in many parts of China) rather than a worse situation (as it has in most of the former Soviet Union).[2]

But is the Chinese path really feasible, given the existing situation in Ukrainian agriculture? What is the existing pattern of property rights, both de jure and de facto? To what extent does the state still retain control over

This chapter is part of a project financed by a grant to Simon Johnson from the National Council for Soviet and East European Research. For their comments we thank Don Clarke, John McMillan, John Whalley, and other conference participants.

1. There is currently an active debate about the precise lessons that can be drawn from the Chinese experience. It seems clear, however, that allowing the acquisition of effective property rights by individuals and families in agriculture was important. See McMillan and Naughton 1992; McMillan and Naughton in this volume; Chen et al. 1992; *Economist* 1992; Naughton, in this volume.

2. Recent theoretical work has demonstrated that under certain conditions, partial or gradual economic reform tends to worsen economic welfare. Specifically, the case that has been treated in detail is that of allowing new forms of business while maintaining price controls (Shleifer and Vishny 1992.)

agriculture, and what scope remains for privatization? Is "privatized agriculture" likely to mean small family farms or large units run as private companies or as cooperatives? Is there any evidence that privatization as currently envisaged in Ukrainian agriculture will tend to improve economic performance and—more broadly—economic welfare for producers and consumers?

In order to answer these questions, we conducted an empirical study in the summer of 1992, based primarily on interviews with directors of farms in Kiev oblast. Follow-up work in the fall and early winter of 1992 has tracked broader developments in Ukrainian agriculture and privatization initiatives. The appendix provides more details on our methodology.

Although our work is still at an early stage, the evidence gathered so far suggests four conclusions. First, there has already been some partial reform of Ukrainian agriculture. Most price controls have been removed and in practice there is now relatively little bureaucratic supervision by ministries. As a result there has been a significant shift of operational control away from central bureaucracies.

Second, the major factor influencing continued bureaucratic control over farms appears to be the ability to supply inputs and control customers. There was a significant difference between farms that had been part of an administrative structure that included both upstream suppliers and downstream processors and those that had been part of a structure that included only farms. In the first case, local bureaucrats retained a considerable amount of control. However, in the latter group, the directors had acquired more significant residual control rights.[3]

Third, there is mixed evidence on the microeconomic effects of these changes. On one hand, we find some evidence of new product strategies and greater evidence of changes in internal organization. On the other hand, there is little indication that managers of the more independent farms behave differently than their colleagues who are still subject to local bureaucratic control.

Fourth, the acquisition of partial property rights by managers has affected the potential for de jure privatization. Managers and local bureaucrats have the incentive to translate their de facto privatization into de jure property rights. They are thus induced to block more "genuine" privatization, in which transferable ownership rights are obtained by individuals other than themselves. As expressed by our interviewees, managerial ownership rights are maximized by maintaining closed ownership forms in which outsiders cannot participate and that preclude any form of hostile takeover.

First, we summarize how external control over farms has declined and

---

3. Following Grossman and Hart 1986, we consider a person to have property rights over an asset if he or she has the residual rights of control—meaning the ability to determine the asset's use, subject to specified contractual provisions.

describe how property rights have developed in the main types of farms. Next we examine the operational effects of de facto privatization by comparing changes in the different types of farms. In the last section we consider the prospects for de jure privatization.

The Decline of External Control

Collectivization of agriculture in the Soviet Union resulted in two distinct forms of de jure ownership in agriculture: the state farm (*sovkhoz*) and the collective farm (*kolkhoz*).[4] A *kolkhoz* was officially a cooperative, owned by all its members, whereas a *sovkhoz* was owned by the state.[5] Under the communist system, however, both were equally controlled by the state.

Agriculture was extremely tightly managed by vertical hierarchies: *sovkhozi* and *kolkhozi* were controlled through separate, but similar, bureaucratic administrations.[6] The Communist Party and its local representatives were heavily involved in all agricultural decisions. Attempts to reconcile the conflicting goals of achieving a socialized system of agriculture and maximizing food production resulted in continuous efforts to "reform" the agricultural system. The division of responsibility between ministries, the role of different organizations, and the names of bureaucrats altered frequently, but there was little substantive change (Dyker 1992). Farms continued to receive detailed production targets, inputs and customers were allocated by plan, and prices were fixed.

However, two substantive changes made during the 1980s remain significant today. First, the 1982 Food Program created the first RAPO—district-level, agro-industrial organization (Aslund 1989, 97). These were amalgamations of local-level *kolkhoz* and *sovkhoz* administrations. During the 1980s similar organizations were created at the oblast and republic level.

Second, in 1987 APK—Agroindustrial Combines—were created in some parts of the USSR and superseded RAPOs. In Ukraine, 38 such organizations were formed as vertically integrated food producers. These organizations united district-level upstream suppliers, farms, and downstream food processors. In the

---

4. Peasants were allowed to cultivate small plots of land—varying between 1/2 and 1 acre—and to sell the surplus in urban areas. This private production helped keep agriculture functioning.

5. In the former USSR as a whole there were 52,000 farms, of which 45 percent were *sovkhozi*. A *kolkhoz* was seen as an intermediate form on the way to becoming a *sovkhoz*, and over time many *kolkhozi* were amalgamated into *sovkhozi*. *Sovkhozi* were and are on average much larger than *kolkhozi*.

6. Some farms were controlled through specific product administrations. These were usually specialist producers—for example, a vegetable-producing farm would be controlled by a specific vegetable administration.

districts where there was an APK they included all farms, including those in a product-specific administrative structure. Initially there were not large differences in practice between the operation of RAPOs and APKs.[7] Both APKs and RAPOs obtained supplies on the basis of their plan targets and were then responsible for distributing these supplies to member farms.

Gradually during the past five years and more rapidly in the last twelve months, the operating environment for agriculture has changed dramatically. Three connected changes have taken place. First, the compulsory contractual obligations of farms have been substantially reduced. Our interviewees reported that during 1991 the system of state plans became instead *goszakazi* (state orders). Prices were negotiated rather than being fixed. In 1992 state orders were fixed at 70 percent of the previous year's level for most products, with farms free to sell any remainder. Prices are "free" in the sense that, with the exception of a few products, such as milk, the government does not directly fix prices.[8]

Second, the constraints on property form, at least for some types of farm, have been altered. In particular, the 1990 all-Union Law of Land provided a legal basis for changing the property form of a *kolkhoz,* by allowing, in principle, members of the *kolkhoz* to collectively own the farm and its land. This was adopted into Ukrainian legislation under the 1991 Republic Law on Kolkhoz Ownership.[9] In addition, the 1991 Law on Farm Economy provided the legal basis for individual farm units.

Third, property rights—in the sense of residual control rights—are no longer effectively held by the party and its associated vertical hierarchies. Probably the most important change was the removal of direct subsidies on inputs and the effective increase in many input prices. The ensuing reduction in shortages resulted in a significant loss of power for local administrations, because farms now became more independent in production decisions. This weakening of the local bureaucracy was exacerbated by the breakdown of interrepublican trade in 1991–92 and the resultant inability of administrators to obtain supplies from other republics.

Administrative control over supplies has always been a major source of

---

7. There was some difference in the precise roles of APKs and RAPOs. The APKs centralized farms' orders and then distributed inputs. Farms in the RAPO structure received deliveries directly from the supplying organizations. However, under the old system the similarities seem to have been more important than the differences between this aspect of RAPO and APK operation.

8. Prices are negotiated in individual contracts between farms and processors prior to delivery. For farms that are in an APK, the negotiations are undertaken by the bureaucrats in the APK, and are thus still effectively fixed.

9. Among policy makers in Kiev, we encountered a surprisingly firm conviction that state-run agriculture is less efficient than "private" agriculture. This may in part be due to the previous parallel system; farms supplied state stores and individual plots supplied markets.

TABLE 1.

	RAPO	APK	Independent
Total interviewed	9	6	1
Suppliers			
Change	7	1	1
No change	2	5	0
Customers			
Change	2	2	1
No change	7	4	0
Organization			
Change	7	4	1
No change	2	2	0
Production			
Change	2	3	1
No change	7	3	0

Note: A production "change" is a change of more than 20 percent in the planting or rearing of a major farm product.

power in the relationship between bureaucrats and farms. The organization or person who controls key inputs can have a major say in how the farm operates—in our terminology, this person holds the residual control rights. Farms that do not rely on administratively procured inputs have no need to produce for state orders.

In this context there is now a marked difference between RAPO farms and those in an APK. As shown in table 1, in seven RAPO farms (78 percent of all RAPO farms) directors reported that they now procured over 40 percent of their supplies for themselves. One *kolkhoz* reported that it obtained 80 percent of its supplies for itself, rather than via the traditional administrative channels.[10]

By contrast, of six interviewed farms, only one APK farm (i.e., 17 percent of all APK farms) obtained more than 40 percent of its inputs for itself. APKs have retained much more control over productive inputs. Assuming that the ability to obtain supplies is an important indicator of residual control rights, this would indicate that the APKs have retained more property rights than the RAPOs.[11]

---

10. In the cases we encountered, RAPOs consistently provided only oil products. In the summer of 1992, all the interviewed farms reported that they still received 100 percent of their oil through the old administrative structures. In fact, access to oil was cited as the major reason for formally remaining in state organizations and fulfilling state orders.

11. As table 3 shows, we found that supplier relationships had changed "significantly" in three *kolkhozi* (50 percent) and also in six *sovkhozi* (60 percent). So far our evidence suggests no link between de jure property form and changes in de facto property rights.

The conclusion is that the disintegration of external control structures constitutes substantial decentralization and even de facto privatization. All farm directors have operational independence, but particularly in the case of RAPO farm directors, substantial control rights have been acquired.[12] In contrast, in APKs the administration holds significant property rights that have probably increased over the past few years.

The subsequent section examines the evidence on what farm directors have done with these new control rights, and in particular whether there has been differential change in farms belonging to RAPOs and APKs. Our goal is to assess whether privatization of this form is associated with economic adjustment.

The Effects of de Facto Privatization

All the farms in our sample—and all the farms in Ukraine—face serious challenges due to the collapse of the old command system. They can no longer rely on administratively procured inputs and guaranteed markets, and will have to adjust to changing economic conditions. "Economic adjustment" can therefore be defined to be the changes in farm operation made in order to handle changing operating conditions.[13] We look at two important elements of economic adjustment: product strategy and internal organization. Product strategy is defined to include relations with suppliers and customers, as well as the composition of farm output. Internal organization includes both the structure of the farm itself and its institutional relationship with other organizations. Our goals are first to assess how much adjustment has occurred according to these criteria and then to examine what has influenced this adjustment. In particular, have the more independent (RAPO) farms shown greater signs of change than APK farms? We are also interested in any possible variation across de jure property form. Have *sovkhozi* shown any signs of being less able to adapt to the new economic environment than *kolkhozi?* If so, can this be attributed to differences in their property forms?

Of the 16 farms we interviewed, ten were *sovkhozi* and six were *kolkhozi*. In terms of current administrative structure, nine were members of RAPOs, six were in APKs, and one was fully independent. Further details about these farms are contained in table 2.

---

12. Unfortunately, because our research relies primarily on interviews with managers, we do not have any reliable information about changes in the relationship between management and workers.

13. We are interested in altered structure, conduct, and performance in Ukrainian farms. While it would be fair to judge economic adjustment solely according to whether it generated superior performance, it is still too early, and macroeconomic conditions are too unsettled, for us to feel comfortable relying on only one indicator.

TABLE 2.   General Information about Sample

Farm Number	Property Form	Administrative Structure	Total Area (hectares)	Speciality	Number of Employees
1	Sovkhoz	APK	2,400	General	385
2	Sovkhoz	APK	3,400	Sugar	600
3	Kolkhoz	APK	3,000	General	260
4	Kolkhoz	APK	5,000	General	520
5	Kolkhoz	None	2,000	General	450
6	Kolkhoz	APK	2,400	Milk and sugar	350
7	Sovkhoz	RAPO	2,000	Veg. and milk	1,200
8	Sovkhoz	RAPO	2,800	Veg. and milk	700
9	Sovkhoz	RAPO	4,900	Calves	740
10	Sovkhoz	RAPO	2,423	Veg. and milk	892
11	Sovkhoz	RAPO	2,000	Veg. and milk	400
12	Sovkhoz	RAPO	3,200	Veg. and milk	1,000
13	Sovkhoz	APK	3,500	Seed Potatoes	730
14	Kolkhoz	RAPO	2,300	General	310
15	Kolkhoz	RAPO	1,390	Sugar and milk	300
16	Sovkhoz	RAPO	1,000	Veg.	540

Product Strategy

Our interviews revealed that only five of the sampled farms had changed their customer relationships in a significant way—meaning they now sold more than 30 percent of their production without state control or that they had changed at least one major customer. As table 1 shows, half the APK farms show significant change in production while only two out of seven RAPO farms do likewise. If anything, more adjustment seems to have occurred in the APK farms, where the bureaucrats retain property rights.

However, two other factors appear to influence the significant variation between farms. First, whether the farm was previously specialized in the production of a particular product, or whether it had a more general production profile. For example, farms that were very specialized—such as the farm that produced only calves for sale to other farms—have had more difficulty changing their customers, at least while maintaining the same production profile.

Second, the farm's location matters a great deal. For example, vegetable and milk farms on the outskirts of Kiev sell a relatively high fraction of their output on *kolkhoz* markets and consequently find it easier to change their product mix. Farms more distant from large urban areas sell relatively less to *kolkhoz* markets and have fewer options.

As far as we could ascertain, there was no evidence that shifts in production profile were more significant in RAPO farms than in APK farms. In table

TABLE 3.   Changes in Sovkhozi and Kolkhozi

	Sovkhozi	Kolkhozi
Total Interviewed	10	6
Suppliers		
Change	6	3
No change	4	3
Customers		
Change	4	1
No change	6	5
Organization		
Change	8	4
No change	2	2
Production		
Change	3	3
No change	7	3

1, we show two RAPO farms (22 percent) and two APK farms (33 percent) with significant changes in their customers. Similarly, in table 1 we show significant production change in two RAPO farms (22 percent) and three APK farms (50 percent).

Table 3 shows that only one *kolkhoz* (20 percent) and four *sovkhozi* (40 percent) had significant change in their customers. Similarly, in terms of total production there was a significant change in three *sovkhozi* (30 percent) and three *kolkhozi* (50 percent).

Organizational Structure

Included in our definition of change in organizational structure was the creation of new organizations, including joint ventures; the formation of cooperatives and small enterprises; the construction of on-farm food processing plants; and the joining of new independent associations. Of all sixteen farms, twelve had made some sort of change along these lines. Three farms had formed joint ventures, one with ICI, one with a fish-breeding enterprise in Kiev, and one with some Polish entrepreneurs to grow mushrooms and flowers. Two of these joint ventures were in RAPO farms (22 percent of all RAPO farms), while one was in an independent farm. Two were in *sovkhozi* (20 percent of such farms) and one was in a *kolkhoz* (17 percent of such farms).

Three farms had cooperatives present on their property, engaged in such diverse activities as gas pipeline repair, road construction, and furniture manufacture. In each case these cooperatives were formed by people who had previously worked on the farm. In each case also they received the land they used without payment, and they were regarded by the director as part of the farm—although de jure they were a separate legal entity. Two of the cooperatives were in RAPO farms (22 percent) and the other was in an APK farm (17 percent). Two were in *sovkhozi* (20 percent) and one was in a *kolkhoz* (17 percent).

There were also three small enterprises, for sausage processing, construction, and brick and furniture production. These small enterprises were also regarded by the director as belonging to the farm. All employees previously worked on the farm and in each case the farm received a share of the profits. One of these was in a *sovkhoz* (10 percent), while the other two were in *kolkhozi* (33 percent).

Seven food processing units were under construction, of which six were intended to be integral parts of the farm and one would be a separate legal entity. In four cases these were intended to process meat, while the other three were for bottling vegetables. Five of the new units were in RAPO farms (56 percent) and two were in APK farms (33 percent). Six were in *sovkhozi* (60 percent) and only one was in a *kolkhoz* (17 percent).

In addition, five of the farms had leased property to new organizations that had not emerged directly from themselves. Two RAPO farms (22 percent) and three APK farms (50 percent)—three *sovkhozi* (30 percent) and two *kolkhozi* (33 percent)—had leased land to such firms. These new firms pursued a wide range of activities, from auto repair to fish breeding, vehicle hire, road construction, and the manufacture of concrete blocks. Interestingly, three of the farms that had these leases had made no significant internal changes themselves.

Overall, our evidence indicates that organizational changes are occurring on farms. Some changes, such as investment in processing units, indicate economic adjustment within the existing product base: an attempt to add value to the farm product, presumably in response to the incentive of liberalized prices. Others, such as the leasing of land to nonagricultural cooperatives and small enterprises, indicate an attempt by managers to gain an alternate return from the land. Interestingly, the level of bureaucratic control does not seem to be important in affecting organizational change (unlike product strategy). Our research revealed no significant variation across APK or RAPO farms, or between *sovkhozi* and *kolkhozi,* although this may be because there were too few farms in our sample. More important facts are directors' personalities and the financial health of farms. The new organizations have been formed by more "go-ahead" individuals. These directors were usually instrumental in permitting the creation of cooperatives and small enterprises on their farms. Those farms in a worse financial position appeared less able to adapt so as to better deal with the new operating environment, presumably because they were unable to afford the investment required in, say, building a processing

TABLE 4. Changes in de Jure Property Rights

	Sovhkozi	Kolkhozi
Total interviewed	10	6
Privatization plans		
Yes	5	4
No	5	2
Begun privatization		
Yes	1	2
No	9	4
Applications for land		
0	4	5
1–10	4	1
>10	2	0
Applications approved		
0%	0	0
<50%	0	0
>50%	3	0
100%	2	0
n.a.	5	6

unit. Financially weaker farms have changed less and remain more dependent on the guaranteed market offered by state orders. Table 4 summarizes the financial situation of the farms in our sample. The three poorest farms interviewed also showed the least change in both product strategy and internal organization. Their situation was characterized by the director of the poorest interviewed *kolkhoz,* who said, "our independence has increased but we don't have any money and so independence doesn't mean very much."

Table 1 summarizes the above information by classifying seven RAPO farms (78 percent) and four APK farms (67 percent) as having changed significantly in organization. Table 3 reports significant organizational change in eight *sovkhozi* (80 percent) and four *kolkhozi* (67 percent).

The Prospects for de Jure Privatization

How does the increasing independence and de facto privatization of farms affect the prospects for de jure privatization? Given the new legal environment, what strategies do directors have for privatizing their farms?

Privatization of Existing Farms

There is currently no legal basis for a *sovkhoz* to change its property form directly—under the 1991 law only a *kolkhoz* can become a joint stock company. Thus de jure property form matters a great deal in defining managerial strategies. A *kolkhoz* director can either do nothing or form a joint stock company under the 1991 law. The *sovkhoz* directors with whom we spoke felt they had three choices: do nothing, convert the *sovkhoz* to a *kolkhoz,* or transfer assets out of the *sovkhoz* and into another organization, such as a small enterprise or a cooperative.

As table 4 shows, nine out of the sixteen farms (56 percent) had what they regarded as privatization plans—four our of six *kolkhozi* (66 percent) and five out of ten *sovkhozi* (50 percent). However, out of the five *sovkhozi* with plans, three were assuming they would be treated just like a *kolkhoz.* A fourth was basing its privatization plans on the argument that it was formed from three *kolkhozi* and therefore was already covered by the 1991 law. The fifth was intending to break up into six small enterprises and to maintain its central administrative structure as an "advisory center."

In contrast, all the *kolkhoz* directors who wanted to "privatize" intended to do so through forming a joint stock company in accordance with the 1990 USSR Law on Land and the 1991 Ukrainian Law on Kolkhoz Ownership Change. In these plans, all *kolkhoz* assets were to be divided into different types of shares, representing the ownership rights of each worker.[14]

First, there are to be *zemel'nii pai* (shares in land). These are to be divided equally among every current *kolkhoz* worker. They are nontradable, but a worker can opt to farm his share for himself. There is, however, no clear mechanism for deciding which physical piece of land the worker is entitled to. The amount of land to be "distributed" per worker varies—from 2.4 hectares to 8 hectares.

Second, there is the *material'nii pai* (share in the capital fund). All nonland assets of the farm are to be distributed among the workers and retired workers according to a complex formula based on the number of years they have worked on the farm. Thus, a veteran of 30 years' service will receive a greater share of the capital fund than a young worker. Although directors say that these shares will become tradable, the mechanisms for making this so are unclear. One *kolkhoz* director predicted that workers who wanted to buy property collectively could use these shares—e.g., they could form a group that together would have a sufficient share of the "capital fund" to buy out the farm garage or repair shop. However, there is again no clear mechanism for translating a nominal share in the capital fund to a claim on a particular fixed asset on the farm.

Third, there is the *denezhnii pai* (money fund). Each worker can invest his or her own money in the farm and "buy" shares, on the basis of which he/she

---

14. We should note that this choice of property form is encouraged by the government, which writes off all of a *kolkhoz's* debts when it becomes a joint stock company.

then receives dividends on the profit of the farm. These shares are internally tradable, but do not represent a claim on any fixed assets of the farm.

In both *kolkhozi* where privatization had begun, the change in legal form appeared to be the idea of the director. These directors were younger and had already made internal organizational changes. Each was also proud to point out that he was now called the president, not the director. As far as we could ascertain, the change in property form appeared to strengthen the director's position in the farm.

Table 5 shows the pattern of privatization plans according to whether farms were in a RAPO or an APK. Of the RAPO farms, 50 percent had privatization plans, while more than 80 percent of APK farms were in a similar situation. Although this evidence is not conclusive, it is true that APKs usually have closer ties to district councils because they contain both farms and agri-businesses. District (*raion*) councils are important because a *kolkhoz* needs their agreement before it can register as a joint stock company.[15]

Probably typical in this regard was the "liquidation committee" for former *kolkhozi* in Samberg, which was run by the APK and then formed into a "Board of Entrepreneurs." The administrators from the APK effectively still had full control. In fact, the APK's control over the process of ownership transformation allowed it to strengthen its position.

In addition, the newly privatized companies still sold to the same processing factories and still obtained their inputs in the same way. Our strong impression was that very little had changed as far as the substance of business activities was concerned.

Who gains and who loses in the transformation of a *kolkhoz* into a joint stock company? The director almost certainly gains because he confirms his future as head of an independent and legally secure new enterprise. Partial privatization is the best way for him to ensure any future division of assets is in his favor. It depends on the director whether the joint stock company is seen as an end in itself or as a step toward the further breakup of the farm.

The administrative structure gains only if it can ensure an active role for itself in the privatization process. APKs seem better able to help themselves in this way than RAPOs, which are already too weak.[16] A strong relationship with the district council is a key asset for the APKs in this process. Above the

---

15. In Samberg, western Ukraine, we interviewed an APK that had privatized all former *kolkhozi* in the raion. Out of seventeen *kolkhozi,* thiry-four new units had been formed—twenty-six farmer associations, i.e., joint stock companies without capital shares; four joint stock companies; two private cooperatives, and one agricultural trade center. There also remained one state farm.

16. Although this is our strong impression, we were unable to interview enough *kolkhozi* in functioning RAPOs to be certain.

TABLE 5. Changes in de Jure Property Rights

	RAPO	APK	Independent
Total interviewed	9	6	1
Privatization plans			
Yes	3	5	1
No	6	1	0
Begun privatization			
Yes	1	1	1
No	8	5	0
Applications for land			
0	3	5	1
1–10	5	0	0
>10	1	1	0
Applications approved			
0%	0	0	0
<50%	0	0	0
50%	3	0	0
100%	1	1	0
n.a.	5	5	1

local level the administrative structure clearly loses from the process: de facto property rights that have been acquired by the farm become de jure rights, and further administrative control over the privatization process is precluded.

There is certainly potential for workers to lose from this process, particularly if shares remain nontradable and the mechanisms for selling shares are unclear. However, an assessment of this issue must also evaluate the alternatives. Would workers do better if there were de facto or de jure individual ownership? Do they want such ownership? The next section takes up this point.

The Creation of New Independent Farms

Under the 1991 Law on Farm Economy, Ukrainian citizens have the right to establish private farms, subject to several conditions. In order to obtain land, a request must be placed with the oblast-level council, which confers with other interested parties, including local government. The final decision is made by the district-level council, which determines how much land a farmer receives and its precise location. The maximum size of a private farm is 100 hectares overall, of which not more than 50 hectares can be arable.[17]

---

17. In addition, land is allocated to a "farming enterprise," rather than to an individual. However, the "head of the farm" receives the "document for the privatization of the land and its possession thereafter." The farming enterprise can contain only the "head of the farm" and his family. (We have not encountered any cases in which the farming enterprise is headed by a woman.)

Once established, the private farmer is essentially independent, can use hired labor, and is exempt from land tax and income tax for three years. However, the sale or transfer of land to anyone other than a family member requires the approval of the district council.[18] Furthermore, farmers can only receive full private ownership after a six-year probation period—and this is at the discretion of the district council.[19]

In order to aid the creation of private farms, a presidential decree required that every *sovkhoz* and *kolkhoz* surrender 10 percent of its land to a Reserve Land Fund. Land from this fund, which is controlled by the district council, can be distributed to potential private farmers.

The process of privatizing land was not proceeding quickly in the summer of 1992.[20] In nine of the sixteen farms, no individuals had applied for land. Five farms had received between one and ten applications, while only in two farms had there been more than ten applications. More generally, the number of private farms is growing fairly rapidly in Ukraine, but from a very low base at the beginning of 1992, and they still account for only a small fraction of arable land.[21]

Why has this process so far been only limited in scope? Is there actually any demand from private farmers for land? Or are the procedures for obtaining land too bureaucratic, while the reallocation of land is opposed by powerful local interests?

Our interviews suggested that potential farmers hold back for several reasons. Some directors claimed there was a lack of machinery appropriate to small-scale farming. While this appears to be true, an obvious solution would be cooperative machinery pools. There are no legal or technical barriers to this form of cooperation about which we are aware. However, we encountered no evidence of such pools for private farms already having been formed.[22]

The demand for land appeared higher closer to Kiev, probably in part because direct sale on the *kolkhoz* market is more feasible there. In addition, the likely future demand for land for urban development increases its attractiveness.

---

18. This combination of provisions prevents the transfer of land to any organization in which the business partners or shareholders are not related.

19. We did encounter two cases in which land was illegally "sold." A contract was drawn up and money changed hands, but the new owner had no proper legal claim on the land. This practice appears to be officially tolerated—it was a farm director who gave us the details.

20. There is anecdotal evidence that demand for private land is higher in western Ukraine and that the process of privatization to individuals is proceeding more rapidly there.

21. On January 1, 1992, there were 81 private farms in Kiev oblast, and by April 1 there were 252 farms.

22. On the farm with twenty-five applications for land we did hear plans for such a scheme.

Given the restrictions on the resale of land, there are limited incentives for workers to claim their share. All workers on farms already have the right to use up to two hectares to produce goods for themselves and for sale in *kolkhoz* markets. Interestingly, the actual average amount of land used per person is under one hectare, and all interviewed farm directors claimed they would give more land if it were requested.

In addition, townspeople can rent agricultural land for their own cultivation, with leases lasting one year. The terms of these leases vary a great deal and may involve side payments that were not reported to us. In some farms that were nearer to Kiev, up to 5 percent of total land was being rented out in this way.

Second, the administrative nature of land reallocation confers considerable power on the oblast and district council. Particularly in the case of APKs, which are directly responsible to the oblast council, there is the potential for an effective coalition to prevent the redistribution of land to individuals. Of the seven farms that had applications for land, only one was part of an APK.[23]

The political situation is further complicated by the presence in every district of a representative of President Kravchuk. Among other responsibilities, this representative is formally charged with accelerating the dispersion of land, in order to fulfill the centrally determined "privatization" targets. We encountered several cases in which the director of an APK had become the president's representative.

In the summer of 1992, there was only a slight motivation to become a private farmer. For people working on farms already, it is only worth becoming an official private farmer if they want to cultivate more than 2 hectares. The bureaucratic procedure for obtaining land is cumbersome and probably requires some level of sophistication in addition to prior political contacts. At the end of the process a farmer has given up the relative security of a job on a large farm. Given the high level of monopolies in food processing, this may just not be worth it.

An additional problem with the current situation is the danger of supply disruption due to a decrease in production on farms in which 10 percent of the land is currently not being cultivated. In one interviewed *sovkhoz*, the director reported the number of livestock had been cut by 10 percent because the amount of fodder was now insufficient. This was the only example we encountered in which a fall in production was directly attributed to the creation of the Reserve Land Fund.

---

23. However, this APK was strongly in favor of land redistribution. More than twenty-five people had applied for land and the whole 10 percent reserve fund had already been dispersed. A further twenty-five people were now waiting for land. We should note that workers on this farm were unusually young—70 percent were aged under 40.

Conclusions

Our empirical research in Ukrainian agriculture indicates there has been a definite shift in residual control rights from central bureaucratic administrators to local administrators. All directors report increased independence in day-to-day activities and decisions, but there is a much more marked change in farms that belong to RAPOs than in farms that belong to APKs. Residual control rights appear to lie overwhelmingly with managers of RAPO farms, but also partly with the administrative hierarchy in APK farms.

Our evidence suggests that most of these farms do not yet show any significant changes in their product strategy. In part this may be because the macroeconomic environment has changed only recently and it takes time to adapt production patterns, especially in agriculture. However, most farms have already made some kind of organizational change: some of these, such as investment in processing units, provide the clearest evidence for economic adjustment. This adjustment, though, did not seem to depend on the form of de facto privatization; we found no significant differences in product strategy and organizational structure in RAPO and APK farms.

We found no noteworthy differences in the extent of property rights now held by managers in *sovkhozi* and *kolkhozi*. However, this distinction matters a great deal for de jure privatization because it determines the legal options that are currently available. *Kolkhozi* can become joint stock companies, but *sovkhozi* have no clear legal route available to them.

In terms of achieving de jure privatization, it may be better to be in an APK than a RAPO. APKs remain well organized and strong relative to district councils. Immediate de jure privatization is more feasible when there is an effective partnership of the APK administration and the farm director. This form of privatization is therefore unlikely to dramatically alter the current decision-making structures.

In contrast, the top-down promotion of private land holding shifts the balance of power away from directors and toward district councils. This has already induced directors to oppose and obstruct this process. However, our interviews indicate that the major constraint so far is the limited demand for land by rural dwellers.

The conclusion is that the de facto privatization that is occurring in Ukrainian agriculture is not resulting in significant improvements in the operation of farms, but it is affecting the potential for comprehensive and "full" transformation of nonprivate property into private property is thus compromised.

The difference between Ukraine and China may lie in the fact that de facto ownership rights in China were obtained at the household level, while in Ukraine they have been obtained by managers at the farm level. This is partly due to the more labor-intensive nature of cultivation in China, but it is also due in part to the way in which agricultural reform initially occurred in the two countries. Ukrainian agriculture will perhaps return to individual ownership, but the important point is that it did not do so in the initial stage of reform. Consequently, establishing full de jure private property rights in Ukrainian agriculture is now likely to prove difficult.

APPENDIX: RESEARCH METHODOLOGY

We began by obtaining a list of all state and cooperative farms in Kiev oblast from a contact in the Ministry of Agriculture. The farms on this list are grouped by district and the details provided include major products and the director's name and telephone number. This list does not state whether a farm belongs to a RAPO or an APK.

Our initial approach was to telephone directors and ask for an interview. This was generally not successful because directors were hard to reach and when we did make contact they were reluctant to schedule an interview without a more formal introduction. Of the more than thirty farms that we tried to contact, we were unable to make contact more than half the time. In ten of the contacted farms, the director flatly refused to meet with us. We therefore obtained only four interviews in this way. Of these four, two were RAPO farms, one was in an APK, and one was independent.

We subsequently approached the Agricultural Department of the Oblast Soviet and requested official authorization to conduct interviews. This permission was readily granted. We then drafted an "official" letter, which was sent on our behalf to the head of the APK in the Balaya Tserkov district, asking that he cooperate with us. With this letter we had no trouble obtaining four interviews in farms belonging to this APK. Similarly, with the help of a second letter we were able to obtain interviews with seven farms in a RAPO close to Kiev. Our findings are heavily weighted toward farms that were in the RAPO and the APK contacted via the Regional Council—twelve of our interviews were obtained through "official" references. However, in both areas we chose which farms to visit and we always made an effort to change a proposed itinerary. In addition, we also saw four other farms more informally and these visits confirmed the general results reported here. However, in so far as the APK or RAPO administration could influence whom we saw, they probably pushed us toward their better farms. Similarly, directors who are willing to speak with a foreign visitor probably tend to be more forward-looking.

There is also an important bias toward farms in the oblast that are closer to Kiev. It was simply too time consuming and expensive to visit farms further away. As a result, our sample overrepresents vegetable and milk production. It probably also contains farms that have a higher demand for land than is typical.

REFERENCES

Aslund, Anders. 1989. *Gorbachev's Struggle for Economic Reform.* Ithaca: Cornell University Press.
Chen, Kang, Gary H. Jefferson, and Inderjit Singh. 1992. "Lessons from China's Economic Reform." *Journal of Comparative Economics* 16: 201–25.
Dyker, David A. 1992. *Restructuring the Soviet Economy.* London and New York: Routledge.
Economist. 1992. "The Least Likely Agricultural Miracle." *Economist,* April 11, 71–72.
Grossman, Sanford, and Oliver Hart. 1986. "The Costs and Benefits of Ownership: A Theory of Lateral and Vertical Integration." *Journal of Political Economy* 94: 691–719.
Johnson, Simon, and Oleg Ustenko. 1992. "Ukraine on the Brink of Hyperinflation." *RFE/RL Research Report,* December 18.
McMillan, John, and Barry Naughton. 1992. "How to Reform a Planned Economy: Lessons from China." *Oxford Review of Economic Policy* 8 no. 1 (Spring).
Shleifer, Andrei, and Robert Vishny. 1992. "The Pitfalls of Partial Economic Reform." *Quarterly Journal of Economics.*

Part 4
The Politics and Economics of Reform Strategies

CHAPTER 12

Distinctive Features of Economic Reform in China and Vietnam

Barry Naughton

China and Vietnam both followed gradual, piecemeal approaches to the reform of their economic systems. Both began reform by tinkering with elements of their planned economic systems, initiated processes of change that slowly gained momentum, and ended by fundamentally transforming their economies into market-based systems. Both began economic reform under the compulsion of severe economic difficulties and then discovered that early reforms not only eased immediate problems, but were successful enough to provide a powerful argument in favor of continuing and deepening reform. China and Vietnam share not only a gradual approach to reform, but also a cumulative, self-reinforcing reform process that led to profound reforms despite the misgivings of ruling Communist Parties.

At the very least, this common experience is surprising. The literature on Eastern Europe is full of references to necessary pain and unavoidable short-run costs. The predominant perception in Eastern Europe is that the market economy is a desirable goal, but that the transition process is extremely difficult. But if transition is inevitably so painful, how could the reluctant Communist reformers of China and Vietnam have been drawn steadily into a transition process to which they were not initially committed? How is it that the transition was accompanied by accelerated economic growth and improved living standards in China and Vietnam? This chapter seeks to provide some basic building blocks that will help approach these questions and contribute to some eventual answers.

The fact that both China and Vietnam underwent "gradual" transitions is not in itself sufficient to categorize their reform experience. Indeed, in chapter 1 of this volume, it was argued that all transitions are in some sense gradual, and that all contain numerous common elements. This chapter does not, then, seek to argue that China and Vietnam both followed a "correct" model of gradualist transition. Indeed, the literature on Chinese—and even more so on Vietnamese—reforms is still too limited to support that kind of argument.

Instead, this chapter addresses a series of preliminary questions: What were the distinctive features of the Chinese and Vietnamese transitions? Do China and Vietnam have enough in common to merit placing them in a category of similar transition experiences? Did the distinctive features of the Chinese and Vietnamese reforms contribute to the "virtuous cycle" of reform that seems evident? Finally, what, if any, are the connections between the main features of reform and the robust performance of the Chinese and Vietnamese economies?

The following discussion is divided into three sections. The first section is a thematic narrative of the Chinese and Vietnamese reform processes. It describes chronologically the main features of economic reform in the two countries. The second section discusses the similarities and differences of the two countries' experiences, and the internal coherence of the reform measures in the two countries. The final section discusses some plausible relationships between reform and economic growth in the two countries.

Main Features of the Reform Process in Vietnam and China

In both China and Vietnam, gathering economic crisis in 1978 led to the first economic reform moves in 1979. The Vietnamese crisis was simpler and more straightforward. Up through 1978, the Vietnamese government pursued a series of policies designed to make the country more socialist. The party continued to push agricultural collectivization in the south through 1978 and early 1979, and pursued the "Socialist Transformation of Private Industry and Commerce" as well. Agricultural policy, perhaps aggravated by bad weather, led to a series of bad harvests that culminated in 1978, while the urban campaigns seriously disrupted the productive capacity of the southern half of the country. The campaign against southern merchants, often of Chinese ethnicity, followed by the invasion of Kampuchea, led to the rupture of relations with China and military conflict, as well as the breakdown of relations with many important aid donors. This pushed the economy over the brink, and led to open economic crisis. At this point Vietnam reversed course and moved for the first time toward significant economic reform during 1979.

The crisis that faced China in these early years was more complex and somewhat less desperate, but no less significant. The trigger was the collapse of the central government investment program, rather than the economy as a whole. Government leaders had long been struggling with chronic slow growth in agriculture. Government planners proposed to circumvent domestic economic bottlenecks through a massive program of technology import financed by oil export. During 1978, the import program unraveled into an uncontrolled buying spree while petroleum exploration failed to deliver new reserves. Planners had no choice but to set aside their entire investment program and cast about for new ideas. Thus, while China did not face an immediate crisis in the sense of declining living standards, it did face a situation in which both the agricultural and industrial elements of the development strategy had run into obvious dead ends. The beginning of reform was an attempt to search for new ways around these obstacles. Chinese reform is conventionally dated to December 1978, when the leadership recognized the unsustainability of existing policies. But reforms really got going during the course of 1979, with significant policy initiatives in both industry and agriculture (Naughton 1995).

Thus both China and Vietnam began economic reform in 1979 with a grab bag of measures designed to bail the economy out of short-run difficulty. Since Vietnam was still in the process of transforming the economic structure of the south by nationalizing most small-scale privately owned businesses, merely stopping this transformation and doing nothing for a while represented a significant shift in orientation. Both China and Vietnam adopted a number of specific measures under the general heading of increasing economic autonomy and decentralizing decision making. These policies were adopted both in industry and in agriculture, but the impact turned out to be more significant in agriculture.

Rural Liberalization Led to Early Successes

In Vietnam, confronting a serious food crisis, the first steps were in the rural sector. The Sixth Plenum of the Fourth Party Congress, in August 1979, allowed both collective farms and state enterprises to engage in a wide range of "experiments," if these experiments led to increased production. Collectivization in the southern half of the country—a shaky process in any case—was effectively abandoned and farmers were allowed to divert much of their labor power to household production tasks. By the end of 1980, only one-third of the collective production teams in the south were still in existence, and the remainder of the farm households had reverted to de facto private farming. By the early 1980s, most agricultural households were operating individually under "production contracts" that stipulated for each a quota for delivery of food grains to the state (Chu 1993, 153–55).

In China, a similar policy of encouraging experimentation with different incentive measures within the collectives ultimately led to the emergence of household contracting (*baogan dao hu*) in various parts of China. Chinese farm contracts at this time were more complete than Vietnamese contracts, in that they covered both land and production. In this system, households were given control over a piece of land in return for payment of taxes and collective management fees (essentially, a local tax) and a promise to sell a certain amount of grain to the state at state-set prices. During 1981 and 1982, the Chinese system was given central government blessing and spread to over 90 percent of China's villages.

In both China and Vietnam, these policies resulted in'surges of agricultural output. The Chinese experience is perhaps best known (Lin 1992; McMillan, Whalley, and Zhu 1989), for the rapid sustained growth of Chinese agriculture between 1979 and 1984 attracted worldwide attention. But Vietnamese success was no less marked, and grain production rebounded strongly through 1982. Output increased over a third from the depressed levels of 1978–79 to 1982–83, and deliveries to the state more than tripled (Lang 1985, 38). Reforms had a rapid output effect in both China and Vietnam, and the initial crises that led to reform were quickly overcome, at least in the agricultural sector.

Competition in Industrial Product Markets

In the standard model of centrally planned socialism, the government has a virtual monopoly over industrial production, as well as foreign trade. This monopoly is used to support the socialist price system, which creates high profitability in the manufacturing sector and enables the government to draw on surpluses in the industrial sector as the primary source of government revenues. The monopoly over industry and the associated price system thus provide the main fiscal source for the government and substitute for an ordinary tax system. In both China and Vietnam, a crucial early feature of the reform process was the weakness of this monopoly, and the consequent importance of competition in markets for industrial goods.

In China, the protected industrial sector was effectively opened to new entrants beginning in 1979. As part of the new rural policies, rural industries were encouraged to start up new product lines in order to boost rural incomes. Large numbers of new firms rushed to take advantage of large potential profits in the industrial sector, and their entry sharply increased competition and changed overall market conditions in the industrial sector. Most of these firms were collectively owned, though some were private or foreign-owned. But local governments also sponsored many new start-up firms during the 1980s, and these firms were often "state owned." The crucial factor was that the central government surrendered in practice its ability to maintain high barriers to entry around the lucrative manufacturing sectors.

The Vietnamese situation was different in its origins, but similar in outcome. The government never established a real monopoly over industry and commerce, particularly not in the south. Aggressive actions had been taken during 1978 to assert control over domestic trade, but these were influenced to a significant degree by the desire to break the economic power of the ethnically Chinese economic elite in southern Vietnam. Those actions led to the emigration of hundreds of thousands of Vietnamese citizens, predominantly ethnically Chinese, and to serious disruption of the southern economy. The state assumed control over large factories and increased its control over commerce, but was never able to establish an effective monopoly. Most small-scale production remained in private hands (indeed, Chinese merchants were encouraged to set up in "productive" activities as they were chased out of commerce). In 1980, 61 percent of the total national trade in all of Vietnam was carried out by private businesses (Khanh 1993, 83-93; Ronnås, in this volume). In the north, ineffective management of state firms combined with the struggle to provide employment for the rapidly growing labor force to produce de facto tolerance for small-scale private businesses. In some cases, control of production actually devolved from state management to dispersed private control: Hy (1993) describes such a process for the northern ceramics center of Bat Trang.

Subsequently, as discussed in the following, Vietnamese policy toward the private sector fluctuated, and there were fitful attempts to enforce a state monopoly over commerce and industry. But throughout the 1980s the nonstate sector coexisted with, and competed with, the state sector. Indeed, the political issue in Vietnam was not so much whether a private sector should be tolerated, but rather whether the state should try to break the economic domination of the private sector. Despite the fluctuations in political line at the top, the private sector on the ground was never in serious danger of extinction.

A "Dual-Track" System for State Firms

Both China and Vietnam operated a dual-track system for a prolonged period during the transition. The dual track means the coexistence of a traditional plan and a market channel for the allocation of a given good. Rather than immediately dismantling the plan, reformers acquiesced in a continuing role for the plan in order to ensure stability and guarantee the attainment of some key government priorities (in the Chinese case, primarily investment in energy and infrastructure). Having a dual track implies the existence of a two-tiered pricing system for goods under that system: a single commodity will have both a (typically low) state-set planned price and a (typically higher) market price. A crucial characteristic of the Chinese and Vietnamese approaches was that *state* firms operated on a dual-track system. That is, state firms had to fulfill a compulsory plan, but after fulfillment of the plan had significant leeway to operate on the market, at market prices.

Informal markets, illegal but tolerated, characterize all planned economies. The dual track in China and Vietnam represented a substantial increase in the size of these markets, as well as their legitimization by the government. Vietnam pioneered this process, with the January 1981 adoption of the so-called Three Plans system for industry. Recognizing the existence of substantial excess capacity in industry, government leaders formally allowed factories to organize production around three different "plans." Plan A referred to the traditional system, in which the state provided inputs and purchased the resulting output at fixed prices. Most profit was delivered to the government. Under Plan B, enterprises were allowed to purchase inputs at higher market prices, and were allowed to sell the resulting output at higher outside-plan prices. Enterprises were still required to produce the products for which they were originally licensed, but they were rewarded with a higher rate of retention of profit. Plan C referred to the authorization given enterprises to produce "minor products" unrelated to their original production assignments. While state commerce had the theoretical right to purchase the resulting output, most was in practice sold on the market, and firms had the right to retain up to 90 percent of the profit so generated. There was a clear ideological hierarchy among these three forms: Plan A was fully socialist and was to have first claim on enterprise resources; Plan B was semisocialist and was seen as a second, high-priced channel of circulation within the state sector; Plan C was to be tolerated, primarily because of the need to provide state-sector workers with additional sources of income. Under pressure of food shortages, the urban cost of living had soared and real incomes had declined substantially. Permitting enterprises to operate subsidiary income-earning activities outside the plan was proposed to offset this decline (Fforde and Van Vylder 1988; Hy 1993, 127–28). Yet the actual incentives incorporated into the system gave state firms a greater interest in Plan C production, because of the higher rate of profit retention. Thus the three-plans system probably contributed to the steady disintegration in state planning in Vietnam during the 1980s.

China, beginning in 1983, tried to give formal structure to its dual markets by defining a somewhat similar tripartite system of compulsory plans, guidance plans, and market activity. The reality of guidance plans varied from region to region, but it was clear that by 1984, most state firms were being assigned a compulsory plan for some output, while nearly all also had additional capacity that was being used for production of above-plan market goods. Thus, virtually all factories, including state-run factories, had been introduced to the market, and had begun the process of adaptation to market processes (See Naughton 1995 for a detailed description). The dual track was especially important for industrial producer goods, where it quickly became the predominant system.

Early Similarities

During the period from 1979 through 1983–84, both China and Vietnam thus went through an early stage of reform that had key common elements. Both were characterized by significant rural liberalization that involved contracting responsibilities over agricultural production to households; entry into industry and (to a lesser extent) trade by nonstate producers that created significant competition; and freedom granted to state firms to transact at market prices outside the plan. These measures implied that a significant share of transactions took place at prices that equated supply and demand. Flexible prices that equated supply and demand quickly came to play an important role in the Chinese and Vietnamese economies. It is essential to recognize what was accomplished in this initial stage.

First, the government's control over the price system was substantially eroded. Without monopoly barriers and facing significant competition, the government was unable to enforce the "socialist price system." In China, the entry of new producers into contestable markets gradually forced a realignment of prices (Naughton 1995). In Vietnam, government inability to impose state control over commerce was accompanied by a similar inability to impose control over the price system. The ultimate result in both countries was that prices were substantially closer to their ultimate market equilibrium relations than in prereform planned economies. As a result, market price signals were readily available in the economy, providing reasonably accurate information to state and nonstate firms alike. Moreover, subsequent price decontrol involved much smaller destabilizing price movements. Without control over the price system, the government was unable to harvest revenues from monopolistic state factories and was forced to cast about for other instruments to raise fiscal revenues. This created additional pressures to move forward with further reforms.

Second, producers throughout the economy had been introduced to the market and the need to operate on the market. Incentives began to shift: state firms were no longer rewarded solely for fulfilling plans, but rather had to rely on the market for some of their income. An important benefit of the legitimacy given to market prices was that transactions between the state and nonstate sector were permitted, and they developed into a remarkable variety of forms. In both China and Vietnam, various kinds of joint ventures and cooperative arrangements grew up, as profit-seeking, state-run enterprises looked for ways to reduce costs by subcontracting with rural nonstate firms or private businesses with lower labor and land costs. Firms and households of all types were increasingly imbedded in a market environment, and an environment was created in which learning and institutional development could occur.

It is also important to recognize what was *not* attempted in these early phases. Neither China nor Vietnam made significant progress toward reform of state-set prices. Neither China nor Vietnam took any significant steps to follow the 1960s Eastern European model of economic reform that envisaged continued state control but shifting to "indirect levers" such as state manipulation of prices and tax rates as a substitute for direct planning. Neither China nor Vietnam had any serious prospect of attempting a "computopia," in which sophisticated planners armed with high-powered computers would produce an improved version of the government-controlled economy. Thus, in both China and Vietnam, the process that we label "reform" was clearly and unambiguously a process of marketization, albeit limited and tentative. It was never confused with a program to modernize and rationalize state steerage of the economy. If anything, Chinese and Vietnamese attempts to mix apparently incompatible elements of plan and market, socialism and capitalism, might remind us of some forms of "Third World Socialism," in which a large-scale state sector coexists with a petty capitalist sector operating primarily on market principles. Such a model is not attractive as an endpoint of reform, since the economic growth record of such countries has been decidedly mixed, at best, but as a transitional strategy, it may be a feasible solution to the problem of getting from the planned to the market economy.

Subsequent Divergence

After 1983, Chinese and Vietnamese reforms diverged, both in the timing of subsequent events and in the specific measures taken. Vietnam responded to early reform success by halting reform implementation, rolling back some reforms, and even making sporadic attempts to increase state control over commerce and industry. By their actions, the Vietnamese leadership showed that the initial reform measures had been primarily expedient, designed to deal with a short-term economic crisis. As the good news about the harvest of 1982 became clear, government policy shifted to resumption of socialist transition. During 1983–85, agricultural collectivization was again pushed in the south. Halfhearted attempts were made to improve planning in industry and draw factories more completely into the planning system, but these had little discernible impact. After 1984, the government tried to push small-scale private businesses into state-sanctioned cooperatives. Given the opportunity, the Vietnamese leadership backed away from reform, and between 1983 and 1986 Vietnam regressed.

China's response to initial success was the opposite. Successful rural reforms gave legitimacy to the reform process as a whole and provided reformers with a working consensus within the top party counsels. Between 1984 and 1988, China moved steadily ahead with reforms, which were particularly prominent in the industrial sector. In part because this second phase of reform built directly on the achievements of the first, the specific reform measures adopted were the direct outgrowth of earlier achievements. The most important measures were "growing out of the plan," and incremental managerial reforms in the state sector.[1] China's premier, Zhao Ziyang,

---

1. In addition, reforms in the area of foreign trade and investment were quite important and successful. See Lardy 1992.

adopted a more explicit dual-track system as a strategy for further industrial reforms. The Chinese government made a generally credible commitment in 1984 to freeze the size of the traditional plan. This guaranteed a long-run dynamic process that would gradually increase the share of nonplan, market transactions in the economy and made the dual-track system into an unabashed transitional device. With this innovation, the dual-track system was converted from a short-run improvised solution to a bona fide transitional device.

The commitment to growing out of the plan was of great importance for the individual enterprise as well. With their plans essentially fixed, enterprises faced market prices on the margin. Even those firms with compulsory plans covering, say, 90 percent of capacity, were in the position that future growth and development of profitable opportunities would take place at market prices. The plan served as a kind of lump-sum tax on (or subsidy to) the enterprise. So long as the commitment not to change it was credible, it really had no impact on any of the enterprise's decision making. Current decisions would be based on market prices. If the enterprise was induced to operate as a profit-maximizing firm, that profit maximization would be carried out on the basis of market prices. In that sense, the plan was irrelevant (Byrd 1987).

Incremental managerial reforms in the state sector included financial incentive mechanisms for the firm as well as programs to realign managerial career incentives. The market framework for the state firm facilitated the maintenance and incremental reform of the management system of state enterprises. As state firms faced increasing competitive pressures, government officials experimented with ways to improve incentives and management capabilities within the state sector. This experimental process focused on a steady shift in emphasis away from plan fulfillment and toward profitability as the most important indicator of enterprise performance. A crucial step was the signing of multiyear profit contracts with state firm managers, which gave them substantial autonomy, as well as a stake in the long-run profitability of the firm. As discussed in chapter 7 of this volume, there is substantial evidence that the combination of increased competition, improved incentives, and more effective monitoring of performance did improve state enterprise performance over the 1980s. Increased flexibility of state firms combined with the steadily growing importance of rural enterprises, private firms, and foreign-invested firms to gradually shift the center of gravity of the economy toward a thoroughly market-based system. Thus, between 1984 and 1988, Chinese reforms moved forward, steadily deepening and broadening the innovations of the earlier reform period. Market forces became steadily more important in the economy, and as the economy became more flexible and responsive, growth rates gradually accelerated. Between 1983 and 1988, the proportion of transactions at market prices increased sharply, while the share of state firms in industrial production declined steadily (see table 1). This was

TABLE 1.   Indicators of Chinese Reform Progress

	1978	1983	1985	1988	1990	1992
Proportion of agricultural procurement at:						
Market prices	6%	18%	40%	57%	52%	—
Guidance prices	2%	14%	23%	19%	23%	—
Fixed prices	92%	68%	37%	24%	25%	—
Proportion of total retail sales at:						
Market prices	3%	16%	34%	49%	45%	
Guidance prices	neg.	11%	19%	22%	25%	90%
Fixed prices	97%	73%	47%	29%	30%	10%
Ownership structure of industrial production						
State ownership	78%	73%	65%	57%	55%	48%
Collectives	22%	26%	32%	36%	36%	38%
Private	neg.	neg.	2%	4%	5%	7%
Foreign-invested	neg.	neg.	neg.	1%	2%	4%

Sources: Prices: *Price Yearbook* 1991, 466; Tian Yuan and Qiao Gang 1991, 203; Sun Xiangyi 1993, 10. Industrial Output: Industrial Statistic Yearbook; Statistical Abstract, various years.

a period when steadily accumulating incremental change began to make a significant qualitative difference in the Chinese economy.

Vietnamese Catch-Up

In Vietnam during this period, the economic effect of reform backtracking quickly became apparent. Agricultural production stagnated between 1982 and 1986, and then dropped sharply in 1987 in the face of poor weather. With stagnant food production and a renewed industrialization drive, the result was rapidly accelerating inflation. By the end of 1985, Vietnam had stumbled into hyperinflation. As inflation raged and the magnitude of the economic problems became increasingly clear, reform returned to the agenda at the Sixth Party Congress in December 1986. The Vietnamese leadership thus learned a double lesson about the benefits of reform: not only did early reform create quick economic results, but in addition, the attempt to backtrack on those reforms quickly put the economy right back into the same problems it had confronted before. Yet Vietnamese backtracking on reform did not substantially improve the performance of the planned sector of the economy. State planning continued to decline, and private businesses continued to grow. But under these conditions, systematic reform of the state sector was impossible. There was no explicit "growing out of the plan" in Vietnam, and managerial reforms in state-run industry were sporadic and inconsistent.

The return to reform in 1986 included the announcement of the policy of "doi moi," or economic renovation. While an undoubted milestone in the evolution of policy, the introduction of *doi moi* did not result in an immediate or unambiguous shift in policy. The Sixth Party Congress did call for the coexistence of multiple forms of ownership and the acceptance of the market. It cut back excessive investment and declared that agriculture, consumer goods, and export promotion would henceforth be government priorities. State firms were exhorted to be financially self-sufficient. But despite the bold principles announced, policy makers seemed unclear about means to achieve those principles, and timid in implementation. The result was two years of inconsistent policy making, continued high inflation, and general lack of direction. It was not until January 1988 that a new land law was adopted that provided for fifteen- to twenty-year land contracts and guaranteed rights to transfer and inherit land. Even this measure came too late: the disastrous 1987 harvest had already caused significant famine in parts of the north.

As a result of the deteriorating situation and the failure of reform half-measures to make a significant difference, the Vietnamese government prepared for dramatic action at the end of 1988. On January 1, 1989, Vietnam carried out a nearly complete decontrol of state-fixed prices. At the same time, government subsidies to ailing state firms were cut off and the currency was devalued. Fiscal and monetary austerity were adopted, and tight limits on credit were allowed to push real interest rates to very high levels. Thus, Vietnam adopted a kind of "small bang" that substituted for the growing out of the plan of the Chinese reformers. It was a dramatic and quite successful step forward (Wood 1989). Motivated largely by the urgent need for macroeconomic stabilization, this method also served the objective of furthering economic reform. In a sense, the sheer desperation of the state's fiscal position was used to make credible its threat to cut off state firms from the support of continuing state subsidies.

At the same time, the Vietnamese initiative differed significantly from the "big bang" of the Eastern European transitions. Price decontrol came after a majority of all prices were effectively set on the market. State firms were cut loose after they had developed market-oriented behavior and after they had already learned to rely on the market for a significant share of income. The Vietnamese stabilization, in other words, did not have to bear the entire burden of the economic transition process. Rather, it was an essential component of a broader transition process that had already been under way for a number of years. Moreover, the dramatic policy measures of early 1989 brought substantial economic success. Not only did inflation come down quickly and stay down, but the government's commitment to a basic market economy was effectively demonstrated. Since 1989, Vietnam has struggled primarily with the problems of a market economy—stimulating and attracting investment, providing stability—rather than with the problem of getting to a market economy (for a description of the contemporary Vietnamese economy, see Dawkins and Whalley, in this volume).

Chinese Catch-Up

Just at the time the Vietnamese were forging ahead, the Chinese seemed to be losing momentum with their incremental strategy of reform. Facing their own inflation problems during 1988, the Chinese leadership shifted to a much more conservative stance. Reforms were put on hold as planners struggled to cool off the economy. The combination of inflation and austerity contributed to the tense political atmosphere that developed around the student demonstrations in Tiananmen Square, with tragic consequences in June 1989. Political and economic reaction seemed to rule the day during 1989. However, this conservative stance survived for only a year or two. By early 1992, at the latest, the Chinese were also willing to move forward boldly with economic reform.

Beginning in 1992, the Chinese moved away from the dual-track system and toward a full transition to a market economy. For the first time, the "frozen" planned economy was cut back, and whole sectors transferred to a market basis. There was no semblance of a big bang: instead, price controls and material allocations were eliminated in individual sectors, sometimes with a multiyear phaseout. Nevertheless, by 1994, price controls remained for only a few products, and even then for only a small proportion of output. Equally significant, the Chinese began to adopt an explicit legal and taxation framework that provided for a "level playing field" among all ownership forms. The adoption of a new tax system, based on nearly uniform rate value-added taxes as well as income taxes, on January 1, 1994, clearly signaled this achievement. Today, the Chinese economy, like the Vietnamese, is predominantly a market economy, certainly insofar as product markets are concerned. Continued institution-building reforms are still urgently needed, as labor, land, and capital markets still work poorly and need further legal and administrative support. In many areas, government-imposed distortions are still important. Industrial restructuring is under way, but still has much to achieve. Nevertheless, the fundamentals of the market economy are in place. In China, as in Vietnam, the crucial and dramatic steps leading to the introduction of the market economy seemed to be achieved with surprising ease. The smoothness of the later steps of the transition argue for the importance and success of the earlier steps. At the same time, both China and Vietnam had to take additional steps: the first phase of initial marketization, though successful, was far from adequate by itself. The particular strategy of this second stage of reform differed between China and Vietnam, but both undertook a second phase of reform to get to the market economy.

Similarities and Differences in the Reform Processes

It is clear that economic reform in both China and Vietnam was a gradual incremental process that unfolded within limits set by political constraints. The continuing power of the Communist Parties of both China and Vietnam did have an impact on the reform process, leading to delays and detours. Shifting alliances and conflicts among Communist Party leaders affected the determination of what types of economic policies were legitimate from a "socialist" standpoint. Moreover, each country was influenced by the other in the shifting definition of legitimacy. The Vietnamese, in particular, have shown themselves to be very aware of and sensitive to Chinese models, even when the two countries were politically hostile. This was particularly evident in 1986 when, along with *doi moi,* the Vietnamese adopted the Chinese definition of the contemporary stage of reform as a "commodity economy on a planned basis." This not very informative characterization was a useful political compromise for both the Chinese and the Vietnamese, because it implied marketization without allowing the market to govern all resource allocation. Factors of production such as land and labor would remain outside the scope of the market, and planners would remain in business. This way station was left behind by Vietnam in 1989, and finally formally rejected by the Chinese in 1992 when they declared their goal to be a "socialist market economy," that is, a real market economy, though with a large public sector. Even in 1994, both countries remain extremely suspicious of privatization, limiting themselves to cautious experiments with the establishment of stock markets that will allow some circulation of shares alongside majority state ownership.

The protracted process of legitimization of the market highlights one of the most striking common characteristics of the transition process in China and Vietnam. The market had to "prove itself" at every step; market reforms had to work or they wouldn't be adopted or continued (see Fang, in this volume, for a theoretical elaboration of this point). Thus, one of the most striking common characteristics was the tentativeness with which the process began, compared with the ultimately profound character of system transformation. A crucial part of the story in both China and Vietnam is that initial reforms bred further reform. The earliest measures were ultimately able to touch off a virtuous cycle of further reform. This process seems more linear in the Chinese case (notwithstanding some cyclical fluctuation in the level of commitment to reform) and more a question of profound hesitation and renewed learning of painful lessons in Vietnam. But in both cases, reforms were not a hurdle to be overcome on the way to a market economy; they were policies that had immediate and visible positive impact on the economy.

It is clear that in both China and Vietnam, the prolonged period of reform allowed time for the revival and consolidation of market institutions. In some of the literature, there is a tendency to take the Vietnamese reforms as beginning with the dramatic policies of 1989.[2] This approach cannot be justified. By 1989, Vietnam was already operating with an economy that had been substantially transformed from the planned-economy model. Government price setting only covered a portion of the economy, concentrated in raw materials. Most importantly, producers and traders oriented toward the market already existed in most sectors. Across-the-board decontrol could succeed precisely because there were already organizations in existence that were responsive to the opportunities created by decontrol.

In a broader sense, we can trace a virtuous cycle at work in the reform strategies adopted by both China and Vietnam. Gradual marketization drove changes in behavior in the initially protected sectors as well. Entry into previously high-profit sectors created fierce competition and downward pressure on the prices in those sectors. In China, the process of entry itself was required to gradually increase the number of price-responsive traders. In Vietnam, the pre-existing petty capitalist sector was ready to take advantage of liberalization. Vietnam was probably closer to equilibrium, in that the small-scale sector had never been eliminated. As a result, the explosive growth of new producers is less evident, notwithstanding the vibrant private sector (see Ronnås, in this volume). In both cases, prices were decontrolled initially in precisely those areas where small-scale production was efficient and technological barriers to entry lowest. As a result, in China at least, the combination of entry and decontrol did not produce strong inflationary pressures. Instead, relative prices fell in the decontrolled sectors, consolidating the momentum for further price control. In fact, price decontrol was associated with the increased supply of a whole range of consumer goods—some new to China—resulting in a "golden period" of reform (Wang Xiaoqiang 1993). A similar dynamic was almost certainly at work in Vietnam as well.

---

2. This tendency is especially prominent in writings by World Bank employees. Leipziger (1992 1, 3) describes the "first bold steps" of 1989 that "followed an earlier half-hearted attempt at reform, which was largely unsuccessful, except perhaps for the fact that it may have whetted the appetite of the reform-minded." Dollar (1993, 6) describes "the main features of the renovation (*doi moi*) introduced in 1989." This is inaccurate not only because *doi moi* was in fact introduced in 1986, but also because many of the features that he describes—rural land tenure reforms, promotion of the private sector, and so on—clearly date to an earlier period. Both papers treat the World Bank's reinvolvement with Vietnam in 1989 as a significant milestone as well.

In the planned economy there were numerous niches waiting to be filled, and many of these niches were best filled by the small start-up firms that we would expect to see in the early phases of reform. This was certainly the case in China, and is probably so in other formerly socialist countries as well. Since those niches were initially empty, the potential rewards to entrepreneurs who arrived first were large. Rapid entry ensured high returns and, at the same time, promised significant efficiency gains for the economy as a whole. In essence, socialist economies create the conditions for an "unbalanced growth strategy": unbalanced state investment raises returns to independent entrepreneurs in associated sectors.

Under the pressure of increased competition and institutional change, state firm behavior starts to change. Changing state firm behavior has many strands. First, under the impact of competition, state firm profitability declines. Losing their former monopoly protection, state firms quickly cease to be government "cash cows" and may even become liabilities. The loss of former protected status shifts the overall incentive environment for state firms. One response to this shift may simply be that the traditional planning apparatus disintegrates. That seems often to have been the case in Vietnam. State firms were under enormous pressure to provide decent minimum wages to their employees. The government, regardless of its intentions, was incapable of providing those kinds of guaranteed incomes and subsidies. Even before the "small bang" of 1989, many state firms in Vietnam were in fact thrown upon their own devices. As a result, they diversified and went into whatever lines of business promised to generate additional income. There was a note of desperation in this process in Vietnam. State-sector worker wages had been severely eroded by inflation. Anything that helped state workers get through their difficulties might be acceptable, at least temporarily.

In China, the process of state firm adaptation to the market was somewhat more orderly, but not qualitatively different. Facing increasing product market competition, the cushion of high monopoly profits that used to enfold all state firms came undone, and the success or failure of individual firms became increasingly evident. Some firms failed to adapt adequately to increased competition and plunged into the red. Other firms adapted successfully. Perhaps most significant is that the difference between successful and failed firms is now evident from their balance sheets. In this context, government monitoring of firm activity continued, but increasingly shifted from monitoring of plan compliance to monitoring of profitability. Erosion of monopoly protection affected government revenues via firm profits, and government officials were forced to intensify their scrutiny of enterprise profitability. The incentive structure of government as "owner" of state-run firms shifted. As a result, firms face greater discipline exerted through the managerial hierarchy. New incentive mechanisms have been created that implement the new objective function of firm overseers. Particularly striking in China has been the use of long-term managerial contracts, in which managerial pay and worker bonus funds are linked to profitability on a three- to five- year term (Naughton 1995; Jefferson, Rawski, and Zheng 1992). While managerial reforms in Vietnam were less systematic, there is little doubt that successful state firm managers in Vietnam were those that were able to generate new revenue sources to maintain the standard of living of their workers. Thus, China and Vietnam were similar in that in both countries, the early steps of marketization touched off a sometimes difficult and protracted process of adaptation to the market that was eventually self-reinforcing.

China and Vietnam share a set of initial conditions that facilitated the adoption of a relatively fragmented, uncoordinated approach to reform. In both countries, bureaucratic control of the economy was relatively weak. In the case of Vietnam, this was due simply to the very low level of economic development and limited degree of industrialization. Even in the 1980s, the state-run industrial sector accounted for a mere 4 percent of total employment. Total industrial employment was about 10 percent of total employment; some 60–70 percent of industry was made up of small-scale and handicraft operations not incorporated into state ownership (Fforde and Van Vylder 1988, 51). Levels of expertise in the state bureaucracy were low—the skilled manpower necessary to make technical economic decisions was lacking. Moreover, the state had been engaged in bitter struggle for almost twenty years with the world's most powerful military force. Unsurprisingly, available human skills were channeled into the national liberation struggle, and economic management resources were further depleted. In Vietnam, the bureaucracy struggled to exert the simplest forms of control over the economy.

China by the late 1970s was far more developed than Vietnam. Employment in the state and urban collective sectors accounted for about one-quarter of total employment, and 40 percent of those workers were in industry. Thus, about 10 percent of the labor force was employed in the large-scale, modern industrial sector. Moreover, China had already constructed a comprehensive industrial base. With the exception of a few goods embodying quite high technological levels that needed to be imported, China had the capacity to produce the full range of investment and consumer goods. Agricultural output per head was substantially higher than in Vietnam. But China's management capability was almost as underdeveloped in relation to its much larger and more diversified economy than Vietnam's management capability was in relation to its smaller economy. In China's case, this underdevelopment was due not to absolute poverty, but rather to the deterioration of the central planning system that had occurred in the years following the Cultural Revolution (i.e., in the period 1966–76).

China's central management organs were decimated in 1970, with manpower at the central level reduced to about one-tenth the level of the mid-1960s. Universities ceased turning out skilled technical personnel for several years. Yet while skill levels receded, industry kept growing, and became more diverse and more decentralized. Inputs of management and technical manpower per *yuan* of industrial output declined steadily. Planning became less an exercise in the detailed control of resources, and more a rough redistribution of resources between regions and sectors. Central planners allocated only about one hundred commodities, in an economy that produced tens of thousands of different products. Planners did not allocate all of the output of even the most important commodities (such as coal), for some was left to local governments to control. At a much higher level than in Vietnam, China's planners nonetheless equally struggled to control an economy that increasingly seemed to be uncontrollable.

In both China and Vietnam, the most obvious manifestation of the weak planning systems was the proliferation of unused and surplus capacity. In both countries, incomplete investment projects proliferated. In both countries, much completed industrial capacity lay idle. In China, it was commonly estimated that about one-third of the industrial capacity was unutilized at any given time because of the shortages of energy supplies. In Vietnam, no similar aggregate calculation is available, but unused capacity has struck numerous observers. For example, the Swedish aid program refused to provide a pharmaceutical plant to Vietnam as originally intended when it was discovered that three similar pharmaceutical plants already existed, each of them running below 50 percent capacity (Fforde and Van Vylder 1988). In both countries, haphazard investment programs, carried out without adequate coordination with available supplies of inputs, led to the coexistence of shortage and useless slack capacity.

China's solution to its weak administrative capacity was to decentralize substantial control over the economy. Thus, local governments shared some of the power to allocate materials and determine investment projects that would be retained in the national capital in more orthodox centrally planned regimes. This decentralization included the encouragement given rural towns and villages to develop their own collectively run enterprises. At a crucial stage in China's transition, rural "township and village" enterprises played the most important role in setting up new firms and creating market competition. There was no similar institutional form in Vietnam; instead, the petty capitalist trader played an analogous role in system transformation.

The most important differences between China and Vietnam relate to the basic pattern in which reforms unfolded, and in particular to the macroeconomic dynamics of reform. We have already noted the difference between Chinese and Vietnamese policy makers in their response to the initial successes of reform. A related difference is the way in which problems of inflation have been dealt with in the course of reform. In China, inflation has tended to be generated during the most "reformist" phases, and these periods of inflationary reform have been followed by consolidation phases in which reform is slowed down. In Vietnam, by contrast, inflation has generally arisen during periods when reforms are not being implemented, and periods of accelerated reform have been associated with decreased inflation. These differences reflect both political and economic differences between the two countries.

In China, reform measures contributed to macroeconomic imbalances, largely because they included decentralization of authority over investment that led to short-run "investment booms." The rapid growth of investment eventually led to a period of macroeconomic austerity, during which time reform implementation was slowed or even reversed. As a result, macroeconomic policies have been of fundamental importance in determining the success or failure of reforms during individual periods. Most significant, stabilization of the economy has been achieved primarily through administrative mechanisms. Quantitative controls on credit and investment are most commonly used to reduce inflationary pressures, and conservative policies are often in favor at these times. There is thus no association between stabilization and liberalization, but rather the reverse.

At the same time, the alternation between expansionary and contractionary phases of the macroeconomic cycle contributed to marketization of the Chinese economy over the long run. The planning apparatus was buffeted by the rapid change in economic conditions, and its importance receded as a result of its inability to respond quickly to rapid changes in the economic environment. The almost intractable task of planning an economy can only be carried out in conditions of artificially imposed stability; without that stability, the inadequacy of attempts to plan the economy become increasingly evident.

In Vietnam, inflation has been associated with the most conservative phases of policy making. Conservative (or rather "socialist") phases have often involved an increased planned investment effort (especially in industry) and reductions in supply, especially from agriculture. These central government attempts to push the economy into "leaps forward" result in inflation. For example, in 1985, inflation rapidly became entrenched and tended to accelerate, and reached annual rates of over 400 percent in the second and third quarters of 1988. As a result, Vietnam adopted the simple and bold method of rapid price decontrol combined with monetary and fiscal austerity. Basic price stability—without price controls—was attained in Vietnam by June 1989. Thus, in Vietnam, an association between stabilization and liberalization was maintained.

This difference between China and Vietnam may in turn be related to another important macroeconomic difference. China has maintained high saving and investment levels throughout the reform process, whereas Vietnamese saving rates have been low. In China, continued high saving was made possible by a gradual takeover by households of national saving from government. Steady erosion in government revenues—ultimately traceable to the dissolution of the government industrial monopoly—led to a sustained reduction in government saving. At the same time, though, steady increases in household income and increasing opportunities in the economic environment led to a rapid increase in household saving. These offsetting changes meant that total national saving remained high, sustaining high levels of investment and growth. Private savings are more than 15 percent of GDP, and total investment has ranged between 30 and 40 percent of GDP during the reform era (Naughton 1995). One consequence has been a vastly enhanced role for the banking system, serving as an intermediary channeling household saving to the enterprise sector.

In Vietnam, by contrast, government saving was quite modest before reform and the country was largely dependent on inflow of foreign saving, primarily from the Soviet Union. (The low level of government saving, in turn, reflects Vietnam's inability to establish a government monopoly over industry and the absence of any other developed tax system.) Private saving and investment seems to have accelerated substantially in Vietnam after 1991, but remains at quite low levels, especially compared to China. In 1992, total national saving reached 13 percent of GDP (Dollar 1993). Low saving in Vietnam reflects the country's poverty (even relative to China) and the underdeveloped state of both fiscal and financial institutions.

These differences may help explain the different macroeconomic patterns observed. Chinese macroeconomic fluctuations can be traced primarily to fluctuations in investment demand. Reasonable supplies of output and saving are available, but the growth of effective demand for investment—ultimately reflecting access to bank credits—simply outstrips available supply. By contrast, Vietnamese macroeconomic fluctuations can be traced in significant part to fluctuations in the supply of output and saving. When reforms are abandoned agricultural output is reduced and real incomes in both rural and urban areas decline. Private saving also declines, and so long as investment is not sharply reduced, inflationary surges result. The supply response is more important in the evolution of Vietnamese cycles, while investment demand is the crucial factor in Chinese cycles.

Reform and Growth in China and Vietnam

The Chinese and Vietnamese economies differ significantly from those in Eastern Europe and the former Soviet states. Although all belonged to a common extended family of planned economies derived from the Soviet model, there were important differences in the level of development and the systemic features of these economies. Some of these differences have important consequences for the ability of these countries to maintain rapid economic growth.

China and Vietnam should be seen as economies with a relatively high human capital endowment (for developing countries) combined with very low wage rates (even for a developing country). Life expectancies and educational levels in China's cities and advanced coastal provinces are not far below those of Eastern Europe, and Vietnam and China's inland provinces have relatively good human indicators compared to their incomes. Vietnam has a life expectancy at birth of 63 years and a literacy rate of 88 percent, both far higher than one would expect given the level of per capita income. Moreover, China and Vietnam are adjacent to the East Asian economic region, the most rapidly growing economic region in the world. Technology transfer can be rapid, and international markets are expanding quickly.

Both China and Vietnam have large rural populations. A little over two-thirds of the Chinese population is rural, and about 80 percent of the Vietnamese population. This portion of the population has never had the same income guarantees that were implicitly extended to urban populations in China and the European socialist countries (the situation in Vietnam, due to the long war, is less clear). The rural population was also not subject to the same intensity of social and economic controls. As a result, the rural population has come to be a more fertile soil for entrepreneurship and economic innovation than has the urban population. This is particularly evident around the periphery of large cities in China. Suburban areas—styled "rural" in the Chinese classification and subject to lesser degrees of social and economic control—have emerged as the most prosperous and rapidly growing parts of the economy. Much of the "rural industry" that has been so dynamic in China is in fact "suburban industry." In suburban areas, economic opportunity, often linked to nearby cities, intersects with looser economic controls. The rural areas provide a kind of space in which economic innovation can proceed, and within which individual entrepreneurs can prosper. Conversely, urban populations are often quite cautious about economic reform. Aware of their privileged positions and income security, urban residents are far less willing to plunge into the dangerous waters of independent entrepreneurship. In this case, the larger rural population seems to give an advantage to China and Vietnam.

Moreover, both China and Vietnam have relatively young populations and abundant labor forces. China has perhaps the most unusual age structure of any population in the world, due to its severe birth control policies. Overall, the population is quite young, with a median age of 25 in 1990. Yet unlike the case in most young populations, the proportion of the total population made up of dependent children is not large. Indeed, the population below 15 years of age is only 90 percent as large as the population between 15 and 29 (Census Office 1991, 13–15). China at present thus has the best of two different demographic worlds. It has a young, vigorous, and adaptable labor force, while also having a low dependency ratio. Vietnam has a more traditional age structure, but one that is very young indeed. Newbery (1993) points out that age structure gives China a significant advantage in terms of the role of the state in providing social security. Because populations are much older in the European socialist countries, the state must maintain a certain level of social security outlays, and that makes it much more difficult for the state to acquiesce in the rapid decline in government revenues that frequently accompanies economic reform. A young population thus implies a smaller stumbling block for economic reform.

More generally, a young population and abundant labor provide ample resources for growth. Conversion of labor from the low-productivity agricultural sector to the high-productivity urban industrial sector is the most potent engine of growth. China is in the midst of this process and Vietnam is just beginning it.

Yet in spite of these similarities there are large differences in the growth experience of China and Vietnam. Vietnamese growth, while rapid in recent years, has been established on a relatively shallow foundation. Vietnam has a much greater problem with lack of infrastructure, low levels of industrial skills, poverty, and rapidly growing population. Moreover, investment, while increasing, is still well below Chinese rates, and the country remains dependent on inflows of foreign capital. China also had an easier time with its foreign trade transition, because China already traded primarily with the capitalist world, whereas Vietnam had to wean itself from dependence on Soviet trade and subsidies. Both China and Vietnam have enormous potential advantages as they undertake accelerated economic growth. But in the Chinese case, the gap between potential and currently realized advantages is much smaller than in Vietnam.

Clearly, the above discussion indicates that it would be foolish to attribute rapid growth in China or Vietnam solely to their reform policies. Yet, it is perhaps most striking that both China and Vietnam have been able to overcome a range of challenges and build upon the diverse advantages that they inherited. After all, there are many countries in the world with robust growth potential that have been unable to realize that potential for various, sometimes policy-related, reasons. At the very least, it would appear that reform policy has played a modest role in enabling the economic systems of China and Vietnam to exploit the resources and advantages that were presented to them.

But in fact, the relationship between reform and growth in China and

Vietnam is even closer. For the association between them is not just evident in cross section (i.e., China and Vietnam have pursued certain reform policies and been rewarded with more rapid long-term growth), it is also evident over time within China and Vietnam. Reform has led to growth acceleration in both countries. Moreover, specific periods in the overall reform process are plausibly related to short-run changes in the economic growth rate. This is most obvious in Vietnam, where reform backtracking has had such obvious negative effects on the economy. But it is also evident in China, where steady acceleration—and occasional surges—of the growth rate in industry have been quite closely linked to progress of reform.

This brief review of the reform process in China and Vietnam must therefore conclude with the observation that the two countries have significant features in common, and that these features are plausibly related to the acceleration in economic growth that the two countries have experienced. The link between reform and growth is not simple, and certainly not monocausal. There are very different patterns of macroeconomic policy and response in the two countries, and both have benefited from good economic fundamentals on the eve of reform. But the basic observation that reforms, once initiated, led to a self-sustaining, virtuous cycle of reform is strongly supported by this review of Chinese and Vietnamese experience.

BIBLIOGRAPHY

Byrd, William A. 1987. "The Impact of the Two-Tier Plan/Market System in Chinese Industry." *Journal of Comparative Economics* 11, no.3: 295–308.
Census Office of the State Council. 1991. *Zhongguo 1990 Nian Renkou Pucha 10% Chouyang Ziliao* [Materials from the 10 percent sample of the 1990 Chinese census]. Beijing: Zhongguo Tongji.
Chen, Kang, Gary Jefferson, Thomas Rawski, Hongchang Wang, and Yuxin Zheng. 1988. "Productivity Change in Chinese Industry: 1953–1985." *Journal of Comparative Economics* 12, no.4 (December): 570–91.
Chu Van Lam. 1993. *"Doi Moi* in Vietnamese Agriculture." In Turley and Selden 1993, 151–64.
Dollar, David. 1993. "Macroeconomic Management and the Transition to the Market in Vietnam." Paper presented at the conference on "Transition of the Communist Countries in Pacific Asia," Asia Foundation, San Francisco, May 7–8.
Eberstadt, Nick. 1986. "Material Poverty in the People's Republic of China in International Perspective." In U.S. Congress Joint Economic Committee, ed., *China's Economy Looks Toward the Year 2000*, 1: 263–322. Washington, D.C.: Government Printing Office.
Ferris, Andrew. 1984. *The Soviet Industrial Enterprise*. London: Croom Helm.

Fforde, Adam, and Stefan Van Vylder. 1988. *Vietnam: An Economy in Transition.* Stockholm: SIDA.

Groves, Theodore, Yongmiao Hong, John McMillan, and Barry Naughton. 1995. "China's Evolving Managerial Labor Market." *Journal of Political Economy* 103, no. 4 (August): 873–92.

Hy Van Luong. 1993. "The Political Economy of Vietnamese Reforms: A Microscopic Perspective from Two Ceramics Manufacturing Centers." In Turley and Selden 1993, 119–48.

Industrial Statistics Yearbook *[Zhongguo Gongye Jingji Tongji Nianjian].* Annual. Beijing: Zhongguo Tongji.

Jefferson, Gary, Thomas Rawski, and Yuxin Zheng. 1992. "Growth, Efficiency and Convergence in China's State and Collective Industry." *Economic Development and Cultural Change* 40, no. 2: 239–66.

Khanh, Tran. 1993. *The Ethnic Chinese and Economic Development in Vietnam.* Singapore: Institute of Southeast Asian Studies.

Lang, Tan Teng. 1985. *Economic Debates in Vietnam.* Singapore: Institute of Southeast Asian Studies.

Lardy, Nicholas. 1992. *Foreign Trade and Economic Reform in China, 1978–1990.* New York: Cambridge University Press.

Le Duc Thuy. 1993. "Economic *Doi Moi* in Vietnam: Content, Achievements, and Prospects." In Turley and Selden 1993, 97–106.

Leipziger, D. M. 1992. *Awakening the Market: Viet Nam's Economic Transition.* World Bank Discussion Papers No. 157, Washington, D.C.

Le Thien Tung. 1989. "The Land Issue: The Internal Debate." *Vietnam Commentary,* no. 7 (Jan–Feb.): 2–4.

Lin, Justin Yifu. 1992. "Rural Reform and Agricultural Growth in China." *American Economic Review* 82, no. 1 (March): 34–51.

McMillan, John, and Barry Naughton. 1992. "How to Reform a Planned Economy: Lessons from China." *Oxford Review of Economic Policy* 8, no. 1 (Spring): 130–43.

McMillan, John, John Whally, and Lijing Zhu. 1989. "The Impact of China's Economic Reforms on Agricultural Productivity Growth." *Journal of Political Economy* 97:781–807.

Naughton, Barry. 1995. *Growing Out of the Plan: Chinese Economic Reform, 1978–1993.* New York: Cambridge University Press.

Newbery, David. 1993. "Transformation in Mature versus Emerging Economies: Why has Hungary been less successful than China?" Paper presented to the International Symposium on the Theoretical and Practical Issues of the Transition toward the Market Economy in China, Haikou, China, July 1–3.

Price Yearbook [Zhongguo Wujia Nianjian]. Annual. Beijing: Zhongguo Wujia.

Stern, Lewis. 1989. "Linh's Economic Reforms: Limits Imposed at Sixth Plenum." *Vietnam Commentary,* no. 9 (May–June): 4–7.

Sun Xiangyi. 1993. "An Account of Price Reform in 1992." *Zhongguo Wujia* 1:9–11.

Tian Yuan and Qiao Gang. 1991. *Zhongguo Jiage Gaige Yanjiu (1984–1990)* [Studies of China's price reform]. Beijing: Dianzi Gongye.

Turley, William S., and Mark Selden. 1993. *Reinventing Vietnamese Socialism: Doi Moi in Comparative Perspective*. Boulder, Colo.: Westview.

Vo Dai Luoc. 1993. "The Fight against Inflation: Achievements and Problems." In Turley and Selden 1993, 107–18.

Vo Nhan Tri. 1990. *Vietnam's Economic Policy since 1975*. Singapore: Institute of Southeast Asian Studies.

Wang Xiaoqiang. 1993. "Groping for Stones to Cross the River: Chinese Price Reform against the 'Big Bang.'" University of Cambridge Department of Applied Economics, Discussion Papers on Economic Transition No. DPET 9305.

Wiegersma, Nancy. 1988. *Vietnam: Peasant Land, Peasant Revolution*. New York: St. Martin's.

Wood, Adrian. 1989. "Deceleration of Inflation with Acceleration of Price Reform: Vietnam's Remarkable Recent Experience." *Cambridge Journal of Economics* 13, no.4 (December): 563–71.

CHAPTER 13

Economic Reform and Performance in Vietnam

Chris Dawkins and John Whalley

This chapter discusses recent economic reforms in Vietnam and the behavior of associated economic performance indicators. Despite apparent initial successes from recent reforms, future Vietnamese economic performance remains uncertain. On the one hand, surrounded by high-growth Asian economies, well endowed with resources and a motivated labor force, and having moved from a country where famine and hyperinflation reigned in the mid-1980s to a rice-exporting country with below 20 percent inflation today, Vietnam seems poised for a spectacular takeoff based on ever broadening economic reform. Accelerating growth rates in the early 1990s, growing flows of inward investment, and moderate to strong trade growth despite large falls in trade with Russia all seem to confirm this conclusion.

On the other hand, a number of factors suggest that such optimism over future economic performance in Vietnam be tempered with caution.[1] While central planning now seems to have no meaningful economic function, the apparatus of state control and intervention remains. High party officials are vigilant not to surrender control completely to the market and as a result, reforms in the state enterprise sector have moved slowly. Inefficiency and financial losses are rampant among large state enterprises.[2] The labor market has encountered substantial disruption as military expenditures have fallen

---

This is a revised version of a paper prepared for a conference on "Evolution of Market Institutions in Transition Economies," San Diego, May 14–15, 1993. It draws heavily on conversations and materials collected during our participation in a CIDA mission to Vietnam in December 1992. We are indebted to Randy Spence of IDRC for arranging meetings on our behalf. Bill Young and Nguyen H. Trung also provided invaluable assistance, and we are grateful to Ian Townsend-Gault and Stephen Tyler for their explanations of the legal and environmental situations in Vietnam. At the conference we benefited from lively and constructive discussion and from written comments provided by John McMillan.

1. The *Economist Intelligence Unit, Country Report No.3,* (1992b) suggests a slowdown in Vietnamese growth performance over the next eighteen months.

2. Hoan Do Dau and Ulf Svennson (1992) estimate that only about 300 of the approximately 12,000 state enterprises are profitable.

and state enterprises have begun to streamline.[3] Such adjustment problems could slow or even reverse enterprise reforms.

Fiscal and monetary disciplines are also fragile. The public sector deficit remains high; tax evasion is an acknowledged problem; the financial system within which monetary discipline is exercised is rudimentary. The government openly acknowledges the problems of rampant corruption and smuggling. Coordination between government levels remains a challenge. The provincial governments in Vietnam exercise substantial power, initiating their own policies and blocking or accelerating central government reforms.

Thus, while the first major steps toward reform have clearly been taken in Vietnam, the follow-through to a period of sustained reform and high growth is by no means assured. The experience could be one of high growth with continued reforms in such areas as state enterprises (as in China), or merely higher growth than before but still low growth compared to Association of Southeast Asian Nations/Newly Industrializing Countries (ASEAN/ NIC) standards.

The Present Economic Situation in Vietnam

The summary of recent performance and the present situation in the Vietnamese economy given in table 1 reflects the sentiment of still-cautious optimism for the country we project in this chapter. While per capita income is low and the specter of high unemployment casts its shadow, strong recent trade performance and macroeconomic reforms seem to have led to substantial growth and high savings rates.

Vietnam is clearly an extremely poor developing country. Current estimates place the annual real per capita GDP around $200, contrasting with levels of $250 to $300 in India, $450 to $500 in China, and $600 to $700 in Indonesia. Based on these figures, and taking population growth rates into account, the base from which development will start in Vietnam is so low that even if Vietnam were to triple real per capita income (an implied real growth rate of approximately 12 percent per year), in 15 years it might only be at Indonesia's current level. Vietnam is thus clearly beginning its development from a very low base. The comparison group might be Korea in the 1950s, Pakistan in the 1960s–70s, or even, perhaps, Bangladesh today.

The true level of Vietnamese per capita GDP (together with other eco-

---

3. This phenomenon is well documented. See, for example, Mallon and de Jonghe 1991, which puts urban unemployment in Vietnam at about 20 percent. The World Bank study (1992), "Vietnam, Restructuring Public Finance and Public Enterprises," also argues that unemployment has emerged as a serious problem. These high unemployment rates are not apparent in visits to Hanoi or Ho Chi Minh City, where most people seem to be engaged in economic activity, even if only in the informal sector.

TABLE 1. Vietnam's Present Economic and Demographic Situation

Overall Economy

per capita GNP—1990	$200 US
Real GDP growth—1992 est.	7.5%
Average annual growth—1986–90	3.9%
Inflation CPI—1992	20%

Government budget percentage of GDP—1991 est.

Revenue	11.1
Recurrent expenditure	12.0
Public savings	−0.9
Public investment	3.0

Balance of payments—1991 est.

Exports	$1,950 million US
Imports	−$2,020 million US
Balance of trade	−$70 million US
Current account balance including grants	−$254 million US

External debt—1990 est.	+$3.1 billion US
	(10.4 billion rubles)

Major exports: crude oil, rice; marine products, coffee, coal; rubber,
        crafts, wood products

Major imports: fuel, capital equipment, vehicles, fertilizers, consumer
        goods

Sectoral Indicators

	% of GDP (est. 1990)	Growth Rate of Production (est. 1990)
Agriculture	46.9	7.2
Industry	28.8	4.6
Commerce	13.6	1.9
Transportation and communication	1.7	0.0
Construction	2.8	5.8
Others	6.3	2.5

Demographics

Population—1991	67.7 million
Population distribution—1991	21% urban, 79% rural
Life expectancy—1990	62.7 years
Access to safe water (% population)	46%
Daily calorie supply	102%
Adult literacy rate—1990 (% population)	88%

Source: "Briefing Note, Socialist Republic of Vietnam," United Nations Development Programme 1992a;
Mallon and de Jonghe, 1991.

nomic statistics) is, however, the subject of some debate. Indeed, a visitor to Ho Chi Minh City who sees wide boulevards, large billboards publicizing Japanese electronics, bustling sidewalk markets, and a sense of vibrancy in some ways comparable to other higher income countries in Asia, might question an annual income of only $200 per head. Other observations add further skepticism about such economic data. Accounting practices in Vietnam are underdeveloped and thus the financial reporting and accounting in state-owned enterprises is likely inaccurate. National income accounts based on these reports would incorporate such inaccuracies. Corruption and smuggling also generate economic activity that goes unreported in conventional national accounts. Furthermore, measures of activity in the private enterprise sector are also underreported since much of it involves unrecorded small- and medium-scale enterprise activity (family-owned).

The methods used to calculate national income provide a further obstacle to reliable estimates of per capita income. In its national income accounts, Vietnam has for many years used the Soviet/Marxist concept of net material product rather than the more conventional Western concept of national income or gross domestic product. Net material product does not include the service sector and also double counts intermediate production in the manufacturing sector.[4]

Taken together, all of these factors make the present estimates of per capita GDP suspect, although not all these missing factors would serve to raise correctly measured per capita GDP. For instance, urban-rural income differentials are large and thus the average per capita GDP is certainly less than initial impressions of Ho Chi Minh City would indicate.

If the base from which future development is to proceed is low, the direction is most certainly up. Growth rates in 1992 were as high as 7 to 8 percent,[5] in contrast with 3 to 4 percent the previous year and around 2 percent in 1990, although, as with real per capita income, substantial uncertainty surrounds these numbers. This growth, however large, has occurred against a background of adjustments that have hit the Vietnamese economy at the same time that reform has been proceeding. These include a major shift in trading patterns, changes in the labor market, and a tightening of government fiscal disciplines. To have achieved such robust growth performance in the face of such major adjustment problems is particularly striking.

The underpinnings of this current strong performance have been microincentive-based reforms and relative macroeconomic stability achieved through

---

4. Thus, not only would production of a car be included in GDP, so would the steel that goes into the production of the car.

5. *Vietnam Investment Review* 2, no.6 (November 30-December 6): 7. "1992 Marks First Year of Real Success" reports a 1992 growth rate of GNP of 7.5 percent.

monetary and fiscal policies. Many development economists have argued that macroeconomic stability was key to the early surges in growth performance in the Asian NICs, particularly in Taiwan and to a lesser extent in Korea. In Vietnam, the inflation rate, which was running at 300 to 400 percent per year in the mid 1980s, is now down to approximately 20 percent per year, and this year's target is a further reduction to 10 percent.

The key to implementing this inflation reduction policy has been an emphasis on fiscal and monetary discipline. The government has reduced expenditures by either cutting or eliminating subsidies to state enterprises, as well as by cutting military expenditures. This reduction in expenditures has been accompanied by efforts to raise revenues. Improved tax compliance through increased enforcement has reduced lost revenues from nonreporting and valuation-avoidance schemes, although problems remain.[6] Future expenditure cuts together with revenue increases are targeted to further contract the deficit.

Trade growth has been especially strong and largely unaffected by the substantial dislocation of trade with the former Soviet Union. The collapse of the Soviet Union sparked the need for a realignment of trading partners; in the late 1980s, well over 70 percent of Vietnam's trade was with inconvertible ruble currencies. The last two years have seen export growth in the region of 15 to 20 percent despite the reorientation of trade away from inconvertible ruble currency trade. Crude oil and marine products have become major export earners along with rice.

Savings rates have also begun to increase, together with an increase in GDP growth rates, reminiscent of experience under the growth surges that occurred earlier in Korea, Taiwan, and elsewhere. In these countries savings rates accelerated into the 20 to 25 percent range shortly after the initial surge in GDP growth rates. Current savings rates in Vietnam are not well documented, but some estimates place them surprisingly high, perhaps around 15 percent, suggesting a potential for even further growth acceleration. Investment flows are also now coming into the country, although probably not at the rate indicated by joint venture approvals.

Unemployment remains the largest negative component of recent economic performance. Estimates of the number of unemployed in Vietnam are as high as 5 million people.[7] Substantial labor market dislocation and adjustment has occurred during the recent reform period, some directly connected to reforms, others not. State enterprises have been forced to trim labor under

---

6. Despite these increased efforts, the General Customs Office estimates that unpaid import-export taxes in 1992 are as high as $29.4 million U.S. (*Vietnamese Investment Review,* November 23–29)

7. See note 3.

budgetary and financial pressures from the Ministry of Finance and the State Bank. Such measures have added to unemployment and reflect the unwilling-ness of state-owned enterprises to hire new labor. Other factors have com-pounded the problem. These include the return of Vietnamese "guest workers" from the former Soviet Union and reductions in military expenditures.

Growth and future prosperity thus seem within the reach of Vietnam. An assessment of the present economic situation in Vietnam would suggest that significant liberalization, and with it economic growth, have clearly taken place over the last five to seven years. Indeed, the process may have pro-gressed far enough that it will prove hard to reverse. However, the base from which this growth must proceed is extremely low, and while growth in trade has occurred, it has not yet been at the levels that were experienced in Korea and Taiwan at their peak.

Despite the positive indicators, many problems remain for Vietnam: weak physical and intellectual infrastructures; corruption and smuggling; and large regional differences.[8] To maintain high growth and to overcome these remaining problems, Vietnam must clearly mobilize a large amount of re-sources. This mobilization will occur through domestic savings, aid flows, and large inflows of foreign capital, all of which have yet to materialize in the amounts needed. Whether a takeover comparable to that we have witnessed elsewhere in Asia will actually occur remains to be seen. The odds may have recently moved in favor of a major growth surge, but such an outcome is far from assured.

The Content of Vietnamese Economic Reform

The economic reforms in Vietnam that underlie the economic performance of today began in 1986 under the doctrine of *doi moi,* or renovation. Reform was, in large part, a response to a decade of major economic distress: starva-tion and famine were endemic in the countryside, inflation rates were well over 300 percent per year, state enterprises were losing large sums of money, and financial and fiscal discipline were weak. In this environment, formalized state planning, as in the Soviet Union from the 1930s to the1970s, was simply infeasible. Little information was available for planning, financial control broke down, and agricultural performance was poor.

The weak economic performance of the early 1970s and 1980s was in large part the motivation for the policy changes that have followed since 1986. At official levels in the party the main reform objective was to substantially raise real income levels without encouraging any move toward capitalism,

---

8. These are dealt with in our discussion of development scenarios for Vietnam and problems and challenges for the future.

which they had been resisting for over 40 years. At the time, the perception in official levels of the party was that private ownership of resources comprised capitalism, and as such was unwelcome. Market-oriented socialism was acceptable, however, and the idea of market-oriented reforms was adopted.

Thus far, market-oriented reforms have progressed in a manner consistent with the socialist orientation of Vietnamese society, although the contradictions involved in this process have grown ever more apparent. Official state planning bodies remain, but since 1986 the cumulative effect of these reforms on their operation has been striking. The State Planning Committee, for instance, the main body concerned with economic planning, still formulates a whole array of complex plans: annual, five-year, ten-year, quarterly, national, regional, sectoral, and others. At the same time, these plans are only indicative, providing indications of where the economy may be headed, but without any imperative content. They contain no orders or requirement of execution on the part of economic agents involved. Centralized authority still resides within the planning apparatus, and hence the official organs of the party, but for now this authority is largely latent. The power that the party retains is considerable, and could in principle be used to resist and even reverse future reform.

The de facto situation introduces further departures from what one thinks of as a command structure. The planning organs lack reliable data, and furthermore cannot adequately monitor the activities of the small- and medium-size enterprises at whom the reforms are aimed. These planning organs also realize the extent to which power slowly devolves away from themselves to more operational ministries (i.e., finance, state bank) under a reformist regime. But at the same time, they see themselves as the custodians of party authority, and hence centralized power. Those controlling these agencies are also aware of the raised expectations for growth, the need for capital inflows, and ultimately the need to allow reforms to advance further in order to allow growth to continue.

Inconsistencies thus arise in many areas. One example is property rights. Thus far, no major privatization of state-owned assets or change in legal ownership of assets has occurred as part of the reforms. In agriculture, to provide incentives for increased output, peasants have been granted long (50-year) leases on land they currently occupy. Legislation to allow trading in leases is under consideration, as is legislation to allow inheritance of leases.[9] Individuals can own assets in the small-scale enterprise sector. With increasing efforts to attract inward foreign investment through joint ventures, ownership issues involving state-owned enterprise now repeatedly arise. Recent talk of a stock market that, like China, may involve trade in

---

9. Ngo Ba Thanh (1992), 20.

claims to income rather than assets, further elevates these property rights issues.

The main components of the reforms that have thus far occurred are as follows.

Price Decontrol

The process of price decontrol in Vietnam has been gradual, spanning a decade and ending in 1989 with the disappearance of the distinction between official and market prices.[10] In 1979, the government began the process by allowing many state-owned enterprises and cooperatives that had fulfilled their fixed-price contractual obligations to buy extra inputs and sell extra outputs in the market. This fledgling market formed the basis for a gradual shift away from the planning apparatus and led the way for a number of more wide-ranging reforms. In 1985 the agricultural price scheme changed to respond to local demand and supply conditions. Industrial input prices, with the exception of steel, petroleum, electricity, and fertilizer, rose to reflect production costs. While a number of consumer goods continued to be rationed, the system of differentiated consumer prices was abolished. Between 1987 and 1989, the prices of production inputs such as fuel and fertilizer rose to international levels. The rationing of essential consumer goods ceased, although a number continued to be subsidized. Although the prices of a few commodities, such as electricity, water, public transportation, communication equipment, and cement and steel are still controlled, they are now allowed to change in response to changes in production costs.

Inflation Reduction and Macroeconomic Coordination

The decrease in inflation from almost 400 percent in 1988 to 20 percent in 1992 is hailed by the Vietnamese as both a major accomplishment of their reforms and a key component part. This has occurred as a result of the policies of two key agencies, the Ministry of Finance and the State Bank. Sharp cuts have taken place in state expenditures through the phasing out of so-called subsidies to state enterprises. These subsidies were largely used to bail out loss-making enterprises under the previous regime. As well, military and other expenditures have also fallen.[11] Anti-inflationary policies aimed at decreasing liquidity have also been undertaken. These have included positive

---

10. This subsection draws heavily on the discussion in Mallon and de Jonghe 1991, and State Planning Committee and United Nations Development Programme 1990.

11. The *Economist Intelligence Unit, Country Report No. 2* (1992a) reports a demobilization of 600,000 troops, as well as a reduction in state enterprise employees of about 600,000 between 1988 and 1992.

real interest rates on deposits, higher interest rates on loans, and a devaluation of the official exchange rate to that of the parallel market.

Substantial efforts have also been made to increase tax collections. Thirty thousand individuals are now active in tax administration in various parts of the country. Prosecutions for tax evasion are a further part of an attempt to increase tax collections. A somewhat chaotic and haphazard system of turnover taxes inherited from the former Soviet Union has been, in part, replaced by a patchwork quilt of ad hoc specific taxes. Clearly, the direction in which much of this tax activity is headed is toward a value-added tax. The Ministry of Finance is working closely with a team of consultants from France, and an experimental value-added tax is to be introduced. The Ministry of Finance has become a key budgetary agency, as it both coordinates and controls the budget, even though it formally reports to the State Planning Commission.

The effect of all these changes has been macroeconomic control, and in particular, a sharp cut in inflation rates. This decrease in inflation has provided a newfound sense of macroeconomic stability, and its contribution to economic growth has been accepted by Vietnamese officials as key, although to some Western economists this position might be somewhat questionable. Apart from the time costs involved in such activities as changing prices and counting more bank notes, expected inflation should not affect the economy unless explicit monetary nonneutralities are present, while unexpected changes in the inflation rate would redistribute wealth from creditors to debtors. In Vietnam, where high inflation has been a constant phenomenon and where access to credit has been limited, one could argue that such a sharp reduction in inflation need not be a priority for growth. Avoiding an increase in the inflation rate, and lowering it gradually rather than abruptly, would seem to be key policies for Vietnam. Such an argument finds support in the development experiences of Korea (in the early years) and Turkey, which have experienced significant growth in the presence of high inflation.

Agricultural Policy Changes

Quite beyond the macropolicy components within which economic reform has taken place in Vietnam, reforms within individual sectors have also been important. Agricultural sector reforms have been especially extensive. They have been critical to sharp increases in agricultural production and Vietnam's emergence as the world's third-largest rice exporter.

In 1988 the government completed the process of decollectivization, and family farms became the basis of agricultural production. Land leases of 50 years have been granted to some of the peasant farmers, and indications are emerging that limited trading may be allowed in some of these leases. These changes, together with price decontrol, have resulted in substantial increases in agricultural production, and agricultural incomes reminiscent of the experience in China with the introduction of the responsibility system in the early 1980s.

Changes to the Tax System

Before 1991, the largest source of government revenues was transfers from state enterprises.[12] Deficits in the late 1980s ranged from 5 percent to 18 percent of GDP and were largely financed through the printing of money, which in turn resulted in triple-digit inflation. In 1988 the government enacted a number of laws designed to reform the tax system and move toward fiscal stability. These included provisions for the uniform treatment of state and nonstate sectors and the implementation of natural resource royalties and taxes.

Reforms in the fiscal system have seen a decline in the importance of transfers from state enterprises and an increase in tax revenues. A surge in exports, particularly rice, together with an overall increase in trade resulting in higher revenues from trade taxes, and efforts to increase compliance, as well as to broaden the tax base, have also contributed to this trend.

While some improvements in tax administration have occurred, a number of challenges for the tax system remain. Compliance rates are very low. Firms have an incentive to inflate cost estimates to avoid profit taxes, smugglers avoid trade taxes, and collection of excise taxes from the many vendors of those goods subject to the tax is difficult. Furthermore, tax regulations are complex, with many exceptions and a complicated rate structure. No legal framework exists within which to settle tax disputes. Changes to the tax system in Vietnam continue, and plans are under-way for the implementation of a value-added tax.

Reforms in the State Enterprise Sector

Major reforms have also been implemented in the state-owned enterprise sector.[13] Although these changes are far from complete in the sense of achieving privatization, they have nonetheless moved the economy toward significant productivity gains.

The most important change has been the application of financial discipline to state-owned enterprises. Enterprises have been placed on a commercial basis and have been made to assume the responsibility for financial losses.

---

12. This section draws on Mallon and de Jonghe 1991.

13. For a comprehensive analysis of reforms in the state enterprise sector see World Bank 1992, "Vietnam: Restructuring Public Finance and Public Enterprises."

Formal bankruptcy does not yet exist for such enterprises, but the state has terminated support for some repeated loss-making enterprises. Cuts in the state investment budget as a result of cuts in expenditures by the Ministry of Finance now mean that enterprises must raise loans to cover losses. Accompanying this new fiscal responsibility has been the price liberalization of most industrial products.

For now, these reforms remain incomplete in a number of ways. Not only does the state continue to own the assets of key large enterprises, but the state-owned sector is also highly concentrated and commingled with an emerging private sector. In addition, large enterprises control some of the private enterprises. For example, units of the military that, in turn, are part of the state enterprise sector, own some of the private enterprises in the transportation sector. Some state enterprises have a large ownership position in some of the private-sector banks. Hence, the concentration of state enterprises may in the long run prove to be a major impediment to further free market enterprise activity.

The wage structure in the state enterprise system remains unchanged and presents a further impediment to market reforms. Regulations are such that the dispersion in wage rates both across and within state enterprises is small, and the wage rates themselves are low. As a result, individuals may often hold two or three jobs with different enterprises, working perhaps only one-and-a-half days per week in each and receiving a full wage for all jobs. Enterprises may even trade jobs one with another on occasion. In this case, one group of employees at one enterprise might hire employees in another enterprise if reciprocal treatment is given to them. Bogus employees also apparently appear on state enterprise payrolls. Such phenomena clearly add to the problems of financial discipline in the state-owned enterprise sector.

In contrast, the small- and medium-sized private-enterprise sector has experienced extremely rapid growth, primarily in the service sector. Restaurants, retail and wholesale trade, transportation, and some forms of light industry, are areas in which an extensive and vibrant private sector now prevails. Some estimates place as much as 25 percent of combined enterprise activity in this sector. Officials in some ministries openly encourage its further growth, since they view small enterprises as substantially more efficient than the state enterprises. That this sector holds great potential for growth is a widely held belief.

Banking and Foreign Exchange Reforms

Banking, and the related area of foreign exchange dealings are also areas that have experienced major reform.[14] The State Bank now operates much like a

---

14. See World Bank 1991, "Vietnam: Transforming a State Owned Financial System, A Financial Sector Study of Vietnam."

conventional central bank, having separated itself from its more functional activities of the past by establishing separate agricultural, industrial, and trade banks. The State Bank now monitors reserve requirements and other features of both its own functional banks and the 17 shareholder banks that are now authorized to operate within the banking system. It sets monetary policy and controls the rate at which it will lend to other banks in the system. It adjusts this discount rate to stabilize and control the monetary regime. An interbank market is planned, with an overnight interbank rate. Foreign banks may also operate in Vietnam, although thus far most have only opened local representation offices.

Along with these banking reforms have come major foreign exchange reforms that have effectively made the Dong a fully convertible currency. Exchange rates float freely in two daily foreign exchange centers in Hanoi and Ho Chi Minh City. Enterprises can hold foreign currency bank accounts and can trade freely in these centers. Indeed, a new ruling indicates that joint-venture operations can hold bank accounts abroad in foreign banks.

Vietnam thus appears to have moved a substantial distance toward a Western-style banking and foreign exchange system, with a Central Bank exercising broad macroeconomic control, interest rates set in a largely free-market environment, and effectively full convertibility of the domestic currency. At the same time, however, much remains in the system that is still underdeveloped. The economy remains largely cash-based. Few individuals hold bank accounts, and most must borrow from informal or curbside credit markets. The largest denomination bill in common circulation is (effectively) 50 cents, with large counting and printing requirements. The regulations governing the system appear for now to have changed more quickly than the system itself.

Foreign Investment Reform

Reforms in the area of foreign investment regulation have been especially dramatic. Large inflows of foreign investment are now actively sought by the Vietnamese through joint ventures between Vietnamese enterprises (both state-owned and private) and foreign firms. Thus far, the majority of inward foreign investment has been in the areas of oil and gas and hotel development, but the aim of policy is clearly to broaden the sectoral coverage, and especially to help with infrastructure development. The stated target is a $24 billion inflow of foreign direct investments and overseas development assistance over the next seven years. Since this number is approximately twice the current GDP of the whole economy, it is an ambitious target. Approval for joint-venture schemes worth approximately $3.6 billion has been granted, although the actual inflow into Vietnam seems for now to be substantially less. This discrepancy arises because Vietnamese enterprises seek approvals without necessarily having foreign partners arranged.

Clearly, then, economic reform in Vietnam has progressed substantially since 1986. Planning remains, but is indicative rather than imperative. Market forces determine prices. Aggregate monetary and fiscal disciplines are bringing stability to the economy, growth rates are up, and foreign investment seems poised to enter. On a political level, the challenge to the authority of the party that the reforms represent has yet to be fully resolved. Party officials who have spent decades fighting capitalism question whether these reforms constitute capitalism and, as such, whether they are in conflict with socialism in Vietnam. Managers of state-owned enterprises faced with downsizing or closure equally resist such change. The unemployment stemming from the adjustment causes further skepticism from those who are directly affected. These concerns however, seem to be concentrated among the older genera- tions. Young people, particularly those in the south, seem uninterested in political activity or any involvement with the party and dedicate themselves largely to money-making activities in the small- and medium-sized enterprise sector. Opposition to and support for reform thus seems delineated along generational (and to some degree regional) lines.

Development Scenarios for Vietnam and Problems and Challenges for the Future

At first glance, Vietnam might appear to be simply an Asian latecomer hoping to follow the earlier dramatic growth surges of surrounding economies such as Japan in the 1950s and 1960s, Korea and Taiwan in the 1960s and 1970s, the ASEAN countries in the 1970s and 1980s, and China today. With all these precedents, the natural assumption is that Vietnam will simply join the list of Asian high performers and quickly achieve high growth rates.

However, despite the high growth rates in neighboring countries, the present situation in Vietnam is different in many ways from experience in these other economies. For instance, neither Korea nor Taiwan relied on or sought to rely on large inflows of foreign capital investment for their early growth. In turn, Korea and Taiwan are each different, insofar as Korea has always had substantial concentration in the manufacturing sector, with, at times, as few as three or four large firms (Chaebol) accounting for around 70 percent of activity. In contrast, Taiwan has always had large numbers of small- to medium-sized enterprises, reminiscent of the current private-sector activity in Vietnam. On the other hand, Taiwanese development began as agriculturally led growth.

The Vietnamese period of agricultural growth also seems more com- pacted than that of its neighbors. Vietnam is attempting to move from initial agricultural reforms and a relatively short-lived surge in agricultural production to more immediate manufacturing-led growth. Agricultural growth dominated Chinese growth performance for some eight years before the current growth explosion in Chinese manufacturing began to take hold.

In turn, in the ASEAN countries, capital flows from Japan and outward processing from Japanese manufacturing establishments who sought to assemble and build components in low-wage ASEAN countries initiated much of the growth. This experience contrasts with the Vietnamese attempt to explicitly develop inward capital flows as an engine of growth. Vietnam also differs sharply in the size and scope of the inward capital flows it seeks. Similarly, the size of the attempted growth surge involving approximately 12 percent growth for the rest of the decade, seems extraordinarily large relative to historically sustainable growth rates, even in Asia.

Clearly, the regional environment of rapidly growing and dynamic economies within which Vietnam finds itself is conducive to stronger economic performance. Its trade growth with its neighbors is marked, and represents an opportunity both for growth and for attracting further inward capital flows. Taiwan, Korea, and to a lesser extent the ASEAN countries, are all contemplating major investments in Vietnam, predominantly in the low-wage areas of apparel, footwear, and other labor-intensive products.[15] Being outside the formal membership of the Multi-Fibre Arrangement makes Vietnam particularly attractive for such investment. Thus, Vietnam's short-term ability to attract inward capital flows from neighboring countries experiencing their own rapid growth and increases in wages rates is a significant source of development potential.

A disquieting aspect of this developmental approach is the number of other countries who are now also seeking to grow using rapid foreign investment inflows. One such case is Pakistan, which is using far more activist policies to attract foreign investment than is Vietnam. Another is Burma, which has announced similar targets for their growth and development to those adopted by the Vietnamese. Bangladesh, India (since the recent reforms), and many Latin and Central American countries are also competing for foreign investment funds. Thus, achieving growth through such heavy reliance on foreign investment will involve new initiatives on a scale that is unprecedented by other countries in the region, and this growth strategy is being used at a time when many other countries are competing with Vietnam for foreign investment resources more aggressively.

---

15. The *Vietnam Investment Review* reports numerous examples of regional investment interest in Vietnam. For example, the December 7–13, 1992, issue reports Malaysian interest in developing an export procession zone in Vietnam, Taiwanese interest in developing a motorcycle assembly factory, Thai interest in infrastructural and draining system projects, and Filipino sea transport and brewing activities in Vietnam.

A period of substantial and high economic growth, as has occurred elsewhere in the region, seems possible for Vietnam as a medium-term development scenario, but it is by no means assured. With the continued situation of uncompleted reforms in the state-enterprise sector, continued complex wage arrangements, provincial government autonomy, and corruption and smuggling, doubts surface about Vietnam's ability to attract the foreign investment levels they seek, accelerate the growth rate as they have indicated, and, in the long run, even complete the reforms that, in turn, are probably a key precondition for the higher growth itself.

The further economic reforms that the Vietnamese are likely to institute in the future also remain somewhat unclear. The direction seems to be one of deepening and strengthening existing reforms, rather than initiating radical new reforms, such as privatization through Czech-style voucher plans. Plans for privatization are emerging in the state-enterprise sector, but these seem to be piecemeal rather than systemwide. Plans do exist to allow full operation of foreign corporations in Vietnam, outside of joint ventures. In the banking sector there are plans to allow the operations of foreign banks to extend beyond representative offices. Whether or not these changes will occur will probably remain unclear until the State Planning Committee issues new policy directives in the coming years.

At the same time, no plans seem imminent for a major overhaul of enterprise wage structures, for further foreign trade reforms, for more initiatives on private property, nor for major budgetary reforms. In short, economic reform will in all probability continue as a patchwork quilt of sector and instrument initiatives, as it has for the past few years. Against this backdrop of ad hoc but extensive reform are some key challenges to strong future performance from the Vietnamese economy.

One of the most daunting challenges to Vietnam's developmental potential is the paucity of the existing physical infrastructure. Roads are few and in poor condition.[16] Railways are single track, extremely slow, and use antiquated equipment. Airports and planes are equally rudimentary. The traffic flow in cities is largely unregulated. No sewage treatment plants exist in the entire country and industrial plants discharge untreated wastes into rivers and lakes. Sewer pipe is almost nonexistent. Urban airborne bacterial counts are extremely high, and it is only recently that the Vietnamese have begun to monitor water and air quality.

The lack of physical infrastructure is mirrored by the limited intellectual capital to carry forward economic reform. Many of the high-ranking current economic policy makers rose to their positions of authority under the central

---

16. Vietnam has 86,643 km of roads and 3,219 km of railways (United Nations Development Programme 1992a, "Briefing Note, Socialist Republic of Vietnam").

planning system and are unfamiliar with many aspects of market economies. Younger meritocrats conduct day-to-day economic policy, but have little training upon which to base their judgments. Although policy training programs are beginning to shift from the Marxist tradition to a market-oriented approach, the educators themselves studied in the former Soviet Union for the most part, and have little expertise in market economics. Furthermore, fundamental conceptual issues such as the nature of property rights, the role of the legal system, the role of the party, and centralized authority all remain unresolved. As Vietnam grows, the complexities of decision making will multiply. All productive levels, from small enterprises to top-level bureaucrats, will have more resources to allocate within a more complex legal and economic framework. Without the intellectual infrastructure to make informed decisions, the scarce domestic and foreign resources will not be used in their most efficient capacities. While physical infrastructure is necessary for growth, without complementary intellectual infrastructure, growth will be held back. Developing adequate intellectual infrastructure to support Vietnamese growth and development is a crucial complement to physical infrastructure development.

The large and growing regional differences within Vietnam might emerge as a key factor that could impede the development process in the longer run. These differences, while undocumented in quantitative terms, seem significant.[17] Much of the industrial growth is concentrated in the south, where resentment over the resources transferred to the north through various taxes and other devices is apparent. The differences between Ho Chi Minh City and Hanoi are especially marked. Hanoi has relatively few vehicles, large numbers of bicycles, little industrial base, and is less developed compared with Ho Chi Minh City, which has large boulevards, is much more cosmopolitan, has more vehicles, and has a wider range of products and shops.

The provinces in Vietnam also seem to have substantial autonomy in terms of their ability to initiate and deal with various kinds of policy initiatives, including approaches to potential foreign investors. Currently the most substantial exercise of provincial autonomy seems to be in the south, a phenomenon that explains, in part, the vibrancy and the greater connection with the outside world. To the extent that this provincial autonomy has been a factor in the growth performance in the south and hence also in the growth performance in the whole economy, it may be a strong portent for the future. On the other hand, given the history of the country and political issues that have been associated with these north-south differentials for many decades, it may portend future economic and political difficulties.

---

17. One Vietnamese economist estimates that the GDP in the north is about 60 percent of the GDP in the south.

A further problem is corruption and smuggling.[18] To some degree, an element of corruption and smuggling may be economically healthy in that in a highly controlled economy it acts as a safety valve in relieving the dislocation generated by government controls. Ultimately, however, these activities will prove costly from an economic viewpoint. The need to bribe corrupt officials greatly increases the cost of doing business in terms of both money and wasted time. Repeated such nuisances are a deterrent to the development of new enterprises. Corruption also impedes the healthy functions of government. It makes macrocontrol of the economy extremely difficult. As tax revenues go uncollected, data become incomplete. Some of the fiscal discipline applied to enterprises becomes redundant. Well-intended regulations of the negative by-products of the market, such as pollution, can also be defeated.

Finally, the sustainability of economic growth in Vietnam remains an open question. Aside from the myriad social and political factors that could destabilize the process are the closely linked issues of growth management. Without the physical infrastructure to absorb new industries, Vietnamese cities may turn into environmental disaster areas. Some would argue that the surge in rice exports has arisen partly as a result of intensive pesticide and fertilizer use, which in a few years will deplete soil fertility. Likewise, the forest and marine resources that, together with rice, form a large component of Vietnam's export base are coming under increasing pressure. Although the Vietnamese government acknowledges the need for resource management and has begun to implement an environmental policy, environmental concerns are likely to emerge as constraints to growth.

Concluding Remarks

There is no doubt that the commitment to growth and development among government officials in Vietnam is, at present, extraordinarily strong and this, as much as anything else, provides the underpinnings to the reform process. The feeling that the country has been outside the global economy for many

---

18. This phenomenon is acknowledged as a problem by the government. Indeed, Prime Minister Vo Van Kiet has made public statements denouncing smuggling and corruption and acknowledging the implication of officials in the process (*Vietnam Investment Review,* Nov. 30–Dec. 6, 1992).

Measures to combat smuggling and corruption are not particularly substantive. They include giving "corrupt elements three months to give themselves up and return any ill-gotten gains to the State," making heads of businesses personally responsible for corruption and smuggling, urging party organizations through the country to fight corruption and smuggling, and holding it as one of their primary objectives and making suspected officials openly declare their incomes (*Vietnam Investment Review,* Nov. 30–Dec. 6, 1992).

decades and that citizens of Vietnam have not had the opportunity to benefit from a higher standard of living despite extraordinary resources and other endowments runs deep. The conflict that exists between such feelings and the ultimate authority embedded in the present party structure still committed to socialism and state control awaits resolution. Clearly, liberalization and economic reform have begun in Vietnam and economic growth has begun to accelerate, even if from a low base. The issue now is whether the reform process has gone far enough that it will be impossible to reverse. What the future may hold, both for this process and for the performance of the economy, and whether or not a takeoff comparable to those that have occurred elsewhere in Asia can be achieved, remains to be seen.

BIBLIOGRAPHY

Australian International Development Assistance Bureau. 1992. *Cooperation, Australia's International Aid Program, 1990–1992*. Canberra: Australian Government Publishing Service.
Economist Intelligence Unit. 1992a. "Indochina: Vietnam Laos." Cambodia Country Report No.2, London.
Economist Intelligence Unit. 1992b. "Indochina: Vietnam Laos." Cambodia Country Report No.3, London.
Fforde, A. 1991. "The Political Economy of Reform in Vietnam—Some Reflections." Manuscript, Australian National University.
Gohl, B., and Nguyen Thanh Ha. 1990. "Vietnam: Development of Scientific Research and SAREC's Support 1976–1989." App. 2, "Universities and Colleges in Vietnam." SAREC Documentation, Research Surveys. Hanoi.
Grub, P D., and Nguyen Xuan Oanh. 1992. "Vietnam: The New Investment Frontier in Southeast Asia." Hanoi.
Hainsworth, G. N.d. "Human Resource Development in Vietnam." In J. Tan and M. Than, eds., *Vietnamese Dilemmas and Options: The Challenge of Economic Transition in the 1990s*. Forthcoming.
Hoan Do Dau and Ulf Svensson. 1992. "Liberalization of the Financial System in Developing Countries, The Case of Vietnam." Department of Economics, University of Lund, Minor Field Study Series; No. 20. Lund.
Hy Van Luong. 1992. "Local Community and Economic Reform: A Microscopic Perspective from Three Vietnamese Villages." Manuscript. Hanoi.
Institute of World Economy. 1992. *Economic Problems Journal*, April, May, June.
International Development Research Centre. 1992. "Vietnam/Indochina/Mekong Sustainable Economic Development Program." Internal Document. Singapore.
International Union for the Conservation of Nature, State Committee for Sciences, Swedish International Development Authority, United Nations Development Programme, and United Nations Environment Programme. 1991. "The National Plan for Environment and Sustainable Development 1991–2000, Framework for Action." Hanoi.

International Union for the Conservation of Nature, State Committee for Sciences, Swedish International Development Authority, United Nations Development Programme, and United Nations Environment Programme. 1992. "Project Profiles Formulated to Assist with Implementation of the National Plan for Environment and Sustainable Development 1991–2000." Hanoi.

Le Dang Doanh. 1992. "Economic Reform and Development in Vietnam." Australian National University, Research School of Pacific Studies, Economics Division Working Papers 92/5. Canberra.

Ljunggren, B. 1991. "Marketing Economies under Communist Regimes: Reform in Vietnam, Laos and Cambodia." Development Discussion Paper No.394, Harvard Institute for International Development, Cambridge, Mass.

Mallon, R., and T. L. de Jonghe. 1991. "Socialist Republic of Vietnam Economic Review and Bank Operations." Manila: Asian Development Bank Internal Document. July.

Ministry of Forestry, Socialist Republic of Vietnam. 1991. "Vietnam Tropical Forestry Action Programme, Forestry Sector Review." Executive Summary, Hanoi.

Ngo Ba Thanh. 1992. "The 1992 Constitution and the Rule of Law in Vietnam Today." Manuscript. Hanoi.

Nguyen Xuan Oanh. 1992. "Some Reflections on Economic Development and Transitional Economies—With Special Reference to Vietnam." Manuscript. Hanoi.

Riedel, James. 1992. "Viet Nam: On the Trail of the Tigers." Manuscript. Washington, DC.

Socialist Republic of Vietnam. 1992. "Constitution." Hanoi.

State Committee for Cooperation and Investment. 1991. "Guidance on Project Document Preparation for Various Forms of Investment." Hanoi.

State Committee for Cooperation and Investment. 1992a. "Legal Writings on Foreign Investment in Vietnam." Hanoi.

State Committee for Cooperation and Investment. 1992b. "List of Projects." Hanoi.

State Committee for Cooperation and Investment and P. Fox. 1992. "Foreign Investment in Vietnam, 100 Questions and Answers." Hanoi.

State Planning Commission and United Nations Development Programme. 1990. "Report on the Economy of Vietnam." Hanoi.

Swedish International Development Authority. 1992. "Sweden-Vietnam Development Cooperation." Internal Document. Stockholm.

United Nations. 1992. "The Annual Report of the Resident Coordinator for 1992." Hanoi. July.

United Nations Development Programme. 1991a. "Vietnam, Development Cooperation, 1989 Report." Internal Document. April.

United Nations Development Programmme. 1991b. "Vietnam, Development Cooperation, 1990 Report." Internal Document. December.

United Nations Development Programme. 1992a. "Briefing Note, Socialist Republic of Vietnam." Internal Document. June.

United Nations Development Programme. 1992b. "Country Programme Management Plan: Vietnam." Internal Document.

Vietnam Investment Review. 1992. 2, no.59–61 (Nov. 23–29–Dec. 7–23).

Vietnam Investor. 1992. 1, no.3, (Oct./Nov.)

Vietnam News. 1992. Issues 476 (Nov. 23), 482–90 (Nov. 28–Dec. 7.)

Vo Dai Luoc. 1992. "Curbing Inflation and the Process of Economic Renovation in Vietnam." Hanoi.

Vu Tuan Anh. 1992. "Vietnam's Social Sciences in the 1990's and Prospects for Cooperation with Foreign Social Science Circles." Working paper prepared for Indochina Planning Conference of Social Science Research Council, New York.

World Bank. 1991. "Vietnam: Transforming a State Owned Financial System, A Financial Sector Study of Vietnam." World Bank Report No.9223-VN.

World Bank. 1992. "Vietnam: Restructuring Public Finance and Public Enterprises." Report No.10134-VN.

World Food Programme. 1992. *1992 Food Aid Review.* Information Publication. Rome.

CHAPTER 14

North Korean Economic Reform: Past Efforts and Future Prospects

Doowon Lee

The inherent problems with centrally planned economies (CPEs), as outlined by Kornai (1980), have left many socialist countries in the depths of economic crisis over the past few decades. This, in turn, has induced most socialist countries to adopt market-oriented reforms, following the precedent of some Eastern European countries like Hungary. These reform efforts by socialist countries make North Korea one of the few countries in the world still adhering to the principles of strict central planning. Even though North Korea has also tried to introduce some material incentives into production, such efforts were not moves toward the market mechanism by any standard, but an attempt to solve its economic difficulties by perfecting the existing system, as Andreff (1989) has described.

The purpose of this chapter is to analyze the historical record of past economic reforms by North Korea and to present the prospects for reform from a political economy perspective. The following section provides an overview of North Korea's macroeconomic performance by examining the previous nine economic development plans, which were first implemented by the North Korean government in 1945. In evaluating the past performance of the North Korean economy, the lack of reliable data along with the difficulties in converting the North Korean data into internationally recognized figures is discussed. Next, a microeconomic analysis of the North Korean economy is presented. The shortcomings of the material incentive system, which was introduced in the mid-1980s in the industrial sector, and the absence of private production in the agricultural sector are studied. Then, the current problems with the North Korean economy and the efforts by North Korea to resolve these problems are discussed. Even though the roots of the current economic problems lie in the closedness of the North Korean economy and the lack of an incentive system (that is, a lack of market incentives), the chronic foreign currency shortage is designated as the most urgent economic problem facing North Korea, and the attempts to resolve this problem by encouraging foreign capital in investment are studied. Furthermore, the political dilemma of succession confronting the North Korean regime, which can hinder its reform efforts, is discussed. In each section, the North Korean case will be analyzed in comparison with the precedent-setting measures of other socialist countries, particularly those of China.

North Korea's Macroeconomic Performance

Estimation of North Korean GNP

In order to evauate North Korea's economic performance, one has to face the problem of a shortage of reliable data. Even compared to other socialist economies, North Korea releases very few reliable economic data to the outside world. Furthermore, the frequency of reporting of official figures by North Korea has been drastically reduced since the mid-1960s, when the North Korean economy began to experience slow growth.[1] Due to this problem of lack of data, as well as the problem of converting the socialist economy's Gross Value of Social Product (GVSP) into GNP, various methods are applied to estimate North Korea's GNP by different institutes. Estimations of North Korean GNP by the Central Intelligence Agency (CIA), National Unification Board (NUB), Chun (1992), and several other sources are presented in table 1.

Using the population data and the estimated GNP of North Korea, we can calculate per capita GNP of North Korea. South Korea's NUB estimation of North Korea's per capita GNP for 1990 was $1,064, while the estimations of Chun (1992) for 1990 and Jeong (1992) for 1989, both of which used the physical indicator method (PIM), were $1,268 and $1,181, respectively. Even though the NUB had long been accused of intentionally underestimating the North Korean GNP, the findings of Chun 1992 and Jeong 1992 show that the bias of the NUB is not that significant. From the estimation of North Korean per capita GNP, we can ascertain that the per capita GNP of North Korea, which was two to five times greater than the South Korean per capita GNP in 1960, according to various sources, was surpassed by the per capita GNP of South Korea in the early 1970s according to NUB estimation, and in the middle of the 1970s according to the U.S. CIA's estimation. Furthermore, almost every estimation shows that the current North Korean per capita GNP is five or six times smaller than that of South Korea. We will now turn to an analysis of the past performance of the North Korean economy, which started better than the South Korean economy but has been surpassed by South Korea and still remains a low-income developing country, focusing on the past nine North Korean economic development plans.

---

1. The only official figures that have been regularly reported since 1948 by North Korea are its government revenue and expenditure figures. For detailed figures, refer to table 4-1 of Hwang 1992.

TABLE 1.   Estimated GNP of North Korea in Millions of Dollars

Year	Population[a]	GVSP[b]	NMP[d]	GNP: NUB	GNP: CIA	GNP: IISS	GNP: Chun
1960	10,789	5,568		1,520	4,800		
1965	12,100	8,734		2,340	7,600		
1970	13,892	14,334	8,700	3,980	10,000	8,510	2,800
1975	15,853	40,357	16,600	9,350	16,000	7,980	
1980	18,025	65,688	33,900	13,500	19,500	13,370	9,700
1985	20,385	71,854	47,800[e]	15,140	23,000[g]	19,240	
1990	21,412	88,688[c]	52,200[f]	23,100			27,100
1991	22,500			22,900			

Source: Tables 3-2, 3-9, and 3-12, of Hwang 1992; table 4-8 of Chun 1992; table 3-3 of Kim 1992.

Note: Gross Value of Social Product (GVSP), Net Material Product (NMP), National Unification Board (NUB), Central Intelligence Agency (CIA), International Institute for Strategic Studies (IISS).

[a]unit: 1,000. For reference, see Hwang 1992 for 1960 to 1985, Eberstadt 1992 for 1990, Kim 1992 for 1991.

[b]estimated GVSP by Hwang 1992; GVSP uses the official exchange rate.

[c]1989 data

[d]officially reported NMP figures by North Korea (official exchange rate)

[e]1986 data

[f]1988 data

[g]1984 data

The Economic Development Plans of North Korea

After independence from Japan, South and North Korea established separate governments in 1948. Since then, each government has competed ferociously against the other to achieve rapid industrialization through different development paths: the inward-oriented North Korean socialist economy with import substitution policies placing priority mainly on heavy and chemical industries versus the outward-oriented South Korean market economy with export promotion policies placing priority on light industry. North Korean economic development can be characterized as successful and impressive during the 1950s and 1960s, followed by the troublesome 1970s and stagnant 1980s. Stalinist central planning and a command economy were the ideological backbone of the North Korean economy in the 1950s and 1960s, with the growing influence of the Chinese economic system during the 1960s. Inspired by the Stalinist command economy during the 1950s, virtually every means of production had been nationalized, and a great deal of ideological stimuli had replaced material incentives in encouraging production. In the late 1950s and early 1960s, massive Chinese-style manpower mobilization and collective leadership in state enterprises was introduced. However, during the 1970s, "Juche Ideology," which had first been introduced by Kim Il-Sung in 1955, became the unchallenged principle of the North Korean economy. *Juche*, which means "self-reliance" in Korean, is an extreme form of nationalism. Juche was first introduced in 1955 by the Central People's Committee to establish ideological independence from the Soviet Union and China.[2] It became the leading principle in economic relations in 1957, in national defense in 1962, and was finally designated as the leading (guiding) ideology of North Korea in Article 4 of the 1972 new constitution.

During the first two one-year plans of 1947 and 1948 and the first two-year plan, establishing a new socialist economic system to replace the old colonial economic system was the main purpose of the development plans. The priority of the three-year plan (1954–56) developed after the Korean War was rehabilitation of the North Korean economy, which had been badly damaged during the war. During this period, massive aid from the Soviet Union, China, and Eastern European countries helped North Korea to achieve its prewar industrial production level by 1954. Recovery from the Korean War and establishing the solid basis for a socialist economy during the three-year plan enabled North Korea to achieve its most successful performance during the first five-year plan of 1957 to 1961.

The North Korean authorities proudly declared the achievement of the major targets of the five-year plan two years ahead of schedule. The successful completion of the plan was mainly due to two factors, the effective mobilization of manpower and continued aid from the Soviet Union and China. During this period, a massive manpower mobilization program called "the Chollima Movement" was initiated by Kim Il-Sung.[3] Resembling the Chinese "Great Leap Forward Movement" of 1958, in which Chairman Mao directed manpower into ambitious heavy industry projects, the Chollima Movement hoped to tap into the revolutionary fervor of the North Korean workers in order to increase output in all sectors of the economy. The effective labor mobilization and continuous ideological stimuli enabled the North Korean economy to achieve plan targets within two-and-a-half years, with the industrial sector's annual growth rate running at 36.6 percent. This resulted in an even more ambitious promotion of heavy industry with the first seven-year plan in 1961.

During the first seven-year plan (1961–67), inward-oriented industrial-

---

2. In the speech of Kim Il-Sung on "Exterminating Dogmatism and Formalism, and Establishing Independence in Ideological Work," made in April 1955, he states, "Although some people say that the Soviet way is best or that the Chinese way is the best, have we not now reached the point where we can construct our own way?" (Bruce Cumings. *The Origin of the Korean War: Liberalization and the Emergence of Separate Regimes* [Princeton: Princeton University Press, 1981]).

3. "Chollima" is a legendary horse that was believed to be able to travel 400 km (250 miles) a day.

ization with greater emphasis on heavy industry was carried out. However, biased resource allocation toward heavy industry with relative neglect of the consumer goods industry produced the problem of unbalanced growth. Despite the official declaration of the completion of the plan by the North Korean authorities, the first seven-year plan was extended to 1970, implicitly reflecting that the original targets had not been met. It was during this development plan that North Korea began to no longer report detailed economic statistics to the outside world.

The problems of unbalanced growth and the lack of advanced technology due to an inward-oriented development strategy made North Korea adopt a six-year plan to resolve these problems. However, despite the alleged completion of major industrial and agricultural targets, a chronic trade deficit and the first oil shock of the early 1970s created a foreign exchange shortage by the mid-1970s, with North Korea beginning to experience debt repayment difficulties in 1975, and bottlenecks in key sectors continued due to the increased complexity and inefficiency of central planning.

Declaring 1977 as a year of adjustment, North Korea started its second seven-year plan in 1978. The major economic goals of this plan included a frugality campaign, an increase in foreign trade, and the modernization of the transportation sector, reflecting the chronic problems of a trade deficit, accumulation of foreign debt, lack of capital, and obsolete technology. In 1984, North Korea declared the completion of the second seven-year plan without reporting detailed figures and announced that it would have a two-year adjustment period before the start of the third seven-year plan, implicitly indicating the unsatisfactory performance of the North Korean economy during this period. In 1984 North Korea also initiated limited economic reforms, which provided some material incentives and autonomy to state enterprises and a semi–open door policy to attract foreign joint-venture projects in North Korea. However, the results of these efforts were far below the expectations of North Korean planners, and this caused North Korea to enact a more vigorous law to attract foreign joint ventures in 1992. The third seven-year plan (1987–93), which has just been finished, began in 1987 with almost the same goals as the second seven-year plan, with modest production targets. However, the foreign exchange shortage in North Korea has been aggravated due to the collapse of many socialist economies and the decline of Soviet and Chinese aid, and the North Korean efforts to attract more foreign capital have not yet been fruitful. Due to such internal and external difficulties, the proposed production targets of the third seven-year plan have not been met, and North Korean Premier Kang has acknowledged—the first such acknowledgement in North Korean history—that the third seven-year plan has failed. In his speech, delivered in December 1993 to the Central Party Committee, Premier

Kang briefly commented that only 78 percent of the industrial production targets were fulfilled. In the next section, we will examine the incentive system for North Korean state enterprises from a microeconomic perspective and briefly discuss the lack of incentives in the agricultural sector.

Partial Economic Reform in North Korea during the Mid-1980s

Sluggish economic growth in North Korea during the late 1970s and early 1980s and economic reforms in China since 1978 have forced the country to try several reform measures in the mid-1980s. However, these efforts were not intended to bring the market mechanism into the North Korean economy. Rather, they were to provide more material incentives within the existing North Korean economic system. The economic reforms of Hungary, Poland, and China can be called transitional reforms toward a market economy, in the sense that they introduced private ownership and abandonment of price controls, both of which are core principles of a socialist economy. However, several reform measures in North Korea in the mid-1980s have not led to such genuine reform efforts. As Andreff (1989) described, North Korea tried to correct its problems by modifying the existing system without damaging the principles of a socialist economy, rather than introduce a new system.

August 3, 1984 Production of People's Consumer Goods Program

For the North Korean economy, 1984 became the year of partial reform. In August 1984, "The August Third Program," which allowed some production of consumer goods outside the confines of central planning, was announced, followed by foreign joint-venture laws in September and the revision of the "Provision on the Independent Accounting System in State Enterprises" in December. The August Third Production of People's Consumer Goods Program can be termed a partial reform based on two aspects: It allowed the production of some consumer goods outside the planned economy, and these products could be sold in the market rather than in state stores. In addition, this program had two more distinctive features. Most of the products produced under this program were basic necessities that used wasted resources as an input. Production decisions were made by local authorities, and products were produced and sold inside the local province. According to a January 1990 article by Choe In-Duk in *Kulloja,* sales of products produced under the August Third Program accounted for 9.5 percent of total consumer goods sales. Even though this program was limited to consumer goods production and the incentives and decision-making authorities were restricted to local bureaucrats and party members, this program did introduce some market forces and thus can be called a partial reform measure.

The 1984 Revision of the "Provision on the Independent Accounting System in State Enterprises"

The revision of the "Provision on the Independent Accounting System in State Enterprises," which was passed in the sixth Central People's Committee in December 1984 reveals the inherent inefficiency problems of North Korean state enterprises. According to the revision, three basic principles were announced: First, it advocated the combination of plans and markets by stating the need for a combination of state planning and commodity-market relations through the introduction of costs, prices, and profits. Second, state enterprises were asked to cover their own expenses from their own revenues. Third, political and material incentives were permitted at state enterprises, depending on the fulfillment of their plans. The first two principles emphasize financial accountability and the independence of state enterprises, which reflects the growing fiscal deficit due to continued subsidies to state enterprises. Even though state enterprises have been allowed to retain a portion of their extra profits since the early 1950s, the third principle of this revision allowed higher profit retention rates for state enterprises.[4] The emphasis on financial accountability verifies the existence of a soft budget problem in the North Korean state enterprises (as with other socialist economies), just as Kornai (1986) predicted. The planning nature of socialist economies makes managers of state enterprises bargain for more inputs and lower target assignments with state authorities, and this bargaining nature inevitably causes soft budget problems that can result in a vicious cycle of input hoarding and fiscal deficits.

A collusive behavior also exists among managers and workers in state enterprises due to the distinctive form of collective leadership. After China adopted a collective leadership system, North Korea followed suit with regards to state enterprises in 1961. China abolished the one-person (manager) responsibility system used in the Soviet Union in 1956, and adopted a system combining collective leadership and manager responsibility. Influenced by China, Kim Il-Sung abandoned the one-man management system and announced his so-called Dae-an Model in 1961, which has a pure collective leadership structure through a state enterprise party committee.[5] Since 1961,

---

4. According to Kang and Lee 1992, the retention rate from extra profits was 10–90 percent in 1960, 13–50 percent in 1962, and 0–20 percent in 1972. Then it was raised to 50 percent in 1985.

5. On the occasion of the introduction of Dae-an Model, Kim Il-Sung said: "The factory's party committee, as the supreme administrative organ of the plant, manages and runs the factory with the direct participation of the party members, the workers, and technicians. No

the Dae-an Model has become the sole management model in the North Korean state enterprises. According to the Dae-an Model, each factory is to be run by a party committee, which is composed of workers, managers, and engineers. The Dae-an Model places higher priority on political guidance over economic and technical guidance by placing the party committee ahead of the executive committee, and it advocates workers' participation in decision making by focusing on cooperation among workers, technicians, and party functionaries at each factory.[6] As it has been empirically shown in China, collective leadership can lead to inertia, which favors the status quo over innovation due to the ambiguity concerning responsibility in the decision-making process and the difficulties of arriving at a consensus. Even though China abandoned the collective leadership approach and moved toward a manager responsibility system in 1984, the fact that Kim Il-Sung himself created the Dae-an Model will make it difficult for North Korea to modify or abandon the model.

In addition to the emphasis on the financial accountability of state enterprises, the December 1984 revision provides more material incentives to workers in state enterprises. Worker income in state enterprises is composed of three portions: (1) basic living costs, (2) bonuses, and (3) monetary prizes. Out of these three components, monetary prizes are paid from the "prize funds." Prize funds are part of extra profits in state enterprises that can be retained by the enterprise. According to the new provision, there are two ways to retain part of the extra profits: enterprise funds and prize funds. Enterprise funds can be used only for production investment and the improvement of collective welfare, while prize funds can be distributed to workers in the form of monetary prizes. Prize funds can be retained by state enterprises only after enterprise funds have been retained from extra profits, and they can be as much as 20 percent of extra profits. According to the Marxian formula of production, the gross value of production is composed of $C + V + M$, where C stands for material costs, V for labor costs, and M for net material income, which means profits. From the composition of the workers' income in state enterprises, a bonus is a reward for the reduction of labor costs, V, while the monetary prize is a reward for increased profits, M. The distinction between the bonus and the monetary prize is a peculiar feature of the North Korean incentive system, which provides incentives both to target accomplishment and profit generation. The bonus amount depends on the target fulfillment

---

single person should take the responsibility of managing the plant, but every party member, worker, and technician in the plant should take part in the operation of the factory's party committee, which is in turn responsible for the administration and management of the factory" (Park and Park 1990, 111).

6. For the detailed hierarchy of state enterprise, that is set by the Dae-an model, refer to figure 20 of Bunge 1981, 132.

rate, which is measured by the ratio of final output to assigned target. Using the above characteristics of the workers' income structure in North Korean state enterprises, we can establish the following equation:

$$Y = B + B \cdot \alpha \cdot [(Q/T) - 1] + (0.2 \, m)/n, \tag{1}$$

where Y is the income of a representative worker, B stands for basic living costs, α is a constant, Q is actual output, T is an assigned target, and n is the number of workers in the enterprise; m is the amount of extra profits, which is $M - M^*$, where M is profit and M^* is planned quota profit that has to be remitted to the state.

With an income structure like the above equation, we can observe that the incentive system for North Korean state enterprise workers is subject to the famous "ratchet effect" and "free-rider problem." The ratchet effect is a dynamic incentive problem, which will occur when a strong past performance leads to a higher current target, with no reward for moving the target upward. The existence of the ratchet effect along with punishment for unsuccessful fulfillment of targets prevents workers from exerting maximum effort and causes them to barely achieve the assigned targets. Bonin (1976) and Holmstrom (1982) proposed allowing managers of state enterprises to self-impose targets instead of receiving targets from the planner to avoid the ratchet effect. However, no such measure can be found in the North Korean incentive system, and from the above equation we can infer that North Korean state enterprise workers are also subject to the ratchet effect. Another incentive problem we can infer from this equation is the free-rider problem. As explained above, the monetary prize is not subject to the ratchet effect because the amount that will be distributed to each worker is not affected by past performance. A monetary prize is a kind of income sharing, which has a superior incentive effect, according to Tyson (1979), but it will lead to the free-rider problem when the number of workers who will share this income (n in the above equation) is significantly large. From the above analysis, we may conclude that the 1984 revision of the "Provision on the Independent Accounting System in State Enterprises" reveals the problems facing North Korean state enterprises, such as a soft budget problem, collusive behavior of managers and workers, the ratchet effect, and the free-rider problem, all of which are commonly observed in socialist economies. Even though the 1984 revision was affected by economic reform in China, North Korea's method of dealing with the existing inefficiency problems in state enterprises was not through market reform, like China, but through modifying the existing system, which makes the long-term effects of this revision questionable.

Kitchen Plots and Peasant Markets: Existence of Free
Markets in Agriculture

The socialization of the agricultural sector began with the Land Reform Act of March 1946. According to this act, the confiscation and redistribution of approximately one million hectares of land formerly owned by the Japanese colonialists took place. After the Korean War, collectivization was vigorously carried out such that by August 1958, all the agricultural means of production were socialized and all farmers joined cooperative farms.

Thanks to collectivization, the effective mobilization of manpower in collective farms, and modernization efforts during the six-year development plan (1971 to 1976), labor productivity in the agricultural sector improved significantly, and North Korea declared itself self-sufficient in terms of major grains by the late 1970s. However, despite the declaration by the North Korean government that agricultural production targets had been fulfilled in every development plan, continuous poor harvests and declining productivity in the 1970s led to insufficient supply of major grains by the late 1970s. According to Kim (1992), it is estimated that North Korea had an annual rice shortfall of approximately 1.43 million tons in 1990, which is about half of the total demand for rice in North Korea. Facing a gradual decline in productivity during the 1960s, the North Korean government allowed each farm household to privately cultivate a small "kitchen garden" surrounding the house and to sell the crops and livestock they raised there in a "peasant market," where prices are determined by market forces. Cultivation of kitchen plots was regarded as a necessary evil, and was implicitly tolerated by the North Korean government until it was finally permitted in the mid-1960s.[7] From the very beginning, the approved size of kitchen gardens was very small because Kim Il-Sung feared that the farmers might be more interested in profit making than participating in the cooperative farm.[8] Even though the absolute and relative size of this privately cultivated land is small compared to cooperative farm size, the existence of a private ownership system and a free market for these privately produced crops is one of the few market-oriented reforms in North Korea.[9] The empirical evidence provided by China proves the impor-

---

7. According to Park and Park 1990 (116–17), Kim Il-Sung stated that in the socialist stage the "peasant market" could not be abolished completely. Kim looks further ahead and offers the theory that the "peasant market will disappear when the country becomes industrialized and there are plenty of consumer goods available to the people."

8. Initially, each farm household could own as much as 260 m². However, as the grain shortage problem became worse, the size shrank to 66–99 m in 1977.

9. When the average amount of land cultivated by each farm household is 1.34 hectares, according to Kim 1992, the existence of kitchen plots of approximately 100 m² implies that no more than 0.75 percent of all cultivated land is privately owned.

tance of such private cultivation and free peasant markets. Judging from China's experience, we can expect that the current "kitchen garden" scheme will be further utilized in the future when North Korea initiates its own version of reform.

Foreign Exchange Shortages in North Korea and Its Open-Door Policy

The 1984 Foreign Joint-Venture Law: North Korea's First Open-Door Policy

Even though the North Korean economy experienced slow growth during the 1980s, North Korea maintained positive growth until the end of the 1980s. However, the above stated inherent problems of the North Korean economy, such as inefficient planning, lack of incentives, bottlenecks in key sectors, declining productivity in agriculture, and food shortages,[10] along with a chronic trade deficit (refer to app. B) and foreign debt depressed the North's economy despite partial reform efforts in the mid-1980s.[11] While the existing problems were serious enough to be considered an economic crisis, the reduction in foreign aid from the former Soviet Union and China and the subsequent demands for trade based on hard currency rather than the previous barter system by the Soviet Union in 1991 and from China in 1993 left North Korea with a serious foreign exchange shortage.[12] Furthermore, the

---

10. North Korea harvested 5.3 million tons of grain in 1991, leaving the country 1.4 million tons short of the 6.7 million tons needed in 1992. Due to this food shortage, food rations have been reduced by 25 percent since June 1991, and a soldier's daily grain ration is down from 800 to only 624 grams (Economist Intelligence Unit 1992a, 36).

11. Recent growth rates for real GNP and trade balance of North Korea are estimated below.

	1987	1988	1989	1990	1991
Real GNP growth rates (%)	2.5	2.9	2.0	−3.7	−5.2
Exports ($bn)	1.47	1.82	1.69	1.86	1.40
Imports ($bn)	2.57	3.20	2.90	2.93	2.31
Trade balance ($mn)	−1,100	−1,377	−1,219	−1,073	−902
External debt ($bn)	1.2				4.7

Source: EIU 1992, 5.

12. Li Lanqing, Chinese trade minister and concurrently a Politburo member of the Chinese Communist Party Central Committee, in a meeting with visiting Kang Jong-Mo, vice chairman of North Korea's External Economy and Trade Commission, said in late 1992 that all trade with China, beginning in 1993, must be paid for in cash by North Korea (*Vantage Point* [January 1993]: 14).

TABLE 2. The Foreign Joint-Venture Laws of North Korea, China, and Vietnam

	North Korea	China and Vietnam
Foreign investor's share	Less than 100 percent	Up to 100 percent
Decision making by the board of directors	Unanimity rule for the entire agenda	Unanimity rule for important agenda items
Labor management	Employment and layoffs through labor administrative authorities only	Direct employment possible (through a labor contract)
Corporate income tax rate	25%	China: 33% (15% in Special Economic Zone) Vietnam: 15 to 25%
Sales of output	Export only	Domestic sales possible

Source: Korea Development Institute 1992, 31.

foreign exchange shortage led to an oil shortage, in a country where oil consumption wholly depends on import.[13] In particular, the import of oil from the former Soviet Union has decreased sharply in recent years: North Korea used to import approximately 800,000 to 1,000,000 tons of oil per year from the former USSR until 1987, but this has since declined to 640,000 tons in 1988, 506,000 in 1989, 410,000 in 1990, and 41,000 from January to July of 1991. Facing this serious problem of foreign exchange shortage and the difficulty of borrowing from Western bankers due to the low credibility of North Korea,[14] along with a need for advanced technology, North Korea enacted the Foreign Joint Venture (FJV) Law in September 1984 to attract foreign capital and technology from Western countries. However, the relatively unattractive terms of the FJV law compared with Chinese and Vietnamese FJV laws and the suspicion of Western investors about the commitment of the North Korean government to the open-door policy resulted in an unsatisfactory number of joint ventures. In the following table, the differences between the North Korean FJV law and the Chinese and Vietnamese FJV laws are presented.

As can be seen from table 2, the North Korean FJV law of 1984 was less attractive than the Chinese or Vietnamese FJV laws in terms of ownership, management, and sales. The results of this FJV law enactment were disappointing to North Korea. Unlike the Vietnamese case, where many companies

13. According to Chang (1992), North Korea imported 2,650,000 tons of oil in 1988, and 17 percent of that imported oil was used in industry while 71 percent of it was used in transportation. Unlike South Korea, North Korea depended on coal (45 percent) and hydroelectric generation (55 percent) for its electricity. The amount of oil imports dropped to approximately 1,100,000 tons in 1992 (*Jungang Ilbo* [in Korean], March 31, 1993).

14. The national credibility rank of North Korea in 1991 was the lowest of 111 countires that were surveyred by *Institutional Investor*, (1993, 3) while the rank of South Korea was nineteenth (Korea Development Insititute 1992, 25).

from its neighboring countries, including Japan, Singapore, and South Korea, rushed into the Vietnamese market after its enactment of the FJV law in 1987, only about 100 joint ventures were signed between North Korea and foreign investors, with an average value of approximately $1 million each by 1990.[15] Furthermore, about 70 percent of these joint ventures were made with the Chochongryon fund, which is a pro–North Korea organization of Korean Japanese, while most of the rest were signed with Chinese or Soviet funds. Therefore, the desired results of inviting advanced technology and capital from Western countries were not met, and the expected increase in exports also did not take place.

The 1992 Enactment of the Three Laws Related to Foreigners' Investment

Faced with the unsatisfactory results of its first open-door policy in 1984 and deepening foreign exchange shortages, North Korea enacted three new laws related to foreign investment in October 1992: the Law on Foreigners' Investment, the Law on Contractual Joint Ventures, and the Law on Foreign Enterprises.[16] These new enactments provided more favorable conditions for foreign investors, who complained about the relatively unattractive terms of the 1984 law. The newly enacted law on Foreigners' Investment is to be applied to those foreign enterprises that are expected to be established in the "Free Economic and Trade Zone (FETZ)" of the Rajin-Sonbong area near Tumen River.[17] According to Article 6 of the Law on Foreign Enterprises, foreigners can set up foreign enterprises in the FETZ by submitting an application to the External Economic Department of the Administrative Council of the DPRK, and these enterprises can be 100 percent owned by foreigners. Furthermore, the corporate income tax rate for foreign enterprises in the FETZ has been reduced to 14 percent from the 1984 level of 25 percent, while the equivalent rate under the Chinese foreign joint venture law is 25 percent (15 percent in Special Economic Zone) and 15 to 25 percent under the Vietnamese foreign joint venture law. Therefore, as far as the FETZ is concerned, the terms offered by North Korea to foreign investors are at least as favorable as the Chinese and Vietnamese conditions. Furthermore, in order to attract investment from South Korean firms, the qualifications for Koreans seeking to

---

15. By the end of 1991, the total worth of foreign joint ventures was approximately $200 million, with 75 to 80 percent of them coming from Chochongryon (*Hanguk Ilbo* [in Korean], May 8, 1993).

16. For the whole text of these new laws, refer to *Vantage Point* 16, no. 2 (February 1993): 21–26.

17. In December 1991, the Rajin-Sonbong area was designated a free economic and trade zone under the Tumen River Basin Development Program, which had been proposed by the United Nations Development Program in 1991.

invest in North Korea have been changed. According to the 1984 law, only Koreans residing overseas could invest in North Korea, but the 1992 law removed this restriction so that Koreans living outside the territory of the DPRK can invest in North Korea.[18] This change has enabled South Koreans to invest in North Korea. However, to minimize the contacts between foreigners and North Korean citizens, hiring of North Korean workers must still be done through the North Korean labor administrative authorities according to the new laws. Encouraged by such North Korean efforts, the Daewoo Group, one of the largest South Korean conglomerates, agreed to set up a joint-venture factory in Nampo, but shortly before the establishment of the factory the South Korean government prohibited any economic cooperation with the North due to the nuclear issue.

Obstacles to North Korea's Open-Door Policy and the Political Dilemma of Opening the Door

As it is observed in the case of Daewoo's Nampo project, the resolution of the nuclear issue, which now prevents any economic cooperation between North Korea and Western countries, including South Korea and Japan, is an essential prerequisite for any positive outcome to the North Korean open-door policy. However, the elimination of the nuclear issue will not be sufficient to stimulate significant foreign joint ventures in North Korea. Even though the South Korean government is very likely to approve inter-Korean economic cooperation once the nuclear issue is resolved, unless South Korean or other Western firms can export those products produced in North Korea through a joint venture with a North Korean counterpart to markets like the United States, there will be less incentive for South Korean or Japanese firms to invest in the North. Currently, the United States government prohibits any economic exchanges with North Korea on the basis of the Trading With the Enemy Act (TWEA), and because of the rule of origin, South Korean firms will not be able to export products produced in North Korea to the United States market.[19] Therefore, for North Korea to truly expect a significant inflow of foreign capital and technology, the resolution of the nuclear issue and improved diplomatic relations with the United States are a prerequisite.

In addition to such external factors that can undermine North Korea's efforts to promote foreign joint ventures, there are some domestic factors that can also derail the open-door policy of North Korea. First of all, fear exists of a collapse

---

18. See Article 5 of the Law on Contractual Joint Ventures (*Vantage Point* 16, no. 2 [February 1993]: 21).

19. Since President Truman designated China and North Korea as enemies of the United States in 1951 during the Korean War, the U.S. government has prohibited any economic transaction with North Korea. This restriction against China was lifted in 1979, when China and the United States established formal diplomatic relations.

among the North Korean leaders in regards to the open-door policy. North Korean society has been completely closed since the end of the Korean War, and only the bureaucratic elite in North Korea have access to outside information. Furthermore, the North Korean government has continued to make the claim to its people that North Korea is a "workers' paradise on earth," particularly emphasizing the superiority of North Korean society over South Korean society. Under these conditions, an open-door policy can provide opportunities to ordinary North Koreans to find out about what is really going on in the outside world, particularly in South Korea. The North Korean people may not be disturbed by the fact that they are worse off than the United States or Japan, but once they find out that they are far worse off than South Koreans, it will be such a shock that it will put the current North Korean regime in danger. The historical record of the collapse of the Central European socialist countries (like East Germany and Romania), as well as the Tiananmen Square Incident or the Massacre in China, also influences the North Korean leaders' fear of collapse. Pyongyang was especially annoyed by the frequent remarks made by Seoul that South Korea should prepare for a unification by absorption, which is based on the assumption that the North Korean regime will collapse. Second, the existence of influential hawks and their perception of the economic crisis in North Korea could also deter the opening of North Korea. It is generally believed that the old leaders in the Workers Party and the military belong to the antireform, hawkish group, while the relatively young technocrats, especially those who have had contact with the outside world, are believed to be pro-reform and dovish. If the hawks believe that the North's current economic difficulties can be solved through nonmarket measures such as missile sales to the Middle East, their resistance against the open door and reform policy can also undermine the doves' efforts at reform.

However, there are some positive signs as well. First of all, the dangerous influence of North Korea's open-door policy on its regime stability can be minimized by restricting the activities of foreign joint-venture firms in the enclave of the free economic and trade zone, as China did during the initial stages of opening. Furthermore, the absence of any visible opposition group inside North Korea will also relieve the North Korean leaders' fears of collapse.[20] Second, the promotion of Kang Song-San and Kim Dal-Hyun to North Korean premier and Politburo member, respectively, in December 1992 also indicates the growing tendency toward reform in North Korea.[21]

---

20. Suh (1993, 4) states, "there is neither a single individual nor a solitary group publicly expressing dissatisfaction against the system, let alone challenging it. The situation in North Korea is quite different from that in the former Soviet Union or China. There is no Andrei Sakharov in North Korea, and unlike the students of Peking University, the students of Kim Il-Sung University do not stand in front of North Korean tanks, they drive them."

21. Kang Song-San initiated the enactment of the first Foreign Joint Venture law in 1984. Due to the unsatisfactory results of the first open-door policy, he was disgracefully demoted to governor of a local province near the Tumen River. But his efforts to pursue the Tumen River

Even though North Korea has made more sincere efforts in its open-door policy, compared to its reform effort, there is one fundamental difference between the North Korean open-door policy and China's open-door policy. Even though both countries' open door policies aim at attracting foreign capital and technology, the motives behind the policies are different. In the Chinese case, the adoption of an outward-oriented development strategy, which imitated the South Korean development strategy in the 1960s, had initiated the open-door policy. Therefore, China attracted foreign capital and technology to promote light industry based on the law of comparative advantage. However, North Korea's motives for adopting an open-door policy were not to promote exports but to acquire foreign exchange needed to continue its import-substitution development strategy. Thus, North Korea attracts foreign capital not to invest in export-promotion industries, but to resolve urgent foreign exchange shortages. The North also seeks advanced technology not for light industry, but for replacing obsolete technology in North Korea's heavy industries. However, whatever motive lies behind the open-door policy of the North, in the sense that it can result in increased exports and further opening of its economy, North Korea's efforts to attract foreign capital will have a lot more positive effect on its economy than any previous measures they have taken.

Concluding Remarks

The relatively better endowed North Korean economy (compared to the South) could achieve considerable industrialization in the 1950s and 1960s by relying on Soviet-style economic planning and the mass mobilization of labor. However, inherent internal problems, such as the imbalance between heavy and light industry, the lack of capital and technology, inefficiency and incentive problems, bottlenecks due to the increasing complexity of planning, and shortages (especially in food and energy), that can be observed in any socialist economy, began to produce signs of problematic unbalanced growth in the 1970s, while the 1980s was a period of stagnant growth. Furthermore, external shocks in the early 1990s, such as the collapse of the Soviet Union, the cutback in aid from the former Soviet Union and China, decreased trade between North Korea and the former socialist countries, and the resulting foreign exchange shortage delivered a critical blow to the already faltering North Korean economy.

Basin Development Plan (TRBDP) have been appreciated by Kim Jung-Il, and he became premier of North Korea in December 1992. Kim Dal-Hyun is also one of the capable technocrats who advocate an open-door policy, and also one of the very few North Koreans who visited South Korea in 1992. Unlike Premier Kang, however, Kim Dal-Hyun was expelled from the Politburo position in December 1993, probably because of the poor progress of North-South Korea economic cooperation, which had shown no progress since the nuclear issue emerged.

As a remedy to the above problems, the North Korean government prescribed deregulation in the mid-1980s to solve internal problems and initiated an open-door policy to cope with external difficulties in 1984 and again in 1992. However, in the sense that genuine reforms, which are market-oriented, have to include moves toward privatization and abandonment of price control, the North Korean economic reform in the mid-1980s was far from this definition of genuine reform, and should be called a partial reform, which attempted to correct problems within the existing socialist economy framework. Contrary to the earlier partial reform measures meant to address its domestic problems, North Korea's open-door policy of 1984 and 1992 is more or less equivalent to the Chinese and Vietnamese open-door policies. However, the low credibility of North Korea, the relatively unattractive terms of its foreign joint venture law of 1984, and restrictions on economic transaction with the United States resulted in a rather unsatisfactory number of foreign joint ventures in the 1980s. The enactment of new foreign joint venture laws in 1992 have not produced any significant results so far because of the issue of political succession and the nuclear issue that North Korea is now facing.

Assuming the removal of the current obstacles, such as the domestic political situation and the nuclear question, that now impede the progress of North Korea's open-door policy, we can predict a much more fruitful outcome for the policy, considering the efforts by the North to attract foreign investors and the enthusiasm of South Korean firms ready to enter North Korea. Given these conditions, the North may well be able to alleviate some of its foreign exchange and obsolete technology problems. However, without genuine reform toward a market economy, the internal problems of the North Korean economy, which are inherent to socialist economies, will be impossible to resolve.

APPENDIX A:
A CHRONOLOGY OF THE NORTH KOREAN ECONOMY

August 15, 1945	Independence from Japan
March 5, 1946	Land reform
June 25, 1950– July 23, 1953	Korean War
April 1954	Cooperative farms are established
February 1960	Chongsan-ni Method is announced
December 1961	Dae-an Method is announced
1965(?)	Cultivation of kitchen gardens is allowed
1977	The size of allowed kitchen gardens is decreased to 66–99 m

1978	Chinese economic reforms begin
1979	North Korea joins United Nations Development Program (UNDP)
1979	Vietnamese reforms begin
August 3, 1984	August Third People's Consumer Goods Production campaign begins
September 1984	Foreign Joint Venture Law is enacted
December 1984	Revision of the Provisions on the Independent Accounting System is announced
July 1985	Associated Enterprises are created
December 1985	Number of industrial ministries is decreased from 34 to 24
December 1985	North Korea joins Nuclear Non-Proliferation Treaty (NPT)
August 1987	North Korea is declared in default by western creditor banks
June 4, 1989	Tiananmen Square Massacre in Beijing
October 3, 1990	German unification
December 1991	Soviet Union breaks up
December 1991	"Free Economic and Trade Zone" of 621 km^2 is designated around Najin-Sonbong area under the Tumen River Basin Development Program (TRBDP) by the UNDP
January 1992	Kim Woo-Choong (chairman of Daewoo Group, South Korea) visits North Korea
May 1992–Jan 1993	International Atomic Energy Agency (IAEA) carries out nuclear inspections six times in Yong-Byung, North Korea
July 1992	Kim Dal-Hyun (North Korean deputy premier) visits South Korea
August 1992	South Korea and China establish full diplomatic relationship
October 1992	Announcement of three basic laws related to foreign investment: Law on Foreigner's Investment, Law on Contractual Joint Ventures, and Law on Foreign Enterprises
March 12, 1993	North Korea withdraws from Nuclear Non-Proliferation Treaty (NPT)
May 10, 1993	North Korea and the United States agree to have high-level talks in Beijing
December 9, 1993	Premier Kang announces the failure of the third seven-year plan

APPENDIX B: NORTH KOREAN TRADE ($ MILLIONS)

	1985	1986	1987	1988	1989	1990	1991
Exports	1,350	1,507	1,470	1,820	1,690	1,860	1,400
Imports	1,720	2,064	2,570	3,200	2,900	2,930	2,310
Trade volume	3,070	3,572	4,040	5,020	4,590	4,790	3,710
Trade balance	−370	−557	−1,100	−1,377	−1,219	−1,073	−902
Trade/GNP ratio[a]	0.20	0.21	0.21	0.24	0.17	0.21	0.16
Trade with China							
Exports to China	222	255	214	212	167	118	79
Imports from China	263	281	305	380	399	398	582
Trade volume	485	536	519	592	566	516	661
(China/total, %)	(16%)	(15%)	(13%)	(12%)	(12%)	(11%)	(18%)
Trade with the USSR[b]							
Exports to USSR	485	642	683	887	891	1,047	171
Imports from USSR	786	1,079	1,265	1,747	1,492	1,516	194
Trade volume	1,271	1,721	1,948	2,634	2,383	2,563	365
(USSR/total, %)	(41%)	(48%)	(48%)	(52%)	(52%)	(54%)	(10%)
Trade with Japan							
Exports to Japan	161	154	218	293	268	271	250
Imports from Japan	274	204	237	263	216	194	246
Trade volume	435	358	455	556	484	465	496
(Japan/total, %)	(14%)	(10%)	(11%)	(11%)	(11%)	(10%)	(13%)

Source: *Vantage Point* 16, no. 3 (March 1993), 11–12; EIU 1992b, 22; EIU 1992a, 5.
[a]For GNP data, NUB's estimation in table 1 is used.
[b]For 1991, it is trade with the Commonwealth of Independent States (CIS).

REFERENCES

Andreff, Wladimir. 1989. "Economic Reforms in North Korea and Viet Nam." *Seoul Journal of Economics* 2, no. 1.

Bonin, J. P. 1976. "On the Design of Managerial Incentive Structures in a Decentralized Planning Environment" *American Economic Review* 66, no. 4 (September).

Bunge, Frederica M. 1981. *North Korea: A Country Study.* American University for U.S. Department of the Army.

Chang, Young-Shik. 1992. "Demand and Supply of Energy in North Korea" (in Korean). Paper presented at the "International Symposium on the North Korean Economy," September 30 to October 1, held by the Korea Economic Daily.

Chun, Hong-Taek. 1992. "A Comparison of South and North Korean Economic Performance" (in Korean). Paper presented at the "International Symposium on the North Korean Economy," September 30 to October 1, held by the Korea Economic Daily.

Eberstadt, Nicholas. 1992. "North Korean Population and Labor Force." Paper presented at the "International Symposium on the North Korean Economy," September 30 to October 1, held by the Korea Economic Daily.

The Economist Intelligence Unit. 1992a. "Country Report: China, North Korea." EIU No. 3.

———. 1992b. "Korea's Coming Reunification: Another East Asian Superpower?" EIU Special Report No. M212.

Holmstrom, Bengt. 1982. "Design of Incentive Schemes and the New Soviet Incentive Model." *European Economic Review* 17, no. 2 (February).

Hwang, Ui-Kwack. 1992. *The North Korean Economy* (in Korean). Seoul: Na-Nam Publishing.

Jeong, Kap-Young. 1992. "The North Korean Economy." *Korea and World Affairs* 16, no. 1 (Spring): 3–24.

Kang, Myung-Kyu, and Keun Lee. 1992. "Industrial Systems and Reform in North Korea: A Comparison with China." *World Development* 20, no. 7.

Kim, Kwang-Suk, and Michael Roemer. 1979. *Growth and Structural Transformation.* Cambridge: Harvard University Press.

Kim, Woon-Keun. 1992. "Agricultural Situation and Prospect in North Korea" (in Korean). Paper presented at the International Seminar on "Agriculture of North Korea and Agricultural Reform in Centrally Planned Economies," held by Korea Rural Economic Institute, September 29–30.

Korea Development Institute. 1992. *Current Problems of Inter-Korean Economic Cooperation and Tumen River Development Plan.* Seoul: Korea Development Institute (June).

Kormai, Janos. 1980. *Economics of Shortage.* Amsterdam: North-Holland Publishing.

———. 1986. "The Soft Budget Constraints." *Kyklos* 39, no. 1.

Lee, Hy-Sang. 1991. "North Korean Economic Reform and Open Door Policy" (in Korean). Paper presented at the Conference on "Changes of North Korea and Inter-Korean Relation in the 1990s," National Unification Board.

Osband, Kent. 1987. "Speak Softly, but Carry a Big Stick: On Optimal Targets under Moral Hazard." *Journal of Comparative Economics* 11, no. 4 (December).

Park, Han-Shik, and Kyung-Ae Park. 1990. *China and North Korea: Politics of Integration and Modernization, Asian Studies Monograph Series.* Hong Kong: Asian Research Service.

Suh, Dae-Sook. 1993. "The Prospects for Changes in North Korea." *Korea and World Affairs* (March).

Tyson, Laura A. 1979. "Incentives, Income Sharing, and Institutional Innovation in the Yugoslav Self-Managed Firm." *Journal of Comparative Economics* 3, no. 3 (September).

Vantage Point. 1993. Vol. 16, no. 1, 2, and 3. Seoul: Naewoe Press.

Yeon, Ha Cheong. 1986. *North Korea's Economic Policy and Operation* (in Korean). Seoul: Korean Development Institute.

———. "Practical Means to Improve Intra-Korean Trade and Economic Cooperation." Seoul: Korea Development Institute (January).

CHAPTER 15

Government Commitment and Gradualism

Xinghai Fang

There has been a debate about the relative merits of a gradual strategy and a
big-bang strategy in the market-oriented economic reforms in (formerly) socialist countries. The debate has taken place on several fronts. They include
macroeconomic control, the coordination of reforms, and microeconomic
efficiency during transition. Regarding the issue of microeconomic efficiency
during transition, advocates of a big-bang strategy deplore the pitfalls of a
gradual, partial reform. Murphy, Schleifer, and Vishny 1992 study a situation
where a partial reform creates the coexistence of state and private firms. Since
state firms cannot negotiate prices freely,when a state firm competes with a
private firm for an input whose price is set below its market value by the
government, a great difference between the marginal product of the input in
the state firm and that in the private firm will result, causing a serious resource
misallocation. Proponents of a gradual strategy, however, think differently.
McMillan and Naughton 1992 contend that if one crack in the traditional
socialist economic system can be made, other parts of the system will be
forced to become more efficient. For example, they point out that the proliferation of private industrial firms in China has exerted great competitive
pressure on the state firms and has made them more productive. As a result of
those increased efficiencies, reforming governments have more room to maneuver in the transition to a market economy. Thus a gradual reform may
prove to be more viable. Tirole 1991 emphasizes the need to sequence reform
steps properly to ensure the microeconomic efficiency of the resulting market
economy. For example, he points out that reform measures promoting competition must be taken before privatization to avoid monopoly in a private
economy.

In this debate, one important factor that determines the choice of a

This chapter is a much shortened version of chapter 1 of my Ph.D. dissertation submitted to
Stanford University in February 1994. I thank very much my committee members and other
faculties in Stanford's Economics Department for their superb guidance. The encouragement
from the editors of this volume is also greatly appreciated.

337

gradual strategy versus a big-bang strategy has not been brought to light: the ability of a reform-initiating government to commit to a reform. Put simply, if a government's commitment ability is low, people affected by the reform, fearing a policy reversal, will not commit many resources toward the direction of the reform. Consequently the results of the reform will not be good. Unfavorable reform results may further weaken the government's commitment ability. Under this kind of circumstance, a big-bang, all-out reform only leads to a rapid decline in output and a quick end to the reform. On the other hand, as McMillan and Naughton 1992 point out, if a spot in the economy can be found where the reform can proceed first and some positive results can be obtained, the reforming government will gain on its commitment ability in subsequent reform measures, thus better ensuring the success of the reform.

This chapter formalizes the above idea. We study a reform that is to shift from socialist collective production to private production. The aim of the reform is to eliminate the free-rider problem caused by the socialist egalitarian distribution of income under collective production. We build an infinite horizon rational expectations reform model to study exactly how government commitment ability affects the public's investment behavior and vice versa. We are particularly interested in delineating the conditions under which a big-bang reform strategy is preferred and the conditions under which a gradual reform strategy is favored. Under the assumption that government commitment ability is positively related to reform outcomes, we find that the path of commitment abilities during the reform process is monotonic. We show that when government commitment ability is above a certain level, a big-bang reform in which the entire population enters into reform at the beginning, is preferred to a gradual reform where the population goes into reform portion by portion. Although both reform strategies will produce a successful reform, in the sense that output after reform is larger than the prereform level, the big-bang reform produces more output than the gradual reform. We then show that in order for a big-bang reform to be successful government commitment ability cannot be below a certain level, otherwise the great likelihood of a policy reversal will reduce investments to a point that output is less than under collective production. When a government's commitment ability is low, we show a gradual strategy in which fraction by fraction of the population goes into reform sequentially is preferred to a big-bang strategy under many circumstances. That is because after a part of the population has gone into private production, the remaining part becomes more efficient due to a less severe free rider problem brought about by the reduced size of the sharing community. The total output of the part under reform and the part remaining in collective production can be larger than before the reform despite the fact the low ability of the government to commit hinders investment of the people under reform. Hence the required government commitment ability for a successful reform is lower than that under a big-bang reform.

The current debate about gradualism and big-bang gives an impression that some reforms have to proceed in a gradual fashion while other reforms must go as big-bang. Gradualism and big-bang appear diametrically opposed to each other. The analysis in this paper shows that for a given reform, the choice between a gradual strategy and a big-bang strategy really depends on the circumstances surrounding the reform. Under one set of circumstances, a big-bang strategy is better; under another set, a gradual strategy is superior.

This chapter is organized as follows. The first section outlines an economic environment in which the analysis takes place. Then we show the existence of the paths of economic agents' rational expectations about a government's commitment abilities and characterize them. Next we study the desirability of a big-bang reform given the initial commitment ability of the government. We show there exists the phenomenon of path dependence in economic reforms (David 1988). In the next section we study whether a gradual, step-by-step reform will do better when the initial government commitment ability is low. The final section concludes and offers some further thoughts.

The Basic Model

There must be some inefficiencies in an economy that call for a reform. Inefficiencies can take many forms. In socialist economies, a major inefficiency is the free-rider problem caused by the socialist egalitarian allocation principle—dubbed as *eating from the big pan*. If no matter how hard you work, you will be paid the same as other people who don't work hard, then why should you work hard? The reform cited in the previous section, by changing from collective production to private production, cures the free-rider problem. Clearly, the interaction between expectations, economic behavior, and reform result that is our subject of study in this chapter depends on what kind of inefficiency a reform addresses. Therefore, a general model in some generic reform environment that is adequate to address our concern here appears rather difficult to build. Instead, we are less ambitious and only study the issues in contexts resembling the kind of reform mentioned above.

We consider a community with N economic units, $N > 1$. These economic units can be households, collective farms, production teams, or industrial firms. Before the reform, they engage in collective sharing according to the socialist doctrine. That is, they share their output equally among themselves. We assume these N units are identical. To bring out the essential insights without becoming entangled in the mathematics, we assume that among the three production factors, labor, land, and capital, only capital is responsible for the output. In fact, we assume output of an economic unit at every period is equal to the amount of capital stock that the unit has at that period. Capital stock depreciates at the rate of $\sigma(0 < \sigma < 1)$ per period.

Economic units are risk neutral and maximize total expected income. The intertemporal discount factor is $\delta(0 < \delta < 1)$.

In the collective sharing mode, a representative unit i tries to maximize the net return of its investment. Its investment decision, I_i, at each period is the following:

$$\max_{I_i} [Y_i - I_i + \frac{1}{N} \sum_{j=1}^{N} (\delta g(I_j) + \delta^2 \sigma g(I_j) + \cdots + \delta^n \sigma^{n-1} g(I_j) + \cdots)], \quad (1)$$

Where we have assumed the following:

1. Investment is out of each unit's income. In the above equation, Y_i and I_i stand for the representative unit's income and investment. Economic units invest separately but have to share the fruit of investment with the other $N - 1$ units according to the socialist egalitarian principle.
2. Investment I is transformed into capital according to $g(I)$. It takes one period for investment to become useful capital. We make the standard assumption that $g(0) = 0$, $g'(I) > 0$, $g''(I) < 0$, $g'(0) = \infty$, $g'(\infty) = 0$.

Solving equation 1 for the representative unit's optimal investment, I_i^*, and focusing on the symmetric outcome, we get

$$g'(I_i^*) = \frac{N(1 - \delta\sigma)}{\delta} . \quad (2)$$

Equation 2 determines unit i's investment, I_i^*. Total capital formation of the N units in each period is $Ng(I_i^*)$.

Steady state total capital stock, K_0, in the collective sharing mode, is

$$K_0 = Ng(I_i^*)(1 + \sigma + \sigma^2 + \cdots + \sigma^n + \cdots)$$

$$= \frac{Ng(I_i^*)}{1 - \sigma} . \quad (3)$$

After a reform from collective sharing to private responsibility, that is, each economic unit enjoys its own output, if it is certain that the reform will continue forever, a representative economic unit's investment decision, I_i, at each period is:

$$\max_{I_i} [Y_i - I_i + \delta g(I_i) + \delta^2 \sigma g(I_i) + \cdots]. \quad (4)$$

Solving the above equation, we have investment I_i^{**} of a representative unit in each period under private responsibility determined by

$$g'(I_i^{**}) = \frac{1 - \delta\sigma}{\delta} \,. \tag{5}$$

Total capital formation in each period now is $Ng(I_i^{**})$. So steady state total capital stock of the community K^* after such a successful reform is

$$K^* = \frac{Ng(I_i^{**})}{1 - \sigma} \,. \tag{6}$$

Equations 2 and 5 show the source of the free-rider problem. It is easy to see that $I_i^{**} > I_i^*$ under our assumptions about the function $g(I)$.

Comparing equations 3 and 6, we see that total steady state output (since output equals capital stock) is larger after the reform than before. We can easily show that average consumption after reform is also larger than before. Therefore, the reform is clearly a good cause that reformers should pursue. We next ask whether this clearly good reform can succeed when economic units have doubts about the durability of the reform.

Let us first specify the rational beliefs of these economic units and the behavior of the government. The government announces at period 0 that the reform starts now and private responsibility begins. We assume the government is not unanimous in pursuing the reform and may not actually stick to the reform in period 1. We can imagine that after the reform is announced, a power struggle between reformers and conservatives breaks out inside the government. If the reformers win, the government sticks to the reform in period 1; but if the conservatives win, the government scraps the reform in period 1. In anticipation of the uncertain outcome of the power struggle, economic units undertake investments at period 0. In period 1, if the government sticks to the reform, economic units will enjoy the benefits of period 0 investments; but if the government scraps the reform, period 0 investments will be completely dissipated.[1] Dissipation could be due to the recollectivization process that will follow after a reform is stopped. Or it could be due to the fact that useful capital under private production can become useless under collective production. If the government sticks to the reform in period 1, it will announce in period 1 that the reform continues. After this announcement, power struggle resumes, which again determines whether the government sticks to the reform in period 2 or not. But if the conservatives win in the power struggle of any period, the reform is scrapped in the period and is dead

---

1. All we need know is that there is some capital dissipation if a reform fails and recollectivization occurs. But for the ease of exposition, we assume complete dissipation.

and buried for ever. No more reforms will follow. We assume the relative strength of the reformers and the conservatives changes in period 1 after period 1 output is realized. If period 1 output increases over that of period 0, reformers' strength is raised; but if period 1 output decreases below that of period 0, reformers' strength is lowered. The change in strength takes place before the period 1 power struggle resumes. In every period, output is compared with the prereform period 0 output, but strengths change relative to the previous period. This process starts at period 0 and continues to infinity.

When economic units make investments at period t, $t \geq 0$, they assess the probability, P_t, of the government to stick to the reform in period $t + 1$. P_t obviously depends on the relative strength of reformers and conservatives at period t. We assume that these economic units are sophisticated enough to correctly assess at period t the true probability of the event that the government will stick to the reform in period $t + 1$, based on the relative strength of the reformers and the conservatives in period t.[2] According to this formulation, P_0 is determined by the initial relative strength of reformers and conservatives. P_t, $t > 0$ changes as the strengths of reformers and conservatives are altered by the outcomes of the reform.

We assume there is a one-to-one correspondence between the relative strength of reformers and conservatives at any period t and the probability P_t.[3] We therefore subsume relative strengths and talk about the changes of relative strength in terms of those P_t's. Specifically, we postulate that the change of relative strengths follows:

$$P_t = F(P_{t-1}, Y_0, Y_t), \ t \geq 1, \tag{7}$$

where Y_t and Y_0 are outputs at period t and period 0, respectively. In equation 7, we require: $0 \leq F(.) \leq 1$, F strictly increases in Y_t and P_{t-1}, $P_t > P_{t-1}$ if $Y_t > Y_0$, $P_t = P_{t-1}$ if $Y_t = Y_0$, and $P_t < P_{t-1}$ if $Y_t < Y_0$. We also require F to be continuous in its variables. One candidate for such a function is

$$P_t = P_{t-1}^{1 - \frac{Y_t - Y_0}{\max[Y_t, Y_0]}}, \ t \geq 1. \tag{8}$$

P_0, which reflects the initial relative strength between the reformers and the conservatives inside the government, is determined by the past history and

---

2. As pointed out by a referee, all we need is for economic units' assessments of probabilities to be monotonic in relative strengths.

3. For concreteness, let's imagine the politbureau, which decides the government's policy, is divided between reformers and conservatives. If one-third of the politbureau members are conservatives, then there is a one-third probability that the government will not stick to the reform.

is outside our model. Equation 7 says that the strength of the reformers is positively related to outputs after the reform. If the output in period t is bigger than the prereform output, Y_0, then the strength of the reformers in period t, relative to the previous period, is enhanced according to equation 7. The strength of conservatives is then negatively related to the outcome of the reform. The above assumption seems to correspond well to what we observe in the real world.

Economic units are assumed to see the initial relative strength of the reformers and conservatives and correctly assess P_0. They also know how the strengths of reformers and conservatives change, namely, equation 7. They make investment decisions according to the probabilities, P_t's, and are aware of the effects of their investments on those probabilities—that is, economic units' expectations are rational (Muth 1961).

Existence and Characteristics of Rational Expectations Paths

The Existence

Given the above specification, each economic unit's investment decision, I_t, at $t \geq 0$ after the government announced the reform at t is

$$\max_{I_t} [Y_i - I_t + P_t \delta g(I_t) + P_t P_{t+1} \delta^2 \sigma \, g(I_t) + \cdots$$

$$+ P_t P_{t+1} \cdots P_{t+s} \delta^{s+1} \, \sigma^s \, g(I_t) + \cdots]. \tag{9}$$

The reason that these probabilities multiply is that once the reform is shelved it never comes back, so for a reform to be on in period t, it has to be on in periods $0, 1, \ldots, t - 1$.

Solving the above maximization problem (equation 9) yields

$$g'(I_i^{***}) = \frac{1}{\delta P_t + \delta^2 \sigma P_t P_{t+1} + \cdots + \delta^{t+s+1} \sigma^{t+s} \prod_{v=0}^{v=s} P_{t+v} + \cdots}. \tag{10}$$

Equation 10 determines each unit's optimal investment, I_t^{***}, at period t. Therefore total capital stock, K_t, at period $t \geq 1$ after the reform is

$$K_t = \sigma K_{t-1} + Ng(I_t^{***}), \tag{11}$$

where K_0 is given by equation 3. That is, we let the reform start from the stagnant (steady) state of the old collective sharing mode.

Since we assume output is equal to the capital stock, equation 7 becomes

$$P_t = F(P_{t-1}, K_0, K_t), t \geq 1.$$

The existence of a rational expectations path is then the following problem: Does there exist a $P = (P_1, P_2, \ldots, P_\infty)$, i.e. $P \in [0, 1]^\infty$ such that

$$P_1 = F(P_0, K_0, K_1),$$

$$P_2 = F(P_1, K_0, K_2),$$

$$\ldots \tag{12}$$

$$P_t = F(P_{t-1}, K_0, K_t),$$

$$\ldots$$

simultaneously hold for any given $P_0 (0 < P_0 < 1)$, while K_t $(t \geq 1)$ is given by equation 11 and K_0 follows equation 3?

It is a fixed-point problem. The above mapping (12) is from $[0, 1]^\infty$ to $[0, 1]^\infty$ and is continuous. The Brouwer's fixed-point theorem only applies to a finite space. But by the Schauder fixed-point theorem, we know there exists a $P^* \in [0, 1]^\infty$ such that the above simultaneous equation system is satisfied. (See the theorem on page 150 of Conway 1990.) We have the following proposition:

PROPOSITION 1. *For our problem summarized in (12), there exist rational expectations paths for any given P_0, $0 < P_0 < 1$.*

The Characteristics

Without proof, the following proposition is stated (for those interested in the proof, please see my Ph.D. dissertation submitted to the School of Arts and Sciences, Stanford University, February, 1994):

PROPOSITION 2. *Both the highest and lowest rational expectations paths of problem (12) are monotonic. That is, if $P_1 > P_0$, then $P_t > P_{t-1}$, $\forall t > 1$; and if $P_1 < P_0$, then $P_t < P_{t-1}$, $\forall t > 1$.*

When Will a Big Bang Succeed and When Will It Fail?

Our reform has a positive probability of stopping at any period t before P_{t-1} reaches 1. A reform that has produced positive results consistently, but is stopped and shelved by conservatives, cannot be said to be a failed reform. Accordingly, we define successful and unsuccessful reforms as follows.

DEFINITION 1. *A reform is called a successful reform if at every period of time when the reform is on, the output at that period is bigger than the prereform output.*

DEFINITION 2. *A reform is called an unsuccessful reform if at all periods of time when the reform is on, the outputs are smaller than the prereform level.*

There is still another case that we will call a no-impact reform.

DEFINITION 3. *A reform is called a no-impact reform if at every period when the reform is on, the output is equal to the prereform output.*

Since we have shown the monotonicities of both the highest and the lowest paths, we will not discuss paths that are not monotonic, that is, paths that produce outputs both higher and lower than the prereform level.

A No-Impact Big-Bang Reform

As a benchmark, let's first show the sufficient and necessary condition under which the reform has no impact. The reform starts from the steady state of the collective sharing mode. That is at period 0, capital stock (by equation 3) is

$$K_0 = \frac{Ng(I_i^*)}{(1 - \sigma)} .$$

Let the initial probability be P_0. If output is always the same as the prereform level, by equation 7, the rational expectations path is the following one:

$$P_0 = P_1 = P_2 = \cdots = P_\infty.$$

For this to hold, capital stock at each period after reform has to be K_0. Therefore

$$K_1 = \sigma K_0 + Ng(I_0^{***}) = K_0, \tag{13}$$

where I_0^{***} is determined by the following equation (from equation 10):

$$g'(I_0^{***}) = \frac{1}{(P_0\delta + P_0^2\delta^2\sigma + \cdots + P_0^t\delta^t\sigma^{t-1} + \cdots)} = \frac{1 - p_0\delta\sigma}{P_0\delta} .$$

From equation 13,

$$Ng(I_0^{***}) = (1 - \sigma)K_0 = Ng(I_i^*), \tag{14}$$

therefore, $I_0^{***} = I_i^*$.

Since

$$g'(I_i^*) = \frac{N(1 - \delta\sigma)}{\delta},$$

and

$$g'(I_0^{***}) = \frac{1 - P_0\delta\sigma}{P_0\delta},$$

we have

$$\frac{N(1 - \delta\sigma)}{\delta} = \frac{1 - P_0\delta\sigma}{P_0\delta}.$$

Solving the above equation for P_0 and calling the solution P_0^*, we have

$$P_0^* = \frac{1}{\delta\sigma + N(1 - \delta\sigma)}. \tag{15}$$

By the stationarity structure of the problem, we know when $P_0 = P_1 = \cdots = P_0^*$,

$$K_t = K_0, t \geq 2,$$

which in turn ensures the above path is a rational expectations path.

So, if $P_0 = P_0^*$, then the following path is a rational expectations path and entails a no-impact reform:

$$P_0 = P_1 = P_2 = \cdots = P_\infty = P_0^*. \tag{16}$$

Along this rational expectations path, output at any period when the reform is on is just as big as the prereform level. The reform is nullified by the unfavorable expectations. We have the following proposition.

PROPOSITION 3. *If a big-bang reform starts out with $P_0 = P_0^*$, where P_0^* is given by equation 15, then there exists a rational expectations path, $P_1 = P_2$*

$= \cdots = P_\infty = P_0^*$, *that is sufficient and necessary for the reform to be a no-impact reform.*

When Is a Big-Bang Reform Destined to Succeed?

How high does P_0 have to be for output at each period after a big-bang reform to be larger than the prereform level? We can only give a sufficient condition at this point.

In order for the reform to succeed, we need to have

$$K_1 = \sigma K_0 + Ng(I_0^{***}) > K_0. \tag{17}$$

Inequality 17 is equivalent to

$$g(I_0^{***}) > g(I_i^*).$$

Therefore, we need

$$I_0^{***} > I_i^*,$$

which is equivalent (by equation 2 and equation 10) to

$$\frac{1}{P_0\delta + P_0P_1\delta^2\sigma + \cdots} < \frac{N(1 - \delta\sigma)}{\delta}.$$

The left side of the above inequality is less than or equal to $1/P_0\delta$. (Setting $P_1 = P_2 = \cdots = 0$)

So we solve the following inequality for P_0:

$$\frac{1}{P_0\delta} < \frac{N(1 - \delta\sigma)}{\delta},$$

$$P_0 > \frac{1}{N(1 - \delta\sigma)}.$$

Defining $\bar{P}_0$ to be:

$$\bar{P}_0 = \frac{1}{N(1 - \delta\sigma)}. \tag{18}$$

Then, if $P_0 > \bar{P}_0$, inequality 17 will be satisfied. According to equation 7, the government's strength-changing rule, we know $P_1^H(P_0) > P_0$, $P_1^L(P_0) > P_0$.

So by proposition 2, both the lowest and the highest paths are monotonically increasing. For this to hold, the output after reform at each period has to be bigger than the prereform level. (Please refer to equation 7 for the reasoning.) We have the following proposition:

PROPOSITION 4. *If a big-bang reform starts out with $P_0 > \bar{P}_0$ (defined by equation 18), then even the lowest equilibrium path entails a success.*

When Is a Big-Bang Reform Doomed to Fail?

Now consider a big-bang reform that starts with a P_0. We ask under what conditions will it fail? The reform begins with K_0 that is given by equation 3. So for the reform to fail, we need

$$K_1 = \sigma K_0 + Ng(I_0^{***}) < K_0. \tag{19}$$

Following the same steps as in the process of showing when a reform will succeed for sure, inequality 19 is equivalent to:

$$I_0^{***} < I_i^*.$$

That is,

$$\frac{1}{P_0\delta + P_0P_1\delta^2\sigma + \cdots} > \frac{N(1 - \delta\sigma)}{\delta}.$$

Because the left-hand side of the above inequality is larger than or equal to $1/P_0(\delta + \delta^2\sigma + \cdots)$, we solve the following for P_0:

$$\frac{1}{P_0(\delta + \delta^2\sigma + \cdots)} > \frac{N(1 - \delta\sigma)}{\delta},$$

$$P_0 < \frac{1}{N}.$$

Defining the following:

$$\underline{P}_0 = \frac{1}{N}. \tag{20}$$

Therefore, when $P_0 < \underline{P}_0$, equation 19 holds. By the government's strength-changing rule, equation 7, $P_1^H(P_0) < P_0$, $P_1^H(P_0) < P_0$. So by proposition 2, both the highest and the lowest paths are monotonically decreasing. Hence, equation 7 tells us that all outputs after reform are less than the prereform level. We have the following proposition:

PROPOSITION 5. *If a big-bang reform starts out with $P_0 < \underline{P}_0(\underline{P}_0$ given by equation 20), then even the highest equilibrium entails a failure.*

Conditions on the Parameters δ, σ, N

In the above derivation, we have not said anything about the magnitudes of P_0^*, $\bar{P}_0$, $\underline{P}_0$. It is easy to see that

$$0 < \underline{P}_0 = \frac{1}{N} < P_0^* = \frac{3}{N(1 - \delta\sigma) + \delta\sigma} < \bar{P}_0 = \frac{1}{N(1 - \delta\sigma)} \ .$$

Therefore, all we need to make these quantities meaningful is

$$\frac{1}{N(1 - \delta\sigma)} < 1,$$

that is,

$$\delta\sigma < 1 - \frac{1}{N} \ , \tag{21}$$

which is not a very restrictive condition, considering N is usually quite big. So if equation 21 holds, $\bar{P}_0 < 1$.

We have not been able to show the behavior of the rational expectations paths when $\underline{P}_0 \leq P_0 \leq \bar{P}_0$. I suspect they will be monotonic as well. The important lesson we learned in this section is that in order for the kind of reform studied in this chapter to succeed, it is crucial to make sure that the result of the immediate period after the reform begins is a success. Once the momentum (positive as well as negative) is built up, it will be self-sustaining.

Gradualism versus Big Bang

We have seen in the previous section that if government commitment ability is low and the whole economy goes into reform at once, the great uncertainty about whether the reform will stick or not alone may render the reform a failure. On the other hand, if we let part of the economy go into reform first while keeping the rest under the existing system and making it more efficient (e.g., the size of the part remaining in the old system is smaller now so the free-rider problem is less severe), as many countries have done, the uncertainty problem will not have such a big negative impact and the required initial P_0 for a successful reform may be reduced. This section formalizes the above idea.

Let's consider the following gradual reform strategy:

> *Strategy G:* At period 0, when the reform starts, the reforming government directs a fraction, α_0, of the community into reform, but tells the rest to remain in the collective sharing mode. During period 1, if the reform is still on, the government directs an α_1 fraction of the people remaining in the collective mode to go into reform, and tells the rest to remain. This process goes on until the whole community goes into reform.

Also without proof, the following proposition is stated (again, please refer to my dissertation):

> PROPOSITION 6: *When $P_0 < \underline{P}_0$, the gradual reform according to strategy G can entail a success in many circumstances while the big-bang reform always fails. The more severe the free rider problem in our community, the more likely the gradual strategy will succeed.*

The specific inefficiency that our reform addresses, the free-rider problem, due to which a smaller sharing community is more efficient, may make some readers wonder whether our positive conclusion about a gradual reform depends on this particular form of inefficiency. But this is not true. Our general principle is that when uncertainty about a reform is very severe, we should not let the whole economy go into reform at once, lest unfavorable expectations feed into themselves and render the reform a failure; instead, we ought to break the reform process into sequential steps, and seek the spots in the economy where some positive results can be obtained quickly to start the reform. In this way, we can avoid the self-feeding of the negative expectations while nurturing positive expectations along the reform path.

It is clear that when $P_0 > \bar{P}_0$, a big-bang strategy is preferable, since then output of a big-bang reform is no less than the gradual reform at every period after reform and larger than the gradual reform at the first few periods. But when $P_0 < \underline{P}_0$, as shown in this section, a gradual strategy such as Strategy G is preferred.

Concluding Remarks

The central messages of this chapter can be summarized as: (1) when uncertainty about the durability of a reform is present and the ability of the authority that initiates the reform to commit to the reform depends positively on the outcome of the reform, there exists a zone of the initial commitment ability under which a big-bang reform will turn out to be a failure, although by itself it is an efficiency-improving reform; (2) if the initial commitment ability falls into the failure zone, instead of a big-bang reform, reformers should seek spots in the economy where a gradual reform can be successfully begun, so that their commitment ability can grow and people's pessimistic expectations can be overcome along the reform path.

Two assumptions have been critical to our argument. The first is the idea that there exist conservatives that oppose a reform. The existence of conservatives can be attributed to either true ideological differences or personal interests being threatened by a reform. The second is the notion that if reform outcomes turn out badly, the forces committed to a reform will be weakened. This of course is a plain fact in all countries undergoing reforms. There are at least three reasons why this is the case. First, opportunistic political opponents always seize on bad outcomes to gain support from the people disappointed by the reform. Second, bad outcomes may be viewed by people with genuinely different opinions as evidence of the infeasibility of reform. Third, reformers themselves may have doubts about the efficacy of a reform; when they see bad outcomes, their doubts grow.

Although this chapter studies the commitment issue in the context of economic reforms in socialist countries, the analytical framework established and the principles derived seem to apply to any form of economic restructuring. For example, when a major corporation embarks on a reorganization of its business, whether the reorganization will be there to stay or not depends on the results of the reorganization. If the board of directors is divided in opinion about the reorganization, then the behavior of the people affected by the reorganization may be strategic and perverse. They may not invest any capital (in particular human capital) toward the direction of the reorganization. As this chapter stresses, the unwillingness of the employees to go along with the reorganization may be enough to render it a failure. Thus, the gradual principle expounded in this chapter will be applicable under these circumstances.

In this chapter we have not considered complementarities among different parts of a market economy. The presence of such complementarities is a main argument favoring big-bang strategies. But there need to be links between parts of a market economy for positive complementarities to be realized. For example, markets for the exchanges of goods, services, and capital need to be set up. If setting up these markets involves irretrievable resources, then the government's commitment ability will be crucial for reforms for the reasons explained in this chapter. However, whether a gradual reform will do better under low government commitment ability is not immediately clear.

Economic reform is fundamentally a process. What happens during the reform process determines the success or failure of a reform. Thus the choice of a reform strategy depends more on the nature of the transition process than on the intended end result of a reform. To advocate a big-bang reform simply because the intended end result is good appears to be rather inappropriate.

REFERENCES

Conway, John B. 1990. *A Course in Functional Analysis*. 2nd ed. Springer-Verlag.
David, Paul. 1988. *Path-Dependence: Putting the Past in the Future of Economics*. Mimeo. Stanford University.
McKinnon, Ronald I. 1993. *The Order of Economic Liberalization*. 2nd ed. Baltimore: Johns Hopkins University Press.
McMillan, John, and Barry Naughton. 1992. "How to Reform a Planned Economy: Lessons from China." *Oxford Review of Economic Policy* 8, no. 1 (Spring): 130–43.
Murphy, Kevin, Andrei Shleifer, and Robert Vishny. 1992."The Transition to a Market Economy: The Pitfalls of Partial Reform." *Quarterly Journal of Economics* 107 (August): 889–906.
Muth, John F. 1961. "Rational Expectations and the Theory of Price Movements." *Econometrica* 29:315–35.
Tirole, Jean. 1991. *Privatization in Eastern Europe: Incentives and the Economics of Transition*. Discussion paper. Department of Economics, MIT.

Contributors

Clarke, Donald C., School of Law, University of Washington

Dawkins, Chris, Department of Economics, University of Western Ontario

Fang, Xinghai, World Bank

Gates, Susan, RAND Corporation, Santa Monica, California

Gitomer, Charles S., Department of Agricultural Economics, University of Minnesota

Johnson, Simon, Fuqua School of Business, Duke University

Lee, Doowon, Department of Economics, Yonsei University

McMillan, John, Graduate School of International Relations and Pacific Studies, University of California, San Diego, California

Milgrom, Paul, Department of Economics, Stanford University

Minton-Beddoes, Zanny, Department of Economics, Harvard University

Naughton, Barry, Graduate School of International Relations and Pacific Studies, University of California, San Diego, California

Nee, Victor, Sociology Department, Cornell University

Qian, Yingyi, Department of Economics, Stanford University

Roberts, John, Graduate School of Business, Stanford University

Ronnås, Per, Stockholm School of Economics

Rozelle, Scott, Food Research Institute, Stanford University

Stiglitz, Joseph, Department of Economics, Stanford University, and Chairman, Council of Economic Advisers

Su, Sijin, Sociology Department, Cornell University

Whalley, John, Department of Economics, Warwick University and Department of Economics, University of Western Ontario

Whiting, Susan H., Department of Political Science, University of Washington

353

Index